Huebner School Series

APPLICATIONS IN FINANCIAL PLANNING I
First Edition

Ted Kurlowicz
Jeff Rattiner
Sophia Duffy
Craig Lemoine
Kevin Lynch
Tom Brinker

THE
AMERICAN
COLLEGE PRESS

HS314–1

This publication is designed to provide accurate and authoritative information about the subject covered. While every precaution has been taken in the preparation of this material, the authors, and The American College assume no liability for damages resulting from the use of the information contained in this publication. The American College is not engaged in rendering legal, accounting, or other professional advice. If legal or other expert advice is required, the services of an appropriate professional should be sought.

© 2014 The American College Press
ISBN-10: 1-58293-158-5
ISBN-13: 978-1-58293-158-6
Library of Congress Control Number 2014930260
270 S. Bryn Mawr Avenue
Bryn Mawr, PA 19010
(888) AMERCOL (263-7265)
theamericancollege.edu
Printed in the United States of America

HUEBNER SCHOOL SERIES

The American College® is an independent, nonprofit, accredited institution founded in 1927 that offers professional certification and graduate-degree distance education to men and women seeking career growth in financial services.

The Solomon S. Huebner School® of The American College administers the Chartered Life Underwriter (CLU®); the Chartered Financial Consultant (ChFC®); the Chartered Advisor for Senior Living (CASL®); the Registered Health Underwriter (RHU®); the Registered Employee Benefits Consultant (REBC®); the Chartered Healthcare Consultant™; the Chartered Leadership Fellow® (CLF®); and the Retirement Income Certified Professional (RICP)® professional designation programs. In addition, The College offers prep programs for the CFP® and CFA® certifications.

The Richard D. Irwin Graduate School® of The American College offers the Master of Science in Financial Services (MSFS) degree, a Master of Science in Management (MSM), a one-year program with an emphasis in leadership, and a PhD in Financial and Retirement Planning. Additionally, it offers the Chartered Advisor in Philanthropy® (CAP®) and several graduate-level certificates that concentrate on specific subject areas.

The American College is accredited by **The Middle States Commission on Higher Education**, 3624 Market Street, Philadelphia, PA 19104 at telephone number 267.284.5000.

The Middle States Commission on Higher Education is a regional accrediting agency recognized by the U.S. Secretary of Education and the Commission on Recognition of Postsecondary Accreditation. Middle States accreditation is an expression of confidence in an institution's mission and goals, performance, and resources. It attests that in the judgment of the Commission on Higher Education, based on the results of an internal institutional self-study and an evaluation by a team of outside peer observers assigned by the Commission, an institution is guided by well-defined and appropriate goals; that it has established conditions and procedures under which its goals can be realized; that it is accomplishing them substantially; that it is so organized, staffed, and supported that it can be expected to continue to do so; and that it meets the standards of the Middle States Association. The American College has been accredited since 1978.

The American College does not discriminate on the basis of race, religion, sex, handicap, or national and ethnic origin in its admissions policies, educational programs and activities, or employment policies.

The American College is located at 270 S. Bryn Mawr Avenue, Bryn Mawr, PA 19010. The toll-free number of the Office of Professional Education is (888) 263-7265; the fax number is (610) 526-1465; and the home page address is theamericancollege.edu.

Ted Kurlowicz, JD, LLM, CLU, ChFC, AEP, CAP, is the Charles E. Drimal professor of estate planning at The American College, where his responsibilities include preparation of courses in estate planning and planning for business owners and professionals. He has helped to develop insurance agent licensing examinations for numerous states and has addressed the national conferences of the Society of Financial Service Professionals, the IAFP, AICPA, NAEPC, and MDRT. Ted has appeared on *Your Money*, a business news broadcast on CNN, and *The Financial Advisers*, a business and financial planning program on PBS.

Ted is an adjunct faculty member at Widener University and Philadelphia University, where he teaches in the Master of Taxation program. He holds a BS from the University of Connecticut, an MA from the University of Pennsylvania, a JD from the Delaware Law School, and an LLM from the Villanova University School of Law. He is a member of the Pennsylvania Bar Association and the American Bar Association. Ted was inducted into the Estate Planning Hall of Fame in 2008 by the National Association of Estate Planners and Councils

Jeffrey H. Rattiner, CPA, CFP

Mr. Rattiner is president & CEO of the JR Financial Group, Inc. Mr. Rattiner was employed as the Director of Technical Standards for the Certified Financial Planner Board of Standards. He was also previously employed as Technical Manager in the Personal Financial Planning (PFP) Division of the American Institute of Certified Public Accountants in New York City.

Mr. Rattiner earned his Bachelors of Business Administration (BBA) with an emphasis in Marketing Management from Bernard M. Baruch College of the City University of New York in 1981, his MBA of Business Administration in Certified Public Accounting from Hofstra University in 1983 and his Certified Financial Planner™ education from the New York University in 1992. He is licensed as a CFP® with the CFP® Board of Standards in Denver, Colorado, and as a CPA in New York and Colorado.

Sophia Duffy, JD, CPA, is an Assistant Professor of Employee Benefits, at The American College. Prior to joining The College, Duffy served as a Senior Auditor with prominent Philadelphia health care, food service and educational institutions. Duffy completed her Juris Doctorate (JD) from the Temple University James E. Beasley School of Law in 2012. She earned her Bachelor of Science (BS) in Accounting from Rutgers University in 2002. In addition to her BS and her JD, she is a Certified Public Accountant, (CPA).

Craig Lemoine, PhD, CFP, holds the Jarrett Davis Distinguished Professorship in Financial Planning Technology at The American College. Craig is an assistant professor of financial planning at The College where his primary responsibilities are developing case study course materials and maintaining the *Fundamentals of Financial Planning* course as well as HS 332 *Advanced Planning Applications.* Craig also teaches graduate investment and mutual funds courses at the College.

Prior to joining the faculty at the College, Craig worked for 10 years in the financial services industry and attended graduate school at Texas Tech University, teaching in the Personal Financial Planning program. Craig has experience in the financial software industry and has worked extensively in the life insurance arena. He has written articles for numerous industry and academic publications including the *Journal of Financial Service Professionals* and the *Journal of Financial Planning.* Craig can be contacted at craig.lemoine@theamericancollege.edu and is always looking for new ideas about financial planning software and advisers using technology.

Kevin M. Lynch, CFP®, ChFC®, CLU®, RHU®, REBC®, CASL®, CAP®, LUTCF, FSS is an assistant professor of insurance at The American College. His responsibilities at The College include writing and preparing text materials for the LUTCF and FSS Programs. He also teaches insurance courses in the Huebner School at The College.

Before joining The College, Professor Lynch worked in the insurance and financial services industry for over 30 years. Originally licensed in Life Insurance in 1981, Professor Lynch has also been licensed in Property & Casualty Insurance since 1984. From 1998 through 2004, he built and operated a "scratch" Property & Casualty Agency, as an agency owner with Nationwide Insurance & Financial. Most recently, Professor Lynch was affiliated with Thrivent Financial for Lutherans, where he served as a Financial Consultant and Regional Management Associate.

Professor Lynch earned a Bachelors Degree from The University of the State of New York, in Albany. He also holds a Master of Business Administration Degree from Central State University, Edmond, OK. He is currently enrolled at Wilmington University, completing requirements to earn his Doctor of Business Administration Degree. In addition, Professor Lynch is completing the course requirements for his eighth American College designation, the Chartered Leadership Fellow® (CLF®).

Thomas M. Brinker, Jr., CPA/PFS, ChFC®, CFE, AEP, is an adjunct professor of taxation at The American College, where he is responsible for teaching and course development in the College's Irwin Graduate School and Huebner School programs. He also is a professor of accounting at Arcadia University (formerly Beaver College) in Glenside, Pennsylvania, where he coordinates the accounting programs in the Department of Business/Health Administration and Economics. In addition to serving at The American College and Arcadia University, Mr. Brinker is an adjunct professor of taxation at Philadelphia University.

Prior to receiving his appointment at Arcadia University, he served as an adjunct professor of accounting and taxation throughout the Philadelphia area, teaching in the undergraduate and graduate programs of Saint Joseph's University, West Chester University, and Widener University. He has received awards for teaching excellence, including the Lindback Foundation Award for Distinguished Teaching, and lectures primarily in the financial accounting and individual tax areas.

Mr. Brinker also is a tax consultant to a suburban Philadelphia CPA firm. His practice concentrates on tax planning and compliance for individuals and businesses. Prior to co-founding his firm, Mr. Brinker was a member of both the audit and tax departments of Coopers & Lybrand and Arthur Young & Company.

A graduate of Saint Joseph's University, where he graduated cum laude, Mr. Brinker also holds master's degrees in taxation (MST) and accounting (MSA) from Widener University, a juris doctorate in international law from Columbia Pacific University, and an LLM in international taxation from Regent University School of Law. In addition,

Mr. Brinker completed course work at the University of Sarasota toward the degree of doctor of business administration in accounting.

He has published articles in numerous journals, including The Journal of International Taxation, The Tax Adviser, The CPA Journal, and The Journal of Financial Service Professionals.

CONTENTS

1. Identify the entity choices available to operate a business.

2. Describe the formation of the business entity types.

3. Discuss how the owners control and manage business entities.

4. Identify the limitations and opportunities for capital formation in business.

5. Discuss the difference between business entities with respect to liability of the business owners.

6. Discuss the impact of the tax of net investment income on business owners.

7. Describe the tax treatment of pass-through entities.

8. Discuss the tax implications of operating a corporation.

9. Discuss the differences between business entities with respect to compensating active and inactive business owners.

10. Identify the causes of continuity problems for a closely held business.

11. Describe the methods for handling the key employee risk.

Selecting the Form of Business Entity

Business owners are faced with a number of choices when selecting the form of enterprise. They may elect to operate unincorporated, as a sole proprietorship, a partnership, or a limited-liability company (LLC); or they may incorporate—as a regular (C) corporation or as an S corporation. The choice of ownership form is revocable, and owners of existing businesses often decide to change the form if circumstances so dictate.

The choice of a form of ownership is a complex decision facing all business owners because it will have a significant impact on the initial start-up cost, the control and flexibility in management, the taxation of the business and individual owners, the ability of the firm to raise capital, and the business risks absorbed by the individual owners.

Forms of Business Organization
• Unincorporated
– Sole proprietorship
– Partnership
• General partnership
• Limited partnership
– Limited-liability company
• Incorporated
– C corporation
– S corporation

Formation of Business Entities

There are typically few statutory formalities involved in forming unincorporated businesses—proprietorships and partnerships. An unincorporated business might have to register the name of the business with the state government authority, and a search should be made to ensure that the name chosen is not already in use.

Since the proprietor is the sole owner of the business, there is no reason for any agreements to be drafted at formation, except perhaps employment contracts for certain hired employees. In contrast, a partnership should be formed with a formal written partnership agreement. These agreements can range in complexity from a simple agreement for a two-partner firm to a complex agreement similar to a corporate charter or bylaws. Professional help is recommended in drafting these agreements regardless of complexity. Obviously the cost of the agreement will depend on the amount of legal assistance required for its drafting. In the case of a large professional partnership the cost may equal or even exceed the cost of a simple incorporation.

limited-liability company (LLC)

operating agreement

The *limited-liability company (LLC)* is a relatively new form of entity. Authorized in all 50 states and the District of Columbia, the LLC is the fastest growing form of enterprise. LLCs are formed under the auspices of an enabling state law. The members file articles of organization with the state authorizing the business. They form an operating agreement to list the specifics of their association. The operating agreement will be a complex document and professional fees will be incurred. Generally, the start-up costs will exceed those of a simple partnership or corporation.

The formation of a corporation is, like an LLC, governed by statutory formalities. The process is regulated by the state of incorporation and always involves specific required procedures and costs. For example, the articles of incorporation and bylaws must be drafted. The articles must be filed with the state, and stock certificates for all classes of stock to be issued must be prepared and distributed. Employment contracts for employees, particularly owner-employees, must be prepared. Subscription agreements might be formed with the original stockholders, or in the case of a formation of a larger corporation, shares of stock will be issued through the services of an underwriter or an investment banker.

For any incorporation, even the most basic, certain filing fees and/or taxes must be paid to the state. Legal fees will be required to pay for advice and document drafting. The cost of the appropriate professional help for the incorporation is money well invested. A typical complaint of shareholders of closely held corporations is that they received bad advice at the inception of the corporation. In any event the cost of incorporation is several hundred dollars at a minimum and may run much higher in more complex cases.

The cost of forming the business enterprise is not significant in the long run. Although incorporation generally involves higher start-up costs and more formalities than other ownership forms, these factors usually do not dissuade owners from forming a corporation. However, the owners of a relatively simple business or professional practice may decide that the costs and formalities of incorporation are an unnecessary expenditure.

Control and Management of Business Entities

closely held business

Owners of a *closely held business* usually hope to maximize their control over the business. The sole proprietorship has only one owner who may run the business without any interference from others and holds powers limited solely by the laws of the state. The proprietor loses control of the business only when the proprietor ceases to engage in the activity or loses capacity to act.

partnership   A partnership is formed under the voluntary association of two or more partners. Inherent in this type of organization is an agreement by the partners on the basic business purpose of the partnership and sometimes the sharing or delegation of specific control functions among the partners.

Each partner typically has the authority to represent the partnership in business matters. This means that an individual partner is capable of frustrating the others by representing the partnership in a manner contrary to their wishes. To avoid such potential conflict, the control of the partnership could be spelled out in the original agreement. However, any partner who becomes dissatisfied may have the right to force dissolution of the partnership by terminating the voluntary agreement to associate with the other partners.

Fortunately the original partners cannot lose control to outsiders against their wills. The sale of a partnership interest to a third party does not automatically create a partnership with that third party since all existing partners must agree to accept the buyer as a partner. Therefore the original partners can ensure that their control of the partnership will not be diluted by outsiders.

An LLC is formed and governed by its articles of organization and operating agreement. Similar to a partnership, management control will depend on the operating agreement. Not all members will have the authority to represent and control the business. Sometimes, the control may be centralized under the guidance of one or more members.

Most LLCs will not permit completely free transferability of the ownership interests. Usually restrictions on transfer will occur and membership will not automatically be conferred on a transferee of an ownership interest. Because of these factors, the control of the current owners should be fairly certain in an LLC.

board of directors   The control of the corporation is vested in the board of directors, which oversees the management of the corporation. The election of the board of directors can generally be dominated by the majority shareholder. Unless minority shareholders can gain representation on the board, the closely held corporation will be under the continuous control of the majority shareholder.

Difficulties occur in the control of the corporation when there is no clear majority owner. For example, the corporation could be owned by a number of individuals or two 50 percent owners. Or a corporation might find it necessary to dilute the control of a majority shareholder by issuing new stock to outsiders to raise badly needed capital. In these instances there are some planning techniques available to the shareholders seeking control of the corporation. In any event the control of a corporation depends on its individual characteristics.

Capital Formation

The ability to raise capital is limited in any small business, regardless of the form of ownership. There are some distinctions worth mentioning among the various forms of ownership with respect to both the method and the ability to raise capital.

Sole Proprietorship

The simplicity of a proprietorship is a double-edged sword. The operating formalities are less burdensome, but the owner's independence can become a drawback for some purposes such as raising capital.

A proprietorship is formed when the owner begins operation by putting personal assets to use in the business. The capital of the proprietorship consists of the proprietor's assets plus any additional amounts the proprietor can obtain through borrowing. Whatever credit is available to the proprietor depends solely on the proprietor's personal financial position, including, of course, the proprietor's business interest. Obviously there is a built-in limit on the amount any one individual will be able to borrow from commercial or private sources. Extremely wealthy individuals, who might otherwise have substantial ability to raise funds, are more likely to form businesses as corporations than proprietorships.

Partnership

Although a partnership has limits similar to a proprietorship in its ability to raise capital, it does have a potentially larger equity base on which to raise capital since it has at least two owners. If the partners have substantial personal assets and are willing to guarantee a loan, a lender is more likely to extend credit to the partnership. It is also easier for a partnership to expand its equity base by taking on new owners. However, this requires the original partners to accept new partners who have all the rights and responsibilities of the original owner.

Limited Partnership

limited partnership
All states have laws permitting the creation of special limited partnerships, which are composed of active participants (general partners) and passive investment partners (limited partners). The general partners all retain personal responsibility for business operations, while limited partners are at risk only to the extent of their investment in the business. Regular (general) partnerships are owned solely by general partners. Limited partnerships can raise capital by selling partnership interests to limited partners in exchange for capital contributions without diluting the control of the general partners. The limited partners invest capital in return for a share of future income and growth of the business but are not burdened with unlimited personal liability for the operation of the partnership. For this reason some ventures requiring large amounts of capital are formed as limited partnerships and may even be publicly traded.

Limited-Liability Company (LLC)

LLCs are particularly advantageous with respect to the ability to raise funds. An LLC features several favorable characteristics of other types of organizations in one enterprise. It provides pass-through tax treatment without requiring that any members retain unlimited liability. It permits an unlimited number of members, unlike an S corporation. For business owners who are concerned about liability from business operations but would like to raise capital from passive investors, the LLC is an excellent choice.

Corporation

In theory the corporate form should be selected for a business that will require substantial capital and expand rapidly. A corporation is a separate legal entity and may own assets in its own right. The corporation can borrow in its own name and may be able to use the various sources of commercial credit to raise any needed capital.

A small closely held corporation with limited assets is unlikely to be able to borrow large amounts secured by corporate assets alone. Commercial lenders are likely to require the individual shareholders of the closely held corporation to personally guarantee loans made to the corporation. In this respect a small closely held corporation is similar to unincorporated businesses in its ability to raise funds.

A distinct advantage of the corporate form over other forms of business enterprise is the ability to raise capital by expanding the equity base. A corporation can take on additional owners to expand its equity capital simply by exchanging equity (newly issued stock) for capital contributions. In addition, this increase in the ownership base of the corporation may allow it to increase its debt while maintaining a safe debt-equity ratio. For these reasons the corporation is generally superior to other forms of ownership for a business that will grow and have large capital needs.

One problem associated with the issuance of stock to new investors is the potential loss of control by the current shareholders. Techniques can be used to perpetuate the control of the current majority shareholders under these circumstances. Of course, it may be difficult to attract investors unless some control is relinquished because new shareholders will have the right to vote their shares. But investors may be willing to take a noncontrolling interest for the opportunity to share in the corporate earnings and appreciation in stock value if business prospects are favorable.

Issues in Selecting Form of Business Organization

- Ease and expense of formation
- Control
- Flexibility in operations
- Ability to raise capital
- Liability of owners
- Income taxation
- Compensation and fringe benefits for owners

Liability for Business Owners and Entities

The operation of a business creates risks from which both the business and the owner need protection. There is the obvious risk that business failure will render the firm insolvent. Furthermore, the operation of a business creates potentially large risks. For example, there are many dangers, both hidden and obvious, on the business premises that could cause injury to employees or third parties. There is the risk that a business's defective products will create liability by causing injury to consumers. Finally, there is the possibility that a business will become liable for injuries caused by its agents and employees.

All individuals are personally responsible for their own actions. If the negligent act of a business owner results in a lawsuit against the business, the individual who caused the harm is always personally liable. However, in some entity forms, nonnegligent owners can be shielded from liability not resulting from their own actions.

Sole Proprietorship

The proprietor faces the greatest risk exposure of any business owner since the business and personal assets of the proprietor are legally indistinguishable and business-related debts are personal debts. The failure of the proprietorship enables the business creditors to satisfy their claims from the proprietor's personal assets. Misfortunes of the proprietor's business can lead to the proprietor's personal financial ruin.

General Partnership

joint and several liability

The general partnership exposes the partners to a liability danger that is similarly unlimited. One characteristic of the partnership form is that more than one owner will share in the losses. The liability of the partners for partnership losses is " joint and several." That is, each partner is liable individually and as a member of the group for any claims against the partnership. Partners sued individually by the business creditors may, however, seek contribution from the other partners for their share of any amounts that were expended to satisfy the claims. A partner's share of any partnership loss depends on the underlying situation. Although the initial partnership agreement should specify the percentage share of each partner of any claims against the partnership, all general partners are ultimately fully liable.

An obvious question is whether the personal liability of a general partner can be limited by the partnership agreement. For example, can the agreement state that a specific partner does not share in any losses of the partnership? The answer to this question is no. The doctrine of joint and several liability provides that the general partner is always ultimately individually liable for claims against the partnership.

Limited Partnership

As a relief from the harshness of unlimited liability in general partnerships, all states permit the formation of limited partnerships. The advantage of the limited partnership lies in the fact that some investors—the limited partners—may contribute capital and participate in the profits without unlimited personal liability. The limited partners may suffer losses, but only to the extent of the capital contributed to the partnership.

The law requires that each limited partnership have at least one general partner. The general partner, of course, is exposed to unlimited personal liability for claims against the limited partnership. To prevent any one individual from absorbing this risk, some limited partnerships are formed with a corporation as the general partner.

Limited Liability Partnership (LLP)

limited-liability partnership (LLP)

A relatively new form of partnership is the *limited-liability partnership (LLP)*. LLP or RLLP (registered limited-liability partnership) laws have now been enacted in all states. An LLP is a partnership that has filed or registered under the state's enabling law to operate with limited liability for all partners. The distinction between the LLP and the limited partnership is that an LLP can be a general partnership and all general partners have limited liability. Under LLP or RLLP laws in general, limits are placed on the liability of partners from the unsatisfied debts and obligations of the firm arising from the negligence and misconduct of other partners. The assets of the partnership itself remain at risk; thus each partner's liability is limited to his or her investment in the partnership. In addition, many states restrict the types of entities that can form as LLPs or RLLPs. For example, some states prohibit the practice of law under this organizational form.

Limited-Liability Company (LLC)

The LLC is a form of enterprise that was developed primarily to address the liability concerns of would-be entrepreneurs. This liability protection is the most important characteristic of the LLC and a key distinguishing factor from a partnership, which provides limited liability only for its limited but not its general partners.

The LLC is the only business entity that allows every member, including managing members, to enjoy limited liability while the entity is treated as a partnership for federal income tax purposes. This insulation is particularly important if the underlying business or asset may involve environmental claims, product liability claims, or similar exposures.

Corporation

The corporate form of ownership provides its owners (shareholders) with personal protection that is unavailable to proprietors or general partners for liability stemming from the operation of a business. Corporate shareholders contribute capital in exchange for equity. Theoretically the capital contributed by a shareholder is the limit of his or her liability for the risks of running the business. The liability arising from the operation of a corporation is satisfied out of corporate assets, regardless of whether they are sufficient to satisfy all claims.

The corporate form is not always a panacea for business owners seeking limited liability, especially in the case of a closely held or professional corporation. Business creditors of these corporations are unlikely to accept solely the corporation's signature on loans to the corporation unless it has substantial assets. For this reason shareholders of a closely held corporation often find that they must personally guarantee the loans extended to the business. To the extent of their personal guarantees, the shareholders remain personally liable for the debts of the corporation. Since corporate shareholder-employees remain personally liable for their own actions, they are not protected from the consequences of these actions, even if occurring in the scope of their employment. This is particularly important in the professional corporation, where malpractice liability for the individual shareholder-employee is a significant risk. The professional is unable to use the corporate form of ownership to protect personal assets from liability caused by his or her own professional malpractice.

The corporate form of ownership does, however, provide significant liability limits for its owners. First, a closely held business with substantial assets may be able to obtain credit solely in the corporate name. The shareholders are liable for debts of an insolvent corporation only to the extent of their capital contribution.

Shareholders are also not personally liable for many of the risks associated with the operation of the business. For example, individual shareholders will not have to satisfy personal injury liability suits against the business not arising from the actions of the individual shareholder. This is a significant liability shelter in the modern liability theater, where courts and juries have taken an expansive view of the law concerning personal injury lawsuits.

Liability of Owners
• Proprietors—unlimited • General partners—unlimited • Limited partners—limited • Members of LLCs—limited • Stockholders—limited

In selecting the form of business ownership, limited liability is always preferable, to the extent that it is available. The need for and the ability to achieve limited liability depend on the actual business being formed. Obviously, passive investors obtain limited liability by (1) purchasing shares of stock in a corporation, (2) investing in a limited partnership interest, (3) investing in an LLC interest, or (4) where permissible, investing in an LLP.

However, owners who actively participate in business activities face a different situation. First, an owner who is actively involved in the business cannot be a limited partner. An owner of a closely held corporation or LLC is often forced to take personal risk for any credit obtained by the corporation or LLC. To this extent even an LLC or corporation does not completely shelter the closely held business owner from liability.

The decision of a professional as to the form in which to operate a professional practice may not be influenced to any great extent by unlimited personal liability. The primary risk of a practice is malpractice liability. Since all individuals remain personally liable for their actions, the professional cannot limit liability for his or her own malpractice by operating as an LLP or LLC or by incorporating. (Note that the state's LLP, LLC, or corporate law must authorize the professional to adopt such organizational forms.) A professional corporation, LLP, or LLC does, however, limit the liability of an owner-employee for actions of others in the enterprise performed while not under the direct supervision of the owner-employee. Since this also shields one professional from liability for the malpractice of another, this limitation can be significant.

Federal Income Taxation of Business Owners and Entities

Taxation of Individuals

pass-through taxation
The taxation of income for federal income tax purposes is a complex topic but is extremely important for business owners. It is often a primary motivating factor for the choice business owners will make with respect to the type of entity they form. Although this cannot be a comprehensive discussion of federal income taxes, we need to discuss some basics such as the marginal tax rates of individuals and businesses. For most closely held business entities, some form of pass-through taxation will be preferable. This means that business income will be taxed directly to the business owners on their individual returns. With few limited exceptions, the only form of entity that is a separate taxpayer with separate rate tables is a regular corporation. The type of business entity will also affect the contributions made to Social Security for earned income or self-employment income for the owners.

medicare contribution tax

net investment income (NII)
Additional tax burdens were enacted to partially fund the Affordable Care Act of 2010. First, a 0.9 percent additional Medicare tax was imposed for earned income of higher wage earners. Second, a 3.8 percent tax is imposed on net investment income (NII). The thresholds for these additional Medicare contribution tax burdens are modified adjusted gross income (MAGI) over $200,000 for individual filers and $250,000 for married filing jointly. These taxes became effective in 2013 and will become an increasing burden because the thresholds are not indexed for inflation. Understanding these tax burdens is extremely important when dealing with business owners because they affect earned income and passive income from the business, respectively. And, the 3.8 percent tax on NII potentially affects sales of a closely held business.

For the purposes of the 3.8 percent taxes, NII is defined as interest, dividends, payments from nonqualified annuities, royalties, rents and capital gains from assets other than those held in a trade or business. The 3.8 percent additional tax rate is imposed on the lesser of the (1) taxpayer's NII or (2) MAGI in excess of the applicable threshold amount.

EXAMPLE
A single taxpayer in 2013 has $400,000 in wages, $150,000 of NII, and MAGI of $550,000. The taxpayer would be liable for $1,800 in additional Medicare tax on his or her wages ($400,000 wages – $200,000 threshold amount, multiplied by 0.9 percent), and $5,700 on NII ($150,000 NII multiplied by 3.8 percent) for a total additional tax of $7,500.

The following items are excluded from the definition of NII:

- trade or business income for an active participant
- self-employment income
- sale or exchange of an interest in a partnership, LLC, or S corporation by an active participant
- inside buildup in deferred annuities and life insurance products
- distributions from qualified plans or IRAs (including Roth IRAs)
- tax-exempt interest

Tax rates for individuals and businesses are illustrated in tables 1-1 through 1-3.

Sole Proprietorship

A sole proprietorship is not a legally distinct form of entity. The sole proprietor simply takes personal assets and applies them in his or her efforts in the business activity. The business does not file a separate tax return. All business income and tax deductions are reported on Schedule C of Form 1040. Business expenses are directly available to offset both business and other income on the sole proprietor's tax return because business deductions are "above the line." The sole proprietor is not a statutory employee and all net income is treated as self-employment income. However, there are some tax advantages available. For example, the sole proprietor can have regular employees who can participate in employee benefit plans. The sole proprietor can deduct (with limitations provided by inflation indexing) premiums for long-term care insurance for the sole proprietor and his or her spouse.

Partnership/LLC

Taxation of Income

distributive share Although the partnership pays no federal income taxes, each partner must report and pay taxes on his or her "distributive share" of the partnership net taxable income for the tax year. The net income is the gross income of the partnership less allowable deductions. For example, the deduction against income from domestic production activities is available for partnerships engaged in such activities. The partner's distributive share is the amount of net income that the partner is entitled to receive under the partnership agreement, even if no income is actually distributed to the partner during the tax year. If the partnership has tax losses, a deduction for each partner's distributive share of the losses may be taken on his or her individual tax return. This share of partnership income or loss is reported to the IRS and the partners on Schedule K-1 by the partnership. Income from a partnership reported on Schedule E of Form 1040 is taxed on the partner's return at individual rates. However, there is no potential for double taxation since there is no taxation at the partnership level. This is a distinct advantage over the corporate form if income is to be paid out to passive investment partners.

EXAMPLE 1

The ABC partnership has substantial income to pay out to limited partners. Assume each limited partner is in the top federal income bracket—39.6 percent.[1] The distributive share to each limited-partnership interest for the year is $10,000. There is no tax at the partnership level, but each partner is taxed $3,960 on a distributive share. Because the limited partner is not an active participant, the 3.8 tax on NII applies causing an additional $380 tax burden.

EXAMPLE 2

Use the same facts as in the example above, except that ABC decides to incorporate. In this case the limited partner (now a shareholder) receives a dividend instead of a distributive share. The income to provide the dividend (again $10,000) is first taxed at the corporate level at rates of up to 35 percent. This leaves $6,500 available to be paid to the shareholder and taxed at tax rates that depend on whether the dividends received are "qualified dividends" and on the tax bracket of the shareholder. In this example, the dividends would be taxed at the capital gains rate of 20 percent. And the 3.8 percent tax on NII would also apply. In this instance, the same $10,000 of business income would result in $5,047 of income taxes—$3,500 of the corporate level and another $1,547 of tax at the shareholder level.

A partner's distributive share of income or loss is not initially determined by rules of tax law. Rather, the allocation of distributive shares is determined by the partnership agreement. The IRS will generally abide by the terms of the

---

1.   Based on 2014 individual income tax tables.

partnership agreement in this respect, unless it finds that the allocation does not have substantial economic effect. In the absence of a specific agreement as to the allocation of income and loss, a partner's distributive share may be inferred by the facts of the partnership, such as each partner's capital interest in the partnership.

EXAMPLE
Nancy and Tim form a partnership in which Nancy contributes cash of $50,000 and Tim contributes a building with a fair market value of $50,000. The partnership begins operation with no formal agreement as to the allocation of income or loss and earns $60,000 in profit in the first tax year. Based on these facts, it may be presumed that Nancy and Tim will share the profits 50-50 in accordance with their relative interest. This means that Tim and Nancy will have to report $30,000 each of taxable income for the year regardless of whether their share of profits was distributed to them.

The partnership, like any other entity, may receive different types of income. For example, the partnership receives ordinary income from its business operations, and it may receive long-term capital gain from the sale of property. Some partnership receipts may be tax exempt, such as the proceeds from a life insurance policy payable to the partnership. The character of all income is passed through directly to the partner. For example, if the partnership has a long-term capital gain, each partner's share of this gain is also a long-term capital gain to the partner. When the partnership receives the tax-exempt life insurance proceeds, each partner's share of these proceeds is also tax exempt.

The partnership agreement may make a special allocation of the various types of income among partners; for example, one partner may be designated to receive all the capital gains. Generally these allocations will be accepted by the IRS if they have substantial economic effect. To have a substantial economic effect, the allocation should create a real impact both on (1) the partner's *distributive share* of total partnership income regardless of tax consequences and (2) the partner's capital accounts. Because special allocations have been abused by taxpayers, the IRS had promulgated complex and restrictive regulations on the subject. In addition, the allocation income from domestic production activities eligible for the new deduction will potentially create possibilities for tax benefits to be shifted between partners. The IRS is expected to provide rules for allocation of income from partnership activities that give rise to the deduction. The financial services professional should be aware that caution should be used in forming special allocations.

EXAMPLE
Boris and Natasha form a partnership. Among the business assets are tax-free municipal bonds and corporate stock. The partnership agreement gives Boris and Natasha a right to 50 percent of the partnership income (tax-exempt income and dividend income). The agreement further provides that all Boris's share will be designated as tax-exempt interest to the extent the partnership has tax-exempt interest. The IRS will regard this special allocation as having no substantial economic effect because Boris and Natasha's actual distributive shares are not affected by the agreement. The result of that conclusion will probably be that both partners will have to reallocate their shares to include 50 percent of each type of partnership income.

Partnership income or loss is reported on each partner's return on Schedule E of Form 1040. In this sense the treatment of partnership income is no different from that of a proprietor's. Income is simply added to or subtracted from the partner's income from other sources in arriving at the partner's adjusted gross income. Partnership capital gains or losses retain their character as described above and are reported by each partner on Schedule D along with the partner's other capital gains or losses.

Table 1-1 Corporate Income Tax Rates

Taxable Income	Rate
$ 0–$50,000	15%
$50,001–$75,000	25%
$75,001–$10,000,000	34%
over $10,000,000	35%
For Taxable Income	
$100,000–$335,000 add	5%
$15,000,000–$18,333,333 add	3%
Personal-Service Corporations:	
All taxable income	35%

Table 1-2 Federal Income Tax Rates on Individual Income for 2014*		
	Taxable Income	**Rate**
Married individuals filing joint returns	$0–$18,150	10%
	$18,151–$73,800	15%
	$73,801–$148,850	25%
	$148,851–$226,850	28%
	$226,851–$405,100	33%
	$405,101–$457,600	35%
	Over $457,600	39.6%
Single taxpayers	$0–$9,075	10%
	$9,076–$36,900	15%
	$36,901–$89,350	25%
	$89,351–$186,350	28%
	$186,351–$405,100	33%
	$405,101–$406,750	35%
	Over $406,750	35%
* Applicable to the owner's income from sole proprietorships, partnerships, LLCs, and S corporations. Taxable income brackets are indexed annually.		

Table 1-3 Surtax on Net Investment Income After 2012*		
	Modified Adjusted Gross Income	**Tax**
Married Filing Joint Return	Over $250,000	3.8%
Single Taxpayers	Over 200,000	3.8%
*Applies to passive income such as dividends from Corporations and pass-through income for nonactive participants in partnerships, LLCs, and S Corporations. Will also apply to gains on sales by nonactive owners.		

Impact of Partnership Operations on Basis

The tax law views each partner's capital contribution as an exchange for a property interest—the partnership interest. This property interest is similar to that held by a shareholder in a corporation but is not evidenced by any share certificates or other intangible objects. However, this interest may be bought and sold as any other property interest.

Since the partnership interest is considered personal property of the partner, it is important to know its basis for tax purposes. When the interest is transferred, any gain or loss recognizable by the partner will be determined by reference to this basis. A partner acquires a basis by making an initial contribution of capital to the partnership at the time of formation in exchange for a partnership interest. Further capital contributions by a partner after the formation of the partnership result in an increase in the partner's basis in the already existing partnership interest. The partner's basis acquired by the contribution is generally equal to the amount of money contributed plus the partner's adjusted basis in any property contributed. Typically the adjusted basis of such property in the hands of the partner is the original cost to the partner less any depreciation deductions and other adjustments taken by the partner.

EXAMPLE

Carl and Jack form a partnership to carry on their construction business. Each partner agrees to put property worth $5,000 into the partnership. Carl contributes his pickup truck, which has a fair market value of $5,000 and an adjusted basis of $4,000. The basis for Carl's partnership interest thus becomes $4,000. Jack agrees to contribute $2,000 in cash plus tools that have a fair market value of $3,000 and an adjusted basis of $1,000. Jack's basis for his partnership interest is therefore $3,000. Thus although both partners contributed property worth $5,000, Carl's basis is $4,000, but Jack's is only $3,000. Any additional contributions made by Carl or Jack will increase their basis at that time.

The significance of basis is apparent. For example, suppose several years later Carl decides to sell his interest in the partnership to Jack for $10,000. Carl's gain can be computed only if his basis is known. Assuming no further adjustments to Carl's basis after formation (an unlikely event) Carl would have a gain of $6,000 ($10,000 less the $4,000 basis).

The determination of a partner's basis in his or her original interest in the partnership seems simple enough. However, a partner's basis for partnership interest can be subject to constant change as a result of the operation of the partnership. These adjustments are part of the complexity of partnership taxation.

Most of the changes in a partner's basis from the regular operations of the partnership result from three rules provided by the IRC. First, a partner's basis for partnership interest is increased each year by the partner's distributive share of the partnership income. Second, the basis is decreased each year by the amount of any distribution received by the partner from the partnership. Therefore there is no change in the partner's basis for the partnership interest if the partnership simply pays out to each partner his or her distributive share of the partnership's income. That is, the basis adjustments for these events cancel each other out. The third rule provides that the partner's basis is decreased each year by his or her distributive share of the losses incurred by the partnership for the tax year. However, the basis is never reduced below zero.

EXAMPLE
Jane has a basis of $50,000 for her partnership interest at the beginning of this year. This year Jane's share of the partnership's profits is $30,000. She actually withdraws $20,000 of this and leaves the rest in the partnership. Jane's new basis for her partnership interest at the end of this year will be $60,000 ($50,000 plus $30,000 less $20,000). If the partnership has losses next year and Jane's share of these losses is $100,000, her deduction for next year will be limited to $60,000, the amount of her basis, and her basis will be reduced to zero. Jane's remaining $40,000 of losses may be carried over to future years and may be deducted in future years to the extent her basis increases in the future.

Two other adjustments to the partner's interest in the partnership should be noted at this time. First, as mentioned above, a partner's basis in the partnership interest is increased by any further capital contributions made by the partner after the formation of the partnership. Second, a partner's basis in his or her interest includes the partner's share of any indebtedness incurred by the partnership. For example, if a two-member 50-50 partnership borrows $50,000, each partner's basis in his or her partnership interest increases by $25,000.

Finally, for tax purposes the partnership itself has a basis in the partnership property contributed by the partners. Among other things, a partnership's basis in its property determines the amount of the depreciation that can be deducted with respect to partnership property. Generally the partnership's basis for the contributed property is a carryover basis. That is, the basis of the property is the same as is adjusted basis in the hands of the contributing partner.

Corporation

Taxation of Corporate Income

dividend

A corporation is a separate taxpayer for federal income tax purposes. The corporation itself must file a tax return and pay federal tax on its taxable income. The owners of the corporation—the shareholders—pay no tax on the corporation's income directly. However, when the corporation distributes income to the shareholders in the form of dividends, the shareholders may pay tax on the dividends, currently at the tax rate for capital gains (for high income shareholders, dividends are NII and subject to an additional tax of 3.8 percent). In other words, corporate income may be taxed twice, first at the corporate level and then again when it is distributed to shareholders.

In some circumstances a shareholder may receive dividend treatment when corporate distributions are made to the shareholder either (1) in exchange for his or her stock or (2) upon dissolution of the corporation.

double taxation

reasonable compensation

The potential for double taxation in the corporate form, while a major planning concern, is not always the obstacle it appears to be at first glance. In many cases it is possible for corporations to minimize the amount of tax paid at the corporate level by minimizing the amount of actual corporate taxable income. In closely held corporations most of the net income from the business can be paid out in the form of salaries and benefits, which are deductible in computing the corporation's taxable income. By paying salaries to shareholder-employees the corporation can pass along income to shareholders without incurring double taxation. Note that double taxation is avoided only if the salaries are deductible to the corporation. A deduction is allowed only for "reasonable compensation," salaries paid to shareholder-employees in excess of reasonable compensation will be treated as dividends that are nondeductible to the corporation.

personal-service business

The question of what constitutes reasonable compensation is frequently a subject of dispute between taxpayers and the IRS. Despite the absence of clear standards a few factors can be noted. If the business is heavily capitalized, then obviously some of the business income must represent a return on capital. In capital-intensive businesses only part of the owner's share of income will generally be allowable as reasonable compensation for services. In a business in which capital is not a significant income-producing factor (personal-service businesses), most or all of the business's income could be paid out to shareholder-employees and deducted as reasonable compensation. This is particularly important because the corporation pays a 35 percent flat rate on taxable income retained at the corporate level for personal-service corporations. These factors should be considered for determining reasonable-compensation levels for employees.

Double Taxation of Corporate Income

- A dollar is earned by the corporation, which pays a tax on it at the corporate rate.

- What's left of the dollar is paid as a dividend to the shareholder, who pays a tax on the dividend.

- The solution: Keep the dollar in the corporation, avoiding taxation at the individual's level; or pay the dollar to the individual as a salary, avoiding taxation at the corporate level.

Retention and Reinvestment of Accumulated Earnings

A corporation is not obligated to pay out its earnings as dividends, so double taxation is not automatic. These earnings may be reinvested in the corporate business or simply accumulated at the corporate level, thereby avoiding a second tax at the shareholder level.

The prospect of accumulating earnings in the corporation for reinvestment or other purposes may produce a limited tax advantage of using the corporate form as opposed to other forms of organization because there is some possibility of income taxed at lower corporate brackets.

The more lightly taxed corporate dollars can also be used to fund a tax-advantaged employee benefit plan with shareholder-employees. In addition, corporate-owned life insurance can be purchased for key person or other corporate purposes with earnings taxed at the lower corporate rates and accumulated in the corporation.

accumulated-earnings tax

Special Corporate Penalty Taxes. The tax advantage of the corporate tax rates on earnings accumulated by the corporation is limited somewhat by the accumulated-earnings tax. Although shareholders' legal actions to force the payment of dividends have met with limited success, the accumulated-earnings tax provides a substantial incentive to distribute income as dividends. Simply stated, the accumulated-earnings tax is a penalty tax designed to prevent tax avoidance through the accumulation of earnings within the corporation beyond the expected needs of the business.

The mechanics of the accumulated-earnings tax are relatively complicated, but the effect is straightforward. A corporation can accumulate up to a "minimum credit" of $250,000 of business earnings and profits without encountering any problem with the accumulated-earnings tax. If a corporation accumulates earnings and profits beyond the minimum credit amount, it must be prepared to demonstrate to the IRS that the accumulation is for reasonable needs of the business. If this cannot be demonstrated, the IRS will impose a tax—the accumulated-earnings tax—on the corporation.

accumulated taxable income

The accumulated-earnings tax is currently imposed at a rate of 20 percent on all accumulated taxable income.[2] The *accumulated taxable income* is basically defined as the taxable income of the corporation less

- corporate tax paid on income
- dividends paid
- amounts accumulated for reasonable business needs or, if greater, the remaining minimum accumulated-earnings credit

Corporate earnings may be accumulated for reasonable business needs beyond the minimum credit amount without the imposition of the accumulated-earnings tax. The Code defines reasonable business needs in a highly circular fashion to include all reasonably anticipated needs of the business. Although the Code is not always helpful for this purpose, there is substantial case law determining what is (or is not) a reasonable business need.

alternative-minimum-tax

In response to the popular perception that many corporations do not pay a fair share of federal income taxes, Congress enacted the corporate alternative-minimum-tax (AMT) provisions. Corporations must pay the alternative minimum tax if it is greater than the regular corporate income tax for the year. To the extent that the alternative minimum tax paid exceeds the regular tax for the year, the corporation may use this excess to offset regular tax liability in future years.

alternative minimum taxable income (AMTI)

The tax is imposed at a rate of 20 percent of the *alternative minimum taxable income (AMTI)* above an exemption amount. The AMTI base is determined by adding certain tax-preference items to the corporation's normal taxable income for the year.

These preferences include the following:

- certain excess depreciation taken by the corporation

---

2.   The accumulated-earnings tax rate is set at the maximum tax rate in effect for dividend distributions.

- tax-exempt interest on certain private-activity government bonds
- 75 percent of the amount by which current adjusted earnings exceed AMTI (computed specifically without this adjustment)

The current adjusted earnings modification is included in the list since corporations often reflect substantial earnings on income statements reported to shareholders and regulatory authorities that are not included in taxable income. For example, corporate-owned life insurance may increase current earnings and profits without a corresponding increase in taxable income when

- annual increases in cash surrender value exceed annual premiums
- death benefits are received in excess of the corporation's basis in the policy

Current adjusted earnings are similar to the corporate earnings and profits and are determined by the corporation's accounting method and may or may not be regularly reported in a formal statement by a closely held corporation. There is some flexibility in planning for this adjustment as long as generally accepted accounting principles are adhered to. Closely held corporations rarely prepare audited public income statements, but the Code permits less formal statements to be used for the purpose of this adjustment. For example, it may be permissible for the firm to use a noncertified statement that was prepared by the business for the purpose of securing credit.

The AMT applies only to "large" corporations. An exemption from AMT will apply to a small corporation. A small corporation is defined as a corporation that has gross receipts below a minimum threshold. The minimum threshold rules provide that a corporation is a small corporation if its average gross receipts for the 3-year period prior to the current tax year are $7.5 million or less.

Taxation of Personal Service Corporations

One of the fundamentals of tax law is that both the labor and capital contributing to the income of a business should be appropriately rewarded. In a typical corporation, the reasonable compensation test prevents over-rewarding the labor by limiting the deductible compensation provided to employees. The accumulated earnings tax is designed to prevent a corporation from accumulating earnings at the corporate level without rewarding the capital investors through dividend distributions. In the case of a personal service corporation, the earnings should technically be created solely by the efforts of the employees and the capital invested should not be much of a factor in producing the corporation's earnings. Congress understood these principles and chose to impose a tax at the highest corporate rate (35 percent) for any retained earnings inside a personal service corporation. As a result of this tax treatment, it makes little sense to retain significant earnings in a personal service corporation.

The S Election

An eligible corporation can make a federal tax election under Subchapter S of the tax code. The tax treatment of an S corporation and its shareholders parallels the tax treatment of partners and partnerships. Each shareholder in an S corporation includes in income his or her share of income items, including tax-exempt income, losses, deductions, and credits. The character of income items—for example, whether they are tax-exempt income or capital gain—carries over to the shareholder. Income items are passed through on a pro rata basis to shareholders, and no special allocations of such items are permitted.

As in a partnership, income items are includible by the shareholder in the income of the taxable year in which the corporation's tax year ends. S corporations must generally use a calendar year for tax purposes, and a shareholder will report the S corporation income on the last day of his or her tax year. If the shareholder is employed by and receives a salary from the S corporation, this salary payment is includible in income when actually (or constructively) received. Salary payments are deductible from business income, thus reducing the income that passes through on a pro rata basis to all shareholders at the end of a tax year.

S corporation losses deductible by a shareholder are limited to the sum of the shareholder's adjusted basis in his or her S corporation stock, plus any basis the shareholder has in debt owed to the shareholder by the corporation. If a shareholder's share of losses exceeds this amount, then the losses can be carried forward indefinitely and taken as a deduction in a subsequent year in which the shareholder has an adequate basis in stock or debt.

EXAMPLE
Jane's share of the net operating loss of Essco (an S corporation) for 2014 is $25,000. If Jane's basis at the end of 2013 was $5,000, she can offset her income from other sources by recognizing only $5,000 of Essco's operating loss—the amount of her basis.

The basis for a shareholder's stock in an S corporation is adjusted in a manner similar to that of a partner's basis in his or her partnership interest. The basis of a shareholder's S corporation stock is increased each year by the shareholder's pro rata share of the corporation's taxable income and is correspondingly reduced by the shareholder's pro rata share of corporate losses. Once the stock basis has been adjusted for corporate income and losses, it is further adjusted to reflect any corporate distributions to the shareholder during the year since such distributions reduce the recipient-shareholder's basis. If all of a shareholder's pro rata share of an S corporation's taxable income is distributed to the shareholder during the year, there is no change in the shareholder's basis. If a distribution from an S corporation exceeds the shareholder's basis for the stock, the excess is taxable to the shareholder as a capital gain. In other words, it is treated as if the shareholder had sold or liquidated stock to that extent.

Although in general an S corporation is treated for tax purposes much like a partnership, there are several significant differences. Two of these involve the treatment of indebtedness of the corporation and the treatment of passive income.

An S corporation shareholder acquires a basis in the debt of the corporation only if the shareholder lends the funds directly to the corporation. If the corporation borrows money from a bank, the shareholder does not acquire any basis as a result of this indebtedness, even if the shareholder personally guarantees the loan. By contrast, a partner's basis is automatically increased by his or her share of any partnership debt, including loans from banks or other outsiders.

Eligibility for Election

Types of Corporations. Only domestic corporations are eligible to make the S election. Although the statute refers to small *business* corporations, there is no specific prohibition for professional personal-service corporations; these entities are eligible to make the S election.

Individual Ownership. In order to qualify for a Subchapter S election, a corporation must conform to a number of formal restrictions imposed by the Code. To make an election under Subchapter S, the corporation must not have ineligible shareholders. The maximum number of shareholders in an S corporation is 100. For this purpose, all family members are treated as one shareholder. In addition, all individual shareholders must be citizens or residents of the United States. The estate of a deceased shareholder may continue to hold S corporation stock for a reasonable period of estate administration.

Requirements for Subchapter S Election
• Must be a domestic corporation
• Must have no ineligible shareholders
• Must have no more than 100 shareholders
• No shareholders may be nonresident aliens

Trusts as S Corporation Shareholders. To facilitate business and estate planning flexibility for owners of S corporations, Congress has provided for several types of trusts to be eligible S corporation shareholders. Transfers of S corporation stock to trusts entail careful planning. It is important to coordinate S corporation shareholders' estate plans with the business ownership because the death of a shareholder could cause the stock held by the decedent to be transferred to testamentary trusts created under the decedent's will.

grantor trust

Grantor (Defective) Trusts. A common type of living trust known as a *grantor trust* is an eligible shareholder of S corporation stock. A grantor trust is one in which the grantor is treated as the owner for income tax purposes. The typical grantor trust is a revocable trust created as a probate-avoidance device. The grantor places selected assets in the revocable trust, and trust assets pass outside of probate at the grantor's death. Thus an S corporation shareholder can fund his or her revocable trust with company stock without jeopardizing the S election. The new law extends the eligibility to revocable trusts for up to 2 years after the grantor's death. Although the revocable trust is the most common form of grantor trust, the tax rules under Secs. 671–678 provide many other forms of grantor "defective" trusts that could be useful for the ownership of S corporation stock.

qualified
subchapter S trust
(QSST)

Qualified Subchapter S Trusts. The law also allows the creation of a *qualified subchapter S trust (QSST)* to hold S corporation stock. The QSST is a useful planning device for splitting S corporation income among family members without relinquishing complete control of the stock. The trust grantor can gift stock to the trust and effectively shift the tax burden to the trust beneficiary. The trustee holds and votes stock until the designated trust termination date, however—perhaps when a donee-child or -grandchild reaches the age of majority. The requirements of the QSST are as follows:

- It must distribute all its income to an individual U.S. citizen or resident. Under its terms there can be only one income beneficiary.
- During the term of the trust, corpus may be distributed only to the current income beneficiary.
- Each income interest in the trust must terminate on the earlier of the death of the income beneficiary or the trust termination.
- Upon termination of the trust during the life of an income beneficiary, the trust must distribute all its assets to that beneficiary.
- The beneficiary must make the S election (the election is automatic for successor income beneficiaries unless a successor affirmatively refuses to consent).

electing small business trust (ESBT)

Electing Small Business Trusts. Tax law permits a special election for trusts that do not otherwise qualify as eligible shareholders of S corporation stock: an *electing small business trust (ESBT)*. The ESBT overcomes some of the disadvantages of the QSST in that the trust may have more than one current beneficiary and the election is made by the trustee rather than relying on the beneficiary. Eligible beneficiaries include (1) individuals, (2) estates, and (3) a qualifying charity (the charity can only be a contingent remainder beneficiary). Only trusts receiving S corporation stock by gift or bequest are eligible to be ESBTs. Thus the trustee of an ESBT cannot purchase the S corporation stock as an investment.

Unfortunately, the ESBT has some tax disadvantages. The S corporation portion of the ESBT must be treated as a separate trust, and items of income attributable to the S corporation stock are taxed to the trust at the highest individual rates. Therefore S corporation income attributable to the trust is taxed at 35 percent and capital gain at 20 percent.

Voting Trusts. The use of a voting trust to ensure that shareholders will vote their stock according to a preconceived plan was discussed earlier in this chapter. It is permissible for a voting trust to be formed by S corporation shareholders; the voting trust is an eligible shareholder.

Testamentary Trusts. Certain testamentary trusts that meet the QSST or ESBT rules are eligible shareholders and can make the appropriate election when funded with S corporation stock by a deceased shareholder's estate. However, the new law also permits other types of testamentary trusts to hold S corporation stock for a period of up to 2 years following a deceased shareholder's death.

Summary of Entity Characteristics

1. Sole proprietorship

Advantages	Disadvantages
• ease of formation • flexibility of operation • owner provided maximum authority • preferred income tax status (no double taxation) • owner entitled to all profits	• unlimited liability • limited and unstable business life • limited availability of capital • limited management resources • difficulty in attracting/keeping quality employees • growth limited to personal energies of owner • transferability/continuity more complex than with corporations

2. Partnerships

Advantages	Disadvantages
• increased management resources • increased availability of capital (compared with proprietorship) • ease of formation and dissolution • preferred income tax status (no double taxation) • minimal government nontax reporting • liability limits (limited partnerships)	• unlimited liability for general partner • limited continuity of life (duration) • sharing of earnings and control (division of authority) • decision-making is more complex than proprietorship • potential payment problems to withdrawing partners • more formation expenses than proprietorships

3. **Limited liability companies**

Advantages	Disadvantages
• limited liability for members • acquisition of capital • potential for single taxation status as a partnership • no membership restrictions • not limited to one class member • unlimited number of members • less administrative burden than corporation • preferred income tax status (no double taxation)	• complexity of organizing and operating • sharing control and earnings • more formation expenses than proprietorships

4. **S corporation**

Advantages	Disadvantages

• limited liability for stockholders
• continuity of operations (perpetual life)
• ease of transferring ownership
• acquisition of capital
• professional management
• preferred income tax status (no double taxation)
	• expensive to start (maintain)
	• limited flexibility of operation
	• legal restrictions
	    – 100 or fewer shareholders
	    – only one class of stock
	    – domestic corporation
	    – shareholder must be U.S. citizen or resident alien

5. **C corporation**

Advantages	Disadvantages
• limited liability for stockholders • continuity of operations (perpetual life) • ease of transferring ownership • acquisition of capital • professional management • shareholder-employees are statutory employees • eligible for employee benefits	• expensive to start and maintain • limited flexibility of operation • legal restrictions with respect to operations and management • tax disadvantages of double taxation

Compensation of Management and Key Employees

compensation planning

A discussion of the planning issues facing the closely held business owner or professional would not be complete without a discussion of *compensation planning*. The business owner or professional operating a business or professional practice is usually motivated by the desire to earn a living. The purpose of compensation and fringe benefit planning is to maximize the usefulness to the owners of any income earned by the business.

Planning the compensation and fringe benefits package of the organization requires a balancing of many different and often inconsistent goals. For example, investing in the future growth and income potential of a business may require the owner to temporarily accept less current compensation from the business.

The Proprietor

The proprietor is entitled to all the profits of the business. Its income is taxed to the owner regardless of whether the income is retained by the proprietor for personal use or reinvested in the business. The compensation of the proprietor—the net income of the proprietorship—can be viewed as consisting of two components—part compensation for services to the business and part compensation for ownership (equity). The extent to which the proprietor consumes or reinvests the proprietorship income depends on the current and future needs of both the proprietor and the business.

Partners

A partnership by definition is owned by two or more individuals. As with the proprietorship, the partners of a general partnership have the right to all income. The actual share of each partner is determined at the end of the firm's tax year when the net income is calculated.

Partners report their distributive share of partnership income on their individual tax returns. As always, a decision must be made by the partners as to the portion of the distributive share that will be reinvested in the business as additional capital contributions. The portion of the distributive share reinvested in the partnership is still taxable to the partners but increases their tax bases in their partnership interests.

guaranteed payments
The circumstances surrounding partnership operations will usually dictate the division of partnership income. For example, the partners who provide substantial services to the partnership should receive a share that reflects their efforts. Service partners often receive fixed payments like salaries but known as *guaranteed payments*.

Partners who provide few or no services to the firm but have contributed large amounts of capital should receive a share of income reflecting their equity interests. The actual distributive share agreed upon may take into consideration the needs of the business and/or the tax brackets of the individual partners. However, the IRS may challenge any partnership allocation that does not properly reflect economic reality. That is, each partner's taxable distributive share must be reasonably related to services or capital contribution.

The partners will probably require cash distributions from the business at regular intervals for living expenses. Partnerships typically make periodic distributions known as draws to partners. The size and timing of these draws should be planned with due consideration to the cash needs of the partners, the cash needs of the business, and the expected annual distributive shares of the partners.

At the close of the partnership tax year the draws taken are compared to the partners' distributive shares. If the distributive shares are larger, partners may receive additional cash distributions. If draws were taken in excess of the distributive shares, the partners will either have to reimburse the partnership or decrease their capital accounts.

Limited-Liability Companies (LLCs)

The compensation of members of an LLC should follow the rules of a partnership, provided that the LLC elects partnership tax treatment. Thus income will flow out to members of an LLC in accordance with the provisions of the operating agreement. Special allocation of income and loss can be made for specific members. In addition, the service-providing members can receive guaranteed payments for their efforts.

For fringe-benefit purposes, members will be treated as self-employed. Thus the tax-advantaged fringe benefits available to members will be limited, similar to the benefits available to partners.

Shareholders

Compensation planning for the owners and owner-employees in corporations presents more options and more complexity than in the case of unincorporated businesses. Part of this is attributable to the need to compensate passive owners through dividends. However, most of the flexibility available in compensation planning for the corporation results from the status of the corporate entity and shareholder-employees as separate taxpayers.

Compensation planning for the corporation and its owners provides both opportunity and complexity. The planner must consider the individual needs of the business client to result in successful compensation planning for the shareholders of closely held corporations.

The form of compensation to the owners of the closely held corporation may consist of cash (salary or bonuses), fringe benefits, or dividends. Since a corporation is a separate taxpaying entity, the manner in which corporate income is paid out to the owners has significant tax effects.

Salary payment to corporate employees, including shareholders, and most fringe benefit contributions are tax deductible to the corporation. Dividends provided to shareholders and payments to an employee above reasonable compensation levels are nondeductible. This results in the double taxation of dividends—and unreasonable compensation for services. That is, these amounts are taxed at the corporate level when the income is earned and again to the recipient when paid. Reasonable compensation to employees in the form of salary or bonuses is deductible by the corporation and therefore is taxed only once when paid to the employee.

The tax treatment of fringe benefits varies depending on the type of benefit. Some fringe benefits, such as group term life or health insurance, provide the ultimate in tax advantages. These types of benefits are deductible from corporate income while providing no taxable income to the shareholder-employee. Some fringe benefits such as nonqualified deferred compensation or split-dollar life insurance plans may not provide a current income tax deduction. However such plans might not be applicable in a pass-through entity where there is not a separate taxpayer.

At first glance, compensation planning for a closely held corporation appears easy. Why not pay out all corporate income in the form of salaries and fringe benefits and avoid the issues of double taxation and corporate tax altogether? While this may be the optimal plan for some closely held corporations, many factors weigh against this simple approach. Among these are the individual tax brackets of the owners, the needs of the business, the obligation to compensate passive shareholders, and the reasonable-compensation limitations.

Business Continuity

key employee   Lack of continuity is a major problem facing a closely held business. There are many reasons for a business to terminate, the most obvious of which is financial failure. However, the death, disability, or retirement of an owner or key employee may also result in continuation troubles for the business.

Common Business-Continuation Problems

A closely held business, regardless of whether it is incorporated, typically relies on the skills and services of relatively few individuals. These individuals have a broad involvement with every aspect of the business and are essential to its very survival. In the absence of proper planning the loss of any of these individuals will usually result in a decrease in income or in termination of the business.

The Death of a Business Owner

In theory the impact that the death of an owner has on a closely held business varies by the type of organization. At the death of the proprietor the business assets will be included in the proprietor's estate along with personal assets. These business assets typically have to be liquidated by the personal representative of the decedent-proprietor for an amount less than fair market value resulting in a reduced distribution to the proprietor's heirs. This situation can be avoided through estate-preservation techniques, such as the prearranged sale of the business as a going concern at the proprietor's death.

termination by operation of law   The death of a partner in a general partnership creates a similar problem. A general partnership *termination by operation of law* occurs at the death of one of the partners. The surviving partners are faced with a dilemma that threatens the future of the business and the careers of the partners themselves. At the death of a general partner the survivors must liquidate the partnership interest of the deceased partner. They are faced with a difficult decision. If the business is terminated, the assets must be distributed according to the relative partnership interests or sold for an amount that might be substantially less than fair market value.

The surviving partners may prefer to form a new partnership and continue the business, but the deceased partner's estate must be paid a fair value for the decedent's interest. The surviving partners are required by law to deal fairly with the estate, even though the surviving partners and the partnership may not have adequate funds to distribute a fair share to the deceased partner's estate without liquidating the business.

The limited partnership provides some relief from the business-continuation problems facing the general partnership because the death of a limited partner has no effect on the business. The limited partnership interest can be distributed to the heirs or sold by the estate, and the business will continue as an ongoing partnership with a new limited-investment partner. The death of a general partner in a limited partnership creates the same situation confronting the general partnership: the partnership is dissolved and its assets must be distributed or sold to provide for the estate and the liquidation rights of the survivors. This situation can be avoided either by (1) forming the limited partnership with a corporation as the general partner or (2) adopting an appropriate continuation plan for the limited partnership.

The LLC generally will have some continuity problems at the death of a member. As with any other business, the death of a key service provider will raise practical problems for the future success of the business. As with partnerships, continuation of the business can be provided for under the operating agreement.

The corporation continues in existence as a legal entity beyond the lives of the individual shareholders. Does this mean that the corporation is the solution to every business-continuation problem? For the closely held corporation the answer is probably not.

A closely held business typically relies on the personal services of the individual owners. Their ownership interest in the business typically represents the owners' largest asset. While the corporation has a life independent of its owners, the loss of a significant contributor to the business can cause termination of its activities. Even if the deceased shareholder was not critical to the everyday business operations, the fact that the deceased shareholder's estate holds closely held corporate stock might present problems. If the stock held by the estate is substantial, the personal representative may want to dispose of this stock so that a cash distribution can be made to the heirs. If the deceased shareholder's holdings represent a majority interest, this sale will result in a new majority shareholder, which might change the direction of the corporation or, at the very least, disrupt the lives of the surviving shareholders.

Some problems may also arise at a minority shareholder's death. First, a minority interest will probably have to be sold at a discount. Second, the new minority shareholders, whether the heirs of the deceased shareholder or a subsequent purchaser, may have goals adverse to those of the surviving shareholders.

The Disability of an Owner

The continuation of a closely held business may also be imperiled by the loss of an owner's services for reasons other than death. Although a proprietorship or partnership does not terminate by operation of law upon the disability of an owner, the physical inability of the owner to perform services may have the same practical effect because the disabled owner's services must be replaced in some way. Since the owner probably has some special skill or knowledge of the business, this replacement may be difficult and very costly. The disabled owner might also require continued salary payment from the business for the period of disability. These added costs come at a time when the business income has diminished as a result of the loss of the owner's services.

Planning for the contingency of an owner's disability may be even more important than planning for his or her death because the occurrence of a disability of at least 3 months is more likely than death at preretirement ages.

Retirement of the Owner

The retirement of a business owner can have the same impact on the business as death or disability. If the business is to continue during the retirement of an owner, a replacement must be found if the owner performed essential services. The owner will also typically desire some kind of compensation from the business during retirement, which could be in the form of either continued salary payments, retirement plan benefits, or proceeds from the sale of the business interest. The loss of the retired owner's services coupled with his or her need to retained income can threaten continuation if not properly preplanned and funded.

Fortunately the owner usually recognizes the need to plan for retirement because retirement is viewed as a certainty, whereas early death and disability are viewed as contingencies and are more psychologically convenient to ignore.

Key Employee Risk

The success of a closely held business often depends on the personal services of key owner-employees and non-owner-employees. The loss of a key employee's services due to death or disability will probably result in a loss of income, at least temporarily, to the closely held business. In addition, increased expenses could result from these circumstances since a replacement employee may have to be recruited at a higher salary and require extensive training. This key employee exposure should be considered in the risk-management process.

key employees   The first step in handling this risk is to identify the key employees. *Key employees* have several characteristics distinguishing them from other employees, including the following:

- A key employee might have a specialized skill critical to the success of the particular closely held business. The skill may be possessed by potential replacements, but replacement employees might have to be recruited at higher salary levels.
- The key employee has a substantial customer or client base, and this employee is responsible for attracting significant amounts of business.
- The key employee might be a source of capital if the loss of this key employee would damage the credit rating of the closely held business.

Identifying the key employee might be more difficult than it seems. Initially the owners of a closely held business are generally material participants in the business and can be classified as key employees. Beyond the owners the key employee risk is often overlooked. The business owners might uncover this risk by considering the damage to the business that would occur if a specific managerial employee was absent for longer than the normal vacation period.

Valuing the Key Employee

Determining the key employee's value to the closely held business is even more speculative than the valuation of the business itself. The actual valuation method employed depends on the characteristic of the employee that creates the key employee status. Determining the value of the key employee who attracts substantial business might be relatively easy. The net income resulting from the business produced by the key employee in excess of the amount of net income that could be expected from a similarly situated less effective employee could be capitalized in some manner. Or if business goodwill is attributed to one key employee, the income level above the amount expected for a similar business can be attributed to that key employee. This income attributed to goodwill can be capitalized to arrive at a current value for the employee.

Key Employee Life Insurance

A business could purchase life insurance on the life of the key employee to cover the risk of income loss and/or increase in expenses resulting from the key employee's death. Term insurance can be purchased if the primary concern is the key employee's dollar value to the business. Decreasing term might be appropriate because the key employee exposure decreases as the insured approaches retirement, since the business can be expected to have his or her services for a fewer number of years.

The provisions of the Pension Protection Act (PPA) of 2006 provide restrictions for employer-owned life insurance to prevent abusive circumstances involving life insurance coverage on employees' lives. If the employee does not meet specified status, and employee notice and consent requirements are not met, the life insurance proceeds will be subject to income tax to the extent the proceeds exceed the policyowner's basis in the policy. First, there is an exception for an insured who was an employee at any time during the 12-month period before the insured's death. Second, there is an exception for an insured who was, at the time the contract was issued, a director or highly compensated employee or highly compensated individual. Thus, key person coverage would generally qualify for traditional income-tax-free receipt of life insurance for the corporation-policyowner, provided the notice and consent requirements are met.[3]

Key employee insurance, however, is usually coupled with some other purpose such as providing a retirement benefit for the key employee. Permanent life insurance is typically purchased to meet this objective. The life insurance death benefit will be received by the business as indemnification for the income loss and/or increase in expenses resulting from the key employee's death. If the insured survives to retirement, the corporation can use the cash surrender value to fund a deferred-compensation retirement benefit. Another approach would be for the business to transfer the policy to the employee at retirement. The business should be the owner and beneficiary of key employee life insurance. This should pose no insurable interest problems since the business will suffer a pecuniary loss at the death of the key employee. The premiums for key employee insurance will be nondeductible, while death benefits will be received tax free. An additional benefit of key employee insurance is that no accumulated-earnings-tax problems should result since the accumulation of earnings to insure the key employee death risk will meet the reasonable-business-needs test. For incorporated businesses key employee life insurance may, however, increase exposure to the alternative minimum corporate tax.

---

3.   The notice and consent requirements of this provision are met if, prior to the issuance of the contract, the employee

     1.   is notified in writing that the employer intends to insure the employee's life and the maximum face amount for which the employee could be insured at the time the contract was issued,

     2.   provides written consent to being insured under the contract and that such coverage may continue after the insured terminates employment, and

     3.   is informed in writing that the employer will be a beneficiary of any proceeds payable upon the death of the employee.

There are two other exceptions that should be mentioned. The adverse income tax consequences for employer-owned life insurance are avoided if

     1.   the proceeds are paid to a family member of the employee or

     2.   the proceeds are to be used by the employer to purchase the business interest held by the employee from the employee's estate.

Tax Aspects of Key Employee Life Insurance
• Premiums are not deductible for employer.
• Death proceeds are tax free to employer.
• There are no accumulated-earnings tax problems for reasonable coverage.

Key Employee Disability Income Insurance

The total and permanent disability of a key employee presents problems similar to those posed by the death of a key employee. The business will also incur an additional expenditure when salary continuation payments will be made to the disabled key employee. To cover the loss of income and increased expenditures resulting from a key employee disability exposure, the business could purchase and be beneficiary of a disability income policy. First, an appropriate elimination period must be selected. One approach would be to select an elimination period equal to the longest vacation or leave of absence that could be provided to the key employee without causing a financial strain on the business. The insurer-participation limits for disability income insurance policies might present a problem. Although the closely held business is the beneficiary of the policy, many insurers' underwriting rules will reduce the coverage available to the insured individually due to the coverage purchased by the employer. This may cause dissatisfaction with key employees who are unable to secure adequate individual coverage as a result of these participation limits. Disability income policies are currently available with high monthly benefit amounts that should alleviate much of the financial loss suffered by a business should the key employee become disabled.

The Adverse Effects of Business Termination

Business-continuation problems can occur for many reasons far removed from simple economic failure. The termination of a business will usually result in a direct adverse impact on all individuals closely affiliated with the enterprise.

The Cessation of Income from the Business to the Owner and Family

It is likely that an owner's interest in a closely held business is the most significant, or at least a major, asset held by its owner. If the owner has an active role in the business, his or her income from the business is probably necessary for the support of the owner and family. If the business terminates while the owner is still alive, a large portion of the business owner's income will also terminate. Until the business owner can find a replacement source of income, this can become a severe financial problem for him or her. The situation may be worse if the business terminates due to the owner's death, leaving the surviving spouse and dependents with no income unless the surviving spouse is substantially employable.

Proper planning can solve most of these problems. A continuation plan might prevent the business from terminating and therefore provide for a continuing flow of income. On the other hand, a properly designed sale of the business, although terminating the owner's interest in the business, could provide adequate proceeds for future support of the owner and family.

Sidetracked Careers of the Surviving Owners and Employees

There are severe problems for the business owner who dies, retires, or is disabled without an adequate continuation plan, but there is another significant problem. When a business terminates, the able-bodied co-owners and employees of the business also lose a major income source. For some, this may not be a problem. For example, employees of a terminated professional corporation or partnership can continue their careers in private practice. Other employees with marketable skills can find equivalent jobs elsewhere. The owners or employees may have unique skills designed solely for the now terminated closely held business. In this case it may be some time before their careers can be continued.

The Discounted Liquidation Value of Business Assets

The termination of a closely held business results either in the sale of the business as a going concern or liquidation of the assets on a piecemeal basis. The forced sale of a business following one of these causes of termination often results in receipt of proceeds that are less than satisfactory for two reasons. First, if a buyer is not found through advance planning, it may be difficult to find the appropriate buyer for the business on short notice. Second, a business terminating after the loss of an owner or substantial contributor has bleak prospects and is likely to be unattractive to potential buyers. A prearranged continuation plan or sale may avoid the possible diminution in value of the business.

When a Small Business Terminates
• Loss of income for owners and families • Disruption of careers of remaining owners and employees • Loss of value due to forced sale of assets

Chapter Review

Review questions are based on the learning objectives in this chapter. Thus, a [3] at the end of a question means that the question is based on learning objective 3. If there are multiple objectives, they are all listed.

Key Terms and Concepts

limited-liability company (LLC)
operating agreement
closely held business
partnership
board of directors
limited partnership
joint and several liability
limited-liability partnership (LLP)
pass-through taxation
medicare contribution tax
net investment income (NII)
distributive share
dividend
double taxation
reasonable compensation

personal-service business
accumulated-earnings tax
accumulated taxable income
alternative-minimum-tax
alternative minimum taxable
  income (AMTI)
grantor trust
qualified subchapter S trust (QSST)
electing small business trust
  (ESBT)
compensation planning
guaranteed payments
key employee
termination by operation of law
key employees

Review Questions

1. What forms of organization can be chosen by the business to carry out an enterprise? [1]

2. How do the formalities of forming a business differ among sole proprietorships, partnerships, LLCs, and corporations? [2]

3. How is the control of business management established in a corporation? [3]

4. Why might business owners anticipating large capital expansion needs consider the formation of a limited partnership or LLC rather than a general partnership? [4]

5. Explain what is meant by limited liability, and identify the types of enterprises that provide this advantage to their owners. [5]

6. Explain how the 3.8 percent tax on net investment income affects business owners. [6]

7. Explain what is meant by a pass-through entity for tax purposes. [7]

8. Explain how overall taxes might be minimized through income splitting between a corporation and its shareholders. [8]

9. Explain what is meant by "double taxation" and how closely held corporations typically avoid this burden. [8]

10. Describe the following special corporate tax provisions:
    a. accumulated earnings tax
    b. corporate alternative minimum tax (AMT)
    c. personal service company taxation
    [8]

11. Describe the income tax treatment of an S corporation. [8]

12. Discuss the methods of compensating business owners in the different forms of business entities? [9]

13. Why does the loss of an owner of a closely held business represent a threat to business continuation? [10]

14. In the absence of continuation planning, what is the status of the following entities after the death of a partner? [10]
    a. partnership
    b. LLC
    c. corporation

15. What are the potential results of the loss of a key employee by a closely held business? [11]

16. Identify the traditional methods for valuing a key employee. [11]

17. Describe the process of protecting the business for a loss of a key employee with permanent life insurance. [11]

Learning Objectives

An understanding of the material in this chapter should enable you to

1. Identify the steps in the transition of the business owner to his or her retirement.

2. Discuss the possibilities for providing income to the business owner in retirement.

3. Discuss the estate planning objectives for the owner of a closely held business.

4. Describe the role of the business owner's advisers in the business succession/estate planning process.

5. Describe the process of forecasting the client's estate tax liability.

6. Describe the discounting techniques for gifts of business interests.

7. Distinguish between the sale of a business interest for installment notes or private annuities.

8. Explain how the provisions of Sec. 6166 can assist the estate of a closely held business owner.

9. Describe the two basic designs for a buy-sell agreement.

10. Explain the tax treatment for buy-sell agreements funded with life insurance.

11. Discuss the differences between purchases and sales of pass-through entities and corporate stock.

12. Identify the advantages of an irrevocable life insurance trust (ILIT).

Transition to Retirement

Prior to Retirement of the Business Owner

A business owner generally relies on the business as the primary source of income for his or her family. Therefore prior to retirement the business must provide the owner with a substantial stream of income. The current income demands of the owner must be balanced with several other goals. First, substantial assets must often be reinvested in the business to provide for future growth and competitiveness. Second, the compensation of key employees, including any family successors, must be sufficiently attractive to retain these individuals. Finally, current federal income tax burdens may force the deferral of some current income through various types of tax-deferred retirement arrangements. Since most business owners will wish to maintain an inflation-protected standard of living, the owner will probably desire a steadily increasing income flow until retirement.

Transition to the Business Owner's Retirement

At some point most individuals will decide to terminate their full-time working careers. Although the owners of businesses tend to work longer than other employed individuals, they still must face the transition to retirement. Since the business owner is the most significant contributor to the success of the business, some long-range planning should be done to ease this transition. First, a successor (or successors) must be identified and groomed. Maybe there are logical successors among the owner's children. Since children will quite often show little or no interest in taking an active role in the family business at first, a parent may need a significant period of time to convince the appropriate children that it is in their best interest to work for the business. Once the junior family members are employed by the business, their development into mature and capable successors may take a number of years. It may be necessary to find executives from the outside to smooth the transition if the family successors are not prepared to take over when their parent(s) retires. An outside board of directors is often recommended for this purpose. If there are no family members interested or capable to succeed the current owner, other potential successors will have to be found. The process of identifying and grooming the appropriate successors should begin as early as possible and certainly long before the owner is approaching retirement.

Assuming the appropriate successors are employed by the business, steps should be taken to prevent these individuals from becoming dissatisfied and thus leaving the business. Providing a substantial salary to the current owner's successors may meet with the other tax-planning needs, particularly if the successor is one of the children. Income taxes can be saved if the business income is divided among several family members. If the reasonable-compensation tests are met, salaries can be paid to the owner's children and taxed at their lower income tax brackets. These funds flowing from the business to the employed children can in some circumstances be used by the children for expenditures that would normally have been provided by the parents. Furthermore, if the business is incorporated, the payment of substantial salaries to family members is an effective method for removing cash from the corporation and reducing exposure to the accumulated-earnings tax.

Once the intended successors have worked for the business for a period of time, they will probably also demand an increased role in the decision-making process of the business. These individuals should be afforded this opportunity since their eventual roles will require creativity and decisiveness. It may also be necessary and advisable to begin providing these individuals with equity interests in the business. These steps are consistent with the phaseout of the current owner's contributions to the business as his or her retirement grows near and may also be consistent with the estate planning goals.

Problems in Transition of the Business
• Identifying the appropriate successor
• Selecting (convincing) appropriate junior generation family members to assume active roles in the business
• Developing the successors
• Compensating both the business owner and the successor(s)
• Giving the successor(s) a gradually increasing role in business decision making
• Coordinating business transition with other estate planning objectives

Other issues must be faced before the business owner transfers the business to his or her successors. It must be determined when and how the current owner will pass the actual control of the ownership interest to the successors. There are really only four choices for transferring a closely held business. Alternate choices for transferring the business to successors include

- the sale of a controlling interest in the business to the successors at retirement
- lifetime gifts of the business interest to the family successors
- the sale of the business interest at death through a buy-sell agreement
- the testamentary bequest of the business interest to family successor

Providing for the Business Owner in Retirement

Another important consideration is how the business owner and his or her spouse will be provided for during retirement. The owner will probably expect the business to provide his or her continuing family needs during retirement. If the expected standard of living is high, a substantial flow of income may be required. The choices for providing this postretirement income include

- benefits from qualified and/or nonqualified retirement plans adopted by the family business
- payments for the continued services of the business owner (for example, consulting fees, director fees, or a part-time salary)
- proceeds from the sale of the business to the successors (such as installment or private annuity payments)
- passive income from any retained ownership interest
- the business owner's other accumulated wealth

It is likely that none of these choices will be adequate unless the necessary funding is made in advance. The funding should be carefully planned since the owner's other wealth accumulation and estate planning objectives must be handled in a consistent fashion.

Estate Planning for the Business Owner

As the current owner of a closely held business prepares to turn over the reins to successors, several estate planning objectives should be considered. These objectives include

- retaining assets (business or otherwise) that provide adequate retirement income while minimizing the size of the taxable estate
- transferring control and future appreciation of the business to the appropriate successors
- reducing the amount of the business owner's assets includible in his or her gross estate
- planning adequate liquidity for the estate
- arranging for an orderly and equitable disposition of the business owner's other assets to meet his or her dispositive objectives

Since the ownership interest in a closely held business is likely to represent the most significant asset held by the owner, it is appropriate for estate planning to focus on this asset. At first, many of these estate planning objectives appear to be incongruent or even mutually exclusive. How does a business owner give up his or her business interest while retaining a substantial income flow? How does a business owner retain sufficient income while also reducing the size of his or taxable estate? How can liquidity be provided to the estate if illiquid assets, such as a business interest, might be included? There are no universal answers to these questions. Furthermore, provisions of the estate and gift tax laws applicable to businesses are often adverse to, and increase the complexity of, meeting these objectives. The facts and circumstances of each particular case require careful consideration before an appropriate estate and business plan can be devised.

A big concern of business owners is how to leave their estates equitably to heirs. Some of the business owner's children will probably not become actively involved in the business. Providing these individuals with significant ownership interests is generally not recommended, because it is difficult to compensate the passive owners adequately for their interests. For example, if the business is incorporated, these passive owners must be compensated as shareholders through nondeductible dividend payments. However, the active family members holding stock must also take these dividends. This is costly and usually inappropriate. Even if the business will be run as a partnership, LLC, or an S corporation, the family members providing substantial services to the business must be adequately compensated before any business income can be paid to the passive owners. The division of ownership in the family business between active and passive family members often creates disputes over their relative shares that may cause an irreconcilable division between family members.

Most individuals hope to provide for their children equitably from their accumulated wealth. If all the children will not become involved in the business, the owner faces a troublesome dilemma. Since the business is likely to represent a substantial portion of the owner's wealth, it may be difficult or impossible to transfer the business to the family successors while also providing assets of similar size to inactive heirs. This problem often leads to procrastination by the business client with respect to the business succession plan. However, financial services professionals generally have adequate products and tools to handle the problem if is recognized. Potential resolutions to the dilemma of providing for all the business owner's heirs include the following:

- An irrevocable life insurance trust can be used to substantially enhance the estate of the business owner without adding to the estate tax burden. Beneficiaries of the trust generally include the inactive heirs and/or the surviving spouse of the family business owner because the active heirs will benefit from the growth in the business.

- The lifetime or postmortem sale of the business can be made to the successors. Since the successor will pay full value for the business interest, adequate liquidity should be available to the estate so that the other family members can be provided a fair share.

- A substantial investment fund can be accumulated by the client outside the business to provide for the inactive heirs. This fund can be partially invested in life insurance covering the life of the business owner to ensure the liquidity of the estate and adequacy of the nonbusiness wealth accumulations.

Finally, if no family members are appropriate successors, the business will either terminate at the death or retirement of the owner, or a sale to individuals outside the family will be transacted. If a sale of the business is preferable to liquidation, the best results occur if the owner plans well in advance.

Advising the Business Owner in the Succession/Estate Planning Process

The business owner is unlikely to arrive at the appropriate business succession/estate planning solution without professional assistance. Most entrepreneurs have a difficult time facing up to their own mortality. They see their very existence commingled with the business and cannot imagine one without the other. This procrastination leads to several of the following problems, which will generally prevent the successful transfer of the business to a successor:

- The business transfer plan will either be inadequate or not communicated to the successors.

- Any planning that has been done will not be coordinated. For example, the wills and trusts executed in conjunction with the estate planning attorney will no longer be appropriate for the transfer of the growing business asset. The entrepreneur's life insurance policies will have inappropriate ownership and beneficiary designations.

- The appropriate successors will not be sufficiently trained to step into the entrepreneur's shoes at his or her death.

- The successors will become dissatisfied with the business since the current owner will control their actions in the business and stifle their creativity.

- The successors will become disillusioned since their future roles with the business are unclear.

- The business itself will stagnate due to the phenomenon of "harvesting." This occurs when the aging entrepreneur becomes less ambitious and puts less energy into the future growth of the business. The entrepreneur may begin to siphon off substantial funds from the business to reap the benefits of his or her earlier sacrifices.

All too often the business owner's professional advisers are unsuccessful in dealing with this problem. This results more from a lack of focus than a lack of ability to meet these needs. Often the adviser defines his or her role narrowly with respect to the business owner. The attorney who works on the estate plan often limits his or her role to the preparation of the documents, such as wills and trusts, to handle the orderly transfer of the business owner's estate at death with minimum adverse estate tax consequences. The attorney for the business is primarily concerned with business contracts and is often unfamiliar with the transfer taxes associated with the estate of a closely held business owner. The accountant that works with the business is concerned with maximizing the business's current net income and market value. The life underwriter is concerned with providing the necessary death and disability protection for the business owner and providing liquidity for his or her estate. Finally, the investment adviser is primarily concerned with the performance of the business owner's investment portfolio. Each of these professionals may be highly competent and perform their individual tasks superbly without addressing the overall problem.

The financial services professional is in a position to assist the business owner. What is needed more than anything else in this process is focus; an adviser who gains the client's confidence as the center of influence should be able to get the task done. If each of the other advisers is satisfied with his or her role in the process, the team will be capable of handling the orderly succession of the family business.

To succeed in this role the financial services professional must become acquainted with (and gain the trust of) the business owner's family and key employees. This individual may come from any part of the financial planning team.

The business owner might want the financial services professional to communicate the plan to members of the family and key employee group. If these individuals have learned to place their trusts in this primary adviser, the plan may be more widely accepted. In many ways this communication process is the most difficult and important step in the succession plan. The inability to face individuals who may be receiving unpopular news is often a stumbling block. It may be necessary to bring in outside professionals such as counselors and psychologists to handle the personal concerns of the family members. The actual implementation of the plan will be a smoother process if the senior family member's intentions for the future of the business are understood by all parties.

Once the plan has been described to the appropriate individuals, the plan must be implemented. At this point it is necessary for members of the financial planning team to perform their individual steps—legal documents must be prepared by the business owner's attorney; the CPA might have to value the family business; the life underwriter will have to secure the necessary coverage to fund the various aspects of the agreement. The key adviser must make sure that these necessary steps are taken. The adviser must be satisfied that the individual steps fit together properly to meet the overall goal. When the advisers are satisfied that all tasks have been completed appropriately, the plan can be executed.

After the plan is in place, the role of the key adviser is not finished. It is probable that future events will cause the need for the plan to be updated or even substantially altered. For example, more insurance funding may be needed if the family business grows. Changes in the status of family members and key employees may necessitate modification of the plan. Finally, changes in the tax laws and business marketplace may lead to further updating. In any event it is the responsibility of the financial services professional to remain on top of the situation.

Forecasting Estate Settlement Costs for the Business Owner

It is appropriate to provide the business owner with a forecast of the costs of settling his or her estate. It will often serve as a wake-up call. In addition to the obvious complexity of planning and settling the estate of a business owner, there is the potential for significant costs that will be difficult to manage with the other dispositive goals that will require liquidity.

Administrative Expenses

administrative expenses   The administrative expenses and other settlement costs vary based on a number of factors. A business owner's estate will be more complex than the average estate. If complex estate settlement matters require substantial professional help, administrative fees could be significant. Any special or unique characteristics related to the estate should also be considered. For example, if the client has substantial recourse loans—loans where the grantor and/or his or her estate are personally liable—such loans unpaid at the time of the client's death could be an immediate cash expense. Other factors, such as appraisal fees, vary from case to case; for example, an estate containing one or more closely held business interests or unusual personal property necessitates the estimation of significant appraisal fees.

Normally, the administrative expenses and other settlement costs (other than death taxes) are stated as a percentage of the value of the estate. This is generally the case whether the estate forecast is done manually or with computer software. For simplicity, most planners estimate the administrative expenses as 2 to 5 percent of the estate.

Forecasting Federal Estate Taxes

gross estate **The Gross Estate.** The first step in forecasting a business's estate settlement cost is determining the amount of the anticipated *gross estate*. The gross estate for federal estate tax purposes is the total of the items included in the estate's tax base. This initial step requires the financial services professional to be familiar with the federal estate tax inclusion rules, state property law issues, and basic principles of property valuation.

The client's gross estate is found by totaling the following items:

- property (such as a closely held business interest) owned outright by the decedent at the time of his or her death
- certain property interests transferred by gift within 3 years of the decedent's death
- property transferred during the decedent's lifetime in which the decedent retains certain rights
- benefits from qualified retirement plans, IRAs, and nonqualified annuity products purchased by the decedent (or paid for by the decedent's employer) payable to a survivor at the decedent's death
- property jointly held between the decedent and a survivor where the survivor obtains the decedent's interest through rights of survivorship
- general powers of appointment held over property by the decedent during his or her lifetime and/or at the time of his or her death

- life insurance in which the decedent held incidents of ownership (or gratuitously transferred incidents of ownership within 3 years of death) or which was payable to the decedent's executor
- property subject to a life interest held by the decedent in which the decedent's spouse or the executor of such spouse's estate made the so-called QTIP election to require inclusion in the estate of the decedent

A thorough listing of the items included in the decedent's gross estate is essential for forecasting federal estate taxes. Without an accurate estimation of the tax base, any subsequent forecasting calculations will produce erroneous results. The financial services professional should have a thorough understanding of these inclusion rules. In most instances, clients do not have any idea how the federal estate tax will affect their property. In fact, clients will be surprised to learn that certain items, such as their pension assets or life insurance, are subject to federal estate or state death taxes.

The financial services professional should also be aware of the forms of property ownership. The different estate tax effects of jointly held property, life insurance, and general or limited powers of appointment can be seen in the discussion above. Many clients are not certain of the form in which they own their property. For example, spouses rarely are sure whether property is titled jointly with rights of survivorship, titled jointly without rights of survivorship, or individually owned by either spouse. For other items, such as retirement plans, clients typically are unsure of, and have no record of, the selected beneficiary designation. The same may also be true for a client's life insurance. It is important that the financial services professional gather thorough and accurate data for each client. A valuable tool in this data-gathering process is a fact-finding questionnaire.

The completion of a fact finder serves several purposes. First, the client gains confidence in the financial services professional who is thorough and knowledgeable regarding the data gathering. Second, the data collected on the client's assets, life insurance, and retirement benefits enable the financial services professional to accurately forecast the estate settlement cost as the client's plan is currently designed. Third, the questions on the fact finder alert the financial services professional and the client to any unusual property ownership interests the client holds that should be given special consideration. Finally, the fact finder helps the client formulate goals, enabling the financial services professional to design and recommend an effective alternative to the client's current estate plan.

Valuing Estate Assets. To accurately forecast a client's estate settlement cost, it is necessary to know not only what assets are included in the estate tax base but also the value of such assets. The estate settlement costs forecast will be accurate only if appropriate values are estimated for each item included in the client's gross estate. The accuracy of the valuation estimates depends on (1) the appraisal skills of the financial services professional doing the forecast, (2) the input available from the client's other advisers, (3) the types of assets held by the client, and (4) the willingness of the client to pay for accurate property appraisals, if necessary.

Many types of assets lend themselves to immediate accurate valuation. For example, the client's estate could consist of cash, marketable securities, and life insurance. The value of all such items can be determined simply and accurately. Other items, such as real estate, closely held business interests, and special types of personal property (such as artwork), involve more complex and uncertain valuation.

adjusted gross estate
Determining the Adjusted Gross Estate. The financial services professional involved in estate planning must thoroughly understand the estate tax calculation procedure. We have already discussed the important first step in the estate tax calculation—determining the value of the gross estate. The calculation of taxes in the estate tax return is not, in theory, markedly different from the calculation in the income tax return. The gross tax base—the gross estate—is reduced by deductions against the gross estate to arrive at the adjusted gross estate. Deductible items should be included in the estate settlement cost forecast because they will be part of the estate's cash needs. In addition, as deductible items, they have the effect of reducing the estimated estate taxes. Items deductible from the gross estate include the following:

- funeral expenses
- unpaid taxes, such as property taxes
- administrative expenses
- recourse debts of the decedent
- creditor claims or other claims against the estate
- losses incurred on estate assets (which are fortuitous, do not occur until the estate is being settled, and are impossible to estimate in the forecast)

marital deduction
Determining the Taxable Estate. The adjusted gross estate determined above is an arbitrary calculation and

is used to measure certain thresholds. For example, the eligibility for Sec. 303 stock redemptions or Sec. 6166 installment payments is based on a percentage threshold of the *adjusted* gross estate. The adjusted gross estate is further reduced by three important deductions—the federal estate tax marital, charitable, and state death tax deduction—to reach the taxable estate. The marital deduction provides choices for providing for a surviving spouse, but also adds complexity. Issues that must be determined in each case include:

- how much should be left to the spouse? Leaving all the estate to a surviving spouse eliminates the federal estate tax but may be inconsistent with other objectives.

- should the surviving spouse be an outright beneficiary or be subject to the controls of a trustee? For example, the transfer to a surviving spouse could be limited to income only (and maybe limited invasion powers). This transfer is known as a "QTIP" trust and would be appropriate if the business owner has children from a prior marriage and these individuals will inherit the remaining principal of the QTIP trust when the surviving spouse dies.

- what should be provided to other family members? There may be other beneficiaries that will be provided for at the business owner's death. There may be children from a prior marriage or there may be children who are successors to the closely held business.

- will the marital transfer be limited to an amount above the deceased business owner's applicable exclusion amount? The use of the business owner's exclusion amount at his or her death coupled with a transfer of the excess estate to a surviving spouse will result in zero estate tax.

- the decedent's estate tax exemption that is unused at the first death can be transferred to the surviving spouse on the decedent's estate tax return. This determination will be made with due consideration to the total estate tax forecast for the married couple.

Determining the Tentative Tax Base. At this point, there is a significant departure from the theory behind the income tax calculation. Lifetime gifts are added to the tax base at this point to preserve the theory of unification between the estate and gift tax systems. Thus, the decedent's estate tax return will appear as though all taxable transfers during the decedent's lifetime were made at the time of his or her death.

Determining a Tentative Federal Estate Tax. The rate schedule (shown in table 2-1) is applied to the tentative tax base to determine a tentative tax.

Because there can be no double-counting of taxes, any federal gift taxes made on such taxable gifts before the decedent's death must be deducted from the tentative estate taxes.

EXAMPLE
Ralph, a single man, dies in 2014 with a taxable estate of $12,400,000. He has no lifetime adjusted taxable gifts. The tentative tax on $12,400,000 is calculated as follows: The tax on the first $1,000,000 is $345,800, as indicated in Table 2-1. The tax on the amount above $1,000,000 is determined by calculating 40 percent (the maximum rate for 2014) of the excess over $1,000,000 ($11,400,000 × .40) or $4,560,000. The final tentative tax is $345,800 + $4,560,000 = $4,905,800.

Table 2–1

Not over $10,000	18% of such amount
Over $10,000 but not over $20,000	$1,800, plus 20% of excess of such amount over $10,000
Over $20,000 but not over $40,000	$3,800, plus 22% of excess of such amount over $20,000
Over $40,000 but not over $60,000	$8,200, plus 24% of excess of such amount over $40,000
Over $60,000 but not over $80,000	$13,000, plus 26% of excess of such amount over $60,000
Over $80,000 but not over $100,000	$18,200, plus 28% of excess of such amount over $80,000
Over $100,000 but not over $150,000	$23,800, plus 30% of excess of such amount over $100,000
Over $150,000 but not over $250,000	$38,800, plus 32% of excess of such amount over $150,000
Over $250,000 but not over $500,000	$70,800, plus 34% of excess of such amount over $250,000
Over $500,000 but not over $750,000	$155,800, plus 37% of excess of such amount over $500,000
Over $750,000 but not over $1,000,000	$248,300, plus 39% of excess of such amount over $750,000
Over $1,000,000	$345,800, plus 40% of excess of such amount over $1,000,000

Determining the Net Federal Estate Tax Payable after Credits. After the tentative tax has been reduced by the amount of gift taxes payable on post-1976 taxable gifts, the federal estate tax payable is reduced by certain credits. Specifically, the credits include the following:

- the applicable credit amount against estate taxes. This amount is the tax that would be imposed on the exclusion amount of $5,000,000 indexed for inflation after 2011. The 2014 exclusion amount is $5,340,000 and this results in a tax credit for 2014 decedents of $2,081,800. Note that this credit is reinstated at death even if some or all was used against lifetime taxable gifts.

- foreign death tax credit. A credit may be allowed against the federal estate tax for taxes paid by the decedent's estate to a foreign country for estate inheritance or other death taxes. This credit may be available whether the decedent is a citizen of the United States or a resident alien at the time of his or her death. This credit is for foreign death taxes paid on properties located outside the United States that are also included in the decedent's gross estate for federal estate tax purposes.

- credit for gift taxes paid on pre-1977 gifts

- credit for tax on prior transfers. This credit provides relief if property included in the gross estate was inherited from someone who died less than 10 years before the decedent's date of death. The credit is designed to prevent federal estate taxes from being paid twice on the same asset within a short period of time. The credit is 100 percent of the federal estate taxes paid at the time of the initial transfer reduced by 20 percent every 2 years. Thus, if 10 years or more have passed since the property was taxed in the initial estate, the credit is completely phased out.

EXAMPLE

Back to the previous example from above. Assume Ralph's estate does not have any credits except the applicable credit amount. His tentative tax was $4,905,800. Applying the applicable credit amount for 2014 ($2,081,800) will result in a net federal estate tax payable of $2,824,000. That would certainly get Ralph's attention if we were providing him a forecast while he was alive.

Designing the Effective Transfer of a Family Business

The business owner can transfer the closely held business through one or more of the following methods:

- lifetime sales
- lifetime gifts
- sale at death
- bequest at death

The transfer of the closely held business will often involve a combination of the potential transfer methods; particularly if the business is to be transferred to successors from the business owner's family. It is difficult to transfer the business in one step during lifetime for a number of reasons. First, the business owner may want to retain control for a period of time. Second, the current owner may wish to retain a stream of income from the business during retirement. Third, if gifts of the business interests are made to family successors, the gift tax system only provides limited exclusions and exemptions to shelter gifts of the business interest from current gift taxation. Finally, family successors may not be prepared to take control. It is important to plan to transfer at least some of the business interest at death to prepare for the contingency of the business owner's premature death.

Lifetime Gifts of Business Interests

Basic Gift Tax Exclusions and Exemptions

taxable gift

annual exclusion

Most people are familiar with the lifetime applicable credit amount ($5,340,000 in 2014). However, this credit only applies to cumulative "taxable gifts". A taxable gift is defined as a gift not excluded or deducted as a result of a special exclusion or deduction provided by the gift tax rules. Another opportunity for gifting property to lower estate taxes is that there is an annual exclusion related to federal gift taxation. This provision offers a unique tax advantage for gifts in the unified estate and gift tax system. It gives the donor the ability to permanently remove property from the transfer tax base without making a taxable gift. The annual exclusion permits the donor to give $14,000 (2014 indexed amount) per year to each selected donee without making a taxable gift.

split gift

Further, if the donor is married at the time of the gift and the spouse consents, the amount of the annual exclusion may be doubled to $28,000 (2014) per year, per donee. (This doubling of the annual exclusion for a married donor is referred to as a split gift.) As a planning point, bear in mind that the per-year element of the annual exclusion refers to a calendar year and not a 12-month period. Furthermore, if the spouse elects to split gifts for a tax year, such gift splitting applies to all gifts made by either spouse during the year (except gifts between the spouses). If gifts are to be split during the year, Form 709 must be filed with the consenting spouse's signature by April 15 of the year following the year the gifts were made.

present interest gifts

There is a limitation on the use of the annual exclusion. It is only available for present interest gifts and not gifts of a future interest. With outright gifts, qualification for the annual exclusion is generally available because there is no future interest problem. However, gifts of closely held business interests will not qualify as a present interest unless the donee has a real opportunity to receive some current income and/or has a real possibility to transfer the interest. Gifts of business interests need to be carefully planned.

EXAMPLE

Margaret Lynn, a widow aged 60, has a large estate (currently valued at $8.5 million) and has been advised by her financial planner to seriously consider initiating a gifting program so that some assets may be removed from her gross estate. She has three children and eight grandchildren. She loves all these potential donees and has no reservations about gifting property to any of them. Because the federal gift tax annual exclusion rule currently (2014) allows $14,000 worth of property to be gifted to each donee per year, Margaret can give a total of $154,000 worth of property each year without incurring any federal gift tax liability ($14,000 x 11 donees = $154,000). If Margaret begins this program next year, continues this pattern of giving for the rest of her life (including gifts made in the year of her death), and lives to her tabular life expectancy (24 more years), she will make 24 years of gifts of $154,000 annually (ignoring further inflation-indexing increases to the annual exclusion). Because the excluded gifts are not taxable gifts, Margaret can make the excluded gifts described above and make a cumulative total of $5,340,000 (2014 indexed amount) of additional taxable gifts without incurring gift taxes as a result of her lifetime gift applicable exclusion. If her donees save the gifts and appreciation occurs, the estate tax savings could be very significant.

Compliance for Gift Tax Purposes

statute of limitations

It is particularly important to make sure that the gift tax compliance rules are followed for the gift of a closely held business interest. A 3-year statute of limitations following the filing of a gift tax return applies to the initiation of an IRS audit of the return. Failure to file an appropriately substantiated gift tax return would not limit the timing of a challenge of the transaction by the IRS. There have been cases where the IRS successfully challenged a gift of a business interest 15 to 20 years later when the transferor passed away.

IRS regulations describe substantiation requirements to ensure the protection of the statute of limitations. The gift tax return will have the 3-year statutory protection only if it is substantiated with enough information to give the IRS sufficient details of the nature of the transaction. A memorandum, including a complete description of the property, should be filed with the return to explain the form of the transfer. The relationship between the transferor and transferee must be disclosed. It is important to include valuation methods, particularly if hard-to-value property (such as a closely held business interest) is transferred. If valuation discounts are taken, the supporting information should provide justification for the discount based on the facts and circumstances of the case. The substantiation rules also permit the submission of an appraisal by a qualified appraiser in lieu of requiring the donor to submit this voluminous substantiation with the return. For most gifts involving hard-to-value property and/or valuation discounts, the return preparer should employ a qualified appraiser.

If the donor is making annual gifts of business interests using the gift tax annual exclusion ($14,000 per donee in 2014), the gift tax return is not technically required for excluded gifts. However, it may be advisable to file a gift tax return anyway to provide the protection of the 3-year statute of limitations.

Importance of Valuation Discounts

It is often justifiable and necessary to discount the value of a business interest determined by one of the above-mentioned valuation techniques. These discounts are appropriate when the value determined by one of the methods is greater than the actual current market value. Reasons for the disparity between actual value and the value of the business interest reached by established techniques are that (1) the interest being valued represents a minority interest, (2) the interest being valued suffers from a lack of marketability, (3) the property is held in individual fractional ownership, (4) the interest being valued has built-in capital-gains tax or other liabilities, and (5) the interest is being liquidated on a distressed basis.

minority discount
The Minority Discount. We mentioned earlier that one basis of value of a business interest is control power. A *minority discount* interest stems from the inability to control the business. The owner or controlling group of owners of a business possesses benefits that translate into market value. The benefits derived from this control are the ability to

- direct the management of the business (that is, elect and sit on the board of directors)
- hire and terminate employees
- establish compensation structure
- determine the goals and operations of the business
- acquire and dispose of business property

- make distributions to partners or pay dividends to shareholders
- terminate the business

The appropriate size of a minority discount depends on the degree to which these control powers are lacking. Many of the control powers are often not an either/or situation for the majority and minority owners. There are many instances in which some degree of control is retained by even a minority interest holder. For example, cumulative voting allows minority shareholders to elect a minimum number of directors. State corporation statutes or individual corporate charters may also require a super majority of shareholders to approve extraordinary corporate actions. In these cases it is not appropriate to fully discount the minority interest. The appropriate degree of minority discount depends on the individual circumstances within the business since the number of owners and the relative sizes of the interests held by the majority and minority groups have an impact on the degree of control possessed by each.

EXAMPLE

LIFO, Inc., has two owners. The majority owner holds 90 percent of the stock outstanding and the minority owner the remainder. The degree of control lost by the minority owner is substantial, and the minority interest is worth far less than 10 percent of the total value of LIFO. Now suppose FIFO, Inc., has four equal shareholders. Each shareholder owns a minority interest, but no discount for lack of control is probably appropriate under these circumstances.

The IRS has accepted the validity of minority interest discounts in many cases, especially in valuing minority interests held by estates for estate tax purposes. As always, minority interests should be valued for this purpose at fair market value (including applicable discounts). Suppose the business is worth $1 million and the decedent's interest is 10 percent. It is highly unlikely that the decedent could have sold the interest for $100,000 on the date of death because this interest did not possess the benefits of control. In this case it would be unfair to assess federal estate taxes as if the value of the interest was really 10 percent of the value of the business.

Both the IRS and the courts have allowed discounts for minority interests, but the facts and circumstances surrounding the valuation are generally closely scrutinized to make sure the discount is appropriate. Some recent studies have revealed that the average discount is approximately 30 percent and can be much higher in appropriate circumstances.

The methods for valuing minority interests are analogous to the methods used to value the entire business. For example, the normal capitalization-of-income methods can be used to determine the value of the business. The value of the minority interest is then determined by reducing the total value to the pro rata share held by the minority owner and applying a discount factor appropriate for the minority interest.

Another technique would be to employ comparative analysis and look for the actual discounts received in transactions involving sales of minority interests in similar situations. In either event the amount of the discount to be applied is highly speculative and should be well documented by relevant evidence if used for tax purposes.

The IRS published a ruling that further solidifies the minority discount in the valuation of a family business.[4] The ruling indicates that each transaction will be valued independently for tax purposes without aggregating the interests held by the taxpayer's family. Thus, each gift of a business interest to a family member will be valued with a minority discount unless a controlling interest is transferred. Therefore, a gift or sale of stock in a closely held corporation that transfers 50 percent or less of the shares in the company can be valued with an appropriate minority discount, even if the transferee's family controls the corporation. Likewise, the transfer of limited partnership interests or nonmanaging membership interests in an LLC can be valued with a minority discount for a family limited partnership or LLC.

marketability discount

Discount for Lack of Marketability. It is generally accepted that a *marketability discount* is appropriate for a lack of an existing market for a closely held business interest. If the business interest cannot be quickly converted to cash, its fair market value may be less than the value determined by one of the conventional valuation methods. The lack of marketability for a closely held business interest may stem from several factors.

First, there may be little or no market for a minority interest. Second, a closely held business interest is not traded on a public exchange and a ready buyer may not be found on a timely basis. Finally, interests in closely held businesses are often subject to transfer restrictions that further limit the ability to convert the businesses into cash. The typical discount for the lack of

---

4. Rev. Rul. 93-12, 1993-1 C.B. 202.

marketability ranges from 10 to 35 percent, but cases have been reported in which the appropriate discount was as high as 90 percent.

blockage discount   Publicly traded corporate stock is also valued as if closely held in some instances. The IRS will allow a so-called *blockage discount* when a large block of corporate stock is valued for estate tax purposes. This discount reflects the suppressed market that would exist if a large block of stock was sold in a short time span. The IRS regulations provide that the large block may be discounted to a price below market quotations to reflect true fair market value in these circumstances.

Fractional-Interest Discount. Cases have established that fractional undivided interests (joint tenancies) may create a valuation discount. The discount is based on the built-in costs of partitioning the property if one joint owner chooses to transfer his or her interest, and it is, essentially, a marketability discount.[5] The cases have held that the fractional-interest discount could incorporate evidence of the historical difficulty of selling the interest and an owner's lack of control. The fractional-interest discount would ordinarily apply to jointly titled real estate. This is certainly important for closely held businesses because business real estate is often held outside the business by the owners or, perhaps, in separate entities such as partnerships or LLCs. It appears from case law that the fractional-interest discount would be 10 to 20 percent and is viable even if the joint interest was transferred just prior to the owner's death.

Grantor Retained Annuity Trusts (GRATs)

The special valuation rules of Sec. 2702 provide an approved form of trust known as a GRAT. This technique is available in circumstances when a donor of property would prefer to retain a temporary interest in a trust while giving the remainder away to family members (or a trust for family members). The GRAT provides the grantor with a fixed annuity for a selected term of years.

The GRAT is generally a grantor trust, and all income tax consequences are passed through to the grantor during the retained interest term. This results from the fact that the grantor could have his or her retained interest in the trust satisfied by distributions. Therefore, the GRAT is not useful for current income-shifting purposes. However, the status of the grantor trust is

---

5.   For example, in *Brocato v. Commissioner*, TCM 1999-424.

important for business-planning purposes since a grantor trust is an eligible shareholder for S corporation stock.

The irrevocable transfer of the remainder interest in the GRAT is a current gift for gift tax purposes. Since the gift provides a future interest to the donees, the gift does not qualify for the annual exclusion. However, the gift is discounted from the full fair market value of the corpus by subtracting the value of the grantor's retained interest term valued under the Sec. 7520 rules. This discounted gift can be sheltered by the grantor's exemption amount. Any retained trust interest other than a GRAT will be valued at zero for gift tax purposes, and the grantor will be treated as having gifted the entire remainder with no discounting.

The rules do require the actual payment of the fixed amount in a GRAT, which may limit the ability to transfer a closely held business in trust. The business must have the cash and surplus to make such payments to the trust. Otherwise, the trustee will have to distribute or liquidate some of the business interest to make the required payments. The failure to make such payments will result in additional gift tax liability for the grantor when he or she does not receive qualified payments from the retained interest. However, if the problems can be resolved, this technique can be useful because the grantor will (a) be able to shift the growth in the business property to his or her heirs at a fraction of its total value and (b) still retain current income rights to the business.

If the grantor survives the retained interest term of a qualified GRAT, the remaining principal, including any post-transfer appreciation, is excluded from the estate of the grantor. Therefore a significant growing property interest can be transferred to family heirs for a greatly discounted transfer tax cost.

If the grantor fails to survive the term, some portion of the trust principal (but less than the full corpus) is returned to his or her estate. The amount returned to the estate depends upon the Sec. 7520 valuation rate at the time of death and inclusion fraction for the GRAT. In any event, the maximum estate freezing potential for a GRAT will only be realized if the grantor survives the retained interest term.

EXAMPLE

Eddie Entrepreneur, aged 65, wants to transfer $1 million in closely held Familyco, Inc., stock to a GRAT for the benefit of his son, Ernie, who is his successor to Familyco. If Eddie retains a 10-year term in the trust with a $70,000 per year annuity payable to Eddie during this term, the retained interest will be treated as providing qualified payments. Since Eddie has retained a qualified interest, the value of the gift of the remainder interest is determined by subtracting the full value of Eddie's retained interest from the total value of the corpus at the time of the GRAT's creation. If Eddie survives the 10-year term, the financial benefits of the gift are as follows:

Trust term	10 years
Value of stock	$1,000,000
Sec. 7520 rate	2%
End-of-year payment	$70,000
Value of retained income interest	$628,782
Taxable gift (value of remainder interest)	$371,218
Assumed growth rate of Familyco stock	9%
Value of property at termination	$1,303,858

Lifetime Sale of the Business

The sale of the corporation provides more choices than the sale of unincorporated business entities. The buyer and seller of a corporation can choose either an asset sale or a stock sale. The purchaser either purchases the desired corporate assets necessary to take over the business activities or purchases a controlling interest in the voting stock of the corporation. There are many factors beyond the scope of this discussion that will dictate the form of sale. The buyer will normally prefer the asset sale. The sale or acquisition of a corporation could also be designed in the form of a tax-free reorganization. This transaction would involve the seller receiving only stock of the acquiring corporation.

The case of unincorporated business sales, the transaction would be treated as a sale of assets by the seller for tax purposes.

The acquisition price in the business purchase could be in the form of cash, property, or notes. The discussion that follows presumes that the buyer will not be able to provide a lump sum in cash or obtain independent financing.

Installment Sales

installment sales   There are several reasons why the business owner may wish to transfer the business prior to his or her death. The owner may wish to retire from the business and make a clean break from all responsibilities as owner. The successors may pressure the owner into such a transfer through their desire to gain freedom and control. Even if the current owner retires from active participation, his or her retention of a controlling interest in the business until death may cause conflict.

Installment Sales of the Business to Successors. An installment sale is a useful device in family financial and estate planning, particularly when a controlling family member wishes to pass on the business to a successor in the family. This type of transfer can lead to estate tax savings in the seller's estate along with income tax advantages. An installment sale for estate planning purposes is one of the methods of freezing the seller's estate and shifting the growth in the value of a business to the next generation without payment of transfer taxes on the growth element.

EXAMPLE
Suppose Eddie Entrepreneur decides to transfer his family corporation, Familyco, Inc., to his son, Ernie. Eddie sells the Familyco stock to Ernie for its fair market value of $1 million. (Eddie's basis for the stock is $100,000.) Ernie executes an installment note providing for annual payments of $100,000 to Eddie over a 10-year period. (For simplicity this example ignores the interest complications.) This sale can result in significant estate tax savings to Eddie. The installment sale will remove the Familyco stock from Eddie's estate. His estate, however, will include any of the cash received from the installment payments (or property purchased by the cash payments) unless Eddie gives away that cash or consumes it before death. In addition, if the installment payments are not fully paid at Eddie's death, the present value of the installments then unpaid is included in Eddie's estate. However, there is a significant potential estate tax advantage to the sale. If the property (in this case, the business) is appreciating in value, the installment sale will remove any growth in the value of the property occurring after the date of the installment sale from Eddie's estate. Consequently, the estate tax value of the business is "frozen" at $1 million. In addition, if Eddie survives the term of the installment sale and consumes (or gifts) the payments received, the estate tax savings will be far greater. Therefore the installment sale can solve what is often a significant estate planning problem.

The Mechanics of Installment Sales. The simplest way to explain the mechanics of an installment sale is to use an example. Suppose that G. Wizz sells the stock of American Flamer Corporation (with a basis of $50,000) for

$400,000 to Octopus Oil Company. The terms of the sale call for Octopus to make a principal payment of $100,000 this year and $100,000 in each of the next 3 years. The contract also calls for interest payments. Under the installment-sale rules, the capital gain is recognized ratably over the period during which installments are paid.

Capital gains= payment received during year $\times \dfrac{\text{gross profit}}{\text{total contract price}}$

The amount of capital gain recognized in any specific year is given as follows:

In this sale the gross profit to Wizz is $350,000 (the total price less Wizz's basis of $50,000). The total contract price is $400,000. Wizz will recognize and report capital gain as follows:

This year : $100,000 \times \dfrac{\$350,000}{400,000} = \$87,500$

Next year and successive years :$100,000 \times \dfrac{\$350,000}{400,000} = \$87,500$

Wizz will report the interest payments as ordinary income as he receives them and Octopus can deduct the interest payments as they are made, subject to the investment interest limitation discussed below.

As this example shows, there are three elements to each installment payment: capital gain (taxed at the long-term capital-gain rate), return of basis (recoverable free of income taxes), and interest income (taxable at ordinary income tax rates).

Taxation of Installment Sale

- Seller's gain can be spread ratably over the period during which installment payments are made.
- Buyer's interest payments are deductible (within limits) when made and taxable to the seller when received.

---

self-cancelling installment notes (SCINs)

Self-Cancelling Installment Notes (SCINs).

The installment note can be designed with a cancellation-at-death provision (self-canceling provision). Briefly, this provision causes the note to be canceled automatically at the seller's death. If properly designed, this provision removes the value of the note from the gross estate even if the seller dies before the installment terms ends. Care should be taken in designing the SCIN. The terms of the cancellation provision should be bargained for and reflected in the purchase price and/or the interest rate imposed. If the seller instead merely cancels or forgives the remaining indebtedness through his or her will, the remaining payments will be treated as a testamentary transfer and included in the estate.

Self-Canceling Installment Notes (SCINs)

- Remaining unpaid installment obligations are canceled at seller's death, so no remaining value of the business is in the estate.
- To achieve this, the terms of the cancellation provision must be bargained for and reflected in a higher purchase price and/or interest rate.

EXAMPLE

Suppose Eddie Entrepreneur decides to transfer his family corporation, Familyco, Inc., to his son, Ernie. Eddie hopes to sell the Familyco stock (fair market value is $1 million) to Ernie. Eddie could sell Familyco to Ernie for an installment note that was self-canceling at his death. Since the mortality risk is borne by Eddie, he should receive more than the $1 million purchase price or receive a higher rate of interest on the principal amount. The increased purchase price will reflect the fact that the seller might not receive all the installment payments. The IRS will be successful in claiming that a gift was made by Eddie to Ernie unless the purchase price or interest rate is increased to reflect the mortality risk borne by Eddie.

Regardless of the form of installment note chosen, the installment sale of a business is a useful estate planning technique if the seller wishes to pass on the business, along with any future appreciation in the business value, to a family member. The installment payments provide cash to the seller for retirement income or for building a diversified investment portfolio without the anxieties of direct involvement in the business. The tax burden of the installment payments is minimized by spreading them out over a period of years. The business itself may generate enough cash for the buyer to make the installment payments. It is important, however, to avoid payments that are so large that they burden the business and make it difficult for the successor to operate it at a profit. Finally, any postsale appreciation in the value of the business accrues to the transferee family member and is out of the seller's estate.

Private Annuity

private annuity   The private annuity is a variation on the installment sale as an estate planning technique. However, the rules and tax implications are somewhat different. A private annuity is a sale of property, such as a family business, in exchange for the buyer's agreement to make periodic payments of a specified sum to the seller for the remainder of the seller's life. The amount of the payments is based on actuarial factors.

EXAMPLE
Suppose that Eddie is aged 65. If he decides to sell Familyco to Ernie in return for a private annuity worth $1 million, Ernie's annual payment, based on IRS valuation methods, will be $69,958 (assuming a discount rate of 2 percent and life expectancy of 85). When Eddie dies, the annuity payments stop, even if he has not yet reached his life expectancy. If Eddie lives longer than his life expectancy, the annuity payments will continue for the rest of his life.

A major advantage of the private annuity is its estate tax treatment. In a regular installment sale some amount will be included in the seller's estate if the seller dies holding the installment note, since the remaining payments are still an enforceable obligation and therefore property of the estate. However, in a private annuity no further payments are due when the seller dies. Therefore it is well established that there is nothing to include in the estate of a seller who dies holding a private annuity agreement. Of course, any annuity payments received by the seller before death become part of the gross estate to the extent that the payments have not been consumed or gifted by the seller. A private annuity is particularly suitable for the transfer of a family business to successors. The guaranteed annuity amount will provide a retirement annuity for the seller, presumably funded by income from the business. Even if the seller does not live to life expectancy (and the sale becomes a bargain for the buyer), the benefit accrues to the family heir. As with a self-cancelling installment note (SCIN), the IRS valuation rules must be used to determine the annuity amount. If the value of the annuity is less than the fair market value of the business, the IRS will claim a taxable gift was made to the family successor.

Bequests at Death of a Business Interest

Estate Tax Implications

The parent may decide to transfer the family business to the successor children through his or her will rather than through a buy-sell arrangement. First, the parent may prefer the *gratuitous* bequest of the business. Second, the owner may wish to delay the transfer of control of the business until his or her death (or the later death of his or her surviving spouse). This delay would protect the surviving spouse because income would be provided from the business until the surviving spouse's death. The usual will of a wealthy business owner will provide this result. The business interest will probably be placed in a marital and/or family trust to benefit the surviving spouse while he or she is alive.

Some additional planning must take place to ensure the success of a testamentary transfer. First, the problem of estate liquidity must be addressed. Since a potentially unmarketable business interest will be included in the gross estate of the business owner and, perhaps, the estate of the surviving spouse, other liquid assets will be needed to pay the death taxes whenever they are incurred.

Second, the heirs of the business owner who do not inherit the business interest must be considered. If the business represents a major portion of the owner's gross estate, an equitable distribution to all heirs may be difficult.

Finally, the family successors must gain the ability to control the business and receive adequate compensation when they take over. This may cause conflicts between the active successors and the surviving spouse, inactive heirs, and the executor. The actual controlling interest in the business may not be received by the active heirs until the subsequent death of the surviving spouse. Fortunately with appropriate planning these difficulties can be minimized by the family business owner.

Liquidity Relief Provisions

6166 installment payment of estate tax

The Sec. 6166 installment payment of estate tax was put in place by Congress to permit an estate that contains closely held business interests to pay estate taxes caused by the business interest in periodic installments. This provision was enacted by Congress to preserve the closely held business. A closely held business would often otherwise have to be liquidated to pay estate taxes if the taxes were due immediately. To qualify to defer estate tax payments under Sec. 6166, the estate must hold a closely held business interest valued at greater than 35 percent of the adjusted gross estate.

Advantages of electing the Sec. 6166 installment payment of estate tax include the following:

- The decedent can leave the business interest directly to the successor family members through his or her will provisions, and his or her estate will receive the benefit of Sec. 6166. The unlimited marital deduction permits the entrepreneur to leave a controlling portion of the business interest in trust for his or her surviving spouse to provide the surviving spouse with substantial income until his or her death while deferring the impact of estate taxes until the second death. The installment plan of Sec. 6166 can also be elected at the second death.

- The estate tax associated with the inclusion of the business interest can be delayed until the death of the second spouse and then deferred in part for an additional 15 years.

- A favorable 2 percent interest rate is applicable to a portion of the deferred estate taxes.

- It is possible for Sec. 6166 relief to be used with any form of closely held business entity.

- The tax liability that is associated with the business interest can be passed to the heirs inheriting the business and might be withdrawn from the business as deductible salary payments in the case of a corporation.

- Sec. 303 redemptions can be made to pay the deferred amount as it becomes due in the case of a corporation.

- Life insurance proceeds with flexible settlement options can be used to provide the installments.

Disadvantages of electing the Sec. 6166 installment payments of estate taxes are as follows:

- A buy-sell agreement cannot be used with this arrangement since the business interest must be included in the gross estate for the purposes of electing Sec. 6166.

- Providing for the decedent's other heirs may be difficult if the business interest is ultimately left to only the active successors.

- Installment payments will put a substantial cash drain on the business for many years.

- There is no income tax deduction for the interest incurred on the deferred taxes.
- The estate must be left open for a much longer period of time while the taxes are deferred.
- There is a false sense of security that the taxes will be easily manageable in the deferred form.

Buy Sell Agreement at Death

Purpose of the Buy-Sell Agreement

A properly designed corporate buy-sell agreement will solve many of the business continuation problems for a closely held corporation. The actual design characteristics of the buy-sell agreement will depend on the goals of the parties forming the agreement. A corporate buy-sell agreement will typically serve some or all of the following purposes:

- A guaranteed market can be created for the stock of a deceased shareholder to provide a decedent's estate with a fair value for the business interest. The agreement can provide the same guaranteed market for the disability or retirement of the shareholder.
- A deceased shareholder's estate will be provided with cash to pay estate costs.
- The agreement can be designed to provide a purchase price that will fix the estate tax value of the decedent's stock.
- The agreement will assure the surviving shareholders that no unwanted or unexpected outsiders will buy into the corporation. It also keeps the executor and heirs from interfering in corporate affairs. This provides for the orderly continuation of the business during the transition to complete control by the surviving shareholders.
- The buy-sell agreement can prevent the termination of a corporation's subchapter S election by preventing the transfer of S corporation stock by the decedent's estate to disqualifying individuals or entities.
- A buy-sell agreement may provide the estate with funds from the corporation income tax free. This is particularly important in the family corporation.

The actual goals of the buy-sell agreement will depend on the circumstances existing in each corporation. The buy-sell agreement for corporations can provide for either (1) an option to buy or (2) the mandatory purchase of the deceased shareholder's stock. To serve the objectives above, a mandatory agreement will usually best suit the needs of the parties.

Design of Buy Sell Agreements

A partnership, LLC, or corporation operates as a separate legal entity distinct from the owners. It holds property as a business entity, while the owners hold their interest in the partnership as intangible assets. This relationship creates two possibilities for a partnership buy-sell arrangement.

cross-purchase agreement

entity agreement

First, the partners, members of an LLC or shareholders of a corporation, can form what is commonly known as a *cross-purchase agreement*. This type of agreement is formed between the owners committing the *survivors* to buy, and the deceased owner's estate to sell, the partnership interest of the first to die. Second, the agreement may provide for the *business entity* to buy and the deceased partner's estate to sell. This arrangement is commonly known as an *entity agreement/stock redemption*.

Cross-Purchase Agreements. The cross-purchase plan involves an agreement between the individual owners and not the entity. Each owner agrees to purchase a share of a deceased owner's interest at death. Each owner must also bind his or her estate to sell the partnership interest to the surviving owners. Generally speaking, the agreement should contain a lifetime-transfer restriction preventing any party from transferring an ownership interest during lifetime without first offering the interest to the other owners. The flow chart below demonstrates the operation of the cross-purchase arrangement for a partnership.

Figure 2-1
Cross-Purchase Plan

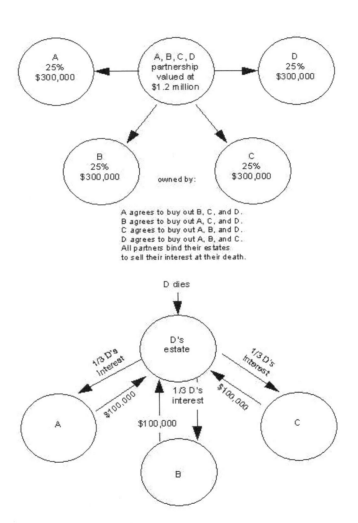

The Entity Approach. Under this approach it is the entity that is obligated to purchase the deceased partner's interest. The agreement provides that the entity will purchase the interest held by any deceased owner's estate. As parties to the agreement, the owners commit their estates to sell their interests to the entity at death. The term *purchase* is a misnomer when used in conjunction with the entity approach. For tax purposes, it is known as a liquidation for partnerships/LLCs or a stock redemption for a corporation. The entity approach for a partnership is illustrated below.

Figure 2-2
The Entity Approach

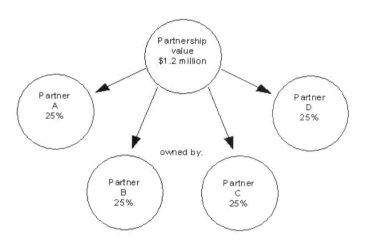

A partnership agreement provides that the partnership will purchase (liquidate) each partner's interest at death. A, B, C, and D form a binding contract for their estates to sell their interest to the partnership at death.

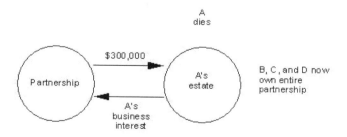

Funding Buy-Sell Agreements with Life Insurance

Buy-sell agreements that are triggered by the death of the business owner are generally funded with life insurance. Other methods, such as a savings fund, will require the set-aside of significant business assets and will generally be inadequate in the case of a premature death. Buy-sell agreements will sometimes provide for the installment purchase of the business interest at a triggering event. The requirement to make substantial ongoing installment payments will place a significant drain on the business and its owners to complete a buyout. Life insurance provides a death benefit at the time the purchase proceeds are required to complete a buy sell agreement at death. Appropriate policy choices can make the cost of life insurance manageable unless some of the owners are uninsurable or substantially rated. Under Sec. 101, life insurance proceeds will be received by the beneficiary free from income taxes except in extraordinary circumstances. The amount of insurance should be as close as possible to the purchase price provided for in the buy-sell agreement.

Advantages of Life Insurance to Fund Buy-Sell Agreement

- Produces the cash for the purchase exactly when it is needed, even if the insured dies early
- Has a manageable and predictable cost, even if the insured lives for many years after creation of the agreement
- Results in favorable income tax treatment of the inside buildup in the policy and receipt of the death benefits

---

Structure of Buy-Sell Agreements Funded with Life Insurance

The design of an insured buy-sell agreement is fairly straightforward. Just follow a simple rule—the purchaser (based on the design of the agreement) should be the premium payer, policyowner, and beneficiary of the life insurance proceeds covering the life of a business owner whose interest must be purchased at the time of his or her death. In the case of an entity-type buy-sell agreement, the business entity should own a life insurance policy on the life of each owner whose interest must be purchased at the time of his or her death. In the cross purchase arrangement, each owner should own a policy on the life of any owner who must be bought out at the time of death.

Cross-Purchase Agreements Funded with Life Insurance. The cross-purchase arrangement provides that the surviving owners will each buy

a prearranged share of a deceased owner's interest. The estate is bound to sell the interest to the surviving owners according to the agreement. The cross-purchase arrangement funded by life insurance requires that each owner purchase life insurance policies on the lives of the other owners with a face amount equal to the share of the business to be purchased. It is recommended that the owner purchasing the insurance be owner and beneficiary of each policy purchased on the lives of the other owners. At the death of an owner the surviving owners will receive the death proceeds from the policies, which will then be transferred to the deceased owner's estate in exchange for the share of the ownership interest.

The deceased owner's estate will include the value of the partnership interest and the value of the policies held by the decedent on the lives of the surviving owners. However, the death proceeds will not be included in the gross estate since the decedent had no incidents of ownership in the policies held by the owner's partners on his or her life.

The tax treatment of the insured cross-purchase buy-sell for a business is fairly simple. The premiums for the insurance to fund the buy-sell agreement will not be deductible for federal income tax purposes. This makes the funding of the insured plan expensive currently from a tax standpoint. For example, if the party to an insured cross-purchase buy-sell agreement is in the current highest marginal individual income tax bracket (39.6 percent in 2014), $16,556 of income will have to be earned to make a $10,000 premium payment.

Fortunately the insurance funding mechanism has some tax advantages. For policies that have cash surrender values, there is no current tax on this inside buildup. When the full face amount is received at the death of an owner, these death proceeds are received income tax free. The income buildup on the policy will be taxable only if the policy is surrendered at a gain prior to the death of the insured. Therefore the insurance held to the death of the owner may provide considerable tax savings.

Entity Agreements Funded with Life Insurance. The entity buy-sell approach provides that the business entity will "purchase" the interest of a deceased owner at death. In the case of a partnership or LLC, this will be treated as a liquidation of the deceased owner's interest for tax purposes. In the case of a corporate entity, the purchase of stock by the entity is treated as a stock redemption for tax purposes. If insurance is used to fund the agreement, the business entity should own the policies and be the designated beneficiary. At a partner's death the proceeds will be received by the partnership and transferred to the estate in liquidation of the deceased partner's interest.

The life insurance used to fund a buy-sell agreement is an asset held by the policyowner. In the case of an entity purchase agreement, the life insurance policies used to fund the agreement are nonoperating assets of the entity and will affect the value of the entity. In fact, the IRS often insists that the insurance portfolio becomes part of the value of the business for the purposes of the buy-sell agreement. In the case of a corporation, life insurance owned by the corporation to fund a stock redemption agreement could expose the corporation to the accumulated earnings tax or corporate AMT.

The tax treatment of the insured entity-purchase buy-sell agreement depends upon whether the entity is a pass-through (partnership, LLC, or S corporation) for a regular corporation tax purposes. In the case of a pass-through entity, the nondeductible cost for life insurance premiums is effectively borne by the owners in proportion to their ownership interest. Because life insurance is an after-tax expense, the owners will be subject to income taxes on the premium amounts in proportion to their ownership interests. In the case of a corporation, the corporation bears the burden of the premium payments and will make such payments out of dollars taxed to the corporation.

Taxation of Purchases and Sales Pursuant Buy-Sell Agreements

Cross-Purchase Agreements. The tax treatment of the purchase and sale of a business interest is simpler in the case of a cross-purchase buy-sell agreement. The purchasers are individuals and will make payments to the deceased owner's estate in exchange for the business interest held by the estate. As such, the purchasers will get a full income-tax cost basis in the purchased interest equal to the amount of the purchase price. For the purposes of the seller, the tax treatment of a sale of a pass-through entity (partnership, LLC, or S corporation) is a little bit more complex than a corporation. Because a pass-through entity is ignored for tax purposes, part of the purchase payments made to the estate of a deceased owner will carry out ordinary income items for the tax year up until the time the purchase takes place. In the case of a partnership or LLC, the amounts received as ordinary income include the estate's share of unrealized receivables and substantially appreciated inventory. For the purchase of S corporation stock, the decedent's estate will receive ordinary income for the pass-through income for the part of the tax year prior to the redemption of the stock.

In the case of a cross purchase of stock in a corporation, the seller is simply treated as selling stock and will be subject to capital gain, if any. If the stock is sold from the estate of a deceased shareholder, the estate gets an income tax basis step up equal to the date of death value if the gain should be either zero or minimal.

Entity Purchase or Stock Redemption Agreements. In an entity purchase agreement for a partnership or LLC, the entity will transfer the purchase proceeds to the estate of a deceased owner. There will be no direct impact on the cost basis of the surviving owners. However, the receipt of the insurance proceeds by the entity will have a positive impact on the income tax cost basis of the owners proportionately. Again, the transfer of the purchase price to the estate of a deceased owner of a pass-through will cause the amounts received for the distributive share of income, unrealized receivables, and substantially appreciated inventory to be treated as ordinary income to the estate. The amount received for the ownership interest will be treated as a capital gain transaction.

In the case of a stock redemption in a regular corporation, we have additional complexities. Because the corporation is the "purchaser," the redemption of stock could carry out accumulated earnings and profits of the corporation. Second, the redemption by the corporation will have no effect whatsoever on the cost basis of the surviving shareholders. Third, the redemption could be treated as a dividend to the estate when the stock is redeemed. These rules are very complex and beyond the scope of this discussion. However, the stock redemption in a family corporation is highly likely to result in unfavorable dividend treatment as opposed to more favorable sale or exchange treatment.

Funding and Value Considerations. The insured buy-sell agreement will retain the advantage of certainty only if the insurance coverage is adequate to fund the purchase price. In general, the valuation provision of the buy-sell agreement will provide for regular increases in the purchase price either through periodic readjustment of the specified price or a formula that measures current value. For this reason the insurance purchased initially will generally not equal the purchase price at the death of the proprietor. An insured buy-sell agreement should contain a provision for adding, or substituting, policies in the agreement. This will allow the purchaser(s) to acquire additional insurance on the owners as the agreed-on price increases.

Life Insurance Trusts for the Business Owner

Gift Tax Treatment of an ILIT

The ILIT has many advantages that could be useful in the estate plan of a family business owner. First, the ILIT provides gift tax advantages. It is arguably the most efficient use of the grantor's annual exclusion gifts. The grantor can provide $14,000 annual contributions to the ILIT for each beneficiary without making a taxable gift. This amount can be doubled to $28,000 if the grantor is married and the grantor's spouse elects to split gifts for the year.

Estate Tax Treatment of an ILIT

An ILIT that is a properly designed, funded, and administered will avoid inclusion in the grantor's gross estate at the time of his or her death. Thus, gifts to fund the ILIT will reduce the grantor's estate and the life insurance proceeds can provide many benefits without incurring federal estate taxes. If the ILIT will benefit grandchildren and extends into future generations, the ILIT could be designed to be sheltered entirely from federal generation-skipping transfer taxes. Thus, a properly designed ILIT will not be subject to any federal wealth transfer taxes. Since the ILIT provides for cash benefits and is not subject to wealth transfer taxes, it enhances the liquidity position of the insured's estate.

ILITs Provide Significant Dispositive Advantages for the Business Owner

The benefits of the ILIT in the family business succession plan would include one or more of the following:

- The ILIT can be funded through tax-efficient gifts and will provide death benefits free of estate taxes.
- Although an ILIT is a completed gift, it has no immediate income tax consequences since the trust provides no taxable income until the proceeds are received at the death of the insured and the proceeds are reinvested in a manner that creates taxable income. During the life of the insured, the ILIT is generally a grantor (defective) trust and any income tax consequences that occur would not burden the beneficiaries until after the grantor dies.
- Estate liquidity/preservation for the business owner. The life insurance, most likely owned by an ILIT, would provide liquidity for

the purposes of settling the estate of the business owner. Wealth replacement for business owner's estate. Life insurance could be used to replace the wealth that was lost to paying the settlement costs incurred by the business owner's estate or wealth that was consumed from the estate during the lifetime of the business owner.

- Estate equalization. Life insurance can provide an inheritance to children who are not active in the family business and this would free up the business owner to transfer all or substantially all of the business interest to the children who are active in the business.

- Since an ILIT is a living trust, the beneficiaries receive distributions from the trust free of the expenses and publicity of probate.

- Although the ILIT is an irrevocable trust, it is a tool for providing flexibility. The grantor cannot retain control over the disposition of the trust without suffering adverse gift and estate tax consequences. However, the grantor does design the terms of the trust and can grant an independent trustee with the ability to manage and determine the distributions from the trust according to the terms provided by the grantor. The grantor can delegate completely independent discretion in making distribution decisions to the trustee. To protect the benefits of the trust from the creditors of the beneficiaries, the trust can be designed to last indefinitely in some states and provide spendthrift provisions. If the ILIT is no longer appropriate or needs to be amended, the provisions of the trust can provide for this contingency. For example, an independent trustee can be given the discretion to appoint principal (that is, the policy) to selected beneficiaries. Or, the grantor can provide a limited power of appointment to a family member to invade the trust. Finally, the trust protector could be named to have the power to terminate the trust or amend its terms.

- An ILIT can be used for business succession planning. Life insurance could be in the ILIT to fund the purchase of the decedent's business interest and hold the business interest for the family according to the terms of the trust.

ILIT as a Business Continuity Trust

Although the ILIT cannot be used to directly pay the estate taxes incurred by the business's estate, the ILIT can be used to provide liquidity to the estate. There are two provisions that can be included in the trust to make the ILIT's cash available to the executor. First, the trustee and the executor can engage in a transaction where the ILIT's trustee purchases assets from the estate at fair market value. In addition, the trustee of the ILIT can make loans to the executor following normal commercial standards using the assets of the estate as collateral. Neither of these provisions will cause the life insurance proceeds to be included in the business owner's estate.

This provides a unique opportunity in the estate of a closely held business owner. The ILIT's trustee can purchase the business interest from the estate at the time the life insurance proceeds are received at the business owner's death. The estate now has the cash necessary for settlement costs and can provide the appropriate inheritances to the business owner's surviving spouse and other heirs. This prevents the executor from either (1) trying to divide up the business interest to fund bequests or (2) engage in a fire sale of the closely held business to settle the estate. The trustee of the ILIT will either (1) manage the closely held business for the family for an appropriate time period or (2) distribute the business interest to the appropriate successors.

Chapter Review

Review questions are based on the learning objectives in this chapter. Thus, a [3] at the end of a question means that the question is based on learning objective 3. If there are multiple objectives, they are all listed.

Key Terms and Concepts

administrative expenses

gross estate

adjusted gross estate

marital deduction

taxable gift

annual exclusion

split gift

present interest gifts

statute of limitations

minority discount

marketability discount

blockage discount

installment sales

self-cancelling installment notes (SCINs)

private annuity

6166 installment payment of estate tax

cross-purchase agreement

entity agreement

Review Questions

1. What are important steps that must be taken for a closely held business owner transitioning to retirement? [1]

2. Identify the possibilities for providing for a closely held business owner during retirement. [2]

3. Discuss the estate planning objectives that must be addressed in a situation where the business owner is contemplating sale of the business or retirement. [3]

4. Identify the typical estate planning objectives for the owner of a closely held business. [4]

5. Describe the difficulty that a professional advisor might face with a closely held business owner in motivating the business owner to begin and stay on task with respect to a business succession and estate plan. [4]

6. Identify the items that are included in the gross estate of the decedent for the purposes of determining the tax base for the federal will estate tax. [5]

7. Explain what is meant by the applicable credit amount and describe how it can be used to reduce a decedent's federal estate taxes. [5]

8. Identify the valuation discounts that might be used to reduce the transfer tax costs of making gifts or bequests of a business interest to family members. [6]

9. Describe the similarities and differences between the sale of a business interest for an installment note, a self canceling installment note, and a private annuity transaction. [7]

10. What requirements must an estate meet to qualify to defer estate tax payments for the taxes created by the inclusion of a closely held business interest under the provisions of Sec. 6166? [8]

11. Describe the structure of the two types of buy and sell agreements for a closely held business. [9]

12. Discuss how the insurance should be arranged for the cross purchase and the entity type buy-sell agreements. [9]

13. Discuss the federal income tax treatment of life insurance policies used to fund a buy-sell agreement. [10]

14. How does the tax treatment for a purchase and sale of an ownership interest under a buy-sell agreement differ for a pass-through entity versus a corporation? [11]

15. What are the advantages of an irrevocable life insurance trust (ILIT)? [12]

16. How does the ILIT specifically assist in the estate plan for the owner of a closely held business? [12]

Learning Objectives

An understanding of the material in this chapter should enable you to

1. Identify the critical facts from a fact-finder narrative in the business planning case.

2. Discuss the efficacy of the choice of entity for a business case with respect to liability issues, taxes, compensation of owners and key employees, and business succession transfer.

3. Describe what is meant by an estate freeze and why it is useful in the business succession plan.

4. Discuss the opportunities in the gift tax system for making transfers of a closely held business interest to the next generation successor(s).

5. Describe the use of the seller-financed sales of a closely held business interest to the family or key employee successors.

6. Discuss a possibility for providing key employees with an incentive to stay with the company.

7. Discuss the problems that divorce presents for a business owner.

8. Identify the issues presented by the premature death of the owner in a closely held business.

9. Design a buy-sell agreement to transfer the closely held business to family or key employee successors.

10. Assist a closely held business owner with identifying the problems presented by an outdated estate plan.

11. Prepare a forecast of a business owner's estate settlement costs and liquidity needs.

12. Assist a closely held business owner in addressing other estate planning objectives.

Case Facts

Ned Saunders is the owner of a closely held family business—Teccom, LLC. This is Ned's second venture as an entrepreneur. After gaining experience working as an employee in other technology businesses, he formed a company that was acquired by a larger firm in 1998. He received a substantial acquisition price, but some of the price was restricted stock that became valueless when the buyer failed. He formed his current business about 9 years ago with a handful of employees. The business has grown through his hard work and marketing efforts.

He currently has 40 employees and also uses independent contractors on some service calls. The business supports and services unified communications for businesses and operates in several states in its region. Ned is the key executive and is involved in virtually all of Teccom's sales. His son, Eric, manages and oversees the operations. The LLC provides pass-through taxation to the owners. Ned's interest is currently 70 percent. Ned's son holds a 10 percent interest. Two venture capitalists that belong to the same country club as Ned own 10 percent each. He and his son have been slowly buying them out. The outside investors provide no services to the company. The business has about $1 million debt that he has personally guaranteed.

Teccom's compensation costs, including Ned and Eric, are approximately $5.2 million currently. Ned identifies about 3 employees as key employees that he would prefer to retain. The company returned a 22 percent profit in its last calendar year. The building used by the business is owned by Ned and is leased to Teccom. The building appreciated rapidly until 2007, but its potential value has sputtered since.

Ned has focused his time on growing the business and increasing the equity held by him and his son. The venture capital members are satisfied with their return and capital gain. He has no known specific plans currently to either sell the business to outsiders or to retire and allow his son to take over. The business purchased a $1 million 10-year term life insurance policy on Ned's life to cover the business debt and satisfy the investors. The term is ending and the cost of continuing this coverage has not been investigated. The shrinking share of the capital investors might eliminate the current need for that coverage as currently structured.

Although Eric represents the natural successor in Teccom, he has been pretty much kept in the dark about any plans that his father has with the business or his estate. He certainly knows that he is acquiring a larger interest in the firm. However, he is also aware that his father previously sold a business and walked away.

Ned has been married to Kathy, his second wife, for 10 years. Kathy is not involved in the business, but all of its growth occurred during the marriage. He married without a prenuptial agreement. His first wife passed away 14 years ago. Ned has two other children, Sheila and David, who have no role in the business and have not expressed any interest in getting involved. Eric is married and has two children. His wife is not currently employed. Sheila is married and has one child. She is a clinical psychologist. Her husband is an attorney and both have significant income. Ted's youngest son David was married briefly and is currently single. David is still struggling to find his way.

Ned executed a will after his marriage with Kathy. It is a simple will that leaves all of his probate assets to his children in equal shares. He named his daughter Sheila as executor under his will. He acquired a $500,000 life insurance policy to fund a bequest to Kathy, but he continues to be the policyowner. He chose the life insurance to provide her inheritance without divesting his children from wealth he acquired while married to their mother. His retirement plan assets are payable to Kathy directly by beneficiary designation. He has acquired significant property, including a residence and a vacation home, jointly with Kathy and views the marriage as solid.

He has not created any trusts as part of his estate plan.

Ned spends most of the time on the road to generate and retain business for Teccom. He expresses a desire to slow down and is under some pressure from Kathy to do so. He has some thoughts about his business and personal estate planning objectives, but has not communicated much of them to his wife and children.

Personal Data

Client	Age
Ned Saunders	60

Client's Spouse	
Kathy Saunders	58

Client's Children	
Eric Saunders	36
Sheila Douglas	33
David Saunders	28

Income Sources	Ned	Kathy
Draw from Teccom	$625,000	
Rent	72,000	
Interest	25,000	
Dividends	185,000	

Asset Inventory	Ned	Kathy	Joint
Savings and checking			$17,000
Treasury bills	100,000		
Mutual funds	1,725,000		
Personal residence			1,250,000
Other real estate	$1,500,000		600,000
Personal Property	100,000	$25,000	250,000
Life insurance			
—Face amount	500,000		
—Cash value	55,000		
Retirement plan/IRA	1,600,000	400,000	
Teccom, LLC est.	$7,500,000		
	(1 million adjusted basis)		

Estate Planning Case Objectives

Your interview attained complete data of Ned's situation as presented on the previous page. Your interview with Ned indicates the following goals:

- to reduce his services to Teccom
- to optimally receive a respectable retirement income from the retirement plans and the business income (if necessary)
- to ensure that Kathy has enough to provide her accustomed standard of living
- to provide relatively equal amounts of family assets to each of the children (or the issue of any children who predecease them) at their later death
- to transfer the controlling interest in Teccom (if the interest is held —or this is not accomplished earlier—until Ned's death) to Eric at a minimum transfer tax cost
- to lower the overall estate tax burden and provide adequate liquidity for his estate

Initial Analysis

After doing our initial interview with Ned Saunders, we've prepared a narrative that you have presumably read thoroughly. There are plenty of facts to be digested with the data concerning his assets and income. The next step is to spend some time brainstorming to determine critical issues.

Evaluation of Business Entity Form—Active Business and Commercial Real Estate

Liability Concerns for Teccom and Ned Saunders

One of the biggest concerns for business owners is personal exposure of the business owner and his or her family to liability. LLCs were created by state laws to provide protection to closely held business owners from personal liability. In theory, the LLC looks like the panacea for business owners that desire liability protection and want pass-through income tax treatment. However, that leaves a bit of the reality out of the discussion. First, everyone is personally liable for actions that they perform. For example, a professional practitioner cannot avoid malpractice for his or her personal actions by organizing as an LLC. However, the LLC does protect members from actions taken by other members and employees of the LLC. In addition, like a corporation, the LLC is bound by any contracts entered into and members are not personally at risk for LLC contracts unless they provide personal guarantees. Herein lies another problem. In a closely held business, lenders will virtually always require personal guarantees from the owners and, perhaps, other family members of the owners.

Federal Tax Concerns for Teccom and Ned Saunders

Most closely held business owners prefer pass-through tax treatment for federal income tax purposes. The LLC in this case appears to meet this objective. LLCs virtually always will choose to be taxed as a partnership under Subchapter K of the Internal Revenue Code. Teccom pays no income tax and Ned, Eric, and the two investors will pay income taxes on all business income. Ned and Eric are taxed on the amounts drawn for their services and then all owners are taxed on the net income based on their percentage of ownership in Teccom.

Income to owners from a partnership is treated as self-employment income. This presents a distinction and, perhaps, a benefit relative to a taxable corporation. The ACA of 2010 created some new taxes that are important to business owners and other taxpayers. The first of these taxes affects earned income from self-employment and wages for statutory employees. An additional 0.9% Medicare tax is imposed on earned income for higher earners. There is no additional tax imposed on the employer. Essentially, this makes the Medicare tax 3.8 percent for earned income over the threshold amount without a ceiling on earnings. For Ned and the other owners, this would apply to self-employment income above a threshold amount (modified adjusted gross income of $250,000 for marrieds filing jointly and $200,000 for single taxpayers). For Ned and the other owners, they will likely have a substantial additional Medicare tax liability.

The ACA also imposes a 3.8 percent tax (Medicare contribution tax) on net investment income (NII) for taxpayers above the threshold amounts, identical to the thresholds for the .9 percent additional Medicare tax. The key to understanding the impact of this tax on business owners is the definition of items included (or excluded) from the definition of NII. For this purpose, NII includes:

- interest
- dividends
- annuities

- royalties
- rents (but excludes rental income from a self-rental activity)
- gains (but excludes gains from sale of an active trade or business that is not a passive activity)

Items that are excluded from the definition of NII include:

- trade or business income
- rent from self-rental activity
- income treated as self-employment income
- sale of a partnership, LLC, or S corporation by an active participant
- distributions from IRAs and qualified plans
- build-up amounts in life insurance and deferred annuities
- income tax-exempt under the IRC
- charitable trusts

The use of an LLC provides some benefit for these new taxes that would not be available in the corporate form. That is, the capital gain resulting from the sale would avoid the definition of NII and reduce the income taxes on the sale of Teccom by Ned or the other owners. (Note: there is some additional complexity to the sale of a partnership or LLC that is not addressed here.) Ned rents a building to Teccom. The rental income is subject to ordinary income taxes, but a self-rental activity is not treated as NII and avoids the 3.8 percent Medicare Contributions Tax.

Compensation Planning for Teccom and Ned Saunders

Sole proprietors, partners (or members in an LLC taxed as a partnership) and more-than-2-percent shareholders in S corporations are not considered employees for fringe-benefit purposes. Such owners are considered self-employed. Therefore, contributions to certain fringe-benefit plans—group life or health insurance—made on behalf of these self-employed individuals are not deductible by the business for tax purposes. (Note: There is an income tax deduction for the health insurance premiums paid by self-employed individuals, but this is a personal rather than a business tax deduction.). With respect to nonqualified deferred compensation, any funds set aside would be taxable to the owners in proportion to their ownership interests. In effect, there would be no deferral for nonqualified benefits As opposed to other employee fringe benefits, the qualified retirement plan rules for self-employed individuals provide similar advantages to those provided by corporate qualified retirement plans and provide virtually the same choices.

For compensation, retirement, and income tax planning reasons, the retirement plan for Teccom should be examined and a structure that provides for maximum deductible contributions for Ned should be considered.

The self-employment status of Ned and the other owners prevents some of the fringe benefits that could be provided in the corporate structure. However, there will generally not be enough compensation planning motives to indicate the conversion to a taxable corporation. This does not mean that compensation planning for Teccom should be ignored. The key employees and other Teccom employees are statutory employees and compensation planning could address concerns about the recruitment and retention of the appropriate individuals.

Business Succession and Transfer in an LLC

An LLC is a hybrid between a partnership and a corporation. Unlike a partnership, it can be designed to provide perpetual life for a business. There are some distinctions for business disposition between a corporation and the LLC. For example, a corporation can be sold in a tax-free exchange if the seller receives only the stock of the buyer in exchange for the stock or assets of the acquired corporation. However, the stock received is often restricted and provides marketability risk for the seller. Perhaps this is what happened to Ned in his previous business sale. In addition, the creation of an ESOP to transfer the interests to current management is not available for an LLC.

The LLC interests can only be sold in a taxable disposition where any gain is recognized by the seller. And, because the LLC is taxed as a partnership, some of the proceeds will represent the pass-through of ordinary income items from the operations that occurred during the tax year prior to the sale. This portion of the proceeds would be treated as self-employment income by Ned. The amount received for his interest in the LLC (the remaining portion of the sale proceeds) is treated as long-term gain to the extent that the proceeds exceed his cost basis in Teccom. The other owners would be in the same manner. However, the LLC provides the advantage that the gain from the sale of an active trade or business is not defined as NII for the purposes of the 3.8 percent Medicare Contributions Tax created by the ACA.

However, most closely held businesses, and Teccom is no exception, rely on the personal services of a few owners and/or key employee managers. This creates a business succession risk if there is no natural successor. That appears to be a problem for Teccom. And this is the biggest business-related risk presented by the case study. We will need to make Ned aware that his biggest priority is identifying and developing a successor. The business-owned key person coverage on Ned covers only Teccom's debt and is term coverage that will expire within two years. This coverage should be reviewed and options presented to Ned by a life insurance professional at the earliest opportunity. Is the coverage convertible to a permanent form? Is the amount adequate to address the loss of Ned? What would term coverage cost at his attained age? From Ned's personal perspective, the ownership of a business that relies on his essential services is an estate planning problem that will be addressed later in the analysis.

Business Succession—Active Business/Commercial Real Estate

Lifetime Transfer to Family Successor or Key Employees

Estate Freeze and Why It Might be Indicated for Ned Saunders

Because business interests have the strongest and most realistic propensity for substantial appreciation in value, planners have always attempted to find a way to place a cap or a ceiling on the value of this type of asset. This has traditionally been referred to as an estate freeze. If a business owner owns all or a portion of a closely held business that has been appreciating in value over the years and he or she has done nothing to place a cap or ceiling on this business interest, the gross estate will be much larger at the date of death than it would have been had a freezing technique been used.

Total removal of the asset by outright sale or a gift from the gross estate prior to the business owner's death is one way to reduce gross estate size. This in turn proportionately reduces estate tax liability, but such a technique is not an estate-freezing technique *per se*. There are few real circumstances in which a business owner would make a gift of an entire business interest at one time. Ned certainly does not appear like someone who is ready to walk away immediately. Nor is Teccom likely to be successful if he does so. A more realistic scenario would not involve a complete, sudden, and abrupt divestiture of the business interest but rather a gradual, piecemeal shifting of the control of the business interest to others. For several reasons, it is unlikely that a senior-generation family member like Ned Saunders would want to pass the entire interest in the family business at one time to Eric or key employees. In this instance, the successors will not be adequately prepared to take over the reins. Moreover, he certainly desires to retain some control over the activities. Finally, Ned clearly wants (or needs) to retain income from Teccom into the indefinite future and an immediate gift of the business to Eric without some retained interest would not suit his goals.

estate freeze   A more appropriate estate freeze is a restructuring of the business owner's assets designed to restrict an individual's eventual taxable estate to its current value. The goal of the estate freeze is to retain some interest that provides the current owner with some control and cash flow while reducing the transfer tax costs. Thus, as the business asset is transferred, it can be done at a predictable estate or gift tax cost.

Estate freezing transfer mechanisms can provide a business the following advantages:

- a reduction in the business owner's federal wealth transfer tax liability
- retained control of the business for a desired period of time
- adequate time for the selection, training, and development of a suitable successor
- the current owner's retention of income from the retained interest in the business or cash flow from the sale of the business interest

Lifetime Transfer of Business Interests to Family Successors

Gift Taxes — Exclusions and Exemptions

The most effective way to reduce a business owner's gross estate is by making appropriate lifetime gifts. For a high net worth closely held business owner, such as Ned Saunders, it is really important to take advantage of the opportunities within the gift tax system to avoid paying unnecessary gift or estate taxes. One of the biggest tax loopholes is the federal gift tax annual exclusion. It permits a transfer of up to $14,000 (as indexed for inflation in 2014) to an unlimited number of recipients annually. If the donor is married and his or her spouse elects to split all gifts made during a given tax year, the annual exclusion effectively is doubled to $28,000 (as indexed for inflation in 2014). Note, it may be difficult to get Kathy to consent to split Ned's gifts to his children unless she is given some incentive; perhaps he needs to make gifts to her also.

All that is required for a gift to qualify for the annual exclusion is that the gift provide the recipient with a "present interest." The present interest requirement could be a little tricky with a gift of a closely held business interest. The transfer of the interest in the closely held business must provide the recipient with current value. For example, Teccom interests gifted to family members must provide a real opportunity to receive income annually or give the recipient the ability to sell the gifted interest for value. With Teccom, the present interest requirement would be satisfied if the business makes regular distributions of cash flow to its owners. Certainly, it probably had a pattern of making such distributions to the passive investors who helped Ned capitalize the business. Most closely held business interest will be subject to transfer restrictions. The present interest requirement would be met as long as these transfer restrictions were not tantamount to a complete prohibition for the recipients to sell their interests.

lifetime exemption

An annual exclusion gift is excluded from the definition of taxable gifts. However, the opportunities for lifetime gifts do not stop there. All individuals are provided with a lifetime cumulative exemption against "taxable" gifts. A taxable gift is a gift that is not excluded or deducted. One such exclusion is the annual exclusion discussed above. Deductions available are the marital deduction for transfers to a spouse and the charitable deduction for transfers to a qualified charity. A lifetime exemption is available against cumulative taxable gifts. This exemption is $5 million (as indexed for inflation to $5,340,000 in 2014) and no gift taxes will be due until the transferor's total lifetime taxable gifts exceed this exemption amount. Certainly, this large exemption amount would permit Ned to make significant gifts of Teccom to Eric. It would be preferable that such gifts be discounted for gift-tax valuation purposes. Any gifts made to Eric might have to be balanced with gifts to other family members. And, his interest in the commercial building is another great possibility for a lifetime estate-freezing gift or sale.

Valuation Discounts for Transfers of Closely Held Business Interests

It is often justifiable and appropriate to discount the value of a business interest for making transfers to family members. This could apply to the lifetime gift or sale of the business interest. Discounts might also be appropriate for the bequest of the business interest at death or the sale at death through a buy-sell agreement. Reasons for the disparity between actual value and the value of the business interest reached by established techniques are that (1) the interest being valued represents a minority interest, (2) the interest being valued suffers from a lack of marketability, (3) the property is held in individual fractional ownership, (4) the interest being valued has built-in capital-gains tax or other liabilities, and (5) the interest is being liquidated on a distressed basis. Of course, not all of these would apply in every circumstance and the transfer-tax value of Teccom is no exception.

The Minority (Lack of Control) Discount. A minority discount interest stems from the inability to control the business. The majority owner(s) possess benefits that translate into market value. The benefits derived from this control are the ability to

- direct the management of the business (that is, elect and sit on the board of directors)
- hire and terminate employees
- establish compensation structure
- determine the goals and operations of the business
- acquire and dispose of business property
- make distributions to partners or pay dividends to shareholders
- terminate the business

The IRS has accepted the validity of minority interest discounts in many cases, especially in valuing minority interests held by estates for estate tax purposes. As always, minority interests should be valued for this purpose at fair market value (including applicable discounts). Suppose the business is worth $1 million and the decedent's interest is 10 percent. It is highly unlikely that the decedent could have sold the interest for $100,000 on the date of death because this interest did not possess the benefits of control. In this case it would be unfair to assess federal estate taxes as if the value of the interest was really 10 percent of the value of the business.

Both the IRS and the courts have allowed discounts for minority interests, but the facts and circumstances surrounding the valuation are generally closely scrutinized to make sure the discount is appropriate. Some recent studies have revealed that the average discount is approximately 30 percent and can be much higher in appropriate circumstances.

The IRS published a Revenue Ruling (93 – 12) that further solidifies the minority discount in the valuation of a family business. The ruling indicates that each transaction will be valued independently for tax purposes without aggregating the interests held by the taxpayer's family. Thus, each gift of a business interest to a family member will be valued with a minority discount unless a controlling interest is transferred. Therefore, a gift or sale of stock in a closely held corporation that transfers 50 percent or less of the shares in the company can be valued with an appropriate minority discount, even if the transferee's family controls the corporation. Likewise, the transfer of limited partnership interests or nonmanaging membership interests in an LLC can be valued with a minority discount for a family limited partnership or LLC.

The appropriate size of a minority discount depends on the degree to which these control powers are lacking. Many of the control powers are often not an either/or situation for the majority and minority owners. There are many instances in which some degree of control is retained by even a minority interest holder. For Teccom, Ned is probably the controlling manager of the business in the operating agreement for the LLC. It is unlikely that the venture capitalists would have provided him with unlimited authority when the LLC was organized. So there are probably some limitations on his authority. It would be appropriate to further examine the LLC operating agreement and to discuss this with Ned. In any event, this would be an issue for an appraiser to deal with when a transfer is planned and implemented.

Discount for Lack of Marketability. It is generally accepted that a marketability discount is appropriate for a lack of an existing market for a closely held business interest. If the business interest cannot be quickly converted to cash, its fair market value may be less than the value determined by one of the conventional valuation methods. The lack of marketability for a closely held business interest may stem from several factors.

First, there may be little or no market for a minority interest. Second, a closely held business interest is not traded on a public exchange and a ready buyer has never been sought nor could one be found on a timely basis. Finally, interests in closely held businesses are often subject to transfer restrictions that further limit the ability to convert the businesses into cash. The typical discount for the lack of marketability ranges from 10 to 35 percent, but cases have been reported in which the appropriate discount was significantly higher.

Teccom is no different than other closely held business interests and presumably has restrictions on transfer (another reason to get a copy of the operating agreement). Typical restrictions include a lifetime first offer provision where someone wishing to sell his or her interest must first offer the interest to the other current owners at an agreed price. This first offer provision would typically be incorporated into a broader binding buy-sell agreement for the business interest. Based on the current facts, there has not been any attempt to market this business to outsiders. Again, an appraiser should be employed to establish the appropriate discount for marketability concerns if the business was going to be transferred by gift or sale to appropriate successors.

Transfer of a Family Business to Grantor-Retained Annuity Trusts (GRATs)

A retained interest trust could solve some of the transfer problems facing a closely held business owner. If the business is to be transferred to a family member, Congress provided some strict rules to prevent abusive estate freezes. A tax-favored trust provided by Congress is known as the grantor-retained annuity trust or GRAT. The GRAT provides the grantor with the right to a fixed amount (an annuity) annually from the trust for the selected retained term.

The GRAT is an irrevocable trust and the transfer to the GRAT is a completed taxable gift for gift tax purposes. It is a taxable gift because the remainder that passes to the remainder beneficiaries at the end of the grantor's retained term is a gift of a future rather than a present interest. Hence, it is not eligible for the gift tax annual exclusion. However, the grantor's lifetime exemption amount can be used to shelter the transfer from gift taxes. What's more, the gift is not the full value of the property transferred because the gift is "discounted" by the value of the annuity retained by the grantor. To help understand the valuation principles that apply to a gift in a GRAT, we need to present the valuation tables and a simple example. Of course, any actual case that planners would address with the client would be illustrated by software. To determine the taxable gift, take the amount of the retained annual annuity from the GRAT and multiply it by the annuity factor (from the table below) for the term of the GRAT. Subtract this amount (it represents what was kept by the grantor) from the total principal transferred to the GRAT. The difference is the value of the remainder or the taxable gift.

EXAMPLE

Eddie Entrepreneur, aged 65, wants to transfer $10 million in closely held Familyco, Inc., stock to a GRAT for the benefit of his son, Ernie, who is his successor to Familyco. If Eddie retains a 10-year term in the trust with a $700,000 per year annuity payable to Eddie during this term, the retained interest will reduce the value of his gift. If Eddie survives the 10-year term, the financial benefits of the gift are as follows:

Trust term	10 years
Value of stock	$10,000,000
Assumed valuation rate	2%
End-of-year payment	$700,000
Value of retained interest	8.9826 x $700,000 = $6,287,820
Taxable gift (value of remainder interest)	$3,712,180
Assumed growth rate of Familyco Stock	9%
Value of property at termination	$13,038,586

As you can see, the transaction is very powerful. A $10 million business interest is transferred for a current taxable gift of $3,712,180, well under the grantor's lifetime exemption amount. Because of the low interest rate currently in effect, the growth in the principal in excess of the current interest rate and annual annuity withdrawal will result in a substantial sum left to the remainder beneficiaries, presumably successors to the business interest. In addition, there is no reason that the value of the business interest gifted to the GRAT cannot be reduced by the minority interest discount or lack of marketability discount that are potentially applicable to a closely held business interest.

Factors for Determining Present Value of Annuities	
2.0% (current Sec. 7520 at the date this was written)	
Term of Years	Annuity
1	0.9804
2	1.9416
3	2.8839
4	3.8077
5	4.7135
6	5.6014
7	6.4720
8	7.3255
9	8.1622
10	8.9826

The GRAT is generally a grantor (defective) trust, and all income tax consequences are passed through to the grantor during the retained interest term. This results from the fact that the grantor could have his or her retained interest in the trust satisfied by principal distributions. Therefore these techniques are useful only for estate planning purposes. They are not useful for current income-shifting purposes. However, the status of the grantor trust is important for business-planning purposes since a grantor trust is an eligible shareholder for S corporation stock.

The rules do require the annual distribution to the grantor of the fixed amount in a GRAT, which may limit the ability to transfer a closely held business in trust. The business must have the cash and surplus to make such payments to the trust. Otherwise, the trustee will have to distribute some of the business interest back to the grantor to make the required annual annuity payments. This could create a significant expense if the business interest would have to be appraised to make the required GRAT distribution. The failure to make such payments will result in additional gift tax liability for the grantor when he or she does not receive qualified payments from the retained interest. However, if the problems can be resolved, this technique can be useful because the grantor will (a) be able to shift the growth in the business property to his or her heirs at a fraction of its total value and (b) still retain current income rights and control with respect to the business. There is no reason why the current business owner cannot be the trustee of the GRAT or choose a friendly trustee.

If the grantor survives the retained interest term of a qualified GRAT, the principal—including any post-transfer appreciation—is excluded from the estate of the grantor. Therefore a significant growing property interest can be transferred to family heirs for a greatly discounted transfer tax cost.

If the grantor fails to survive the term, some portion of the trust corpus (but sometimes less than the full principal) is returned to his or her estate. When interest rates are low at the time of death, as they are currently, the inclusion of the annuity right will result in the full amount of the GRAT's principal at date of death value. Thus, the premature death of the grantor creates a liquidity problem that should be addressed.

Although the GRAT could certainly be useful in the Ned Saunders case, the following advantages and disadvantages should be addressed in presenting the GRAT to Ned and the interested parties:

Advantages of a GRAT

- Provides Ned with an estate-freeze opportunity
- Provides Ned with annuity for transition/retirement
- Provides Ned with retained control temporarily
- Provides gift-tax valuation leverage based on the discounts to the contributed principal and the value of his retained annuity
- Provides estate reduction for Ned because of his continued payment of income taxes
- Shifts post-gift appreciation on the property to the remainder beneficiaries

Disadvantages of GRAT

- Transfer is irrevocable
- Other gifts may be necessary if some family members do not benefit from GRAT
- Legal and tax appraisal expense
- Principal faces normal investment risk and the transaction provides advantage only if the principal appreciates above the Sec. 7520 interest rate at the time the GRAT is created
- Distributions may have to be made from difficult-to-value principal
- Ned's death prior to the expiration of the GRAT essentially unwinds almost all of the forecast benefits of the GRAT

Lifetime Sales of Closely Held Business Interest to Family Members or Key Employees

Installment Sales of Closely Held Business Interests or Other Property

An installment sale can be a useful technique for planning purposes. It is a taxable sale of a business or of property where the income tax reporting of gain is accounted for under the installment accounting provisions of the Internal Revenue Code. An installment sale is any sale in which at least one principal payment is received in a year other than the year of the sale. The installment reporting provisions are typically used when the definition for an installment sale is satisfied. However, the seller can elect to use normal accounting for an installment sale and recognize all gain in the year of sale.

Advantages of Installment Sales

- The taxable gain from the sale of property in exchange for an installment note is delayed and recognized gradually over the installment period. Appreciated property can be sold without immediate recognition of the full taxable gain. The flexibility of an installment sale's reporting rules permits a taxpayer to defer gain recognition and, to some degree, plan the timing of capital-gain taxes from the sale of property.

- The installment sale also provides potential estate-freezing advantage for the seller. It is a particularly useful device for family estate planning, which usually occurs when a senior family member wishes to pass property on to a successor in the family. If performed properly and if the installment note is equal to the fair market value of the property at the time of the sale, the installment sale shifts the postsale appreciation to the junior family member without any transfer taxes due on the transferred property.

- The installment sale permits the buyer to defer some or all of the principal payments on the sale. This is particularly important for buyers without the funds for the entire purchase price.

- The buyer gets a guaranteed cost basis for the purposes of depreciating the purchased property or mitigating the gain on the subsequent sale of the property.

- Independent financing of the purchase may not be available to the junior family member in normal financial markets. Quite often, the purchase and sale would be impossible without the payment deferral and seller financing provided by an installment sale.

Income Tax Considerations of the Installment Sale

The sale of appreciated property in exchange for an installment note results in some or all of the purchase price being paid at some future date. From the seller's standpoint, the future payments can be broken down into three components for income tax purposes. One component of each annual payment on the installment note is treated as a return of the seller's original basis in the property. This return of basis is not taxable because the seller is merely recovering the cost of the property. A second component of each payment received is treated as taxable gain. The third component of each payment is considered interest, which is taxable to the seller as ordinary income. Under the installment sale rules, the taxable gain component is recognized proportionally over the period in which the installment payments are made. The formula for recognizing gain from any particular installment payment is as follows:[6]

$$Capital\ gain = Payment\ received\ during\ the\ year \times \frac{Gross\ profit}{Total\ contract\ price}$$

The interest paid by a buyer on an installment sale is potentially deductible for income tax purposes. In this instance, the purchasers (Eric and/or key employees) of Ned's LLC interests could deduct the interest as a business expense if they will materially participate in Teccom. However, the interest received by the seller is the most highly taxed income in the Internal Revenue Code. The senior generation seller, such as Ned, would probably prefer not to receive substantial interest in the installment sale of a business interest. The good news is that the Internal Revenue Code provides rules for interest rates and these can be relied on for a family transaction. The current interest rates are historically low. This would help Ned and Eric or other family members if the interest in Teccom and/or Ned's commercial real estate were transferred through an installment sale

related-party installment sales

Related-Party Installment Sales. Certain transactions can cause the seller to accelerate the remaining deferred gain on the installment sale. One such transaction is the subsequent sale of the property by the initial buyer. This "second disposition" rule applies only if the original installment sale is to a related party. Related parties consist of the seller's spouse, children, grandchildren, parents, grandparents, siblings, and controlled entities (partnerships, corporations,

---

6. This formula is simplified to some degree to demonstrate the gain-recognition process without adding federal income tax complexity beyond the scope of this chapter.

trusts, and estates). The second disposition by the initial buyer causes immediate gain recognition, as if the original seller has received the funds from the second disposition. This rule applies only if the second disposition occurs within 2 years of the first, unless the property sold consists of marketable securities. The second disposition of marketable securities by a related party triggers gain to the original seller if the disposition occurs at any time during the installment period. Any installment sale to Eric (or other family members) of Teccom units or the commercial real estate would be affected by this rule. If Teccom was sold to the key employees through an installment sale, this would not be a problem.

Estate Tax Considerations of an Installment Sale

The installment sale is particularly useful as an estate freeze when a senior family member sells property to a junior family member. This transaction is one of the methods of "freezing" the seller's estate and shifting the growth in family property to the next generation to avoid transfer taxes on the growth. The property sold in the transaction and any subsequent appreciation on the property is not subject to gift or estate taxation in the seller's wealth transfer. All that remains in the hands of the seller is the installment note which has a declining balance. If the seller survives the term, no property will be left to be taxed in the seller's gross estate. Anything sold by Ned in an installment sale freezes his estate tax value to the declining balance of the note and the growth on the business would become the property of the buyer.

Self-Canceling Installment Notes (SCINs)

A variation of the traditional installment note is an installment note that includes a self-cancellation provision at the seller's death. The SCIN is designed like an installment note and is subject to normal installment sale reporting rules, but it is automatically canceled by the terms of the sale contract if the seller dies before all the remaining principal payments are made. Because the buyer benefits from the seller's premature death, the SCIN would typically be used in an intrafamily sale. However, the intrafamily sale always invites IRS scrutiny. The SCIN must be equal in value to the property transferred, or a gift is made to the buyer to the extent that full and adequate consideration is not received in the transaction. Because the buyer potentially makes fewer payments if the seller dies before the note is satisfied, the IRS normally takes the position that a premium must be added to the interest paid by the buyer to reflect the seller's assumption of the mortality risk. An additional problem occurs if the capital gain has not been entirely realized by the time of the seller's death. The remaining taxable gain will be accelerated to the estate even though no further payments are received.

A SCIN could certainly be useful for Ned in transferring interests in Teccom or his business real estate. If he sells a controlling interest to Eric for a SCIN, the other family members can be honestly told that Eric is buying his interest. The benefit to Eric is that the controlling interest in Teccom might be purchased at a significantly reduced sum if Ned dies prematurely.

A SCIN might be even more useful in the transfer of the commercial real estate. The sale may be made to a group of family members who can benefit from the rental income and appreciation from the real estate after the purchase. Again, this would meet the estate freezing objectives for Ned.

Sale of a Closely Held Business Interest or Other Property for a Private Annuity

The private annuity is a variation of the installment sale with unique estate planning benefits. However, the rules and tax advantages are somewhat different. A private annuity is a sale of property, such as a family business, in exchange for the buyer's agreement to make periodic payments of a specified sum for the remainder of the seller's life. The obligor cannot normally be in the business of providing commercial annuities. The amount of the payments is based on the actuarial mortality and interest rate factors determined under the rules for annuities, term interests, and remainders that follow. A private annuity is virtually always used solely for transfers of family assets from senior family members to successor-generation heirs.

Estate Tax Considerations

The major advantage of the private annuity is its estate tax treatment. In a regular installment sale, some amount is included in the seller's estate if the seller dies holding the installment note. The remaining payments are an enforceable obligation held by the estate, and therefore they are a valuable asset to the estate. As discussed above, the inclusion of the installment note can result in serious adverse income tax consequences in addition to estate taxes. However, in a private annuity, no further payments are due when the seller dies. It is well established that there is nothing to include in the estate of a seller who dies holding a private annuity agreement. Of course, any annuity payments received by the seller and not consumed before the seller's death become part of the seller's estate.

Some of the transfer-tax advantages are lost if the annuity is not equal in value to the property transferred. This raises a series of valuation issues. First, the value of the life annuity obligation must equal the fair market value of the property transferred, or a taxable gift will result. The gift would be equal to the excess of the transferred property's fair market value over the value of the annuity. Certainly the property must be valued carefully. In addition, once the property is valued appropriately, the life annuity must be valued according to the principles provided by the Internal Revenue Code for the valuation of annuities, term interest, and remainders that follow. This should be fairly straightforward. However, a life annuity valued under these actuarial tables assumes a normal life expectancy. What is the effect of the seller's impaired health? A shorter life span than predicted by the actuarial valuation tables will have estate tax advantages in a family situation. The estate reduction value of the private annuity is greater if the senior-generation seller dies soon after the sale. A sizable property interest could be transferred at a substantial discount if the seller receives few payments. If the annuity was valued appropriately, the premature death of the seller does not result in additional estate or gift taxes. However, the IRS has issued regulations that the actuarial tables cannot be used if there is a less than 50 percent chance that the seller will survive one year. Thus a private annuity will probably require immediate payment equal to the fair market value of the property if death is imminent. However, normal valuation rules may probably be used if the seller's health is impaired but expert medical testimony can establish a reasonable possibility of the seller's survival for one year.

Income Tax Considerations of a Private Annuity

Unlike the installment sale, the gain in the property sold in exchange for the private annuity is recognized immediately when the deal is closed. Another disadvantage of the private annuity concerns the cost basis received by the buyer. The buyer's cost basis may be an important consideration in any purchase and sale transaction. The basis will offset the taxable gain if the buyer later sells the property. If the property is depreciable, a larger basis increases the depreciation deduction potential. At the time the sale is transacted, the buyer gets an immediate income tax basis equal to the value of the annuity obligation. But this initial basis assumes payments over the seller's life expectancy. What happens if the seller dies earlier or later than life expectancy or if the buyer sells the property before the original seller reaches life expectancy? In these circumstances, the buyer's basis is reduced to the amount of payments actually made.

Private annuities are fairly unusual transactions. In this instance, the immediate recognition of gain on the sale of Teccom or the commercial real estate will probably be unattractive for Ned. In addition, the life annuity promise made by the family buyer(s) will be an unwanted burden unless Ned was not expected to live to life expectancy or beyond. Nothing in the fact pattern indicates this likelihood.

Retaining Key Employees

Retaining the key employees is essential for every business. Whether the business will remain in the family and pass to successor generation heirs or will be sold to the key employees or an outside third party, the key employees are essential for sustaining the success of the business. Certainly, in this instance, Ned has identified three key employees that should be retained to enhance any succession plan. We have discussed gifts or sales of Teccom to Eric (and perhaps other family members), but there is also the possibility that the business could be sold to a key employee or a group of key employees. As nonfamily members in what appears to be a family business, they are likely to have concerns for their future. Ned has previously sold a closely held business before starting Teccom. The key employees may be comfortable with Ned but might not be as interested in working for Eric down the road.

Sec. 162 bonus life insurance plan In a corporate structure, nonqualified deferred compensation benefits would be a natural fit to provide golden handcuffs. In an entity with pass-through taxation, such as Teccom, LLC, it certainly would be unattractive for Ned and the other owners to pay income taxes on compensation that was deferred for future benefits to the key employees. Two possibilities that might provide the incentive to the key employees to stay with the company involve bonuses/increased compensation. First, increased compensation through a simple bonus could incentivize the key employee(s). This could be combined with increased responsibility and that would be useful in this case because no one is adequately trained in Ned's essential sales function. Reasonable bonuses are deductible under Sec. 162 as a reasonable and ordinary business expense. That introduces the second incentive opportunity—the Sec. 162 bonus life insurance plan.

Sec. 162 life insurance plans have the advantage of simplicity, which holds down their administrative costs. The key employee participants in the plan apply for, own, and name the beneficiary on permanent life insurance policies covering their lives. Alternatively, the key employee could create an irrevocable life insurance trust (ILIT) to be the policyowner if estate taxes are a concern. The premiums for such policies are provided through bonus payments by the employer. The employer either pays the premium directly to the insurer or gives the amount necessary to pay the premium as a bonus to the employee, who is then billed directly by the insurance company.

The Sec. 162 bonus life insurance plan involves ownership of an individual life insurance policy by an insured-key employee. This is a flexible and portable policy that will potentially have significant value. However, the policy is only valuable as long as the employer or someone else continues to make the premium payments. It is a useful retention device because the employer, in this case Teccom, is paying the premium to maintain the policy's value. If the key employees terminate employment, they have a policy which will continue to grow value only if they pay the premiums out of their own pockets. This would provide the incentive for the key employees who participate to stay with the employer providing the Sec. 162 bonuses.

The Problems Presented by the Divorce of a Business Owner

The possibility of divorce is a significant problem and the property division issues are amplified if a closely held business interest is included in assets subject to division. The marriages of any one of the business owners could end in divorce. This presents some interesting questions. Did any of the business owners have prenuptial agreements in place prior to their current marriages? Were any postnuptial agreements created? Was the business interest addressed in any such marital agreements? If not, what amount of the business interest held by a married owner is subject to equitable distribution or community property rules? If the business interest is subject to division at divorce, this could cause a severe liquidity problem for the business owner. If insufficient liquidity prevents the liquidation of the former spouse's interest, he or she could become a hostile and unwanted partner. If feasible, a postnuptial agreement should be considered where local law permits. This would take arm's-length negotiation and full disclosure of all financial facts concerning the business. In addition, a former spouse should be included as a party to any buy-sell agreement to require the purchase of the former spouse's interest if divorce occurs and the former spouse receives an interest in the business as a result of the property settlement. We'll discuss buy-sell agreements a little later.

In the case of Ned Saunders and his son Eric, both are married and neither has a prenuptial agreement. This is a significant problem because the ownership of Teccom would be subject to equitable distribution or community property rules depending on the state. What's worse, most or all of the increase in value of the business has occurred during their marriages. Although this problem affects both Ned and Eric, let's focus on Ned's divorce possibility. Teccom represents approximately half of his current net worth. If Kathy were to get half of this in divorce, this is a significant liquidity problem for Ned. Certainly, he could try to negotiate and give Kathy other assets if divorce occurs, but the composition of the assets would make this difficult.

Planning for the Death of the Closely Held Business Owner

Although the death of a member of an LLC does not automatically terminate the entity, it certainly would jeopardize the future of the business if the decedent was a key service provider. This is certainly the case with Ned Saunders. Ned's death would create some troublesome estate settlement implications that would not be faced by an estate that did not hold a closely held business interest. Ned's current plan would be problematic if he passed away without redesigning his wealth transfer documents. More discussion on that will occur later.

The business interest held by the estate of the closely held business owner is treated like any other personally-owned property in probate. Unless a buy-sell agreement effective at death has been executed, the business interest is transferred according to the provisions of the will or, in the absence of a will, by the provisions of the state's intestacy laws. The business interest held at the time of death will be included in the gross estate and subject to federal estate taxes. The value of the business depends on the status of the business at the time of death. Its value could be reduced dramatically if the decedent was an essential service provider. The type of business interest and the percentage of ownership held by the estate will also affect its value for federal estate tax purposes. Certainly, the discounts we discussed earlier (minority interest or lack of marketability) could be applicable to reduce the value in the gross estate. If the estate holds a controlling interest, the minority interest discount would not apply. In either event, the estate will incur a substantial appraisal expense and be subject to liquidity pressures if the business is not immediately marketable.

The news is not all bad. Congress has provided some relief provisions that could be applicable to the estate holding a closely held business interest. In the case of Teccom, the provisions of Sec. 6166 could be used to defer the estate taxes caused by the inclusion of the closely held business and some taxes could be deferred for up to 15 years. However, the relief provisions should only be relied upon as a stopgap if other planning has not been completed prior to the business owner's death.

In most instances, when addressing a case such as Ned Saunders and Teccom, it is prudent to secure adequate life insurance as quickly as possible to provide estate liquidity. With Ned's net worth, the life insurance should be owned by an irrevocable life insurance trust (ILIT). This will give the family and the business a fighting chance in the event that Ned passes away before other planning has been implemented. We'll have more to say about the ILIT later when we discuss Ned's estate planning objectives.

Buy-Sell with Family Successor(s) or Key Employees

Because Ned is not ready to hand over the reins of Teccom and nobody is prepared to fill his shoes, it is unlikely that any lifetime transfer techniques could feasibly be adopted to cause a significant amount of his Teccom interest to be transferred immediately. Having a premature death resulting in estate settlement where half of the estate is comprised of a closely held business interest is a recipe for disaster. Although we anticipate that Ned will ultimately take steps to move his Teccom interest during his lifetime, it is appropriate to discuss the possibility of a buy-sell agreement to manage the possibility of his premature death. If Ned does not die prematurely and has taken steps to transfer a significant amount of his Teccom interest during lifetime, the buy-sell agreement could be modified or terminated when appropriate.

The current purchaser under the proposed buy-sell agreement would probably be Eric. Presumably it would make no sense for Ned to be a reciprocal buyer under the buy-sell agreement because he already holds the controlling interest and is investigating exit strategies during lifetime. However, the potential certainly might exist for key employees to become purchasers if they want to become investors in Teccom's future. In a one-way buy-out arrangement, the cross-purchase design will meet the required objectives. We will need to be flexible and give Ned time to discuss this with potential successors.

Analysis of Type of Buy-Sell for Teccom

"wait-and-see" buy-sell agreement

The buy-sell agreement could be designed as an entity purchase or a cross purchase agreement. There is also a hybrid structure known as a "wait-and-see" buy-sell agreement. The wait and see type of agreement essentially has both structures but allows the parties to choose whether to use the entity's funds or the surviving purchaser's funds to transact the agreement. For Teccom, the cross purchase agreement probably would be the more favorable choice. It is simpler from a drafting and a tax standpoint. The cross-purchase buy-sell agreement provides the following advantages:

- Ned's controlling interest can be transferred to the chosen purchaser; initially, we'll presume this is only Eric but certainly the agreement could be modified to include one or more of the key employees.
- Ned can participate only as a seller.
- The purchaser would get a fixed cost basis equal to the entire purchase price. This would be less certain and more difficult to accomplish with the entity purchase structure.
- The life insurance funding a cross-purchase buy-sell agreement would not be owned by Teccom and run the risk that the IRS would inflate the estate-tax value of Ned's interest at the time of death by the amount of the proceeds.
- Eric's purchase of life insurance on Ned's life to fund the agreement could be funded by an adjustment to his compensation. The entity purchase would have to be funded with life insurance owned by Teccom and Ned would be subject to 70 percent of the income taxes associated with the nondeductible premium payments.

Funding Options for Teccom's Buy-Sell Agreement

It is unlikely that Eric or the key employees would have sufficient liquidity to purchase Ned's Teccom interest if he died prematurely. Outside financing is a possibility but may be unavailable at the time the chosen purchaser(s) needs the funds. Seller financing through an installment sale is a possibility. However, in this case the seller would be Ned's estate and the sale and its terms would have to be provided for in the agreement or negotiated between the buyer (presumably Eric) and the executor of Ned's estate. Currently, Ned has selected his daughter Sheila as his executor. This would put the heirs in an uncomfortable negotiation because only Eric has the incentive to continue to hold the business in the family.

Obviously, funding for a buyout triggered by Ned's premature death would lead to a recommendation for life insurance. The life insurance to fund the cross purchase buy-sell agreement should be owned by Eric (or any other purchaser) and the face amount should be chosen as close to the purchase price as economically feasible. At this time, we do not know all the facts concerning the lifetime transfer of Teccom should Ned survive for many years, but we continue to assume at this point that he has good intentions to remove himself from the business during his lifetime. Under this scenario, we should investigate all available life insurance products, but certainly some form of blend of term insurance would make the funding affordable. We could adapt if circumstances indicated that Ned was unwilling or unlikely to give up the business until death and investigate permanent life insurance under that scenario.

Special Considerations for Family Buy-Sell Agreements

The transfer of a family business to next generation purchasers invites the scrutiny of the IRS that the sale is a disguised gift or bequest. The purchase price and other terms of the purchase and sale agreement should be based on commercial standards that would apply in a arm's-length transaction between unrelated parties. If the sale of Teccom was designed with the key employees as the purchasers, we would not have this difficulty. However, we are currently assuming that Eric would be the purchaser. Strategies for designing a successful buy-sell agreement between family members include the following:

- The agreement must have a bona fide business purpose.
- The agreement should have lifetime transfer restrictions that would prevent Ned from obtaining more money in a lifetime sale of his Teccom interest than the purchase price effective in the buy-sell agreement at death.
- The sale must be binding on Ned's estate.
- The purchase price or formula to determine the purchase price should be designed with the intent to result in fair market value at the triggering point.
- The agreement must be comparable to agreements entered into at arms length.

Illustrating Estate Planning Problems to the Business Owner

A critical step in motivating the closely held business owner to act with respect to business succession planning is to demonstrate the problems that would occur if he or she dies prematurely. It is necessary to illustrate the impact on the business owner's estate planning goals. The critical question is, "If you were not here tomorrow, is this what you would want to have happen?"

What is Wrong with Current Picture?

It can be helpful to begin the analysis of the current estate plan by reviewing the business owner's current wills and trusts and doing an audit of all beneficiary designations. Then, sketch the transfers in a diagram (perhaps a PowerPoint illustration) to demonstrate to the business owner how he or she has currently answered the "who," how," and "when" questions with respect to the transfer of assets. Then it is possible to discuss the problems associated with each and every transfer. Based on the notes we have from the case facts narrative, the current estate plan of Ned Saunders provides the following transfers.

Ned Saunders--Current Dispositions

Ned's Will	Life Insurance	Retirement Plan	Joint Property
All Probate Outright to Children Equally	$500,000 Outright to Kathy	All to Kathy Outright	All to Kathy By Survivorship

Forecast the Federal Estate Tax Liability of Ned Saunders

After we have demonstrated to our business owner the proposed transfers under the current estate plan, we must also take a careful analysis of the facts and forecast the potential settlement costs and liquidity issues that face the business owner's estate. In this case, the estate tax liability is going to be real and reflects the fact that Ned has a blended family and will not be using the federal estate tax marital deduction to fully shelter his estate from federal estate tax liability. The federal estate tax alone only presents part of the problem. There is another important step that must be illustrated to the business owner. We must carefully analyze the facts and determine whether or not the estate has a liquidity shortfall for (1) paying off creditors, (2) paying the costs associated with settling the estate, and (3) providing the desired inheritances to heirs in the appropriate manner. It is time to examine Ned's facts carefully.

Addressing Estate Planning Objectives

At this point in the discussion, it is important to work with the business owner to focus some random thoughts from the initial consultation into clear objectives and goals. Earlier we presented the deficiencies of Ned's current estate plan. We will need to discuss the gaps between estate planning goals formulated and the current estate plan. A suggested list of objectives includes:

- reducing Ned's involvement in Teccom
- providing for the retirement of Ned and Kathy in the manner to which they've grown accustomed
- providing the appropriate share of his estate to Kathy
- transferring the business to Eric (or key employees) during lifetime
- providing fair inheritances to all of his children in the appropriate manner
- reducing the costs of settling Ned's estate to provide the most efficient inheritances possible
- ensuring adequate liquidity to solve the problems of the estate

We have discussed the shortcomings of Ned's current estate plan in detail in other learning objectives. It's time to go to work!

Designing Appropriate Estate Plan for Ned Saunders

Although this is not a case study that focuses primarily on estate planning, we will need to address some things to solve our business owner's problems. Our suggestions might include:

- adopting an irrevocable life insurance trust (ILIT) to address the immediate liquidity needs that would occur if Ned passes away prior to accomplishing the business transfer. The terms of the ILIT and Ned's will should be designed so that the liquidity can be made available to his estate without family discord.

- increasing the share of his estate passing to Kathy to provide her with adequate funds for a comfortable retirement. This should be done with due consideration to the fact that these assets will be diverted from Ned's children temporarily or, perhaps, permanently

- restructure the transfers to Ned's children. In this design, we should give consideration to balancing equal distribution with fair distribution. In addition, we also should consider asset protection goals. To the extent possible, we would like to make the transfers protected from the children's creditors, divorce, and, at least with respect to one child, his own deficiencies.

- begin the lifetime transfer of Ned's interest in Teccom in earnest. We have addressed many of these possibilities in earlier learning objectives. Due consideration will have to be given to potentially balancing gifts to Kathy and Ned's other children not involved in the business.

Current Estate Tax Illustration

Illustration 1

Gross Estate Calculation

Ned Saunders

Assumed date of death   7/2014

Checking & savings account	$8,500
Securities	1,725,000
Personal Residence	625,000
Other real estate	1,800,000
Other personal property	225,000
Life insurance	500,000
Teccom, LLC	7,500,000
Retirement benefits	1,600,000
Gross estate	13,983,500

Illustration 2
Estate Tax Liability

Ned Saunders

Assumed date of death	7/2014
Gross Estate	$13,983,000
Funeral & administration expenses	216,500
Adjusted gross estate	13,767,000
Marital deduction	3,158,500[7]
Charitable deduction	0
Taxable estate	10,608,500
Adjusted taxable gifts	0
Tentative tax base	10,608,500
Tentative tax	4,189,200
Unified credit	2,081,800
State death tax credit	0[8]
Federal estate tax	2,107,400
State death taxes	$0

7.   Assuming no election against Ned's Will
8.   Assume Ned's state does not impose an estate tax

Illustration 3
Liquidity Analysis

Ned Saunders

Assumed date of death	7/2014
Life insurance proceeds	$500,000
Retirement benefits	1,600,000
Other liquid assets	1,733,500
Liquid assets available	3,833,500[9]
Federal estate tax	2,107,400
Funeral & administration expenses	216,500
Loan Guarantee	1,000,000
Cash requirements	3,323,900
Estate liquidity	$509,600[10]

---

9. $2,108,500 of the liquid assets are payable nonprobate to Kathy who has no real incentive to solve the other liquidity problems of the estate. It is also worth noting that anything taken from the retirement accounts to pay expenses would trigger income tax on the distribution.

10. See note above. Without the nonprobate assets payable to Kathy, the estate's real liquidity would be a negative amount ($1,598,900). Certainly, the tax and expense apportionment clause is critical and the probate process is likely to get contentious.

Chapter Review

Review questions are based on the learning objectives in this chapter. Thus, a [3] at the end of a question means that the question is based on learning objective 3. If there are multiple objectives, they are all listed.

Key Terms and Concepts

estate freeze
lifetime exemption
related-party installment sales

Sec. 162 bonus life insurance plan
"wait-and-see" buy-sell agreement

Review Questions

1. From the case facts narrative of Teccom and Ned Saunders, identify some critical issues that must be addressed. [1]

2. Discuss the use of the LLC as the entity choice for Teccom and the impact of the following concerns: (a) liability for Teccom and Ned Saunders, (b) federal tax exposure for Teccom and Ned, (c) compensation planning for Ned, the other owners, and employees, and (d) business succession and transfer issues for Ned and Teccom. [2]

3. Describe what is meant by an estate freeze and why employing an estate-freezing mechanism would be indicated in the transfer of Ned's interest in Teccom. [3]

4. Describe the opportunities presented by the gift tax system and how the system may be useful for Ned to make lifetime gifts of Teccom or other property to family members. [4]

5. Suggest how a GRAT might be employed to meet some of Ned's objectives in the transfer of Teccom or the business real estate. [4]

6. Describe the circumstances that would indicate the use of an installment sale in the purchase and sale of a closely held business. [5]

7. Would an installment sale to Eric or key employees be indicated at this time? [5]

8. Discuss how the use of the Sec. 162 bonus life insurance plan might provide an incentive to Teccom's key employees. [6]

9. Discuss some of the planning steps that might be considered by Ned and Eric to plan for divorce. [7]

10. Describe the problems for Ned's estate if he dies prematurely before much planning can be implemented. [8]

11. Discuss the design for a buy-sell agreement between Eric and Ned for Teccom effective at Ned's death. Your answer should include a discussion of funding and the purchase price. [9]

12. Identify the pitfalls that might occur if Ned Saunders died prior to making any changes to his current estate and business succession plan. [10]

13. Examine the data sheet provided with the case narrative and (a) determine the value of Ned's gross estate, (b) his federal estate tax liability, and (c) the liquidity position of his estate if he died today. Assume that Ned's state imposes no state inheritance tax and that funeral and administrative expenses will be 2 percent of his probate estate. [11]

14. Provide a sketch of estate planning recommendations for Ned Saunders. You should address planning for liquidity, Kathy's survivorship, and the transfer of his bounty to his children. Be specific as possible with respect to transfer vehicles such as trusts and the terms of such transfers. [12]

Learning Objectives

An understanding of the material in this chapter should enable you to

1. Learn the financial commitment undertaken during the divorce process.

2. Determine the costs of divorce.

3. Discuss the financial responsibilities of divorce on the parties.

4. Identify ways to pay for divorce.

5. Identify the use of budgeting during the planning process for divorce.

6. Clarify the distinctions between common law and community property.

7. Examine property settlements in the context of divorce.

8. Discuss the inclusion of investment assets, insurance and fringe benefits in the divorce settlement.

9. Understand how to value closely held businesses for the divorce settlement.

10. Determine how to search for past or frozen retirement plans.

11. Differentiate among retirement plan categories and the plans themselves.

12. Describe nonqualified plans.

13. Understand the methods used to value retirement plans.

14. Determine what constitutes spousal support.

Cost of Divorce

Many spouses underestimate the real cost of divorce. It represents a major financial undertaking since there is a preliminary and a final stage. The preliminary stage is the temporary period where household expenditures continue to occur, and the final stage is the actual divorce date where each party signs off on final numbers.

For starters, monies that previously funded one household now must fund two. The parties are working from the same pot of money and now have to stretch it that much further. And it isn't as easy as just dividing the cost in two. The mathematics of divorce do not quite work out that way. The process may be long and drawn out. the "temporary costs" of funding the process itself cancontinue for a period of time longer than anticipated.

Paying for the divorce is no easy task. If there is a primary breadwinner during the marriage, the costs will usually fall disproportionately on his or her shoulders. However, there are generally no winners, financial or otherwise, as a result of thedivorce process—only losers.

Accounting for Disbursements

Disbursements paid are often unpredictable during the divorce process. There are recurring everyday expenses that have been paid routinely for years, as well as newly added costs that are only incurred during the divorce process. We can break the costs into two types:

Everyday Life Expenses

Everyday life expenses include fixed expenses such as mortgage, rent, utilities, insurance, and taxes, as well as discretionary expenses such as food, clothing, transportation, car expenses, credit card payments, travel and entertainment, vacations, contributions, personal care, dues, and so forth.

Divorce Costs

Divorce costs are new and often excessive expenses which include hiring an attorney and specialty fees such as business valuations, mediators, arbitrators, vocational experts, and therapists.

One or both parties must now budget to pay these expenses as they are incurred. These higher numbers reflect the added expenses of going through the divorce process. That is easier said than done for most people. If paying for everyday expenses represents a challenge, additional divorce-related expenses—for both spouses—can make it unbearable. What is even worse is that the main breadwinner may now have a dual responsibility to pay for his or her expenses and the soon-to-be ex's. A well thought-out financial plan is needed to distinguish what to pay for, how to pay for it, and for how long.

Financial Responsibilities

Who pays and what is paid comes down to which spouse is in the best financial position. What is paid is determined by the ongoing current expenses and perhaps other costs identified during the divorce process. Many times, the courts and the attorneys determine that the higher wage earner should be responsible for the expenses of the divorce.

The party responsible for paying most of the expenses, (payor spouse) needs to be aware of bad financial behavior on the part of the other spouse (payee spouse) such as running excessive joint credit-card debt with frivolous purchasesA careful eye must be kept on the nonpayor spouse's current or planned expenditures, particularly for nonessential items or services.

One of the primary responsibilities of the payor spouse is to continue to pay for expenses during the divorce process. That period of time starts from the beginning of the filing through the filing date of the divorce. These amounts would include everyday household expenditures that occur and perhaps new expenses incurred during the period to help the payee spouse transition into another mode of life or determine how to proceed now that the divorce appears imminent. The expenses related to this temporary or tentative period are usually itemized in a temporary order.

The Temporary Order

temporary order   A temporary order may be used to limit the amount of money that can be spent by the dependent spouse. It will establish a set amount of support which may limit what each spouse is able to spend.

The temporary order could set the stage for what is to come, especially if the divorce gets delayed and takes longer than originally expected. This is especially true in matters of child custody and visitation. Temporary orders should be created between husband and wife. If terms are agreed upon between husband and wife including financial and visitation issues, it is important to formalize these matters in writing. Each party should be clear on what both parties are supposed to do. They should be expected to uphold their end of the agreement. However, in a contentious situation, the attorneys, and often judge or mediators, get involved.

Length of Time of the Temporary Order

The length of time for payments under the temporary order is based on how long the divorce process continues, and whether financial needs are met during the process. A good attorney will try to expecite the process to limit the costs and the emotional wear and tear.

Financial Responsibilities: Pre-Divorce

Before either spouse files for divorce, not much can be done to protect joint assets. If a spouse deliberately does some damaging or wasteful things with the joint assets, there could be repercussions from a judge. Each spouse has a legal responsibility not to do anything that would harm the other with regard to joint interests. Joint property must be managed for the benefit of both parties. Unfortunately, it does not always work that way.

If one spouse takes half of a joint account, although causing intentional harm, it could be considered appropriate. That spouse should keep the money in a separate account under his or her name and show what the money was used for because this money will have to be brought back into the final accounting of assets to be divided. If the spouse takes all of the money in the account, that may be construed as hiding assets which the courts will not look favorably upon. Further, if this causes undue hardship to the other party, a judge or mediator may insist that part or all of this money be returned to the account, given to the other spouse or, at a minimum, brought back into the final accounting of assets to be divided.

Half of the joint assets in the account belong to each spouse. If one spouse withdraws money from the joint account, does that put the other spouse in some type of danger? If done in anticipation of the divorce, the answer would be yes. The attorney for the other spouse would have to prove that. As a sidebar, if the divorce was amicable up to this point, it will certainly not be afterwards.

Financial Responsibilities: Post-Divorce

After divorce papers have been filed, the court automatically issues an order that restricts both parties from taking or transferring any jointly-owned property. Each spouse is required to leave joint savings, checking, and investment accounts and other joint properties untouched unless both spouses jointly agree to use these assets. Make sure the spouses agree in advance about how any joint monies should be used and to get it in writing so that there are no issues down the road as to whether or not it was mutually agreed upon.

If one spouse takes more than his or her fair share, that money may need to be repaid later or worked back into the settlement, as stated above. Unfortunately, this happens quite often. The spouses can protect themselves in these situations by notifying the bank, brokerage house, or insurance company that there is a divorce in the processand that withdrawals or transfers of any monies from any of these accounts should not be allowed without the written consent of both parties. Further, the financial institution must be sent a letter stating that it must adhere to and honor the court orders that are an automatic part of the divorce.

The same can be done regarding retirement accounts by contacting the ex's plan administrator and for home equity lines of credit by contacting the bank or financial institution. Also, if the ex-spouse trades securities or performs other financial transactions over the internet, send an email to the trading firm advising them that a divorce action has been filed and that no further transaction should be made on the account without both spouse's authorization.

Budgeting During and After a Divorce

The first step in planning this reality is to develop a budget. This will earmark the monies necessary for this long and drawn out process, and help determine what each spouse will pay for during the divorce process. The reality is that there is a fixed amount of income and that has to go towards paying down current and future expenses. Not every financial decision needs to be made at this time. Some things will begin to fall into place during the process.

A budget is a necessity because it tracks the spouses incomes and the amounts they spend. Also, it will be required during the process to determine the needs of each party. Be careful since one or both sides will attempt to exaggerate their numbers. Each spouse should be proactive in looking at the budget his or her soon-to-be ex-spouse provides because he or she knows better than anyone the accuracy of those numbers. Make sure that expenses are only claimed by one spouse as there is obviously no need for both spouses to pay the same mortgage, credit card bill, etc. Once the financial information submitted by your soon-to-be ex has been reviewed, make notes and comments for your attorney so it is clear what the real income and expenses are. This will most likely be very different from the inflated numbers the other spouse generated.

It is easier to work together with a spouse when undergoing the development of a budget but that may not be possible. An honest approach tends to benefit both parties, but emotions may not allow that to happen for the reasons stated above. If that cannot happen, then the spouse should calculate his or her expenses accurately and estimate what the other's living expenses should be.

Step 1: Figuring Out Income

List all income for both husband and wife. Look at W-2 wages, 1099 self employment income, rental income, interest, dividends and capital gains, and perhaps other sources as a starting point. This process may provide a rude wake-up call. After this step is completed, determine how much money can be spent. Make sure taxes are factored in.

As a general rule, each spouse should keep income separate from the other. If the spouse does not have a separate bank account, immediately open one and begin depositing the paycheck into it. If it's the main breadwinner, keep it separate and deposit into it. Then, if necessary, transfer funds to pay for family expenses. As soon as permanent separation exists, that income becomes that person's separate property. Having separate accounts clearly indicates that each spouse is living separately and the income deposited directly into the separate accounts belongs to the income's earner.

Step 2: Figuring Out Expenses

Next, the spouse should list all the major categories of his or her expenditures. Fixed expenses, which are present in roughly the same amount every month, should be the starting point. Examples include mortgage, rent, insurance and taxes. Other expenses one tends to have more control over are listed afterwards. These expenses can be determined by examining checkbooks, charge statements, or simply keeping a cash log of every expenditure on a memo pad whenever you go out and write down the amount as you spend.

Step 3: Surplus or Deficit

Once the income and expenses are figured out, then you need to determine whether a surplus or deficit exists. With a surplus, hopefully some of those excess funds can be used specifically in the divorce process. If a deficit exists, then monies from other areas need to be reduced in order to fund the expenses of divorce.

litigation budget   Lastly, an alternative to the expense portion of the divorce above is to have the attorney develop a litigation budget. Broad-based categories should be developed including items for discovery, negotiations, alternative dispute resolution, trial preparation, and trial. If there are unresolved or complex issues, litigation costs can easily be upwards of $50,000, even in a fairly amicable divorce. Due to these high costs, litigation should be avoided, if possible.

Paying for Divorce

Once you have firmed up the budget with amounts that will be in line with the process ahead, now comes the hard part—paying for the divorce. The following represents a series of options to consider:

1. Begin liquidating joint assets under the premise that they will provide money which can temporarily be placed in a liquid account (such as a money market or savings account) to pay the fees associated with the divorce. Of course, if the assets are jointly held, then the opposing spouse must sign off on it. The rationale is that funds must be available for payments and ultimately both spouses can be held responsible for paying those debts either during the divorce process or afterwards.

2. If the spouse is not the primary wage earner, put the attorney fees on a joint credit card. Be aware that this action may cause great hardship down the road. However, because it is a joint debt, the opposing spouse will still be liable for this joint debt. The rationale for placing these expenses on the joint credit account is that the primary wage earner will be responsible for most of these bills as the lower wage earner has no money to pay the bills.

3. Apply for and take out a joint loan to pay those bills. Perhaps a home equity line of credit makes sense. A home equity line of credit is a pre-approval from the bank stating that you have sufficient equity in your home and strong credit scores to borrow against the house for whatever reason.

4. It would make sense to take out a mortgage or home equity loan in advance for what each attorney may estimate the legal fees to be. Add up the two legal fees, and take out a mortgage for about 125 percent of that amount, thus allowing for cost overruns. If the attorneys are not paid, they could attach a lien on the house.

Further, since the home equity loan or mortgage is secured against the house, the interest is tax-deductible.

5. Tax deductibility of expenses helps minimize the sting. It is generally not a good idea to go into debt, especially to pay for divorce related expenses. However, if it is a joint obligation, then perhaps the debt can be shared by both spouses once the final settlement is reached. The debt and assets typically are split, and hopefully each party will take a share of both the debt and assets. Keep in mind, however, that unless the property securing the mortgage or home equity line of credit is sold, or money is used from another source to pay off those loans, there will still be liens again the house for which ever party obtains that asset in the final settlement.

6. Use retirement assets to pay for divorce expenses. Even though there are restrictions and repercussions, and permission may be needed to use retirement assets, they become part of the pool of monies to be divided between the spouses. If borrowing against qualified retirement dollars is allowed, then that would be a wise move. However, if monies come from an IRA or other personal retirement account, then borrowing is not allowed. In addition, a 10 percent penalty on top of the ordinary income tax liability from the withdrawn funds would be payable to the IRS.

7. Rental real estate or other assets can be sold. Selling rental real estate may be a good solution because the tax implications of selling the property later may not adequately be taken into consideration if the property is simply transferred to a spouse as part of the marital settlement.

   Capital gains and recaptured deprecation with rental real estate will effectively lower your tax basis and thus increase your tax liability. Accounting for that during the process will make both parties liable for the tax consequences so that one party will not get stuck footing the tax bill alone as would happen if the property was sold after the divorce. For example, if the spouses owned a piece of real estate jointly since 2000 and now, roughly 13 years later, some of the depreciation on the property may have been used up, the adjusted basis is reduced. Therefore, when the property is sold, it contains more profit.

8. Another possible source to satisfy the divorce expense is joint assets, depending on whether or not divorce papers have been filed. Both spouses would have to agree to it in writing before this could occur. Once the filing occurs, both spouses are legally

prohibited from doing anything that would harm the jointly-owned interests. Jointly-owned property must be managed for the benefit of both parties. Taking care of joint assets is viewed as a fiduciary responsibility, similar to that of financial advisors managing their clients' money.

9. The spouse could use his or her own solo assets to pay for divorce. For example, 50 percent of a retirement account can be borrowed (if allowed) or withdrawn. However, that may not be a good idea for several reasons. For starters, money may be borrowed only from certain plans, and there are specific limits as to how much can be withdrawn. With a 401(k) plan, that amount is 50 percent of the account balance up to a maximum of $50,000. However, this money must be paid back within 5 years to avoid having to take the money as a withdrawal. In addition, depending on the retirement owner's age, there may be penalties for early withdrawal and taxes that result from the withdrawals.

   Lastly, judges may conclude that one spouse was intentionally trying to reduce the asset base, which may result in inclusion of those withdrawn funds as part of the final financial settlement. It also must be determined whether the retirement account is sole or joint property. If it is considered a joint asset, an argument can be made that taking half of the account is within that spouse's right, especially if those funds are used to pay attorneys fees and other divorce expenses.

10. As a last resort, separate property can be used. However, do not confuse solo assets with separate property. Separate property is what is brought into the marriage. As long as that property is kept apart from the other spouses's property, it will remain separate property. These include assets or debts that either spouse had before the marriage. Generally, each party keeps the separate property and is responsible for the separate related debts. However, in some states separate property can be divided at divorce.

    Separate property is property titled in that spouse's name and is allowed to be kept separately as long as it's not commingled it with the spouse's property. Separate property also includes gifts and inheritances brought into the marriage or received during the marriage as long as it is again not commingled with the spouse's property. In some states, the increase in separate property will be considered marital property.

Financial Issues of Divorce

property settlement   Financial settlements of divorce can usually be broken down to the immediate division of assets and liabilities through property settlements and the ongoing series of payments, such as spousal and child support.

Approaching the Discussion of Property Settlements

Most of the initial uncertainty regarding divorcstems from how the marital property will be divided. Dividing propertycan be done the easy way through cooperation with the opposing spouse, or the hard way where the couple can duke it out. Looking at the big picture and figuring out what makes the most sense for everyone is the easy choice—if the couple and their advisers can make it happen.

When all is said and done, spending 3 hours of legal time at $350 per hour for an item that costs $30 is clearly not a good strategic financial maneuver. Sure there may be sentimental value attached to certain items, but it is just "stuff" which can be easily replaced in a cheaper way and as part of a fresh start. It all comes back to looking at the big picture and picking the right battles. Remember, fighting over every item will wear some individuals out and they won't be as effective at getting the bigger ticket items.

IRC Sec 1041 (Property Settlements)

Property Settlements

IRC Sec 1041   Property settlements fall under IRC § 1041, which states that a transfer is incident to divorce if it is made within one year after the marriage terminates, or it's related to the marital termination. A property transfer is presumed related to the marital termination when required by a divorce or separation instrument (either original or modified), and the transfer is not more than 6 years after the marital termination. The purpose of Sec. 1041 is to avoid capital gain to the transferor-spouse.

If a taxpayer transfers property to a third party on behalf of his or her former spouse, the property is treated as if it was transferred to the spouse or former spouse, and the spouse or former spouse immediately transferred it to a third party provided the transfer is required by a divorce or separation instrument or the transfer follows a written request of the recipient spouse. Transfers of an interest in a health savings account (HSA) or medical savings account

(MSA) are not considered taxable transfers. After the transfer, the interest is treated as the spouse's HSA or MSA.

Sec. 1041 does not apply in the following situations:

- Taxpayer's spouse or former spouse is a nonresident alien;
- Certain transfers in trust; and
- Certain stock redemptions, which are taxable to a spouse under the tax law, a divorce or separation instrument, or a valid written agreement.

Purchases Between Spouses

Under Sec. 1041, the selling spouse is not taxed on the transfer, but the buying spouse cannot increase the basis of the property, even by amounts he or she may have paid to the other spouse for the property. Thus, a spouse who buys property from another spouse is disadvantaged as compared to a third party purchaser.

Common Law vs. Community Property

The state of residence can be a factor in the division of assets. All of us live either in a common law state or a community property state. Either way, the objective is to fairly divide property that the couple owns together. Let's take a look at the differences.

common law   In common law states, courts are supposed to apply equitable distribution standards to divide property equitably or as justice requires. These laws give judges more latitude and property awards tend to vary greatly, although a 50/50 split is considered the norm.

Equitable does not mean equal. An example of this would be the following. Let's assume a marriage acquired only two assets; a $500,000 business that the husband has operated alone and a $400,000 house shared together. Upon divorce, it is possible (hopefully not probable) that the judge can award the husband the business if he was the main person involved and provide the ex with the house to relatively equal out the distribution. That can be considered as equitable although definitely not equal. Forty-one states have equitable distribution laws.

community property

Community property represents a unified or undivided interest in property. It follows the premise that marriage is an equal partnership and that all property acquired during the marriage (whether assets or income) are split 50/50 regardless of who actually earns it. The same principles apply to debt. Therefore each married spouse owns an equal undivided interest in all of the property accumulated utilizing either spouse's earnings during the marriage.

As with any set of laws, there are certain exceptions. Property acquired before the marriage, or through gifts or inheritance received during the marriage, retains its separate property status if preferred. If any separate property is commingled, or can no longer be traced as separate, it will be assumed to be community property. In addition, in some states, if you buy separate property, such as a house, then get married and pay for the expenses of the house (such as mortgage, taxes or utilities) as a marital asset, under community property upon divorce the law will state that there were joint contributions from both spouses toward the upkeep of the house and some portion of the house will end up as community (marital) property. It may not be 50 percent, but it could be substantial.

The rationale for enforcing community property laws under these circumstances is that if the property was separate but both parties contributed to the care of that asset, then both should enjoy the benefits of the ownership if they split up.

Nine states are considered to be community property states. These include Arizona, California, Idaho, Louisiana, Nevada, New Mexico, Texas, Washington, and Wisconsin. In addition, Alaska allows residents and nonresidents to enter into community property agreements permitting in-state property to be treated as community property. In these states, only property that was accumulated during the marriage will be divided, with a few exceptions, and the property will be divided equally at 50/50, asset by asset whenever possible.

Wages, incomes, and bonuses are community property and are considered credit obtained during the marriage. Therefore, homemakers are not penalized for not working outside the house. Claims of "I earned all the money" therefore are not relevant since it is assumed that each spouse contributed to the household income.

There are seven specifics regarding community property that you should be aware of.

1. If one spouse takes money belonging to community property and pays off a separate debt, then the community property will be paid back that amount when the parties split.

2. If one spouse receives a financial settlement or award as a result of a community property activity (for example, that spouse receives an award from a lawsuit brought about as he was driving his kids to school and had his car hit by another driver), then the entire award will be considered community property.

3. Community property regimes vary considerably from state to state. In other words, there are nine separate community property laws, not one set of laws that nine states adhere to. So make sure that you understand the specifics of your home state.

4. Community property does not have an automatic right of survivorship. When the first spouse dies, one half of the value of the property will pass through the probate process for retitling, per the direction of the decedent's will or the state intestacy (dying without a will) law. Each spouse's one-half interest will also be included in his or her own federal gross estate.

5. Community property status can be dissolved through death, divorce, or by agreement between the spouses. Specifically one spouse can gift his half of the community property to the other spouse, thereby creating separate property owned entirely by the spouse who receives the property. Because there is an unlimited deduction for gift taxes, gift tax liability would not be created. However, this type of gift tax may occur when a couple moves from a community property state to a common law (separate property) state in which the couple intends to remain. Otherwise, community property once created retains its community property status. Further, any property acquired utilizing the earnings of either spouse, subsequent to the couple's move into the community property state, is considered community property.

6. General rules to remember are "once community property, always community property" (even if they move to a common law equitable distribution state), and "once common law, always common law" (even if you move to a community property state) except in the following situation. In five community property states, a quasi-community property system is recognized for a couple moving from a common law state to a community property state.

quasi-community property

Quasi-community property is property that would be community property had the couple been living in the community property state

Applications in Financial Planning I

at the time of acquisition. Quasi-community property is treated just like community property at the death of either spouse, or at the time of divorce. Before either one of these occurrences, the quasi-community is treated as separate property. The five quasi-community property states are Arizona, California, Idaho, Washington, and Wisconsin. That means if you move from a common law state (for example, New York) to a quasi-community state (for example, Arizona), then your property takes on the characteristics of the state to which you move (Arizona), which is a community property state.

7. Community property owners receive a full 100 percent step up in value at death from each spouse's half as opposed to common law where the heir receives a 50 percent step up in basis (the decedent's share only). This creates a new tax basis which is higher than the old one. This is called community property with right of survivorship.

Separate Property

separate property   As stated previously, property acquired alone by a spouse prior to marriage, or received as a gift or inheritance during the marriage, is considered to be separate property. Separate property is not subject to division by the court (with few exceptions). In certain situations, a married couple can own property even within a community property state as separate property. In these cases, this property would not receive a new tax basis on both halves at the death of the first spouse.

If the separate property appreciates and taxes are paid jointly by the couple on their income tax return, then a gray area exists. Many times the appreciated portion of the property can be considered marital property while the original separate property remains just that.

For example, let's assume that the ex-spouse received a $2,000,000 inheritance and took the money and invested it earning 5 percent per year for a total income of $100,000. If the couple files a joint tax return, and pay taxes on the $100,000 jointly, then the appreciation in the asset can be considered to be a marital asset under community property law. To avoid that scenario, figure out what the tax liability is on the property. Let's assume $15,000.. The ex would then write a check to the community property account for $15,000 from the ex's inheritance account to cover the tax liability on that money. This way, by keeping it separate and having the ability to trace the tax liability directly to the ex should keep the $100,000 of income as continued separate property.

Common Law Marriage Issues

Couples who act like they are married, hold themselves out to the world as married, and intended to be married are considered legally married. Examples of this type of behavior include filing joint tax returns, referring to each other as "husband" and "wife," and using the same last name.

common law marriage   If your client lives in one of the states that recognize common law marriage and meets the criteria, then he or she is considered legally married and must get a divorce to end the marriage. Before entering into this type of relationship, visit with an attorney who's an expert in this area.

There are many assets and liabilities that get divided under property settlement rules. A discussion of them follows.

Valuation of Assets

The Primary Residence

This is a very difficult decision. Since you cannot split the family residence down the middle, you must determine what result you want to achieve after the divorce. Among the possibilities for dividing the house include:

- selling the house outright, paying off the mortgage, paying taxes if any, and dividing the net proceeds
- transferring ownership from one spouse to the other where one spouse buys out the other
- one spouse keeps the house for a certain period of time, such as until the youngest child enters college, and then sell it
- gifting the house to the child.

No matter what decision is agreed to, the house must be appraised. That result is the fair market value to begin negotiations. The mortgage balance must be subtracted from it.

If the spouses agree to sell it, then a real estate broker should be contacted. Consideration for the real estate brokers commission, closing costs, and tax considerations should be factored in to determine the net equity each spouse will walk away with.

The selecting of a real estate agent, agreement on an asking price, the ability to show the house, and reviewing all bona fide offers should be done jointly by the spouses.

If one spouse decides to hold on to the house, then that net amount goes into that spouses' column for dividing assets. The other spouse will walk away with the amount equal to the house derived from other assets from the couple. Negotiating this buyout should incorporate adjustments for the real estate agent's fee, deferred maintenance, spousal support considerations, refinancing issues, and other things pertinent to that particular house.

However due to the significant tax consequences involved, a full discussion of this topic can be found under the Divorce and Taxes chapter.

Personal Belongings

Hopefully what each spouse owns will be received by that spouse, but unfortunately, that is not always the case. List these assets individually to justify a starting point for their division. Examples include jewelry, furs, furniture, kitchen items, clothing, sporting event tickets, club memberships, subscriptions, frequent flier miles, and personal effects. Pets are considered property and the judge will award a pet to one of the spouses (if it can't be agreed upon before hand). Also, the sharing of pets can be an option.

Some of these possessions may already be in the spouse's possession if living separately. If not, perhaps each spouse can pick items from a select list if the spouses are on speaking terms.

The value of these assets should then be divided up on the balance sheet spreadsheet indicating in which column that asset should go. With regard to automobiles, trucks, motorcycles, and other vehicles, the driver usually ends up with the one he or she drives. Ensure that any automobile loans are reflected in the division of this property and make sure that the name on the title is transferred to the rightful owner, and that the insurance is properly adjusted. After totaling all of these items, if a difference exists, then the other spouse should be awarded other assets of comparable value to equalize the balances as much as can be done. Remember, it does not pay to spend legal fees fighting over a particular item, when it could be repurchased for a much lower cost.

Investable Assets

After-tax investments, such as mutual funds, stocks, bonds, art, rental and vacation real estate, gold, and other items are difficult to value because of their constant fluctuations. Since the divorce will not be completed for a period of time, the question becomes how should you proceed in valuing this property? You can assign a value to each asset as of the date of separation, divide the actual asset or account whereby each spouse would receive a portion of the total asset, such as splitting equally a mutual fund. Don't forget to include the tax ramifications of the transition for when the asset is sold. Lastly, try to detach yourself from the sentimental appeal of the asset, if possible.

Life Insurance

If spousal or child support is provided pursuant to the divorce, ensuring that the payee spouse owns a policy on the payor spouse provides income protection in the event of the payor's death, and protects future cash flow regarding spousal support and child support payments. The agreement should state time limits for buying the insurance, or, if the spouse already has life insurance, then the payee spouse must contact the insurance company to change ownership and beneficiary designations.

Disability Insurance

To protect the earned income stream of the payor, ensuring the payor spouse has disability insurance coverage, will again, continue to assure payments to the payee spouse, thus protecting spousal and/or child support future payments.

Fringe Benefits

Settlement of fringe benefits is a very uncertain area because courts have disagreed about how to classify particular benefits (from using the company car to providing certain free benefits to select employees) at divorce.

1. Health Insurance. A court may provide coverage for children as part of the child support package.
2. Disability Insurance. If employer paid and provided disability benefits are available, benefits received from fringe benefit this are taxable.
3. Group Term Life Insurance. This benefit is generally not transferable upon leaving the employer, but may be portable to

upper management. The first $50,000 of benefit can be excluded from the employee's taxable income.

4. <u>Health Savings Accounts</u>. These are nontaxable accounts funded by employers and employees to pay for medical expenses. Employee contributions are tax deductible up to specified amounts, can accumulate tax-deferred, and are received tax free if used for medical reasons. They may accumulate large balances over time.

5. <u>Cafeteria Plans</u>. These plans offer a variety of fringe benefits purchased through employer funds, such as group term life insurance, disability insurance, health insurance, child care, 401(k), or even cash. The type of benefit is selected in advance of the calendar year. Only the cash option generates taxable income to the employee.

6. <u>Severance Plans</u>. These are payments given to the employee upon being terminated by the employer. These amounts generally either reward employees for past performance with the employer, or help them cover their expenses while looking for a new job.

7. <u>Group Legal Services</u>. These plans offer employees low cost legal services, including advice, representations and referrals in a negotiated rate by the employer. Costs are paid for through union dues or payroll deductions. These benefits do provide for taxable income.

8. <u>Educational Assistance Programs</u>. Employees receive benefits covering tuition, and fees for various educational offerings. These programs can be offered through outside institutions or even through in-house programs.

9. <u>Employee Assistance Programs</u>. These programs provide coverage for employees and their families needing assistance for issues covering anxiety, depression, money and credit problems, substance abuse, and legal problems.

The Closely Held Business

If a business was built or grew significantly during the marriage and joint funds were used for investment, the extent that the business will be considered marital property will have to be determined. If separate funds were used, it can be a tricky scenario. In either case, if the value of the business appreciated, it is more likely that the increase in value will be considered marital property.

closely held business valuation

To determine whether the business should be considered marital property, these key business valuation questions will have to be answered:

- Was the business established before or after the marriage?
- Did it grow substantially during the marriage?
- If the business did grow, was the ex a stay at home spouse who did not work full time in the business?
- Was separate property from either spouse invested in the business?
- Was it a joint business run by both spouses?

The conclusion is that if any part of the business is designated to be marital property, then a value must be placed on it.

If your client is the business owner, he or she may not want the spouse to take any part of the business. Any value the opposing spouse has in the business will need to be satisfied with an equivalent amount of other assets in trade. Other joint or separate assets, such as money the client put into a pension plan may need to be rolled over to your spouse in whole or in part. If there are no other assets, the client may have to borrow money or possibly sell out your portion of the business. And there is a chance that no market will exist to sell the business, especially when it is necessary.

Whatever the client decides to do, the one thing the business owner will certainly feel is that the business belongs to him or her. Period! Any business owner can attest to that. He or she will not want the ex to receive anything business related. The client may also feel that it is not part of the marital estate, but the courts will not be as kind and will generally refuse that position.

For example, I knew a successful financial planner who lived and operated a business in a community property state and was married for 20 years. After his divorce, his wife received 50 percent of the business even though she never stepped foot in the business during that 20-year marriage. Because he could not afford to buy her out right away, she initially owned 50 percent of the business after the divorce and all decisions related to the business had to be made jointly.

So how do you go about the valuation process? First, obtain a copy of the business tax returns. The returns will show the business structure and the income and expenses of the business interest, which should help with the flow of the valuation. However, there are many ways to accomplish the valuation, and unless the client owned the business prior to marriage as separate property, it will be counted as part of the final settlement.

As a sole proprietor, one person LLC or S Corporation, essentially the client is the business. She can make the argument that if it weren't for her, there would be no business, and most people would agree—even the business valuators. For example, if the client becomes disabled or dies, there is no business.

Unfortunately, the business valuators don't value the business in that way. Advisors should be aware that the business can get "double dipped" if the lawyer is not on top of this. Here's why: the opposing spouse will get credit for a percentage of the business interest (assume 50 percent) as part of an equitable distribution and then will also be entitled to take part of your client's earnings or income for support! Therefore, it is counting twice against the business owner.

Don't enter into a relationship with a valuator without understanding the fee that will be charged and exactly what you will get in return for payment. Taking this action does not mean that the client should blindly hand over all his books and records to the appraiser and expect this person to figure it out, leaving you out of the loop. Qualified professionals should be able to explain their recommendations and assessments in terms the client can understand. They should be willing to decipher through the alternatives available, explain why certain decisions are recommended, lay out the risks involved, and answer questions fully. If the client is uncertain about the validity of the appraisal, get another opinion.

To get comfortable with this huge undertaking, interview different business valuation firms and determine the method they use to value the firm. Get references from other clients who went through the process with that firm. In some cases, the client will find out that the business valuator will not understand the type of business and will derive a number not really relevant to how the business works.

It is important to have the client's attorney present during the questioning both before hiring a valuator and during the appraisal process. If the attorney is present, any information discussed between the client and the business valuator will be considered privileged (confidential) information. Without the attorney, that privilege is lost.

fair market value

There are various methods that business valuators can use. One is the *fair market value method*. Under Treasury

Regulations, this is what a willing buyer and seller can agree upon as the final price. Since businesses are not identical and are tailored to be different from other existing businesses, it can be tough to get meaningful comparisons to other business valuations.

The downside with this approach is it's based on what the business would sell for in cash. Most businesses do not sell for cash. Most are financed. Business valuators will also typically look at the accounts receivable and the debts of the business when considering fair market value. There can be an element of subjectivity included in business valuation as well.

capitalized earnings   There are so many types of businesses out there and each one may require a different approach in valuation. When a business has limited assets but constant cash flow, as is typical of a professional practice, *capitalized earnings* is the favored method to use. On the other hand, when a business such as a manufacturing or retail enterprise has a large amount of capital tied up in assets but a more limited cash flow, the focus generally should be on the market value of the assets. Other types of businesses have a balance between assets and cash flow, and for these, calculation of value should be by an *excess earnings method*. IRS Rev. Rul. 59-60 deals with methods of valuing closely held corporations such as a professional practice.

Furthermore, in a divorce you are not putting the business up for sale now nor are you able to find a willing buyer and seller. The Treasury regulations state that neither party should be forced to buy or sell. In a divorce situation, this is definitely not the case. In fact, nothing out of the ordinary is to be done by the person running the business. What's happening in a divorce is that one of the two spouses is essentially selling one-half of the business. What makes it difficult is that both parties do not have the same knowledge of your business.

An alternative approach which is probably safer is to look at the business's *future earning capacity* which asks what the likely amount of earned income will be in the future. That is also risky but probably a better method than seeing what was earned in the past. Historical information is always outdated the moment is released. For example, just because a mutual fund earned 20 percent last year doesn't mean that the same fund should expect to earn 20 percent this year. Either the fund will or it won't. Knowing that the business will earn something different in the future is a safe bet. Since you do not have knowledge of what will really happen in the future, the business value may be much higher (or lower) than the projected income assumed.

Another approach for valuators is to look at *sales of comparable businesses*. There are books and computer programs that can also assess the value of similar types of businesses. These formulas are generally expressed as multiples of gross revenues, operating income, and other factors and sometimes can be taken from general rules of thumb. Sometimes business brokers can lend a hand based on what they have seen in the marketplace.

Still another approach can have the business be *valued for tax purposes* (which is nothing like valuing for divorce purposes) under Rev. Rul. 59-60. This approach requires the valuator to answer certain key questions about the business. These questions address the type of business, history since inception, general economic business conditions outlook and the prospects for your business, the financial condition of the business, its earning capacity, whether large quantities of stock were sold, if goodwill is present, and the market price of similar type corporations.

Closely Held Business Valuation Documents Needed

Be prepared to show your business valuator the following documents. If not, the client's lawyer can also request these documents from the ex's lawyer, and vice versa.

- Last 5 years of individual tax returns and documents (Form 1040)
- Last 5 years of business tax returns and documents [Form 1120S (S Corporations); 1120 (C Corporations); 1065 (partnerships, limited liability companies, limited liability partnerships)]
- K-1s for 1065 or 1120S
- Income (profit and loss) statement
- Balance sheet
- Listing of shareholders or partners who own a piece of the company
- Capital accounts of the partners if the business is a partnership
- Retained earnings statement
- List of cash accounts and any investments
- List of aged accounts receivable (money due the business)
- List of aged accounts payable (money the business owes others)
- Business plan and projections
- Key officers' compensation
- Key officers' life insurance
- List of existing contracts
- List of partnership agreements in affect

Goodwill—the increase in earnings or value brought about through repeat business—may be another factor in the valuation equation. To determine if goodwill exists, questions such as "Do you have a steady stream of repeat clients or customers constantly knocking at your door?" need to be answered. Goodwill can be broken down into enterprise goodwill if it deals with selling product or professional goodwill if it deals with patronizing the same CPA, CFP®, doctor, lawyer, etc. This is very tough to determine. If you run a service business, then some states may include professional goodwill as part of the marital estate.

Another place where goodwill shows up is when one spouse sacrificed a career by either being an at-home spouse, or worked various odd jobs or whatever while the other spouse went to school or obtained professional licenses or certifications. That ex may feel he or she deserves a part of that business because of his or her sacrifice to the big marital picture. Many attorneys will try to view the entire marriage and its components (that is, business interests) as a complete partnership and thus try to determine a dollar value for the spouse staying home to raise the kids and split as part of an equitable distribution.

Understanding the Closely Held Business Valuation Report

Valuation reports can be oral or written. If the two spouses agree on the business valuation, oral reports would be the best way to go since it ultimately saves both spouses money. If the spouses don't agree, it is more than likely that a written report will need to be prepared which describes the nature of the business and all the facts and documents relied on to reach the final appraisal. Ultimately, it will be needed for court but not having to go to court where the business valuator testify will certainly save lots of money.

If either of the spouses are unhappy with the business valuation findings, either one can opt to get a new valuation or hire an expert to challenge how the business valuator arrived at their numbers. The expert will serve on the witness stand countering the original business valuator's method, logic and rationale. Before you make that call, you really need to see what the true differential is and whether it is worthwhile pursuing. Sometimes the dollars are not there to support this challenge or redo. If the couple is headed for court to resolve the property settlement, then, as many spouses have found out, wasting money on a second valuation should be done only if it is a necessity.

The closely held business valuation report should include the following:

- full description of the business
- method of valuation
- name and qualifications of the evaluator
- names of relevant documents that were reviewed
- full explanation for the rationale for the evaluation
- date the business was valued
- reason for the valuation
- relevant industry standards

When Both Spouses Work and Own the Business Together

When divorcing spouses co-own a closely held business, there is a bigger challenge since each spouse would probably want to continue owning the business after the divorce becomes final. It is likely that the spouses would not want anything to do with each other after the fact. However, if both spouses are relying on this income as their principal source of revenue, should they divide the business initially or separate and keep the business intact? That's a tough call. Other issues begin to develop including if one spouse takes over the business, then how does the other spouse get compensated for that? Should he or she continue to draw profits or a salary from the business? Should they work out a buyout for the present value of the future interest for the spouse no longer involved with the business? What happens when both spouses while married ran personal expenses though the business (like car expenses, travel, entertainment, etc.)? How do you account for that situation? The bottom line is that if the business can be kept afloat and not taken down with the divorce, it may be wise to work out some acceptable arrangement.

Some courts reason that professional goodwill is personal to an individual and not capable of being divided as an asset. In any case, professional income is always the basis of a support order. The courts won't make a distinction between income from goodwill and ordinary income. So even though it may not count as a division of a marital asset, it will always be countered as income for support purposes.

Stock Redemptions

stock redemption   The rules get much more complicated when dealing with spouses who have interests in a large corporation. Treas.

Reg. Sec. 1.1041–2 acknowledges that, depending on the circumstances, a stock redemption can be:

- a sale of stock that if held for more than a year would result in a capital gain or loss (IRC Secs. 302 and 316)
- a constructive dividend subject to ordinary income treatment (IRC Secs. 302 and 316)

Interestingly, Treas. Reg. Sec. 1.1041–2 permits the spouses to decide who has to report the constructive dividend or capital gains created by the redemption. Make sure your client's attorney and business valuator draft this extremely well and tight. Unfortunately, Treas. Reg. Sec. 1.1041–2 only applies to corporations. Partnership redemptions, as we will see, fall under IRC Sec. 736.

Partner Liquidations

partner liquidation

A partner liquidation is similar to a partnership liquidation except that cash paid triggers IRC Sec. 736. Sec. 736 requires money payments to be characterized as a

- distributive share or guaranteed payment, or
- payment for an interest in partnership property

This allocation generally is made under the partnership agreement. The total allocated to Sec. 736(b) cannot exceed the fair market value of the partnership's assets at the time of liquidation.

If there is no allocation provision in the partnership agreement, payments are first treated as coming from Sec. 736(b) to the extent of the value of the partnership interest.

Under IRC Sec. 736(a), cash payments made to a retiring or deceased partner (an ex-spouse) are:

- a distributive share if figured by reference to partnership income, thus reducing the amount of partnership income available to the continuing partners, or
- guaranteed payments, if not determined by reference to the partnership income, thus producing a deduction from gross income to arrive at partnership taxable income.

Sec. 736(b) payments are made when the cash payment is exchanged for the interest of the retiring or deceased partner in partnership property. It is treated as a current distribution by the partnership and not as a distributive share or a guaranteed payment. Liquidating cash payments under Sec. 736(b) are considered a return of capital to the extent of a partner's basis in the partnership, and capital gain is recognized to the extent of any excess.

The income payments received in lieu of the retiring partner's interest in current or future partnership income and are treated as:

- guaranteed payments, if they are not determined by partnership income and are either capitalized or deductible by the partnership and ordinary income to distribute
- distributive shares if determined by reference to partnership income and are excludible from the continuing partners' income and may constitute ordinary income and/or capital gain

Stock Options

stock options   In most states, stock options granted to a spouse while married become part of the marital property. If that is the case, they need to be valued just like any other assets. Stock options are considered to be additional forms of compensation that need to be factored into the entire income package. They are really viewed as deferred compensation since this compensation is tied to the future increase in the value of the company stock. The critical issues that develop include whether to include the option value as part of the distribution of property and/or whether to include the income as part of support.

Stock options are an employee spouse's right to formally buy company stock at a specified price during a specified time period. They can only be issued to the employee and thus cannot be transferred as part of the divorce settlement. Stock options generally remain outstanding for up to 10 years. Employee stock options are subject to vesting. If the employee leaves employment, the vesting period would not be satisfied and all those options not vested would then be forfeited. The vested portion would remain intact. If the stock goes down in value, the employee will not exercise the option since it would create a loss.

There are several types of options but the main two are incentive stock options (ISOs) and nonqualified stock options (NSOs). ISOs are options granted by an employer to compensate key employees and executives of larger corporations to buy stock at some specified time in the future. ISOs generally are not issued to closely held business owners because they get their value when the options are sold and there typically is no readily available market for closely held business owner stock. NSOs can be issued to both employees and independent contractors and are designed in any manner suitable to an executive or to the employer with few government restraints.

nonstatutory stock options

incentive stock options

Said another way, the IRC divides stock options into two categories. These include nonstatutory stock options, which do not meet specific IRC requirements for special tax treatment, and statutory stock options, which include employee stock purchase plans (ESPPs) and incentive stock options (ISO).

That makes analyzing options more difficult because the higher the stock option valuation, the more the ex receives in comparable assets since the employee has no choice but to keep the option. It's no different than the closely held business owner having to keep the business and include the value of the business on his or her side of the martial valuation statement.

Key Stock Option Questions

To determine whether stock option valuation is even an issue in divorce, you'll need to answer these four questions:

- Is the stock option part of marital property? In other words, was it earned and received during the marriage?
- How is the option valued?
- When is the option valued?
- What are the tax consequences when the option is exercised?

Your client must come up with a proper valuation of the stock options to adjust for the opposing spouse's entire compensation package, including stock options, retirement benefits, flexible benefit packages, and other perks given to that working spouse. You'll also need to understand the date as to when the option is valued. Is it at the hearing date, the date of separation, the date of trial, the date of divorce decree? As we have all seen with major stock market declines recently, the date of valuing stock options is critical. Again, these are very tough questions to answer.

The tax issues can be significant because of the difference between ordinary income and capital gain tax rates upon exercise and sale. Incentive stock options are not taxed as wages when the options are granted or exercised, but they can have alternative minimum tax consequences. ISOs are only taxed when sold under IRC Sec. 522. Nonqualified stock options, on the other hand, are taxed as ordinary income upon their exercise because they are considered to be additional wages. In any event, while the options are accruing there are no tax consequences to the employee. However, under IRC Sec. 83, the taxpayer spouse can elect to recognize income earlier which then makes future appreciation eligible for lower capital gain rates as long as certain holding period requirements are met. As with other investments, losses are limited.

Formerly, stock options were always taxed to the employee spouse (the person who earned it) based on the assignment of income doctrine under IRC Sec. 1041. However, Rev. Rul. 2002-22 now provides that statutory stock options and nonqualified deferred compensation are considered property subject to IRC Sec. 1041. Thus, the transferee spouse is taxed at ordinary income tax rates when he or she exercises the options and the employee spouse is not taxed.

The problem with stock options is that they are not easy to value. One reason is because of future market fluctuations. Second, unlike wages, where you receive a W-2 and know exactly how much you have earned during the year, it is not as clear cut with stock options. To make matters worse, courts also recognize that options can be granted for past or future service and as such a value will need to be assigned during the appropriate time period. If there is a potential for a huge valuation and income potential assigned to the stock option, some parties to divorce will tell their employer to hold off on granting them options until the pending divorce is final. Good attorneys will know how to argue either side. As a general rule, it is preferable not to transfer stock options but agree to distribute net after-tax proceeds after the stock is sold. This will result in a true fair market value being realized without speculation as to future performance of the stock.

Stock options are not always black and white. There is a huge gray component present. For example, if an option is awarded to you during the couple's separation but the aware relates to past performance (which is when they were married), is it considered marital property? What about if the marriage ends before the options vest? That's also a tough question to answer. Your client will definitely need to determine when the services were performed to help determine what to include. Special valuation people are needed to assist in this area.

Many attorneys and judges do not know how to value these options. An expert should definitely be called in to determine the value. You can even have the stock options appraised by an independent appraiser.

Retirement Plans

Retirement plans make up one of the largest sources of assets for a married couple. As a result, it can be a huge source of contention for divorcing parties. Furthermore, since the purpose of retirement plan assets is to accumulate for retirement, decisions must be made as to what to do with these accounts during the divorce process.

Strategy: Before proceeding in this area, here are a couple of thoughts on what to contemplate:

1. Should a portion of the balance (such as 50 percent) be handed over to the other spouse now?
2. Should the retirement plan remain with the current owner and a comparable amount from other assets be paid to the other spouse?
3. If it is a pension type of plan that provides monthly or annual income, should nothing be done currently to the ownership of the plan? In this instance, the nonparticipant spouse would begin receiving this income stream perhaps many years down the road?
4. Does the retirement owner want protection in the event of the other spouse's remarriage or death?
5. Has one spouse worked previously in another job whereby there was a retirement plan offered. If so, is that spouse entitled to any future benefit?

Facts: Retirement assets accumulated during the marriage generally tend to fall under marital property and are thus subject to a marital split. Retirement plan benefits earned prior to marriage generally stay as separate property. However, if one spouse has been with the same company (both prior and during the marriage), a formula must be determined to determine what percentage of benefits the other spouse is entitled to receive. Each retirement plan must be valued independently. Depending on the length of time worked, each plan will have its own vesting schedule.

Some plans may operate differently than others. For example, some plans are divided at divorce through the use of a QDRO.

Plan Types: There are many retirement plans that might be considered in a divorce. They can fall under qualified, personal retirement, and nonqualified categories. They could be found through existing employment or from prior jobs that spanned over many years. It is not uncommon for an older couple getting divorced to have multiple retirement plans.

Vesting Rules. Being vested means that the participant spouse is entitled to all the benefits your employer has contributed to the plan. The participant actually owns the employer benefits and is entitled to receive them at retirement or when employment terminates. The participant spouse can be fully vested or partially vested for employer benefits, depending on the type of vesting schedule used. The employee always owns all the employee benefits that he or she personally contributed. If the participant spouse is not vested, consider contacting an attorney to determine whether the state characterizes nonvested retirement benefits as marital property.

Double Dipping Payments. Be careful that the other spouse does not get paid twice for the retirement benefits received as income. If the spouse is given a portion of your client's retirement benefits as part of the property settlement, the retirement benefits should not be considered part of income when spousal support is calculated. One way to protect against this is to include a provision in the settlement exempting your retirement payments from being considered income for the purposes of spousal support. Remember, the plan can be divided as a marital asset or can be treated as a stream of income for the participant. Make sure that both are not divided in the divorce process!

Types of Retirement Plans

There are many types of retirement plans to become familiar with. Descriptions of many of the more common ones appear below. Once one is familiar with the benefits and disadvantages of each plan, then valuing and dividing up the assets of those plans becomes easier.

Qualified Plans

Qualified plans (QP) are generally employer-based plans. These include defined-benefit plans and defined-contribution plans.

defined-benefit plan

Defined-Benefit Plans. In a defined-benefit plan, the employer promises a retirement benefit or pension to the employee when the employee spouse reaches retirement age. The payment amount is either preset under the terms of the plan or determined by a formula that takes into account age, years of service, or both. Generally, defined-benefit monies come available when the participant spouse retires. When there is a divorce, it is necessary to decide what percentage of the payment each spouse will ultimately receive.

defined-contribution
plan

Defined-Contribution Plans. In a defined-contribution plan, the employer pushes the onus of investment risk on to the employee. That is why these types of plans are more popular now than defined-benefit plans. With a defined-contribution plan, a certain sum of money is put away on behalf of each employee spouse. It is deposited into a separate account established in the employee's name. The employee owns this individual account and knows what the account balance is all the time. Since the risk is with the employee, the employee must do a good job of managing that money.

With a defined-contribution plan, the contribution the employee makes is defined, but the benefit is not since it is based on the amount accumulated in the plan at the time the benefits are paid or withdrawn. The participant spouse knows that an amount of money will be received at retirement. However, the exact amount is unknown and may increase or decrease depending on the value of the investments. The value of the defined-contribution plan can be determined as of the date of divorce, because it is possible to distribute the money right then and there. That's because it has a present as opposed to a future value.

Traditional or Roth 401(k) Plans – Your Own Funding Towards Retirement

A 401(k) plan, whether traditional or Roth 401(k) plan, is a qualified profit-sharing or stock-bonus plan under which one can contribute monies up to government guidelines to fund his or her own retirement. This "cash-deferred arrangement" allows a person to grow tax-deferred monies earned inside these accounts and allow for these monies to be a direct reduction in taxable income in the year the contribution is made.

Employers set up 401(k) plans when the employer wants to shift the investment burden over to the employees and minimum fund the policy. Younger employees stand to reap the biggest benefit since they have many years until retirement and can continue to defer tax on these monies until funds are withdrawn.

Employees aged 50 and over can make an additional "catch up" contribution. Employees are always 100 percent vested in any monies they put into the plan. Any employer contributions are not vested until the employee has satisfied the vesting requirement.

403(b) Plans

A 403(b) plan, also called a traditional or Roth 403(b) plan or a tax-deferred annuity, is a tax-deferred employee retirement plan than can be adopted by certain tax-exempt organizations and public school systems. Employees have accounts in a TDA plan to which employers contribute or employees contribute through payroll deduction, similar to a 401(k) contribution.

A nice feature with the 403(b) plan is that in addition to the regular catch up provision afforded qualified plans (such as 401(k) plans) and IRAs, a special catch up provision exists if you have underfunded your 403(b) plan and have been an employee for at least 15 years with the organization. In this case, the employee can make an additional $3,000 per year for up to 5 years.

Personal Retirement Plans

personal retirement plans

Personal retirement plans (PRP) differ from qualified plans (QP) in several ways. Personal retirement plans have less stringent government reporting requirements (per ERISA rules) than qualified plans. PRPs do not have to file annual employer tax returns called the Form 5500, where QPs do. A person cannot borrow from a PRP plan where he or she may be able to borrow funds with a QP. PRPs do not qualify for 10-year income averaging where QP may. Personal retirement plans provide for immediate vesting (as soon as contributions are put into an employee's account, they belong to that employee), whereas with a qualified plan there may be a vesting schedule that forces the employee to wait until the monies become the employee's. That is set by the employer in advance. Also PRPs may be creditor protected up to a limited amount, whereby QPs are always creditor protected in full.

Personal retirement plans include individual retirement accounts (IRAs), simplified employee pension plans (SEPs), and SIMPLE plans.

The Traditional IRA. If a person has earned income (wages, self-employment and spousal support), she can contribute to an individual retirement account (IRA). A traditional IRA is a type of retirement savings arrangement under which IRA contributions (up to certain limits) and investment earnings are tax-deferred until withdrawn from the IRA. A person can contribute to the maximum amount each year, and if over age 50, there is a special annual catch-up provision that can be added to the maximum contribution.

The Roth IRA. To encourage people to put money aside for the future, the government offers tax benefits to retirement savers. Usually, it's done with pretax dollars. However, in 1997, the government provided an alternative—a way to save on an after-tax basis and still grow tax-free. That alternative is called the Roth IRA. Since then, Roth accounts have also been expanded into many other types of accounts, such as Roth 401(k) and Roth 403(b) plans.

To qualify as tax-free, a distribution may be taken:

- after you have had a Roth IRA for 5 tax years, and
- on or after the date you reach age 59½, due to your death or disability, or for qualified first time homebuyer expenses up to $10,000. The expenses can be for you, your spouse, your child, grandchild, or ancestor of you or your spouse.

And other Roth IRA distributions are taxable to the extent of your account earnings. Unless an exception applies, any distributions prior to age 59½ will be subject to the 10 percent early distribution penalty tax in addition to the taxable amount. Unlike traditional IRAs where distributions must begin by age 70½, distributions from a Roth do not have to begin until the holder's death.

Simplified Employee Pension Plans (SEPs). SEPs are employer-sponsored plans under which plan contributions are made to a participating employee's IRA. These contribution amounts are usually higher than the IRA contribution.

If an individual is self-employed and earns the maximum amount that you can use towards an IRA contribution, you can put away as much as if you had a defined contribution plan. Therefore, the limits are much higher than what you can put away under a SIMPLE or IRA plan. Also, if you have a slow earnings year, you may be able to skip future contributions where in most qualified plans you cannot do that. All qualified plans (except profit-sharing plans) require annual contributions. That could be an exhaustive drain on cash. However, the flip side is that if you continue to miss making contributions, then you will be lacking in retirement monies come retirement age.

Savings Incentive Match Plans for Employees (SIMPLE Plans). SIMPLE IRAs are employer-sponsored plans under which plan contributions are made to a participating employee's IRA. Tax-deferred contribution levels are higher than for IRAs but probably lower than SEPs. SIMPLE plans also provide an employer with the flexibility to decide whether to make contributions annually. Lastly, SIMPLE plans provide for an over age 50 catch up provisions (like qualified plans).

Nonqualified Retirement Plans

nonqualified plans   Nonqualified plans are mainly deferred-compensation plans, whereby the participant agrees to defer part of current compensation to a later date. This reduces the taxable income for the year. Monies are not taxed until distributions are made to the participant (like other retirement plans). However, the monies remain with the employer until distributions are made. The participant is a creditor of the company, and if the company should default, the participant will have to line up with all the other creditors against the company to claim his or her contributions. A participant should be wary of this type of plan if the employer is not in good financial health.

457 Plans. A 457 plan is a nonqualified plan for government employees. Such plans receive the same favorable tax-deferred tax treatment on employee contributions like traditional 401(k) and 403(b) plans.

457 plans also have their own favorable catch up provision. In this case, in the 3 years prior to the year (and not including the year) of retirement, a participant can double his or her contribution for each of those 3 years (up to annual guidelines). In addition, a participant can take the over-age-50 catch up provision as well.

Social Security

Social security benefits are generally not considered marital property and are not divisible at divorce. However, if your client is married to the opposing spouse for 10 years or more, then that spouse will be entitled a portion your client's Social Security benefit upon his or her retirement age. Furthermore, your client's benefit will not be affected by whether the spouse is receiving a benefit based on the amount he is entitled to collect or whether or not your client has begun collecting benefits.

If your client is of normal Social Security retirement age (currently age 66), then opposing spouse can receive 50 percent of the benefit. If the opposing spouse is aged 62 (early Social Security benefits) and the client is of full retirement age to begin collecting, then the spouse can get a minimum of 37.5 percent of the benefit. For every month that the ex waits, that benefit is increased. Full retirement benefits will be paid at age 67 for those taxpayers born 1960 and thereafter.

In addition, if the spouse collects as a result of your client's death, he or she is entitled to 100 percent (or essentially the full retirement benefit). (Now that can present a moral hazard!) Lastly, if the opposing spouse worked at least 10 years, then he or she is entitled to his or her own benefit. Of course, the ex can collect only the higher of the two and not both. Otherwise spouse swapping would gain even more popularity!

To apply for benefits under the opposing spouse's record, your client will need his or her Social Security number, date and place of birth, and parents' names. For more information, contact (800) 772-1213 or visit www.ssa.gov

Understanding Qualified Domestic Relations Orders (QDRO)

qualified domestic relations order
A QDRO is a court order that provides specialized instructions to a plan administrator as to how to pay a nonparticipant or nonemployed spouse (such as a divorced spouse, child, or other dependent), who is also called the alternate payee (someone other than the named beneficiary in the pension plan) all or a portion of a pension plan benefit after the divorce becomes final. Therefore, the ex-spouse will be considered the alternate payee on all the documents resulting from the division of the participant's retirement plan accounts.

Requirements for a QDRO

For a document dividing a retirement plan to be considered as a QDRO, it must specify:

1. the name and last known mailing address of the employee spouse (the participant).
2. the name an mailing address of the nonemployee spouse (the alternate payee)
3. the amount or percentage of the participant's benefits to be paid to the alternate payee, or the manner in which the amount or percentage is to be determined
4. the number of payments or the period to which the order applies
5. the name of the plan to which the order applies

Limitations on QDROs

A QDRO cannot do any of the following:

1. require a plan to pay any benefit or option not otherwise provided by the plan
2. require a plan to provide benefits that exceed the value of the participant's interest as determined by an actuary
3. require the payment of benefits to an alternate payee if those benefits are already payable to another alternate payee (such as a different ex-spouse) under a previous qualified order
4. specify who will be responsible for payment of taxes

Valuation of Retirement Plans

Now that you have a handle on the many types of retirement accounts in the marketplace, and the need for a QDRO to help divide certain retirement plans, the next step in the process is how to value each.

Valuing retirement assets depends on the type of retirement plan being valued. With certain retirement plans, like defined-contribution plans, these numbers are easy to value based on the statements the individual receives each month. However, with defined-benefit plans, it is much more difficult because there is no real value until that person retires. There may be a vested balance based on formulas derived in the plan. But how much can be counted in the divorce settlement may be difficult to determine.

Methods for Dividing a Pension

There are three methods for dividing retirement accounts: the buyout method, the wait-and-see method, and the reserved jurisdiction method.

buyout method   *Buyout method.* With this method, the participant spouse purchases the interest of the nonparticipant spouse by ultimately keeping the pension interest and providing the nonparticipant spouse with an equivalent amount of assets. Also called the immediate offset method, this can be accomplished by either providing a lump-sum payment to the nonparticipant spouse or by giving that person an equivalent amount of marital assets from other sources. Because a dollar amount must be known, under this approach, the value of the retirement accounts must be valued and determined in advance of the final divorce decree. The benefit to this approach is that each spouse is completely free of the other with regard to receiving retirement dollars in the future since it is all taken care of now.

wait-and-see method   *Wait-and-see method.* With this method, the pension assets are on hold until a future date and then are split at the date of retirement. That date is when the monies are ultimately received by each spouse. The upside is if something happens, if the numbers are not where each spouse thought they would be, then each spouse shares in the risk while the monies are accumulating. The downside here is that the spouses will continue to be drawn together and may have possible contact with each other until the monies are ultimately divided up. A valuation is not needed here (unlike the buyout method). Rather, all that is required is the future benefit be known to each spouse.

reserved jurisdiction method   *Reserved jurisdiction method.* This little-used method asks the court to wait and delay until a later date before valuing and dividing the pension because there are too many unknown variables at this time thus making an accurate current valuation unlikely. Examples include where the employee spouse may receive stock options that become vested at a later date, bonuses to be paid dependent on other factors, and other sources of compensation that cannot be determined until later on. This approach is worthwhile if you don't want to hastily value a retirement number and find out that it is completely without merit.

Using Retirement Assets to "Buy Out" (Balance Out) Equity

Let's continue with the first method listed above, the buyout method, and how that probably is the best solution to providing each spouse with a workable asset. For example, assume that parties to a divorce have a few assets to divide. These include a house valued at $500,000, automobiles at $50,000, personal property at $200,000, after-tax investments of $200,000, and pension value at $750,000. In order to equalize the balances, the spouse with the pension benefit may have to give up most if not all of the other assets to even the playing field. In this example, the spouse with the pension would only receive approximately $100,000 of the remaining assets. This would then allow the spouse with the pension to keep all of his or her pension rights.

A more difficult scenario would be the following. Assume that the pension benefits were valued at $210,000 by one expert and $250,000 by the other. Although, the difference is rather small (when compared against divorce fees), the judge or the parties may decide to split the difference or call in a third expert that both parties can agree upon.

Another solution would be for the court to simplify the division of property by using a QDRO. Using a QDRO helps the court to simplify the division of the remaining assets which results in the awarding of one-half of the plan to each party when each party retires. In these cases, the financial hardship is lessened at the time of the divorce in which only the more liquid assets are allocated evenly to each party. If multiple retirement plans exist, not all of them have to be divided through a QDRO. The bottom line is that each party receives half of the overall value.

The result of this approach is that it is clean and simple. Each party receives an equivalent amount of dollars that work best for his or her scenario.

An Ex's Remarriage or Death and Your Client's "Vested" Pension Benefits

Sometimes if an ex remarries and a QDRO is not properly drawn up, it could spell disaster. That's because under Federal tax law retirement benefits are automatically paid to the surviving spouse which is now the new spouse. The former spouse will need a provision in the QDRO to name him or her as the alternate payee, which again is the person entitled to the retirement benefits after the participant worker spouse's death.

Inclusion of this clause essentially states that he or she will remain the surviving spouse for these retirement benefits only no matter if death or remarriage occurs. This way the nonparticipant spouse will be protected and ensured of receiving the retirement benefits that were agreed to at the time of your divorce.

Discovery of Retirement Plans

discovery   Attorneys can do a great service for their clients if they uncover each and every type of retirement plan accrued during the marriage. The importance of discovery in both the valuation of retirement plan benefits and QDRO-related issues is another aspect of the process that shouldn't be overlooked. Here are some of the issues that can be used to uncover these plans.

1. *Frozen plans.* Plans that were previously offered and then frozen when ERISA came along were usually subsequently converted to annuities and paid in addition to the current plan benefits. These plans, while not showing outwardly on the books of the employer, nevertheless are legitimate plans that should factor in the division of property.

2. *Overlooked plans.* Many times if a spouse has contributed to a 401(k) plan, it is assumed that it is the only available plan. In fact, many defined-benefit plans go unnoticed. Since defined-benefit plans pay out a monthly benefit, don't provide a statement or benefit accruals, it sometimes can be very difficult to find these types of plans when evaluating that spouse's overall retirement benefits. Many times larger companies will have both defined-benefit and defined-contribution plans.

3. *Discovery questions.* The starting point for the attorney of the nonparticipant spouse should be to ask to develop a listing of all past employers of the participant spouse and list all retirement plans associated with each employer. This helps determine a value of the retirement plan which can then offset against the family's other marital assets, or to begin developing a QDRO. If the participant spouse has been with various employers a short period of time (generally before vesting occurs), it's probably safe to assume that no retirement plans existed with that employer.

The next step is to develop a nongeneric questionnaire indicating the plan administrator to list all those possible plans that the participant plan may have had an interest or accrued benefit in while working at the employer. The key to this approach is to determine the value of the benefits that were accrued during the marriage.

Spousal Support

spousal support   Spousal support (also referred to as alimony or maintenance) represents a payment made to an ex-spouse, which is not paid as part of an IRC Sec. 1041 property settlement, under a divorce or separation instrument. It does not include voluntary payments that are not made under a divorce or separation instrument. It may be made in one lump sum or in installments. It can also be temporary or permanent. There is no time frame necessarily tied to it. Spousal support rules can be found under IRC Sec. 71(b).

Spousal support is designed to help the lesser earning spouse or the at-home spouse to gain the necessary training and provide sufficient time to re-enter the workforce and earn as much as that spouse is capable of. This rehabilitative maintenance bridges the gap until the payee spouse is capable of supporting him or herself

Spousal support payments are concerned with the future needs of each spouse. In determining the ability to pay, a judge may consider whether the payor can afford to pay what is needed and still have enough to live on in a manner that the payor was previously accustomed to.

Many factors are involved in the awarding of spousal support. These include:

- the length of the marriage
- each spouse's age
- vocational skills of each spouse
- time necessary for the spouse to get up to speed in his or her occupation
- standard of living during the marriage
- health
- occupation and needs of each spouse
- conduct of the parties during the marriage
- who will maintain a household for the children
- liabilities of each spouse
- the sacrifice of one spouse's future earning capacity because he or she was an at-home spouse raising the children and he or she put their career on hold
- the economic circumstances of each spouse

It is important to be aware of your state's laws regarding how spousal support works.

Determination of Spousal Support

When courts calculate the amount of spousal support to be paid by a spouse, each spouse's ability to earn an income is usually taken into account. Past actual earnings are taken into account, sometimes without regard to future earning capacity. Another factor may be the spouse's ability to earn more in the future.

The court will look at the nonworking spouse's ability to earn outside the home given his or her marketable skills. If the opposing spouse refuses to work outside the home but is capable of doing so, that factor will also be taken into accountwhen awarding spousal support.

The age factor may come into play especially if one spouse has been out of the workforce for a long time. Health issues also enter into the decision, especially if it is not feasible for the other spouse to work. A spouse closing in on retirement or with poor health may not be in a position to pay spousal support. Courts will factor that in when arriving at the actual number.

How Long is Spousal Support Paid?

Spousal support can be awarded for any length of time depending on the circumstances. Generally, spousal support is paid for a period of years or ends at death or when the other spouse gets remarried. In fact, in some states, if you are living with a spouse in a marriage-type setting and have not remarried, payments can stop as well.

Spousal support can also be awarded on a temporary basis pending the outcome of a divorce. If one spouse is making voluntary payments to the other, that amount could be used as a precursor or establish a pattern or routine for the payment of spousal support in that amount. Therefore, that amount becomes finalized based on what has been happening throughout the divorce process. The court may reason that since the payee spouse has been getting along on that amount during the divorce process, then that amount of payment should therefore remain the same and continue as beforehand.

Remarriage

When the payee spouse gets remarried, spousal support payments stop because the court views the payee spouse in that situation as receiving more money than what was received beforehand. If the payor spouse remarries, however, the payee spouse will probably not be able to adjust the amount of spousal support currently being received unless the payee spouse can show need.

Initial Payment of Spousal Support

Spousal support is generally paid monthly, but it can be paid on a weekly basis or as a lump sum paid in advance. By paying it as a lump sum, the payer is locking him or herself in and won't be able to alter that decision later on. But it also can be a blessing in disguise.

When paying spousal support as a lump sum, the amount is determined by the length of time the spousal support payments would be required to be paid based on past state case law. Then those payments are discounted back to a dollar value as of today at an assumed discount (interest) rate. In other words, The recipient takes the present value of the future cash flow payments.

Modification of Spousal Support Payment

Other than payout of spousal support as a lump sum, spousal support can be modified. It can be changed by the spouses by modifying the spousal support terms of the final decree. It can also be made without court approval, although that is never a smart way to go. It can also be made by one of the spouses filing a request for modification with the court. The party requesting the change will have to show proof for why the change is necessary. The rationale behind this rule is it helps stabilize the prior arrangements and prevents the court from becoming too overburdened with change requests.

Spousal support can be increased or decreased based on changing circumstances. Examples of changing circumstances include:

- cost of living adjustments (COLA)
- escalator clause in the agreement tied to the payer spouse's increase in income
- payer spouse's loss of job
- payer spouse's reduction in income due to a severe downturn in business
- payee spouse's change in needs
- payee spouse's increasein income
- payee spouse's disability or illness

Hiring a Vocational Expert

If the opposing spouse did not work during the marriage but had a prior career, your client may want to employ the services of a vocational expert to forecast the future earning potential of that spouse. The amount of spousal support may be reduced as a result, since the numbers will tend to get netted out against each other and the difference will be used in the spousal support calculations.

Vocational experts can help spouses who are facing a change in circumstances to identify what type of work they wish to pursue, what additional education or training they will need, their chief capabilities and limitations, how long training will take, realistic expectations as to starting salaries, and whether outside issues, such as mental health counseling will be necessary before the spouse will be fully capable of self-support.

Deductibility

Spousal support is deductible by the payer and must be included in the spouse's or ex-spouse's income. Each spouse should consider the tax ramifications of receiving and deducting spousal support payments.

To be considered spousal support, a payment must meet certain requirements.

Spousal Support Requirements

There are seven requirements to be met for payments to be considered spousal support. They include the following:

1. *Payments must be made under a divorce or separation instrument.*

   Divorce means a divorce decree or a separate maintenance instrument written incident to that decree. It also includes a written separation agreement or a decree or any type of court order requiring a spouse to make payments for the support or maintenance of the other spouse. An interesting tidbit is that a premarital agreement that provides for support can be considered spousal support if incorporated into the decree or separation agreement.

2. *Payments must be made in cash.*

   Cash payments that qualify as spousal support include checks and money orders. However, transfers of services or property, execution of a debt instrument, or the use of property do not qualify as spousal support.

3. *No designation of the payment from one spouse to the other is considered to be spousal support.*

   Both spouses can designate qualifying payments not to be considered as spousal support. This is done by having a provision in the divorce or separation instrument stating the payments are not deductible as spousal support from the payer spouse's income and are excludable from the payee spouse's income. Any written statement signed by both spouses is treated as a written separation agreement. For temporary orders, the designation must be made in the original or a later temporary support order. Lastly, both spouses must attach a copy of the written instrument to their tax return filing in each year the designation applies.

4. *If separated under a decree of divorce or separate maintenance, the spouses cannot live in the same household.*

   If separated under a decree of divorce or separate maintenance, the spouses cannot share the same living space or household.

5. *Payments must end at the death of the payee spouse.*

   Payments made to a spouse must end at death if they are considered to be spousal support. If the spouse makes payments for any period after his or her spouse's death, none of the payments made before or after death are considered to be spousal support. Unless state law automatically requires payments to end at death, the divorce or separation instrument should state that there's no liability for continued payments after death.

6. *Payments cannot be considered child support.*

   The decree or separation instruments must clearly state a fixed amount for child support, or the entire payment will be deemed spousal support. Where confusion exists as to whether past child support or spousal support has been paid, the presumption is that child support has been paid.

7. The spouses cannot file a joint tax return with each other.

   Payments are not considered spousal support if the spouses file a joint return. Therefore, couples who are married on the last day of the tax year must file as married filing separate or head of household for any payments to be considered spousal support.

Spousal Support Recapture (Front Loading of Spousal Payments)

Many payer spouses demand that their ex-spouses take larger payments in the form of spousal support on an ongoing basis (typically within the first 3 years) as opposed to receiving those monies up front. The payer spouse may come up with an excuse stating that the payee spouse can't handle money, he or she will blow it, or that it's easier to pay the payee spouse on a pay-as-you-go-plan.

The real reason why payer spouses would do this is because the payer spouse wants to deduct those excessive monies when paid out as spousal support as opposed to being included as part of a property settlement under IRC Sec. 1041. This only applies to the first 3 years of spousal support payments. The reason the rule is capped at 3 years is that the IRS says most of these cases occur during the first 3 years after the divorce becomes finalized and they want these disguised payments to be part of the original property settlement negotiated at the time of the divorce.

Little does the payer spouse know that any payments considered excessive will have to be recaptured. This means that it is not deductible to the payer spouse and not taxable to the payee spouse.

If the payer spouse is subject to this rule, then the payer spouse must include as income in the third year the part of the spousal support payments that were previously deducted in the prior 2 years. That means the ex-spouse payee can deduct in the third year the part of the spousal support payments such spouse previously included in income.

The 3-year period starts with the first calendar year a payment qualifying as spousal support under a divorce decree, separate maintenance or a written separation agreement was made. Payments made under temporary support orders are not included here. The 3-year period includes the second and third year whether or not payments are made during those years.

Calculating the Recapture

The recapture rule is triggered in the third year if the spousal support paid in the third year decreases by more than $15,000 from the second year, or the spousal support paid in the second and third year decreases significantly from the spousal support paid in the first year.

Payments not included in the recapture calculation include payments made under a temporary support order; payments required over a period of at least 3 calendar years which represent a fixed part of business, property or self-employment income; and payments that decrease because of the death of either spouse or the remarriage of the payee spouse.

It should be noted that spousal support recapture rules only apply when the payments are decreasing in amount each year. Therefore if payments in year two are more than payments in year one, no recapture scenario exists.

Let's run through an example. This is a tough calculation. The format can be found in IRS Publication 504.

Example: Recapture of Spousal Support

Jonathan pays his ex-spouse, Susan, $80,000 spousal support during the first year, $60,000 during the second year, and $40,000 during the third year. Calculate the amount of spousal support recapture.

Note. Do not enter less than -0- on any line.

1. Spousal support paid in 2nd year	1. $60,000
2. Spousal support paid in 3rd year	2. $40,000
3. Floor	3. $15,000
4. Add lines 2 and 3	4. $55,000
5. Subtract line 4 from line 1	5. $5,000
6. Spousal support paid in 1st year	6. $80,000
7. Adjusted spousal support paid in 2nd year (line 1 less line 5)	7. $55,000
8. Spousal support paid in 3rd year	8. $40,000
9. Add lines 7 and 8	9. $95,000
10. Divide line 9 by 2	10. $47,500
11. Floor	11. $15,000
12. Add lines 10 and 11	12. $62,500
13. Subtract line 12 from line 6	13. $17,500
14. Recaptured spousal support. Add lines 5 and 13	*14. $22,500

*If you deducted spousal support paid, report this amount as income on Form 1040, line 11. If you reported spousal support received, deduct this amount on Form 1040, line 31a.

Chapter Review

Review questions are based on the learning objectives in this chapter. Thus, a [3] at the end of a question means that the question is based on learning objective 3. If there are multiple objectives, they are all listed.

Key Terms and Concepts

temporary order	stock options
litigation budget	nonstatutory stock options
property settlement	incentive stock options
IRC Sec 1041	defined-benefit plan
common law	defined-contribution plan
community property	personal retirement plans
quasi-community property	nonqualified plans
separate property	qualified domestic relations order
common law marriage	buyout method
closely held business valuation	wait-and-see method
fair market value	reserved jurisdiction method
capitalized earnings	discovery
stock redemption	spousal support
partner liquidation	

Review Questions

1. How should a divorced party evaluate the issues and the financial commitment necessary to pursue a divorce? [1]

2. What are the costs that arise during the divorce process? [2]

3. What are the financial responsibilities that need to be considered during the divorce process? [3]

4. How are the financial responsibilities determined for each party during a divorce? [3]

5. What are some of the methods used in paying for divorce? [4]

6. Identify and evaluate financial planning strategies using during the divorce process? [5]

7. How does common law differ from community property law? [6]

8. How are property settlements determined and valued in a divorce? [7]

9. What are some of the options the spouse has when dealing with the primary residence? [8]

10.   What are some of the key issues that arise when attempting to value closely held businesses? [9]

11.   Identify documents needed during the valuation of a closely held business? [9]

12.   How should partner liquidations between the spouses be approached? [9]

13.   How can a spouse determine whether a prior retirement plan existed? [10]

14.   Explain why the type of retirement plan is of concern in dividing property during a divorce? [11]

15.   Describe some of the methods used to value nonqualified plans [12]

16.   What are the differences among qualified plan assets? [13]

17.   What are the methods that can be used to divide pension plan assets? [13]

18.   What are some of the approaches that should be considered prior to dividing retirement assets? [13]

19.   When would it make sense to use retirement equity to balance out the division of other assets split during the divorce process? [13]

20.   What is considered spousal support? [14]

21.   What can a spouse count on when accounting for Social Security benefits of the ex? [14]

22.   What would a spouse potentially subject him or herself to front loading spousal support thus giving way to possible recapture consequences? [14]

Learning Objectives
An understanding of the material in this chapter should enable you to

1. Discover what is considered child support.
2. Determine the tax consequences of divorce.
3. Evaluate the income tax ramifications of property settlements.
4. Define a blended family.
5. Understand the dynamics of a blended family.
6. Identify financial and estate considerations unique to blended families.
7. Learn the requirements of a prenuptial and postnuptial agreement.
8. Determine when a QTIP trust is a worthwhile tool for blended families.
9. Learn retirement planning considerations unique to blended families.
10. Identify the process and challenges for financial advisors in dealing with divorced clients.

Child Support

child support   Child support is the amount of money that the noncustodial parent pays to the custodial parent to help pay for the everyday needs of the child or children. These needs include housing, food, clothing, and education. Child support rules can be found under IRC Sec. 71I.

All states have specific guidelines that must be followed in the determination of how much child support is to be paid and allocated to each of the children of the marriage. Parents cannot opt out of child support laws. That's because all children have the right to be supported by their parents. As a result, parents cannot agree in advance to waive or alter significantly the amount of child support paid.

Child support must be paid in cash to the custodial parent or to a third party, such as the child's private school, in accordance with the parents' binding agreement or the court order.

To determine how much child support can be counted on, visit the appropriate state website.

Factors in Determining Child Support

There are many factors to consider when determining child support payments. Consider the child's physical, emotional, or health state; the child's actual expenses including health care; physical custody arrangements; and the support of parent to other former households including spousal support and child support.

Also consider other financial obligations of the parent which are not tied into child support, such as the income capabilities of each parent, child's future college costs, child's summer vacations, camps, or costly recreational activities.

Lastly, calculate a parent's extraordinary needs, such as high medical expenses and travel expenses associated with one parent assuming full or partial child rearing responsibility.

Taxation of Child Support

Child support is neither taxable to the recipient spouse nor deductible to the payer spouse. Per the IRC, all worldwide income earned by any U.S. citizen is considered income from whatever source derived. The only exception to that rule is when the Code specifically states that something is not reportable as income. Most of the exclusions consist of social exclusions which are for the betterment of society and really are not designed to have true income consequences. They are considered more like reimbursements. Child support is one of those exclusions.

Modification of Child Support

Like custody orders, child support orders are not set in stone for the remainder of the child's youth. Courts will modify support if circumstanced have changed substantially since the time of the original order.

The courts can adjust the child support either up or down to reflect the changing circumstances—such as increased or reduced income—of the noncustodial payor parent. If the custodial parent brings the noncustodial parent back to court, he or she can have a rude awakening if the money the custodial parent now receives is reduced.

Temporary Child Support

Temporary child support is typically awarded by the court at the outset of the case to ensure that the children do not have a reduction in their standard of living pending the outcome of the divorce dispute.

An important planning tip is to make sure that the custodial parent seeks an appropriate level of temporary child support because if they do not, they run the risk that the amount of support initially awarded could become the final amount of child support.

Child Support Ends

Child support ends when the child reaches age 18 to 21, depending on state law, and/or if the child becomes emancipated. Becoming emancipated means that the child gets married, becomes self-supporting, abandons the parental home, goes into the military, reaches the age of majority, or it is appointed by court order.

Failure to Pay Child Support

Penalties for failure to pay child support are quite substantial. Every state imposes criminal penalties on parents who fail to pay child support and the states can pro-actively monitor that the payments are made going forward. States can garnish wages, cancel driver's licenses, gain access to federal and state tax refunds, or even arrest the payer parent for failing to pay child support. In addition, states can block the transfer of property, enter liens against property, or revoke professional licenses.

Using a QDRO to collect child support from a retirement account has tax implications. While child support is not a taxable event, withdrawals from a retirement plan are. Thus, payments made from a retirement plan to fund child support will result in taxable income to the spouse receiving the child support.

Income Tax Issues

The tax ramifications surrounding divorce are monumental. If the divorce is not drawn up properly, the tax consequences can eat up much of what the spouses thought they were receiving in the divorce. First, let's talk about the divorce.

Property Settlements (IRC Sec. 1041)

Under IRC Sec. 1041, no gain or loss is recognized on a transfer of property from one spouse to the other if the transfer is incident to divorce. Nonrecognition treatment applies even if the transfer was in exchange for cash, the release of marital rights, the assumption of debt, or other consideration. There are no income or deduction issues that arise from the general division of property. The income tax issues may arise when property is given beyond the initial settlement through alimony or child support.

The nonrecognition rules of Sec. 1041 do not apply to nonresident alien spouses. The rationale is that since nonresident aliens would not have to pay U.S. tax on the sale of property outside the country, there would be no reason for them to receive property tax-free incident to a divorce.

Transfers in Trust

The nonrecognition rule of Sec. 1041(a) does not apply to the transfer of property in trust when the transferred property is encumbered by an obligation in excess of the property's adjusted basis and such obligations are assumed or property is taken subject to its liabilities by the transferee.

When a taxpayer spouse makes a transfer in trust, gain must be recognized to the extent that the liabilities assumed by the trust, plus the liabilities to which the property is subject, exceed the total of the adjusted basis in the property transferred. Also, gain or loss is generally recognized on a transfer in trust of an installment obligation.

Passive Activity Loss Property

When a spouse gives passive activity property to his or her current spouse or ex-spouse, the basis in the gift is increased immediately before the transfer by the amount of any passive activity losses allocable to the property. These losses cannot be deducted for any year pursuant to IRS Pub 504. In a community property state, half the property would get a basis adjustment under this rule.

Deferred Tax Liability

The courts rarely consider the deferred tax liability impact of property divisions unless the taxable event is likely to occur in the near future or a sale is ordered by the court. The rationale is that taxes are considered highly speculative and subject to change or offset. If the tax impact is uncertain, the later taxes may be ignored. If this is a critical issue for the client, the only way to have them considered is in negotiation or mediation settlement.

Record-keeping Requirements

The transferor spouse must at the time of the transfer supply the transferee spouse with records sufficient to determine the adjusted basis and holding period (the length of time the property has been held) of the property.

Where potential credit recapture exists (such as with rental real estate), the transferor spouse must also supply the transferee spouse with records sufficient to determine the amount of the potential tax liability. However, no sanctions are specified for failure of the transferor to comply with these rules. Therefore, consideration should be given to incorporating these rules into the divorce decree.

Gift Tax Issues

The transfer of property to a spouse or former spouse is not subject to gift tax if it:

- is made in settlement of marital support rights
- qualifies for the marital deduction
- is made under a divorce decree
- is made under a written agreement, and the divorce takes place within a specified period
- qualifies for the annual exclusion

Property Basis

When one spouse transfers property to the other spouse, the receiving spouse picks up the basis from the transferor spouse. There is no step up in basis if the fair market value is higher at the time of the transfer than what it was at the time of acquisition. Step up in basis only occurs at death.

The transferee spouse receives the marital basis even if the asset is subject to liabilities exceeding that basis. This can result in a future tax liability. A Sec. 1041 transfer is treated as a gift for income tax purposes. The transferee spouse receives no added basis when receiving the property.

Filing Status

filing status

Income tax filing status is determined as of the last day of the tax year. The filing status also depends on marital status at year end. This is important because applying the appropriate filing status will save significant taxes when filing the tax return.

Therefore, if the spouses get legally divorced on December 31st, then each person can file either single or head of household (if that person qualifies). If two people get married on December 31st, they can file either married filing jointly or married filing separately. Then why can spouses file jointly if married only one day of the entire year?

If a spouse is considered unmarried, his or her filing status is single, head of household (if certain requirements are met), or qualifying widower. A couple is considered married for the entire year if they are separated and have not yet obtained a final divorce decree by December 31st. An exception to this rule is if the spouse lives apart from the soon-to-be ex-spouse; then that spouse may be considered unmarried and able to file head of household. What is the advantage of that? Head of household has more favorable tax rates than married filing separately.

Before your client even decides which filing status to use, he or she should get an estimate of what the tax liability will be at year end. He doesn't want any surprises. There are many tax programs that can help sort through the numbers. Otherwise, a CPA can work out the numbers.

There are five tax filing statuses. They are single (S), married filing jointly (M/J), married filing separately (M/S), head of household (H/H) and qualifying widow(er) (Q/W). Notice that all the filing statuses have two letter abbreviations other than single Let's take a look at comparing the different filing statuses.

Single

This filing status subjects your client to the highest tax rates. This filing status should be used when there are no dependents (children or parents)to claim as deductions. Given the same taxable income as a married couple filing jointly, more overall tax is paid by the single person.

If both spouses have significant income, then it may be better to delay the divorce until the following year so they can file under the more advantageous married-filing-jointly status in the current year. Staying married until the beginning of the following year could save money in the current year.

Married Filing Jointly

A divorcing spouse will be required to file one of the two marital filing statuses if not legally divorced yet, with few exceptions. There are liability issues to be aware of, even though it may be cheaper to file with the status married filing jointly. When filing jointly with the ex-spouse, both are both considered jointly and individually liable and responsible for any tax, interest, and penalty issues that arises from the filing of that return before the divorce. This means that one spouse may be liable for 100 percent of the entire tax liability even though the other may have earned all of the income. Furthermore, this liability applies even if the divorce decree states that the one spouse would be responsible for any amounts due on previously filed joint returns.

Generally, married filing jointly provides for greater tax relief and the least amount of tax liability, primarily in situations where one spouse is the predominant bread winner. Filing jointly could institute a marriage penalty. This occurs when both spouses earn roughly equal amounts because that can push them up into a higher overall income tax bracket.

If the spouses file jointly, they are 100 percent liable for any taxes due from the filing. Both spouses must sign a joint return. If one spouse refuses to sign and files a separate return, then the other spouse must as well.

Lastly, if the spouses are likely to receive a tax refund, that amount of money is considered a marital asset and subject to property division.

Married Filing Separately

If your client is concerned about the liability from the ex spouse, then filing married filing separately would be a better alternative. When in doubt, file separately. Filing separately makes a spouse only responsible for his tax liability reported on his tax return. If one of the spouses had certain high itemized deductions, such as medical expenses, casualty losses, or miscellaneous expenses (all subject to deductibility limitations), then it may be cheaper to file separately.

After the due date of a return, the spouses cannot file separate returns if they previously filed a joint return.

Lastly, your client's filing status will also depend on when the divorce process started and when it's likely to be completed. The spouses can file jointly in any year the divorce has not become final, but once it is final, then they must file independently. If your client has dependents, such as children, then he or she will probably file head of household status.

Qualifying Widow

This is a filing status used by the surviving spouse for the two years following the death of a spouse. In the year of the spouse's death, the couple still files either married filing jointly or separately.

Head of Household

Head-of-household filing status is a better alternative than single if your client qualifies. Generally, the taxpayer must be unmarried or considered unmarried as of December 31st. The taxpayer must also have paid more than half the cost of keeping up a home that was the main home of any unmarried children for more than half the year or have provided more than 50 percent of the support of the taxpayer spouse's parents if they are considered dependents. Children away at school are not affected by that provision.

Children include an unmarried child, grandchild, adopted child, and foster child. Foster children have to live with the taxpayer the entire year. If the children are married, head-of-household status can still be used if your client claims these children as exemptions on his or her tax return.

Relationships that qualify under the head-of-household status are listed below.

Seven Ways to Pass the Qualifying Relationship Test

1. Cchild, stepchild, legally adopted child, eligible foster child, or descendant of any of them
2. Brother, sister, half brother, half sister, stepbrother, or stepsister
3. Father, mother, grandparent, or direct ancestor, but not foster parent
4. Stepfather or stepmother
5. Brother or sister's son or daughter
6. Father or mothers's brother or sister

7. Son-in-law, daughter-in-law, father-in-law, mother-in-law, brother-in-law, or sister-in-law.

Any of these relationships that were established by marriage are not ended by death or divorce.

Parents and Qualifying Relatives

Parents can be claimed as dependents even if they don't live with the taxpayer. In fact, they could be living in another state or even in a nursing home. Qualifying relatives can be any relatives from whom an exemption is claimed. There is no age requirement. The key here is that the taxpayer has to provide greater than 50 percent of their support.

Four Ways to Pass the Qualifying Relative Requirements Test

The qualifying relative must:

1. Not be the taxpayer's child (for example, 20-year-old son is not a qualifying relative, since he is a qualifying child);
2. Be a member of the household or pass the relationship test (the qualifying relative must either live with the taxpayer all year as a member of the household, or be related to the taxpayer as described above);
3. Pass the gross income test by earning under the personal exemption amount for that year); and
4. Pass the taxpayer support test in which the taxpayer pays more than 50 percent of the qualifying relative's support during the calendar year. To calculate, compare taxpayer's provided support to the entire amount of support received from all sources.

Remember, the taxpayer support test does not apply to qualified children.

Exemptions

Exemptions come in two types: personal and dependent. A personal exemption is one the taxpayer can claim for himself. An annual dollar amount, adjusted for inflation, is provided for each year that the taxpayer claims himself on his tax return. Dependent exemptions are ones discussed above, including children, grandchildren, parents, and if married again, the new spouse.

In the case of divorce, which parent gets to claim the child as an exemption? Generally, the rules are complex, especially if joint custody is awarded. If parents are awarded joint custody of a child, they should have the divorce decree clearly state who is entitled to the exemption. When the parents do not have an agreement, the parent having actual custody for the greater portion of the year gets the dependency deduction under IRC Sec. 152(e).

Is there any way for the dependency exemption to be awarded to the noncustodial parent?

The answer is yes if all of the following apply:

1. The parents:

    a. are divorced or legally separated under a decree of divorce or separate maintenance;
    b. are separated under a written separation agreement; or
    c. lived apart at all times during the last 6 months of the year.

2. The child is in the custody of one or both parents for more than half of the year.
3. The divorce decree or separation agreement provides that the noncustodial parent can claim the child as a dependent or the custodial parent signs a written declaration (Form 8332) that he or she will not claim the child.

Form 8332

The custodial parent can sign Form 8332, *Release of Claim to Exemption for Child of Divorced or Separated Parents,* or similar statement, agreeing not to claim the child's exemption.

The exemption may be released for:

*   a single year
*   a number of specified years (for example, alternate years), or
*   all future years

The noncustodial parent must attach the release to his or her return. If the exemption is released for more than one year, the noncustodial parent must attach the original release to the return the first year and attach a copy each of the following years.

Sale of the Principal Residence

When the principal residence is sold, the general rule is that single taxpayers can exclude up to $250,000 of capital gain, married-filing-separately taxpayers can each exclude $250,000, and married taxpayers filing jointly can exclude up to $500,000 of capital gain as long as they have lived in the house for 2 of the last 5 years (It's 2 of the last 10 years if they are in the military). In addition, during the 2 year period ending on the date of the sale, neither spouse excluded gain from the sale of another home.

Remarriage

What happens if one spouse ends up getting remarried prior to the sale of the home jointly owned with the former spouse? If that situation occurs, then the remarried spouse can use the new spouse's time in the home to meet residency requirements in order to use the married-filing-jointly exclusion amount.

Exception to the Two-Year Rule

An exception exists to the 2-year rule if the house is sold due to unforeseen circumstances. In such cases, the gain on the house can be prorated.

Unforeseen circumstances include moving for any of the following reasons:

- job change
- health issues
- divorce

Since divorce is listed among the criteria, the gain can be prorated and some of the gain can be deferred (but not up to the full $250,000/$500,000 exclusion). Here's an example of how that works:

Stan and Carly Williams purchased a house for $320,000. Eight months later they were legally divorced. Carly, who is now single, and is the sole owner of the house, decides to sell the house for $400,000 after the sixth month. How much of the gain would be taxable to Carly?

Step 1:

Sales Price	$480,000
Cost	$320,000
Profit	$160,000

Step 2:

$250,000 single exclusion x 8/24 = $83,333 can be excluded from the sale of the house

Step 3:

Profit	$160,000
Excluded Gain	$83,333
Taxable Gain	$76,667

Note 1: The 8/24 represents living in the house for 8 months out of 24 months (2 year requirement).

Note 2: If Carly sold the house at the end of 2 years (instead of 8 months), then the entire gain (up to $250,000) would have been excluded from capital gains tax.

For more information on the tax implications from the sale of a primary residence, see IRS publication 523 or visit www.irs.gov for more information.

Tax Deductibility of Divorce Costs

Under Code Sec. 1041, property transferred to either spouse is not deductible because it is part of the initial property settlement. Under Code Sec. 1012, legal fees paid specifically for a property settlement can be added to the basis of the property received.

Also, legal fees and court costs for getting a divorce are not deductible under Reg. Sec. 1.262-1(b)(7).

However, investment advice received during the divorce process from the attorney can be deducted as long as a separate itemized receipt specifies that specific portion of the fee as investment advice.

Tax Implications of Living Together

Couples living together cannot file jointly. To file joint returns, they would have to be legally married. A few states have provisions for common law marriages but such cases are rare. Working couples with similar incomes will often find a tax advantage in not marrying. However, couples with only one income source or with widely different incomes will come out better taxwise if they do tie the knot.

Like-Kind Exchanges IRC Sec. 1031

like-kind exchanges

Like-kind exchanges are designed so that investors do not cash out their investments, but instead roll them into more expensive property. In return, the IRS would allow these investors to defer the tax on their gains from selling the first property and to roll it into a second more expensive property.

The key for using like-kind exchanges is that is must be qualifying property and must work within the stringent set of rules mandated by the IRS. The three essential elements of a like-kind exchange are:

- the properties must be exchanged
- both the property exchanged and the property received must be held by the same taxpayer for productive business use in the taxpayer's trade or business or for investment, and
- the properties must be "like kind" with one another

The only requirement necessary outside of the above described rules is that whatever asset is sold, an asset more expensive must be purchased in order to defer the gain. If an asset is purchased that costs less, then gain will have to be recognized to the extent of the difference right away.

Like-kind exchanges apply to divorce in the following manner. If one spouse takes over the rental real estate, that spouse can trade it for another piece without incurring taxes on both the capital gains and the recaptured real estate. Exchange could be desirable if the spouse who ends up with the property decides that keeping that property entails too many bad memories and is looking to start over and replace the property with another one representing a new beginning.

The gains on such property can be quite enormous. For example, if your client held rental real estate for more than ten years and depreciated it each year (which is a requirement), then her recapture tax alone could be astronomical, let alone the fact that if she sells the property for more than she paid for it, she would have significant capital gains tax as well. It all adds up. Worse yet, she may not have the funds to pay the taxes currently. Therefore, if she wants to keep that type of property for her own enjoyment (that is, rental at the beach, in the mountains, and so forth.), she can have her cake and eat it too. In addition, it does not have to be one-for-one exchanges. For example, she can have three properties with a total sales price of $1 million and perform a like-kind exchange for one property costing $1.2 million.

As long as she spends more than she is taking in, it qualifies for like-kind exchange treatment. So the exchange can be five properties for one, or more.

In order to do the like-kind exchange, a qualified intermediary must be used. That person or entity can be a title company, real estate broker, attorney, or someone in a similar capacity. The intermediary has to physically hold the money and release it to the seller of the property the client, using the like-kind exchange, ends up purchasing.

In addition, there are time constraints on the process. That means after she sells it, your client has to identify as many as three properties she plans to purchase. She doesn't have to purchase them all, but she does have to purchase one of them. She has 45 days from the date of escrow to identify the property she plans to purchase and has 180 days to close on any one of them from the date of escrow. If the like-kind exchange doesn't work this way, she runs the risk of having the entire gain taxable immediately.

Installment Obligations (IRC Sec. 453B)

installment obligation

IRC Sec. 453B provides for the recognition of gain on the disposition of an installment obligation. A transfer between spouses or former spouses incident to divorce does not result in the recognition of gain or loss under IRC Sec. 453B(a) except for transfers made in trust. The transferee spouse is entitled to the same tax treatment on the installment obligation as the transferor spouse under IRC Sec. 453B(g)(2). The rationale is that the transferee will stand in the transferor's shoes.

Nonqualified Stock Options (IRC Sec. 83)

A nonqualified stock option is one that does not meet specific IRC requirements for special tax treatment. Such options may be granted to employees or independent contractors for services. Ordinary income is realized when the option is exercised or disposed of to the extent that the stock's fair market value exceeds the option price. However, under IRC Sec. 83, the taxpayer can elect to recognize income earlier which would then allow future appreciation to be eligible for capital gain rates. Losses are limited to capital loss rules which are $3,000 for filing married filing jointly or single and $1,500 for married filing separately.

Formerly, stock options were always taxed to the employee spouse who was the person that earned it based on the assignment of income doctrine and not under IRC Sec. 1041. However, Rev. Rul. (R.R.) 2002-22 now provides that nonqualified stock options and nonqualified deferred compensation are considered property subject to IRC Sec. 1041. As a result, the transferee spouse is taxed at ordinary income rates when he or she exercises the options and the employee spouse is not taxed.

Stock options are difficult to value because of future market fluctuations. Therefore, it is preferable not to transfer stock options but instead agree to distribute net after-tax proceeds after the stock is sold. This will result in a true fair market value being realized without speculation as to future performance of the stock.

Tax Credits Regarding Children

1. *Child Tax Credit.* This is a credit that the spouse who claims the child as a dependent can get on the tax return. The credit is equal to $1,000 per child under the age of 17.

2. *Dependent Care Credit.* This is a credit for a maximum of two children for child care in a two parent household where both parents are working or in a one parent household where the single parent is working. The credit is equal to the first $3,000 of expenses for one child and $6,000 for two or more children. The credit range goes from 20 percent to 35 percent based on the spouse's adjusted gross income (AGI).

3. *Adoption Expenses Credit.* This is a credit for the costs associated with adopting children. Qualifying expenses would include adoption fees, attorney fees, court costs, social service review costs, and transportation costs. This also includes children adopted overseas.

The spouse can claim the credit in the year qualifying expenses were paid or incurred if they were paid or incurred during or after the tax year in which the adoption was finalized.

Education Tax Credits

1. *American Opportunity Tax Credit.* This credit counts for the first 2 years of college (freshman and sophomore years only). The maximum amount is $2,500 per year calculated as follows: The first $2,000 of expenses are covered at 100 percent, and then the next $2,000 of expenses are covered at 25 percent for $500. This credit is subject to income limitations phase-out.

2. *Lifetime Learning Credit.* This credit is a flat 20 percent of an amount up to the first $10,000 of expenses. This credit cannot be

claimed if the child is already getting the American Opportunity Tax Credit. This credit is typically used by individuals after the first 2 years of college. Juniors and seniors would typically try to qualify for this credit. The lifetime learning credit is also available for those seeking new job skills, or maintaining existing job skills through graduate training or continuing education. This credit is also subject to income limitations phase-out.

Introduction to Blended Families

When two parents with children of their own get together, blending the two families into one can be tough for everyone involved. Emotions can run high and trust can be in short supply, particularly if one or both families are coming out of a messy divorce. And yet, when the dust settles and everyone adjusts, a blended family can be a wonderful source of support and love.

blended family   The Merriam Webster Dictionary definition of a blended family is a family that includes children from a previous marriage of the wife, husband, or both parents. An example of a blended family is a woman with two children from a previous marriage who marries a man with three children from a previous marriage.

Many issues surround the blended family. That is because two independent lifestyles and family units are coming together and the need to protect each family becomes that much greater. Americans marry, divorce, and cohabit more than any Western society. They also start and stop relationships more quickly. When parents remarry (forming a blended family) and divorce again, the negative effects of parents' marital transitions are cumulative[11]. The well-being of children goes down as the number of marital transitions goes up.

The Emergence of Blended Families

There are more blended families than ever. Americans are also creating new types of households by starting second families later in life, adopting kids or caring for grandchildren. And the trend is only accelerating.

Many graduate schools of psychiatry, psychology, and social work provide no specific training in dealing with these particular dynamics of blended families.

---

11. Kurdek & Fine, The Relation between Family Structure and young adolescents' appraisals of family climate and adjustment and parenting behavior, *Journal of Family Issues*, 1993,

Often, the methods and information appropriate to the nuclear family can be destructive if applied to the highly specific dynamics of the blended family system. Our cultural forms, rituals and assumptions still relate primarily to the intact, first marriage family, and the most ordinary event, such as filling out a form or celebrating a holiday, can become a source of acute embarrassment or discomfort for members of remarried families.

Blending families or even simply merging the finances of two childless adults can be difficult. Each person comes into the marriage with a unique set of circumstances and the emotional attachment that often comes with our assets. For those considering remarriage, the difficult financial issues need to be sorted out *before* a newly merged family is started. Although settling complicated issues such as inheritance and property division can be unpleasant, it's usually better to deal with these thorny issues sooner rather than later.

Confronting Reality

Remarrying couples enter into a marriage hopeful and optimistic, but sometimes unprepared for some tough realities. By addressing these issues in advance, you can help the couple get started on the anticipation of "happily ever after."

Aside from the strategies for dealing with the financial implications of blended families, discussing the issue itself can be difficult. A good way to begin is to have honest discussions with the future spouse and, if appropriate, family meetings should be held with affected children in which wishes are clearly stated .

It's important to remember that when each spouse is determining how to leave money, fair does not always mean equal. These discussions ensure that each spouse does not lose sight under mistaken assumptions.

Dynamics of the Blended Family

The dynamics of the blended family may not be the same as those of a nuclear family. The blended family will not and cannot function as does a natural family. It has its own special state of dynamics and behaviors. Once learned, these behaviors can become predictable and positive. The expectations and dynamics of the intact or natural family onto the blended family should not be superimposed by the step-parent. Also, remember the children are not the stepparents, nor will they ever be.

Blended parents are not replacement parents. Mother and father (no matter how bad the natural parents may have been) can still have a role in the development of the child. It is important to go slow and not come on too strong.

Discipline styles must be sorted out by the couple. What may be acceptable to the natural parent may not work for the stepparent. Clear job descriptions should be established between the parent, stepparent and respective children to determine the specific job of each parent in the household. As in any financial planning matters, unrealistic expectations can significantly destroy any possible relationship and create rejections and resentment.

There is no model for the blended family relationship. There are no ex-parents, only ex-spouses. The blended family should begin to get information on how to best handle the prior spouse. The conflict of loyalties must be recognized right from the beginning. The conflict is particular to blended families, and is a massive body of confused emotions. If the child in the blended family begins to have warm feelings toward the stepparent, the child will pull away and negatively act out. The child could act out the following; "If I love you, that means that I do not love my real parent." The feelings are normal and must be dealt with. The pulls of "Who am I loyal to first?" go full circle in the blended family. A strong approach could be for the stepparent to have a guarded sense of humor and use when necessary, especially since the situation is filled with the unexpected. The most important thing is to take care of the new marriage. The last thing anyone wants is a second divorce.

The Statistics Are Staggering

One out of two marriages ends in divorce. Sixty percent of second marriages fail, and 73 percent of third marriages fail according to the U.S. Census Bureau. Sixty-six percent of marriages and co-habitation situations end in break up when children are actively involved, according to Stepfamily Foundation statistics. It is predicted that 50 percent of children in the U.S. will go through a divorce before they are 18. Approximately half of all Americans are currently involved in some form of blended relationship. According to the Census Bureau, more Americans live in blended families than in nuclear families.

In his 1994 study, "The Changing Character of Blended Families," Professor of Sociology Larry L. Bumpass of the University of Wisconsin challenges the common perception that the blended family is defined by marriage. His research states that:

- About half of the 60 million children under the age of thirteen in this country are currently living with one biological parent and that parent's current partner.

- Nearly half of all women, not just mothers, are likely to live in a blended family relationship, when we include living-together families in our definition of the blended family.

Therefore, we have already become a nation of blended families.

Blended Family and Remarriage Statistics

- 40 percent of married couples with children (that is, families) in the U.S. are blended couples. (At least one partner had a child from a previous relationship before marriage; this includes full and part-time residential blended families and those with children under and/or over the age of 18). The percentage of all married couple households is 35 percent. (Karney, Garvan, & Thomas, 2003)

- Approximately one-third of all weddings in America today form blended families. (Demographic estimate, Deal). In 2001, 38 percent of all U.S. marriages were remarriages for one or both partners—15 percent for both, 23 percent for one. (Wendy Manning, personal communication Jan. 2010, National Center for Family and Marriage Research).

- Anywhere from 52 percent to 62 percent of all first marriages will end in divorce, says the National Stepfamily Resource Center. Meanwhile, roughly three-quarters of divorced people will remarry—and about 65 percent of remarriages will involve kids from the previous marriage.

- 42 percent of adults have a blended relationship—either a blended parent, a blended or half sibling, or a blended child. This translates to 95.5 million adults. (Parker, 2011) by the Pew Research Center

- 13 percent of adults are blended parents (29–30 million); 15 percent of men are blended dads (16.5 million) and 12 percent of women are blended moms (14 million.) (Parker, 2011) by the Pew Research Center.

- More than 40 percent of American adults have at least one blended relative, such as a son or daughter from a spouse's former relationship, in their family.. (Pew Research Center analysis published in January 2013). Experts say that is up dramatically from just 50 years ago.

- Remarriage has become commonplace with 79 percent of women and 89 percent of men marrying again within 5 years.

- 43 percent of marriages today in America involve a second or third remarriage.

- One million American children experience divorce every year.

- 68 percent of remarriages involve children from prior marriages.

- 70+ percent of remarriages involving children end in dissolution within 5½ years.

- 2,100 new blended families are formed every day in the U.S.

- Over 65 percent of Americans are now a blended parent, a blended child, a blended sibling, blended grandparent, or touched directly by a blended family scenario.

- Blended families are the most common form of family in the U.S.

- There are 35 million Americans in the U.S. today who are remarried. There are an additional 36 million Americans who are divorced or widowed (possibly finding themselves in a remarriage at some point). (US Census, 2007).

- One-third of individuals who got divorced in 2008 were redivorcing—that is, divorcing again.

- Only about one-third of blended family marriages last until death do them part. 60 percent of second marriages and 73 percent of third marriages end in divorce.) U.S. Bureau of the Census, 2006)

- Serial transitions in and out of marriage/divorce/cohabitation is now typical of family life in the U.S. but has significant consequences for children. (Cherlin, 2009)

- Americans marry, divorce, and cohabit more than any Western society. They also start and stop relationships more quickly.

- 16 percent of persons born after 1970 will marry, divorce, remarry, and redivorce.

- By age 15, 29 percent of U.S. children experience two or more mother partnerships (either marriage or cohabitation).

- The more parental partnerships (transitions in and out of couple relationships) that children experience, the lower their over-all emotional, psychological, and academic well-being.

- There are 35 million Americans in the U.S. today who are remarried (US Census, 2007).

    1. At that time, 12 percent of men and 13 percent of women (15 years old and over) were remarried twice.

2. An additional 3 percent of men and 3 percent of women were remarried three times.
3. Thus, 15 percent of men and 16 percent of women were remarried at least twice.
4. Therefore, of all men and women (aged 15 and above) 15.5 percent were remarried at least twice which equals 34.9 million people (34,865,642 to be exact).

- There are an additional 36 million Americans who are divorced or widowed who will possibly find themselves in a remarriage at some point. (US Census, 2007).

    1. 9 percent of men and 11 percent of women (aged 15 and older) were divorced in 2004.
    2. 2 percent of men and 10 percent of women were widowed.
    3. A total of 10 percent of all people, then, were divorced and 6 percent of all people were widowed.
    4. Together, 16 percent of Americans aged 15 or older (35.9 million people) could potentially remarry.
    5.   All together, 70.8 million Americans are remarried or potentially remarried.

- The divorce rate for remarried and blended family couples varies but is at least 60 percent. Second marriages (with or without children) have a 60 percent rate of divorce and 73 percent of third marriages end in divorce (U.S. Bureau of the Census, 2006). At least two-thirds of blended family couples divorce.

- 16 percent of persons born after 1970 will marry, divorce, remarry, and redivorce (also see Cherlin, A.J. Marriage, divorce, remarriage. Rev. ed. Cambridge, MA: Harvard University Press, 1992).

Sources for statistics not specifically identified above:

Pew Research Center, 2013

The Bonded Family, 2004-2013.

The Barna Update

U.S. Bureau of the Census, 2006, 2007

Wendy Manning, personal communication Jan. 2010, National Center for Family and Marriage Research

Blended Family Financial Pitfalls to Avoid

Since blended families are on the rise, then so are the financial pitfalls that can come with mixing family and money. Second marriages have their own challenges and potholes, particularly concerning money, and especially when stepkids are involved. Any time a family is blended together the potential for conflict exists. Financial conflict is always the worst kind in any relationship. Indeed, money differences may well have been responsible for the breakup of the first marriage.

When stepkids enter the picture the pitfalls get even deeper. For example. questions such as the following may arise:

- Who pays for what?
- Whose kids are costing more?
- Is that our dental bill, your dental bill, my dental bill?
- Did your kid wreck the car, or did our kid wreck the car?

These are all money issues, so blended families must have a system for sorting out who is responsible, and when.

These examples are not small and irrelevant. According to the Stepfamily Association of America, 43 percent of unions are a second marriage for at least one partner, and about 65 percent of remarriages involve kids. Blending kids, ex-spouses, money, and investment styles, each example requires its own strategy.

Money style differences are generally the point where things will start to unwind for the blended family. It may be more important to look first at whatever money issues are already on the books as the marriage begins. If there are different styles of handling finances, this is a critical issue to discover well before the remarriage.

There are at least four different money styles. Overlap exists on many of them.

- savers—those who insist on having money set aside at all times
- spenders—those who believe that if there are checks in the checkbook, they still have money and care little for cash on hand
- money-indifferent spouses—those who don't know much about money and don't care to, because it's beneath them to deal with it
- combination—those who combine at least two of the preceding, depending on their income level or fear of poverty

Money Management Tips and Planning Strategies

Here are some tips on how to avoid the inevitable tension that can arise over where all that money is coming from, and where it's going on a daily basis.

- Make sure the family money style is understood. Certain styles simply will not mix. A spender will have a tough time with a saver, or a money-indifferent spouse will have no interest in paying bills, so the other spouse had better be prepared to do it. Regardless of which stylistic tensions there are, when money is spent on the natural child, the irritation from the stepparent can come out of nowhere, causing incidents that can erode the marriage. Knowing ahead of time what to expect helps ease the tension.

- Make every effort to think of the children as "our kids." This exercise will be difficult at first for each parent, but it's more important than it appears. Start using that terminology right away. The other side of this is to avoid the phrase "your child" at all cost. "See what your kid did this time"; or "See how much your child is costing us,", are not ways to start a conversation. When the child has caused a financial loss, such as a wrecked car, damaged property, lost personal item, dentures, private tutor, cello lessons, any kind of unexpected cash outlay, referring to the child in those terms is unacceptable. The occasion should be used for the opportunity it is. Instead of "your child," it should be "our daughter or son." The new spouse will be grateful for the consideration.

- Avoid keeping score. Children cost a lot of money, and the costs seem to escalate as they get older. Blended parents who subconsciously or otherwise keep score of the overall costs will not contribute to familial bliss. The ability to put aside financial reality, which will seem chaotic at times, is essential to family harmony. On the other hand, if the kids are old enough to understand, it is appropriate to bring them into the discussion any time a major financial event has occurred. Indeed, it's detrimental to hide those events from them.

- Don't keep secret cash or hidden accounts from the new spouse. This is a difficult adjustment period for many people, especially those who consider themselves more sophisticated about money than their partner, or just more financially literate. The temptation is to hold back a certain part of the future spouse's income or assets until the new relationship is established, and then possibly open up. This policy is fraught with peril. At what point, and how is the new spouse told about that private account? Or what if one of the children needs something in the meantime, and money appears to be tight? If the tendency is to want such protection, especially against possible encroachment from stepchildren, then a prenuptial agreement is needed to address that. Otherwise, full disclosure is always the best policy.

Holidays and Family Traditions

Every year, many blended families run into the problem of figuring out how to visit multiple households on Thanksgiving, Christmas and other holidays. Holidays and family traditions, such as annual Labor Day reunions, often go out the window when families are blended. The holidays are supposed to be perfect, with lots of time spent together, but it's not always possible based on visitation times and blended family finances.

Holiday visits can also be a perfect setup for sibling rivalries and relationship stress. Whether because a grandparent won't accept the new family and buys more presents for some kids than for others, or because an ex-spouse lavishes a child with presents to win affection, the holidays can quickly become anything but a season of cheer. Sometimes there just isn't any flexibility, so blended family parents have to release old expectations and traditions and focus on creating new ones based on the things in their control, which are their attitude and emotions.

Arguing over how much to spend on individual children or feeling frustrated by an ex-spouse's financial role for the holidays and otherwise are common issues for the 65 percent of remarriages that involve children from a previous marriage, according to the National Stepfamily Resource Center. Proper financial planning is warranted to create appropriate strategies for the blended family.

Financial Planning for Blended Families

Personal Financial Planning

A brand new personal financial plan should be created, reflecting the objectives of both spouses and the needs of the blended family. Past financial plans should not be used since they were previously written with the needs and objectives of the prior families focusing on the issues identified by the ex-spouses or perhaps when they were single individuals.

These financial issues need to be discussed before the marriage to ensure that the financial aspect of the new union can be addressed covering the wants and needs of each spouse. As mentioned previously, money issues are one of the big stumbling blocks to keeping remarriages and blended families intact.

Insurance Planning

Health Insurance

Probably the most important issue for blended families is to ensure that all family members are covered under the family health insurance policy. It's critical to check over the wording in both spouses' health insurance policies to make sure that all family members are covered the way parents wish.

Life Insurance

Ensuring that beneficiary designations are correct after a remarriage is extremely important. Life insurance policies may have been purchased prior to the remarriage and may contain old or unwanted beneficiaries, such as the former spouse. The newly married life insurance policyowner must now decide if the beneficiary(ies) should change or whether the policies will continue to represent separate property and benefit the natural children of each parent.

Amounts of life insurance should be examined to determine if the newly blended family is covered sufficiently. Since expenses overall will be increasing, additional life insurance could be justified to pay for college and other obligations that the new parents may decide are appropriate. Tying the amount of life insurance needed into the objectives stated during the financial planning process is critical.

Disability Insurance

A review of each spouse's disability policy and the benefit amount under each are warranted.

Homeowners Insurance

Change the names on the homeowners policy to include both spouses.

Automobile Insurance

Ensure that all family members (including driving age stepchildren) are listed on the automobile insurance policy.

Umbrella Insurance

Ensure that all properties owned by both spouses are included under the policy. Each residence (if both are kept) and rental properties (even if each is separate property) should be covered. This is critical liability coverage since it goes beyond the existing homeowners and automobile coverage.

Cash Flow Planning

Contingency Planning

Many would agree that signing divorce papers rarely ends the relationship with the former spouse. Legal battles can rage on and siphon money for years. The newly formed family units should set a contingency fund or budget on an ongoing basis to account for these possible contingencies.

Budgeting

A second marriage will likely cost more than the first one. There's the initial desire to buy new in order to create a new home together. There are also more children and more daily expenses. Annual expenses such as vacations and travel will also increase. Every blended (and natural family for that matter) should create a daily and yearly budget, as well as a long-term financial plan.

The budget should include a savings plan for the family. Families should do everything possible to abide by the budget, but recognize that emergencies come up. Some families choose to eliminate credit cards to avoid debt and temptation. In order to make sure the budget is working, families should discuss their finances regularly. This guarantees stability and openness.

Sometimes putting these items into place for the blended family can be overwhelming. We can assist on the financial matters but also ensure that the family work with a certified family law attorney to provide needed guidance and help ensure things are set up correctly.

Establish a Household Game Plan with a Sufficient Number of Bank Accounts

Blended families should work out a practical method for handling money. A common example is to establish a joint household account and joint savings account for life together and keep other accounts separate. This enables expenses relating to the blended family to be paid for together and other interests to be kept separate.

Decide ahead of the marriage who pays for what. Determine who is responsible for which children, and how each major expense and financial responsibility will be assigned and handled. Depending on income, a simple sliding scale may work just fine. Blending families doesn't necessarily mean blending bank accounts. The only drawback to this arrangement is, that if one of the spouses lacks money handling skills, they may have to acquire them.

The recommended approach is to keep separate accounts but also have a shared bank account, with each partner depositing a percentage of income or a fixed amount each month. This makes it more equitable to both sides. The shared bank account is used to cover family expenses—mortgages, vacations, cars, everyday expenses and emergencies.

It also means each side may pay for his or her own children's expenses, so there is no resentment if one spouse feels they are paying too much for their partner's children. Also, separate accounts protect the spouse from the other partner's debts, including any alimony or child support payments.

Separate accounts also allow each partner to keep assets acquired before the marriage. For a parent saving for a child's college education, this is important. Separate accounts may also be better for obtaining financial aid. Separate accounts also protect both sides if the second marriage doesn't work out.

Income Tax Planning

Deciding on Which Spouse's Home to Live in

If each spouse own a home, the decision of whether to sell one home and live in the other, or for both spouses to sell both their houses and buy a new home together must be made. Before selling, the spouses must factor in federal and state tax considerations. The exclusion on the capital-gains tax is larger for married couples than for singles. It is $500,000 for married couples and $250,000 for single individuals. To benefit from that exclusion, the homeowners must have lived in the house for two of the past five years. Further, if a spouse remarries and now is part of a blended family, then the new spouse can count towards satisfying the marital requirement to exclude up to $500,000 of capital gain. So depending on the value of the home, it may make sense to keep the house a little longer after getting remarried.

Filing a Tax Return

The new spouses need to determine how they wish to file income tax returns going forward. Some spouses prefer to keep all of their financial matters separate and not commingle or give the appearance of commingling through the filing of a joint tax return. Some spouses may not even want to share that information with the other spouse. Others realize that the income tax rates are cheaper when filing jointly versus separately.

Some spouses may not want the possible increased liability of filing a joint return since all liability is now considered joint and severable.

Investment Planning

The new spouses should create an investment policy statement and investment plan from the financial plan they create. Both spouses should ensure that they are comfortable with their approach. In many instances, one spouse may be more or less conservative regarding investments than the other, but they should sign off together on the way their soon-to-be joint assets will be invested.

These assets may be invested differently than the assets each spouse plans to maintain as separate property and discloses in the prenuptial agreement. In this case, the assets only need to follow the direction of the owner spouse because they will not become marital property.

Using a Prenuptial Agreement before Remarriage

prenuptial agreement

Each spouse may wish to have a prenuptial agreement prior to entering the marriage. A prenuptial can help the spouse sort out finances regardless of whether the marriage ends in divorce after 6 months or with the death of one spouse after a long, happy union. Not only does a prenuptial spell out what each spouse owns and can expect if that spouse ends up single again, but it also lets one spouse waive rights to any property—for example, a family business or an investment account—that the other wants to preserve for his or her kids. Without a prenuptial, state property-division law bestows a share of the marital property on the other spouse, no matter how the marriage ends.

EXAMPLE

Individuals come into a marriage with children and assets of their own. This causes decisions regarding inheritance and other financial matters to take on a new level of complexity. Parents will generally want to make sure their wealth will benefit their own biological children. If the new spouse also has children—especially teenagers or adults—typically there may not be a strong urge to have those blended children share equally (if at all) in the estate of the spouse with the greatest amount of assets. Frequently, there may be some concern about leaving an estate outright to a surviving spouse. These issues become more apparent when there is a large age spread between the husband, the wife, and the kids.

Many couples entering a second marriage are a little bit weary, but also a little bit wiser. Signing a prenuptial or a postnuptial agreement if already married, enables spouses to clearly lay out what belongs to whom. While some people view these agreements as a sign of doom, they can often help clarify not only ownership, but also financial and marital obligations. Knowing they've worked out these issues often helps people feel safer and more secure in the marriage. And when new issues come up, these agreements can be used as a reference for new contracts written up.

The prenuptial agreement must provide for full disclosure of each party's assets and essentially put everything out on the table. This way, since we determined that 60 percent of second marriages and 73 percent of third marriages end in divorce, each party is prepared just in case of the unfortunate.

EXAMPLE

Some blended families may decide to put their respective assets in several pots, where the husband decides to set up a college fund account for his two sons and another that sets aside money for their future children. This approach could be used as a framework for the goals that the family wishes to accomplish. If the couple has children of their own, their education needs and costs will be covered before any inheritance gets divvied up.

The prenuptiual process involves tabulating and documenting individual assets and values, and becomng comfortable that this solution will effectively preserve what each party brought into the relationship if things don't go as planned and property needs to be split up again.

If the prenuptial route is chosen, each party will need a lawyer to represent their interests. The parties should sign off on the pre-nuptial well before the wedding. Otherwise, a judge might conclude that one of the spouse's was pressured and refuse to honor it.

While prenuptial agreements may not sound terribly romantic, using one to clearly state who has what going into a marriage is often one of the most effective tools remarrying individuals can use to head off trouble. Particularly for someone coming into a marriage with significant wealth, these agreements can help prevent the agony and expense of disputes in the future.

Post-Marital Agreements

postnuptial agreement

If the spouses's never got around to entering into a prenuptial agreement, there is always a postnuptial agreement that could still work. Each spouse could sign this document after the wedding, although each one has less leverage with the other, especially once the marital knot is tied.

Spouses who prefer to preserve assets for him or herself, or the children, by keeping the property each spouse acquired before the wedding separate from the marital mix should be aware that the definition of "separate" depends on state law and maybe the courts. Spouses should research how their state interprets separate and commingled property, or check with a lawyer.

Estate Planning

Estates, Inheritance, and Wills

Blended families must take extra precautions to do proper estate planning. It's possible to accidentally disinherit natural children. Even if the parents don't think sufficient money exists to warrant planning, many blended family situations should provide for it. The couple should meet with an attorney and make sure all the kids from the various marriages are considered. Topics to consider include financing college educations, inheritances and, even more important, issues of custody. An important family asset can easily make its way from one family's hands into another's if beneficiary designations and trusts aren't well documented and kept up to date.

Beyond the use of prenuptials to keep assets separate, a well-crafted estate plan will ensure that the assets go where that particular spouse wants them to go. These plans involve the use of wills, trusts, and sometimes, life insurance.

EXAMPLE
In the scenario of an older husband with children of his own who marries a considerably younger woman, the concern is how his estate plan can ensure that both the spouse and the kids receive benefits after he dies. A frequent fear is that the surviving spouse will have very little desire, and in the absence of good estate planning often no legal obligation, to ensure that her blended children will receive the inheritance the deceased had intended to leave them.

Another alternative involves the creation of an irrevocable life insurance trust (ILIT) which is funded with assets of the creator spouse. The trustee is directed to purchase a life insurance policy on the life of the creator, with the death benefit going to the trust. The trustee can then distribute the proceeds according to the creator's wishes, perhaps apportioning the payout among children and the surviving spouse.

It's vital to check and revise the wills, too, and make sure the wording includes all children, both natural and adopted.

Inheritance Issues

There are many ways of ensuring that property is passed on correctly after death, whether to the new spouse, children from an earlier marriage or children from the current marriage. Life insurance, wills and trusts allow for designated beneficiaries.

Using a combination of approaches allows a family to provide for the surviving spouse while still providing for the children. For example, spouses can give each other lifetime use of the house, as well as the money to maintain the home, through a bypass trust or a qualified terminable interest property (QTIP) trust. Once the spouse dies, the specified heirs inherit the house.

In order to provide for all children, a parent can make the older children from the first marriage beneficiaries on a life insurance policy and leave the rest of the property to the children from the second marriage. Retirement plans, such as 401(k) plans or IRAs can also be considered in the inheritance question but they have different rules and taxes so couples figuring out how to divide these monies should speak to a professional financial planner.

QTIP Trust

One estate planning approach is a qualified terminal interest in property, or QTIP. A QTIP allows a decedent to qualify a transfer for the martial deduction at his death yet still control the ultimate disposition of property.

A QTIP trust holds property for the benefit of a surviving spouse and makes income distributions to the surviving spouse at least annually. At the surviving spouse's death, the trust property will transfer to the remainder beneficiary as determined by the grantor of the QTIP trust, the first-to-die spouse.

In a blended family situation, the parent with the natural children could protect those children, or perhaps others of the natural parent, after that parent's death, if that parent feels that his natural children deserve, or are entitled to a larger share of that parent's estate. This will enable property to be distributed by the natural parent in accordance with his or her main wishes. It could also allow for certain assets to pass to intended heirs, and perhaps others to be split equally or in some proportion based on the blended family. It spells out exactly what should happen in advance without any conflicts developing after the death of the natural parent.

To qualify as a QTIP trust, the executor of the decedent's estate must make an election on the estate tax return to qualify the trust for the marital deduction. The election defers any estate tax on the property until the death of the surviving spouse. Even though it is a terminal interest, the QTIP trust will qualify for the unlimited marital deduction since the surviving spouse will be required to include in his gross estate the fair market value, at the surviving spouse's date of death, the assets in the trust. Despite the fact that the assets are taxed in the surviving spouse's gross estate, the assets will pass according to the terms of the trust created by the first to die spouse. Second, income must be paid out annually to the surviving spouse for his or her lifetime. Third, the surviving spouse must have the authority to alert the trustee to sell nonincome-producing investments and reinvest those proceeds in income-producing investments. Fourth, during the surviving spouse's lifetime, no one can have the right to appoint the property to anyone other than the surviving spouse. And finally, the decedent's executor must file an election to treat the trust as a QTIP trust on the decedent's federal estate tax return Form 706.

Upon the death of the surviving spouse, the executor of the surviving spouse's estate may require the trustee of the QTIP trust to pay out of the trust assets, any estate taxes attributable to the inclusion of the trust assets in the surviving spouse's gross estate. This provision is included in the law to prevent one spouse from forcing the other spouse to pay estate taxes attributable to his assets.

Disinheriting Children

With many children brought into the mix from the natural parent and the step-parent, and perhaps other children of either parent not living with the blended family, one parent may decide that some or even all of the children should be disinherited. A trust document, the QTIP, or property left through contract or operation of law, can be used to ensure that the parent's property goes to the appropriate children.

Retirement Planning

Qualified plan beneficiary designations need to be changed to the new spouse after marriage. That's because the spouse is the automatic beneficiary in a qualified plan, unless a spousal waiver is signed. In fact, under contract law, if the account owner does not remove the divorced former spouse as the beneficiary in a qualified plan, then the former spouse, and not the current spouse, will wind up with the account balance if not changed.

For personal retirement plans, such as SEPs, SIMPLES, and IRAs, as well as nonqualified plans, most state laws allow the account owner to leave those funds to the person of choice, which may not be the spouse. Natural children can remain as designated beneficiaries allowing the account owner the ability to protect and keep those funds away from the blended family.

Planning for All of the Children

Child Support

One of the most contentious issues facing blended families is child support. It's estimated that it will require least $250,000 to raise one child through college age in this country. Multiply that by several children and the task could be daunting.

Blended parents do not have an obligation or a responsibility to pay for child support. The only exceptions to this rule are the following:

- The blended parent has sought visitation rights.

The blended parent has interfered with the stepchild's ability to obtain support from the natural parent, or

- The blended parent has agreed to pay child support in a divorce agreement.

According to the U.S. Census Bureau's latest statistics, roughly $35 billion in child support went unpaid in 2009. The average due to dependent children was $5,960 annually, yet only 61 percent of that money was actually paid. Custodial parents who receive child support get only about $300 per month on average.

Parents initially see child support as a fixed number that never goes down and may actually go up. The downturn in the economy over the past few years has left many parents who owe support either unemployed or making less, which can alter the lifestyles of everyone involved. Many parents see their financial situation deteriorate after the divorce. And if a support modification is sought, the custodial parent (along with the new step-parent) has to find a way to make up the lost dollars. That can cause a lot of resentment between ex-spouses as well as relationship and financial stress for new spouses.

Education Funding

Many stepparents may resent paying for college, especially after that parent has paid for college previously. Not only is the cost of college, whether public or private, for four years (or more) significant, but that obligation takes away resources that could be earmarked for other purposes. Financial aid or loans can help lighten the load for the parents, but those types of resources may not be available.

The most effective investment vehicle for college funding is the 529 plan. With the 529 plan, monies accumulate income tax-deferred and can be withdrawn income tax free if used for college. Depending on the state plan and the most expensive school in the state, approximately $350,000 (based on the cost of the most expensive school in the state for five years worth of schooling) can be contributed per beneficiary. In addition, five years worth of present interest annual gifts can be made and counted for as made all in year one (tax exclusion of $14,000 per year for 5 years, or $70,000 today). That amount is then applied against the lifetime gift tax exclusion keeping the exclusion (currently $5.34 million in 2014) totally intact.

The owner can control the account and can change beneficiaries at any time. Scholarship money can come out without the 10 percent excise tax penalty (only the increase in the account value would be taxed as income), a state tax deduction could be had in certain states, and the parent can change the beneficiary to him or herself. All of these reasons make this type of education funding the best solution to pay for college.

Financial Aid

Blended families applying for college aid often run into major obstacles. It gets tricky very quickly. Children from blended families are oftentimes less likely to go to college and graduate because they are used as a weapon to hurt the other parent. Marital status and residency, as well as whether a public or private college is being considered, can dramatically increase the complexity of financial aid calculations.

Many parents are caught by surprise because they don't know how the process works. If, for example, the custodial parent has remarried, the blended parent's income will be included in the calculation, which can reduce the amount of federal aid a child receives. However, an unmarried custodial parent may in fact be eligible for a larger amount of federal aid.

Selecting one of the 250 schools that require the noncustodial parent to complete a "profile form" can be a major challenge for blended families. Some noncustodial parents are unwilling to cooperate for fear that divulging information about their income may prompt an ex-spouse to seek more support.

Advising the Divorced Client

Process and Challenges

Planning for a divorce is perhaps one of the most challenging aspects of working as an advisor due to the adversarial role in working with the couple going forward. The advisor will have to evaluate each spouse's potential needs in an uncertain financial future and decide whether to represent either one. Each spouse may try to intentionally hurt the other—financially, emotionally or otherwise—or try to gain access to more than his or her rightful share of financial assets and future income. Further, either spouse can drag the advisor into a litigious role and possibly subpoena that advisor on the grounds of working in conspiracy with one spouse over the other.

Many issues will need to be addressed including how assets and liabilities should be divided among the parties as part of the property settlement, and how future payments involving spousal and child support should be determined. The potential tax effects of the amount to be paid—which could be determined either as an annuity or as a lump sum—need to be evaluated. Income needs of each spouse that tie back to the financial plan and the creation of a new financial plan will need to be assessed, especially in situations where one spouse does not have the same earning capacity as the other. Since two households will now be formed, essentially from the same pool of money, stretching the dollar for most couples becomes a priority.

Some spouses may benefit from retaining certain assets that, for example, throw off an income stream that can assist one spouse in receiving monies to cover current and anticipated expenses going forward.

The tax considerations of those actions will need to be addressed. Attorneys may not be the most qualified professionals to address these issues simply because of the lack of financial training in dealing with future tax implications that can arise. Examples include the depreciation recapture and future capital gain issues resulting from the sale of assets after the divorce is completed.

Ethical considerations can pose the greatest challenge since perceptions of conflict of interest may arise if one spouse feels that the advisor is favoring the other spouse. Questions arising from either spouse should be communicated by the advisor to both spouses. This way the advisor is not providing information to one spouse and not to the other, minimizing the appearance that the advisor is favoring one over the other. The advisor should not try to take the place of an attorney or other qualified individual under any circumstances. The advisor should be available to make a series of recommendations but continue to point out that anything suggested by him or her needs to be brought back to and cleared by that spouse's attorney.

Any advisor should clearly identify his or her client—the one to whom the advisor owes the primary duty of care or a fiduciary responsibility. This may be extremely difficult to accomplish in a divorce situation since the advisor owes a great degree of loyalty and care to each spouse individually. The advisor may also have to work with other interested parties, such as attorneys and CPAs, to help in the division of the overall financial structure. Joint representation of both spouses due to ethical constraints or conflict of interest, therefore, is never a good idea.

The blended family represents a significant challenge since two separate families are essentially becoming one. Since each family has had a set pattern and general way of conducting itself as a separate unit, blending the two separate units into one can present the ultimate in financial and emotional demand on the couple. Proper planning prior to entering into this type of arrangement is a must and should be coordinated with all advisory and legal parties involved.

Developing a Life Plan

A life plan is a road map for how the needs and wishes of the divorced spouse will be carried out. It is a statement of future intentions that need to be accounted for in the division of assets, liabilities and the distribution of future income and division of expenses. The plan will be prepared by the divorced spouse to address aspects relating to budgeting future income needs to cover anticipated expenses and the division of assets and liabilities that can be justified in a way that is fair to each party.

With a blended family, the life plan challenges each spouse to repeat parenting skills from the prior marriage in a new situation. The time, attention and dedication spent during the first go-round of raising a family is revisited. With this scenario comes new financial and emotional challenges that need to be addressed in advance of and during the new blended family relationship.

Getting Organized

It is critical to get a handle on a number of specific issues to assist the divorced spouse in future planning. The planner must help the divorced spouse organize data so a comprehensive life plan can be established and implemented. Determining the personal requirements of the divorced spouse such as the division of assets and liabilities and the distribution and receipt of income and expenditures is of paramount importance. It is necessary to estimate the financial needs as accurately as possible. The complexity of the new plan requires accuracy and completeness of the evaluation. The advisor needs to be prepared to make recommendations across a vast array of topics. There are a number of questions that might be placed in a checklist to gather data for this purpose.

With a blended family, organizational skills may be more important for the spouse this time around. Each spouse entering into this type of arrangement is suggested to review all legal and financial documents with the respective attorney or advisor, disclose critical information if signing a prenuptial agreement, and determine how postnuptial transactions will be handled.

Checklist

1. Change the names on all assets transferred to the spouse.

2. Change the names on all liabilities transferred to the spouse now responsible for that debt.

3. Change the deed on real estate to the spouse who ends up with the property. (This is especially necessary in order to apply for financing to buy out the other spouse.)

4. Transfer the car titles to the spouse who ends up with the car. Make sure all documentation for paperwork regarding paid off loans or other liens is available.

5. Update all insurance policy beneficiary designations.

6. COBRA health insurance if the nonworking spouse needs to take advantage of ex-spouse's benefits. Coverage can be extended for up to 36 months.

7. Update retirement plan beneficiary designations. Refer to the list prepared for the court disclosing all the different types of retirement plans so no plans are forgotten during the process.

8. Make sure a QDRO is completed to split the money from a qualified retirement plan. IRAs don't need to complete QDROs.

9. Update the will and other estate planning documents. The most current will is the one that is valid because it supersedes all previous wills. Change health care proxies and powers of attorney so the ex can't control any of your client's decisions going forward.

10. Confirm that all bank and brokerage accounts have been separated into each spouse's name.

11. Make sure the ex has been removed from any joint credit cards. Otherwise, debts that are rung up could be your client's responsibility.

12. Keep meticulous records of all transactions involving the ex spouse.

13. Remove all personal assets from the prior residence before the divorce becomes final.

14. Spousal support may be modified.

15. If child support needs to be modified, your client should discuss it with his or her ex. Only as a last resort, try mediation or going back to court.

16. If living with a new person in a blended family relationship, a cohabitation agreement should be used. All issues in should be in writing to prevent any future misunderstandings before marriage either while alive or at death.

17. Before remarriage, a prenuptial agreements is a necessity. It sets the expectations from the beginning so everyone knows what to expect. The client must always manage the other side's expectations both before becoming a blended family and after (if there is an after).

18. Forming a blended family through remarriage is tricky business. Make sure the kids and even the ex are ready for it. The client should prepare for it before it happens.

The Team Players

There are many participants in the planning team in a divorce case. The number involved in each specific instance will depend upon the circumstances of the case. The following is a list of possible participants and the roles that will be played by each.

Attorney(s)

It is imperative that each spouse have representation during the divorce process. This should be the first stop made by each spouse before selecting other members of the team. Each spouse should hire an attorney to represent current and future interests. The attorney is most knowledgeable in how the divorce process works, and the implications of settling or going to trial. The attorney can set strategy based on the facts and circumstances surrounding the case. The attorney may be able to spell out the ramifications of specific past and future events, the cost attributed through the entire divorce process, and the possible settlements that can be reached in advance.

An attorney familiar with state law specifics should be chosen. For example, a divorced client living in a common law state should not engage an attorney from a community property state, or vice versa, because the attorney may not be familiar with different state laws. The advisor can assist the attorney on financial matters, but should never be the end source of any decision making since the advisor will not know the legal ramifications of his or her actions.

Business Valuation Expert

If either spouse has a business, then the business will need to go through a proper business valuation. The amount determined through the business valuation will then show up as a corresponding asset by the business owner on the balance sheet and the other spouse would receive a corresponding amount of assets to balance out the distribution. For example, if the business is worth $500,000, then $500,000 of assets in the form of a residence, retirement plans, or other investments would be received by the other spouse. Each state has a different way professional practices are evaluated and show during a divorce.

A business valuation represents a very detailed analysis of anywhere from 3-to-5 years worth of tax returns, and analyzing other records. In many instances, the valuation is based on past earnings performance and not future earnings prospects. Therefore it may not be truly representative of what is to come. In addition, forensic accounting may be necessary if foul play or fraud is suspected.

Vocational Expert

A vocational expert is an individual specializing in valuing the financial income capabilities of a nonworking or part-time working spouse. This team member is critical because he or she can help reduce the amount of financial support (both spousal and child support) that may be required to be paid by the payor spouse if the payee spouse is capable of earning a living going forward. The potential earnings of the payee spouse can be factored into the payment amounts and potentially making them less than anticipated.

CPA(s)

The evaluation of tax issues resulting from the valuation of property will be a significant consideration, thus requiring the help of a certified public account. Business and investment properties present tax issues not common for many individuals, such as depreciation recapture, capital gains, capital loss carry forwards, basis calculations, like-kind exchange carry forwards, and other important but often unrecognized or forgotten items. A CPA can play a huge role in the final division of assets and liabilities. Also, tax preparation will be required for each divorced spouse.

CLU, ChFC, CFP, or Other Financial Services Professional

There may be significant investment or insurance planning necessary in the case involving a divorced spouse. Issues that may arise include purchasing or adding to disability insurance since there is no one else to rely upon for paying bills in case the spouse becomes disabled; purchasing additional life insurance and changing any beneficiary designations on existing life insurance policies; retitling and reevaluating automobile, homeowners, umbrella, long-term care and business insurance.

The divorced spouse may need to refine his or her investments by repositioning assets to possibly generate income. That is because the newly divorced spouse may need to generate a specific amount of income per month to cover household and discretionary expenses. The current positioning of the assets may not allow the divorced spouse to accomplish that.

Even with the attorney playing an active role, it is likely that the financial services professional will have a substantial amount of contact with the divorced spouse. It is important that this individual understand the basic team structure and the role of the other professionals in the divorce process.

The financial services professional may be uniquely exposed to ethical issues with respect to the financial assets available to the divorced spouse and future ongoing income needs.

Breaking Down a Divorce Case into Life Stages

From a legal and financial planning standpoint, a divorce case can be broken down into two stages.

The first stage is to evaluate, summarize, and recommend strategies based on the divorced spouse's current financial situation. That means taking all the client information available (and perhaps searching for more) and developing a balance sheet to help with the property settlement under IRC Sec. 1041. The balance sheet represents a snapshot in time of what is owned and owed by the couple at a specific date. The balance sheet will list all assets owned by the couple and the debts responsible by the couple. Assets are owned items recorded at fair market value. Liabilities are debts recorded at their face amount.

The financial plan initially developed by the spouses may not be relevant simply because the needs and wants of each spouse will have changed over the years, especially with the impact of the divorce pending.

The second stage is to determine what the spouse will need to live on going forward and determine a game plan for achieving that objective. The second objective will not be attainable until the divorce becomes final, which could take several years. A revised financial plan just for that particular spouse is recommended since many of the objectives and perhaps some of the financial considerations have changed since the first time the financial plan was done.

In this stage, a cash flow statement is developed showing all income received and expenses paid over a period of time. A one-year time horizon probably would work best. Each income and expense categorized item is listed separately with some income and expense items ultimately changing hands from one spouse to the other.

Sample Forms

Budgeting

budgeting

Budgeting is the process of creating and following an big picture plan for spending and investing the resources available to the client. In simplest terms, the process works via the establishment of a working budget model followed by a comparison of actual and expected results. By constantly monitoring the budget, the advisor and client can recognize problems as they occur and even anticipate them. Budgeting provides both a means of financial self-evaluation and a guideline to measure actual performance.

Budgeting does have some disadvantages, however. For example, many individuals have a psychological aversion to the record keeping required and may not maintain sufficient information for the budget to be useful. Obviously, to the extent the data utilized are inaccurate, the conclusions drawn from the budget may be misleading. For some clients, a rote dependence on budgeting numbers inhibits creativity, stifles risk taking, and encourages mechanical thinking.

Here are some guidelines for establishing a budget:

- Make the budget flexible enough to deal with emergencies, unexpected opportunities, or other unforeseen circumstances.
- Keep the budget period long enough to utilize an investment strategy and a workable series of investment procedures—typically one calendar year.
- Make the budget simple and brief.
- Follow the form and content of the budget consistently.
- Eliminate extraneous information.
- Estimate especially with insignificant items.
- Tailor the budget to specific goals and objectives.

- Utilize methods of tracking expenses that are already part of the client's daily activities such as using quicken or keeping track on a smart phone.

- Remember that a budget is also a guideline against which actual results are to be measured. Unexpected results should be analyzed: they may be the norm and deserve to be incorporated in a revised budget.

- Pinpoint, in advance, variables that may influence the amounts of income and expenses. Income may vary because of expected annual raises and increases or decreases in interest or dividend rates. Expenses may vary because of fluctuating living costs, changing tastes or preferences, or changing family circumstances.

- Budgeting is a psychological process—a study of "what can be," not "what is." Mental accounting may not reflect actual spending habits and behavior.

Monthly Expenditures	Amount
Auto loan payment	$
Auto maintenance	$
Child care	$
Clothing	$
Contributions	$
Credit card payments	$
Dues	$
Entertainment	$
Food	$
Household maintenance	$
Income and Social Security taxes	$
Insurance	$
Personal care	$
Property taxes	$
Rent or mortgage payment	$
Retirement plan investments	$
Savings/investments	$
Transportation (gas, fares)	$
Utilities	$
Vacations (monthly allotment)	$
Other	$
Total Monthly Expenditures:	$

Monthly Receipts	Client (1)	Client (2)
Wages or salary	$	$
Capital gain (long-term)	$	$
Capital gain (short-term)	$	$
Dividends (mutual funds, stocks, etc.)	$	$
Interest (CDs, savings account, etc.)	$	$
Pension	$	$
Rental and/or royalty	$	$
Social Security	$	$
Other taxable	$	$
Other nontaxable	$	$

Total Monthly Receipts: $_____

Net Cash Flow = Total Monthly Receipts – Expenditures	$

Income Allocation

Identify the amount of gross (before-tax) income from each of the following:

- salary
- bonus
- incentive payments
- commissions
- self-employment
- real estate cash flows
- dividends—closely held corporations
- dividends—publicly traded corporations
- interest—savings accounts
- interest—taxable bonds
- interest—tax-free bonds
- trust income
- other fixed-payment income
- variable sources of income

Basic sources of information regarding items of income include, among others, check stubs from work, bank and investment account statements, prior years' income tax returns, and personal financial position statements that show income-generating assets as well as previously owned assets that have been sold. Clients that use Microsoft Money®, Quicken®, or other personal finance software packages have the ability to develop personal financial statements using that software. Even if the client is only using the software to facilitate transactions using the electronic bill payment feature, it still provides a cash flow history that the advisor can use to prepare a cash flow statement. The advisor's ability to use the client's software to generate financial statements could shorten the time spent in the data-gathering phase of the financial planning process and improve the accuracy of the statements.

Financial professionals should also consider net (or after-tax) cash flow items such as gifts, tax-refunds or other nontaxable payments. These net cash flows should be recorded on the cash flow statement, and noted that they are not subject to federal or state income taxes.

	1 Total Income (Community/ Separate)	2 Allocated to Husband	3 Allocated to Wife
1. Wages (each employer)			
2. Interest Income (each payer)			
3. Dividends (each payer)			
4. State income tax refund			
5. Capital gains and losses			
6. Pension income			
7. Rents, royalties, partnerships, estates, trusts			
8. Taxes withheld			
9. Other items such as : Social Security benefits, business and farm income or loss, unemployment compensation, mortgage interest deduction, etc.			

Balance Sheet

Since net worth is determined by subtracting total liabilities from total assets, preparing a client's financial position statement involves

- identifying each of the client's assets and liabilities
- valuing each asset and liability as of the date of the statement

- recording those values in an appropriate format that shows the client's net worth as the difference between total assets and total liabilities

Balance Sheet. Please attach all brokerage, financial advisor, and mutual fund investment statements. Also attach any other necessary documentation.

Determining Net Worth—Analyzing Assets and Liabilities

Personal Assets:	
Name of Asset	Current Value
Primary residence	$
Secondary residence	$
Automobile(s)	$
RVs (boats, campers, etc.)	$
Household belongings, etc.	$
Other personal assets	$

Cash Reserves:						
Bank Name	Name of Asset	Current Value	Rate of Return (%)	Maturity Date	Annual Additions	Purpose*
	Checking accounts	$				
	Savings accounts	$				
	Credit union accounts	$				
	Money market accounts	$				
	Certificate of deposit #1	$				
	Certificate of deposit #2	$				
	Certificate of deposit #3	$				

Brokerage Accounts:

Brokerage Name	Current Value	Stock, Bond, Mutual Fund, Other	Ownership	Current Balance
				$
				$
				$
				$
				$
				$
				$

Retirement Investments:

Name of Asset	Current Value	Rate of Return (%)	Ma-turity Date	Annual Additions	Pur-pose*
Company ret. plan:					Retire-ment
Company ret. plan:					Retire-ment
Company ret. plan:					Retire-ment
Company ret. plan:					Retire-ment
IRA: _____					Retire-ment
IRA: _____					Retire-ment
IRA: _____					
Other: _____					
Other: _____					

Nonretirement and Business Investments:					
Name of Asset	Current Value	Rate of Return (%)	Matu-rity Date	Annual Additions	Pur-pose*
Real estate: _____					
Real estate: _____					
Real estate: _____					
Real estate: _____					
Personally-owned business					
Other business interests _____					
Note receivable _____					
Note receivable _____					
Note receivable _____					
Life ins. cash value: _____					
Life ins. cash value: _____					
Life ins. cash value: _____					
Other: _____					
Other: _____					
Other: _____					
Other: _____					

Liabilities:					
Name of Liability	**Initial Balance**	**Current Balance**	**Monthly Payment**	**Interest Rate**	**Payoff Date**
Home mortgage					
Home equity loan #1					
Home equity loan #2					
Second home mortgage					
Auto loan #1					
Auto loan #2					
Credit card: _____					
Credit card: _____					
Credit card: _____					
Credit card: _____					
Real estate loan: _____					
Real estate loan: _____					
Real estate loan: _____					
Business loan: _____					
Business loan: _____					
Business loan: _____					
Retirement plan loan: ____					
Retirement plan loan: ____					
Other loan: _____					
Other loan: _____					
Other loan: _____					
Other loan: _____					
Other loan: _____					

Chapter Review

Review questions are based on the learning objectives in this chapter. Thus, a [3] at the end of a question means that the question is based on learning objective 3. If there are multiple objectives, they are all listed.

Key Terms and Concepts

child support
filing status
like-kind exchanges
installment obligation

blended family
prenuptial agreement
postnuptial agreement
budgeting

Review Questions

1. What is considered child support? [1]

2. Should either spouse write-off any of the cost pursuant to a divorce? Why or why not? [2]

3. What are the tax implications of spousal support? [2]

4. Explain the tax ramifications of property settlements? [3]

5. When would the divorcing parties consider using IRC Sec. 1031 (like-kind exchange) during a divorce? [3]

6. Describe the various types of blended families? [4]

7. What are some of the financial planning strategies that are appropriate and how could they work for blended families? [9]

8. What are the requirements for a prenuptial agreement [7]

9. When would a postnuptial agreement make sense? [7]

10. How is a QTIP designed? [8]

11. How can a QTIP be an effective tool for a blended family? [8]

The Case Study — Mike and Ellen Sawyer

Mike (47) and Ellen Sawyer (44) of Breckenridge, CO have been married for 25 years. Mike runs a successful ski and bike shop and Ellen works as a teacher at the local high school. They have three children: Lindsay (10), Risa (8) and Devon (6).

On June 30, 2013, Mike and Ellen decided to get a divorce. Each spouse has been living separately since that time. On August 1, 2013, Mike moved in with his girlfriend Carla and her family. Carla has three children: Sam (9), Diane (7), and Jackie (5). Mike and Carla plan to get married in 2015.

Mike and Ellen have agreed to joint custody of the children where Mike would have the kids on Tuesday nights, Thursday nights and every other weekend.

Each spouse is attempting to maximize the amount received at the end of the divorce. Each side has hired an attorney who will be spearheading that spouse's effort. A balance sheet of assets and liabilities follows on the next page:

Ellen received an inheritance on 6/12/10 of $230,000 when her mom passed away. She has kept the money in a separate account in her name only.

Cash Flow

Mike earns $180,000 per year from his business. Business profits amount to $20,000 per year.

Ellen earns $40,000 per year as a teacher.

Mutual funds pay income of $8,500 per year.

Stocks pay income of $6,000 per year.

Bonds pay income of $2,000 per year.

Bank accounts in total pay $750 per year.

Rental real estate shows losses of $6,000 per year while breaking even cash flow wise.

Mike and Ellen do not make any contributions towards after-tax savings accounts.

Insurance

<u>Life Insurance:</u>

Mike: $500,000 annual renewable term policy; $300,000 universal life policy with $20,000 CSV

Ellen: $100,000 whole life policy with $10,000 CSV

<u>Disability Insurance</u>

Mike: Individual, own occupation policy for 60 percent of his gross salary

Ellen: None

<u>Health Insurance:</u>

Mike has health insurance for family under preferred provider organization (PPO) policy.

$500 family deductible; $2,000 stop loss limit.

<u>Homeowners Insurance</u>

The family has HO3 and HO15 coverage on the primary residence.

$500 deductible

<u>Automobile Insurance</u>

The family has $250k/$500k/$250k coverage on all automobiles.

$500 comprehensive and $1,000 collision deductibles

<u>Umbrella Insurance</u>

The family has a $2,000,000 policy

<u>Long-Term Care</u>

Neither spouse has long-term care insurance

<u>Business Liability Insurance for Mike</u>

$5,000 premium per year

Retirement

Mike contributes $20,000 per year to his SEP plan. Employer match is 25 percent or $5,000.

Ellen contributes $17,500 per year to her 403(b) plan. No employer match.

Each spouse would like to retire at age 65.

They do not want to factor in Social Security in any retirement calculations.

They would each like to retire at 70 percent of their gross income.

General Information

Primary Residence: $450,000 original loan amount, 15 years, 4 percent interest rate, payment is $3,328.59/mo. Real estate taxes are $450/mo, homeowners insurance is $200/mo.

Vacation Home: $300,000 original loan amount, 30 years, 5 percent interest rate, payment is $1,610.46/mo. Real estate taxes are $400/mo, homeowners insurance is $140/mo.

Rental Property: $400,000 original loan amount, 30 years, 4.5 percent interest rate, payment is $2,026.74/mo. Real estate taxes are $375/mo., dwelling policy insurance is $125/mo.

Each spouse expects inflation to average 4 percent annually.

Each spouse expects salary to increase by 3.5 percent per year.

Income Tax Bracket

Federal: 33 percent marginal tax bracket filing married filing jointly.

State: 4.63 percent Colorado state income tax bracket

Estate Planning

Mike and Ellen each have a will leaving all property to the other and naming the other spouse as primary guardian. Each spouse lists his/her respective brother as backup guardian for the children.

Mike and Ellen each have living wills/health care proxies naming the other as the primary decision maker.

All property is owned as joint tenants with right of survivorship.

Anticipated funeral expenses to total $20,000 and administrative costs to total $35,000 for each spouse.

Investment Information – Prospective

	Expected Return	Beta
Aggressive stocks	12%	1.8
Growth stocks	9.5%	1.3
S&P 500	8%	1.0
Value Stocks	7.5%	0.8
Bonds—Corporate	6%	0.5
Bonds—Municipal	4%	0.4
Money Market (Bank) Funds	1%	0.1

Objectives

Mike's objectives are as follows:

1. Keep his business.
2. Keep the vacation home.
3. Keep the rental property.
4. Receive as much cash and cash equivalents as possible.
5. Hire a vocational expert to place a higher value on Ellen's future income potential in order to reduce his future income obligations to Ellen for both spousal and child support.
6. Marry Carla during 2015.
7. Protect his assets and income when their blended family is formed.
8. Pay Ellen a lump sum for spousal support instead of a monthly amount and to factor in the tax consequences of that payment.

Ellen's objectives are as follows:

1. Provide an adequate income stream to maintain the lifestyles of her and the children.
2. Take the differential in assets by balancing out the retirement accounts, and/or receiving most of the investments.
3. Ensure that her inheritance remains separate property.
4. Have Mike pay off credit card debt and remaining balance on her car.
5. Receive an adequate amount of temporary support to minimize the disruption to her and the children's lifestyle.
6. Keep the primary residence and have Mike pay off the mortgage on it.
7. Have Mike perform a valuation of his business in order to determine its true worth.
8. Cover income needs per month of $60,000 including spousal and child support.
9. Have Mike pay for college for all three children.

All assets and liabilities are listed on the balance sheet.

Mike and Ellen Sawyer: Balance Sheet

Assets

<u>Current Assets</u>

Checking account	$15,000	
Savings accounts	$40,000	
Money market accounts	$20,000	
Cash surrender value life insurance	$30,000	
Total Cash and Cash Equivalents		*$105,000*

<u>Investable Assets</u>

Mike's business	$875,000	
Stocks	$60,000	
Bonds	$50,000	
Mutual funds	$85,000	
Rental real estate	$600,000	
Mike – SEP	$150,000	
Ellen – 403(b)	$180,000	
Mike – IRA	$70,000	
Ellen – IRA	$45,000	
529 assets for college	$25,000	
Total Investable Assets		*$2,140,000*

<u>Personal Use Assets</u>

Primary residence	$700,000	
Vacation house	$500,000	
Automobiles (both cars)	$75,000	
Personal property	$55,000	
Total Personal Use Assets		*$1,330,000*
Total Assets		**$3,575,000**

Liabilities

Short-Term

Credit card debt	$8,000	
1 year remaining of Ellen's car pmt. balance	$4,200	
Total short term liabilities		$12,200

Long-Term Debt

Mortgage – primary residence	$430,000	
Mortgage – vacation home	$280,000	
Mortgages – rental property	$370,000	
Total Long-Term Debt		*$1,080,000*

Total Liabilities	$1,092,200

Net Worth	**$2,482,800**

Chapter Review

Review Questions

1. How will the Sawyers' treat the division of property under IRC Sec. 1041?

2. What are the financial and tax ramifications with payments Ellen will receive going forward?

3. What planning recommendations would you make to try to equalize the distribution?

4. What can Mike do regarding the inheritance received by Ellen during the marriage?

5. How would Mike's business be valued and what are the important considerations to contemplate and documents to be reviewed and evaluated during this process for the closely held business owner?

6. What ethical considerations would you advise in working with divorced clients?

7. What issues does Mike need to consider regarding his newly-formed blended family?

8. What can Mike do to protect himself in his remarriage to Carla?

Learning Objectives

An understanding of the material in this chapter should enable you to

1. Describe the concept of gross income, and explain the difference between exclusions and deductions.

2. Distinguish between above-the-line and below-the-line deductions in computing adjusted gross income (AGI).

3. Distinguish the standard deduction from itemized deductions.

4. Describe itemized deductions that may be applicable to families with special needs individuals and the requirements for each.

5. Describe the rules for personal and dependency exemptions, and explain the structure of federal income tax rates.

6. Identify the key credits available to families with special needs individuals, and discuss the requirements for their use and the extent of the tax benefit.

7. Explain the nature and purpose of the alternative minimum tax (AMT).

The Principle of Gross Income

gross income   Gross income includes every item of value, whether consisting of money or other property, that is either made available to or comes into the possession of the taxpayer. In other words, anything of value is considered to be gross income for income tax purposes unless—and this qualification is very important—the Internal Revenue Code contains a specific provision that excludes a particular item from the taxpayer's gross income.

This is why the provision in the Internal Revenue Code that provides the gross income rule is referred to as a "shotgun" clause. Although the provision lists 15 different items that are includible in a taxpayer's gross income, the provision states that gross income includes, but is not limited to, these items. Gross income means "all income from whatever source derived."

However, certain items of money or other property are not includible in a taxpayer's gross income. These items include gifts, income from tax-exempt bonds, workers' compensation benefits, and many other items. Such items are called exclusions from gross income. It is important to remember that the reason such items are excluded from a taxpayer's gross income is that there is a specific section in the Internal Revenue Code that says so. In other words, no item of money or other property can be excluded from gross income unless there is a code provision stating that it is to be excluded. Therefore, it is fairly simple in most cases to determine whether an item is includible in the taxpayer's gross income.

deduction   It is also important to distinguish the concept of an *exclusion* from that of a *deduction* for tax purposes. As noted above, an exclusion is an item of value that the taxpayer receives that is not includible in the taxpayer's gross income. A deduction, on the other hand, is an item of expense (not an item of receipt) that reduces the amount of income that is subject to tax.

EXAMPLE

Cheryl has the following items of income and expense for the current year: a $35,000 salary from her job as a paralegal, a $5,000 gift from her aunt, and an alimony payment of $3,000 to her former husband. The $35,000 salary is includible in Cheryl's gross income. The $5,000 gift is not includible in her gross income because there is a provision in the Internal Revenue Code that says that gifts are not includible in the recipient's gross income. The $3,000 alimony payment is deductible from Cheryl's gross income in determining how much of Cheryl's income will actually be taxed, because the Internal Revenue Code contains a provision that states that alimony payments are generally deductible.

Exclusions from Gross Income

There are many items that the Internal Revenue Code states are excludible from a taxpayer's gross income. Among these items are the following:

- gifts and inheritances
- income from certain bonds issued by states and municipalities
- workers' compensation benefits
- death proceeds from life insurance contracts

- benefits paid from medical expense insurance policies
- Social Security benefits (for taxpayers below certain income levels)
- amounts received under certain dependent-care-assistance programs and educational assistance programs
- certain qualified scholarships

An item that is excludible generally does not have to be reported in any way on the taxpayer's return.

Tax-Exempt Transactions

tax-exempt

tax-deferred

Perhaps one of the best types of tax planning techniques is that of creating a transaction that produces a monetary benefit without the taxpayer being taxed on that transaction. Within this general category there are two basic types of transactions. The first is where taxation is altogether eliminated, and the second is where taxation of the transaction is merely deferred. The first type can be described as a tax-exempt transaction. Such transactions are generally based on some specific exclusion from gross income. The second type of transaction is considered a nonrecognition transaction.

An example of a tax-exempt transaction is the receipt of income from a public-purpose municipal bond. The income from such bonds is excludible from the taxpayer's gross income for federal income tax purposes. As previously discussed, however, all income is includible in gross income unless there is a provision in the Code that specifically excludes it. There is such an exclusion for certain municipal bond income (IRC Sec. 103).

Financial market forces generally dictate that unless the taxpayer is subject to a high marginal income tax rate, the interest rate on such bonds will not be greater than the after-tax rate on taxable obligations. Therefore such investments are generally of interest only to upper-bracket taxpayers.

Another example of a tax-exempt monetary gain is the exclusion of the first $250,000 ($500,000 if married, filing jointly) of gain on the sale of a personal residence if certain requirements are met.

Nonrecognition Transactions

nonrecognition transactions

There are many types of transactions in which taxation is merely deferred rather than eliminated. These transactions may generally be referred to as *nonrecognition transactions.* Typically, such a transaction involves the sale or exchange of property at a gain realized by the taxpayer. However, because of a provision in the Internal Revenue Code, the realized gain is not currently recognized (reportable on Form 1040).

How do such transactions merely defer, rather than eliminate, taxable gain? In order to understand the mechanics of the nonrecognition transaction, the basic tax treatment of a sale or exchange of property must be understood.

How Nonrecognition Transactions Differ from Taxable Transactions.

Some sales and exchanges are governed by specific provisions in the Internal Revenue Code, which provide that the gain realized shall not be recognized for tax purposes. The purpose of nonrecognition transactions is not to eliminate taxation, but merely to defer it. Deferral is accomplished depending on the taxpayer's basis in the property. Generally, a taxpayer's basis in property is equal to the cost of the property. In the case of an exchange of property, the taxpayer's cost for the property received in the exchange is really the fair market value of the property surrendered in the exchange. However, if the exchange is one in which gain is not recognized, the taxpayer's basis in the new property will generally be the same as the taxpayer's basis in the old property. This preserves the unrecognized gain and allows that gain to be taxed when the new property is later sold in a taxable transaction.

EXAMPLE

Robert owns a condominium that he holds as a rental property. He paid $100,000 for the property and added $20,000 worth of improvements. For purposes of this example, depreciation deductions are not considered. The value of the property is now $180,000. Robert exchanges the property for another condominium in a transaction that qualifies for nonrecognition treatment under the Internal Revenue Code. The property received in the exchange is also worth $180,000. Robert's realized gain is $60,000 ($180,000 value of property received minus $120,000 basis in property given up). Robert's recognized gain is zero because the exchange qualifies for nonrecognition treatment. However, Robert's basis in the new property will be the same as his basis in the old property ($120,000). As a result, if the new property is sold later, the gain that would have been recognized if the exchange was taxable earlier will be recognized later, when the new property is sold. On the other hand, if the exchange was taxable, Robert would pay tax currently on the $60,000 of gain, but he would have a basis of $180,000 in the new property.

Clearly, the deferral of taxation in such a transaction has significant value. Moreover, the deferred gain may never be taxed if the taxpayer does not sell the property received in the exchange at a later date. The intent of the nonrecognition provisions is merely to defer taxation. But there is no assurance that Uncle Sam will ever get his tax money, particularly if the taxpayer keeps the new property until death.

The example above is just one type of transaction that qualifies for nonrecognition. Other examples include certain exchanges of insurance policies and involuntary conversions. These transactions, and the specific rules that govern their tax treatment, are beyond the scope of this reading.

Transactions That Result in a Taxable Loss. Some sales of property will result in a loss rather than a gain to the selling taxpayer. This will happen when the amount received for the property is less than the taxpayer's basis in the property. In such cases, the amount of the loss will generally be deductible for income tax purposes if the property sold is either business property or property held for the production of income. If the property is held for personal use, the loss resulting from a sale of the property is generally nondeductible.

EXAMPLE
Alexandra owns stock in the Hi-Five Corporation, a publicly traded corporation that sells sneakers. Alexandra paid $5,000 for the stock 2 years ago. This year, she sells the stock for $3,500. Alexandra has a realized loss of $1,500 ($5,000 basis minus $3,500 amount realized). Alexandra may deduct the $1,500 loss on her tax return this year.

capital losses

Tax Treatment of Capital Losses. When a capital asset is sold at a loss rather than at a gain, special rules apply. Basically, capital losses can be deducted only against the taxpayer's capital gains. In other words, a taxpayer cannot deduct capital losses against ordinary income (such as his or her wages for the year). However, in the special case of individual taxpayers, net capital losses can be deducted against ordinary income in an amount up to $3,000 per year. Net capital losses in excess of $3,000 can be carried over to future tax years.

Capital Gains

taxable gain

taxable loss

Computation of Gain or Loss. When property is sold, it is necessary to determine what portion of the sale proceeds will be subject to taxation. In general, the gain realized from a sale of property is equal to the total amount realized from the sale, minus the taxpayer's basis in the property.

basis

What does the term basis mean? Broadly stated, basis is the amount that the taxpayer has invested in the property. Therefore, basis is generally the amount that the taxpayer paid for the property, plus the cost of improvements to the property, if any. Stated another way, the basis of property is generally equal to its cost. As a result, the gain realized from a sale of property is the sales price minus the taxpayer's cost.

EXAMPLE
Nancy bought 1,000 shares of stock in Cleanseco, Inc., a household cleanser manufacturer, 2 years ago. She paid $5,000 for the stock. This year, she sells the Cleanseco stock for $10,000. The amount realized from the sale is $10,000. Nancy's basis is $5,000. Therefore, the realized gain from the sale is $5,000 ($10,000 – $5,000)

The fact that the portion of the sales price that represents a recovery of the taxpayer's basis is not taxable illustrates a basic principle of tax law, namely, that money received that represents a return of capital is not treated as gross income. The Internal Revenue Code contains many provisions which reflect this basic principle. It is really a matter of common sense: Getting back money that the taxpayer has invested in property should not result in taxation, because there has been no profit returned to the taxpayer, only the original investment.

Ordinary versus Capital Gain and Loss. Some different rules apply to sales of a taxpayer's assets, depending on whether the gain or loss is treated as an ordinary gain or loss or a capital gain or loss.

ordinary gain or loss

capital gain or loss

Capital Gain versus Ordinary Income. What is the difference between capital gain and ordinary income? Basically, capital gain is income that is realized through the sale or exchange of a capital asset. The definition of a capital asset does appear in the Internal Revenue Code, although the Code defines a capital asset by stating what it is not rather than what it is. In any event, a capital asset can generally be described as any property held by the taxpayer other than property held for sale by the taxpayer, or intellectual or artistic property created by the taxpayer. Special tax rules apply to the sale of property used by a taxpayer in a trade or business. These rules will be discussed below.

Under the law currently in effect the maximum rate applicable to capital gains on assets held by individual taxpayers for more than 12 months is generally 15 percent and 20 percent (for those taxpayers in the 39.6 percent marginal tax bracket), as opposed to the much higher maximum marginal tax rate of 39.6 percent that is applicable to ordinary income. However, a 0 percent rate applies for those taxpayers in a 10 percent and 15 percent tax bracket. In addition, gains from collectibles and real estate gains attributable to "unrecaptured" depreciation are taxed at the higher rates of 28 percent and 25 percent, respectively.

qualified dividends   ***Qualified Dividends Taxed at Long-Term Capital Gains Rates.*** Dividends represent income that has already been taxed at the corporate level before being distributed to individual stockholders. Under the 2003 Jobs and Growth Tax Relief Reconciliation Act, dividends paid to individual stockholders typically were designated as qualified dividends, and are generally taxed at the same rates that apply to long-term capital gains (0 percent, 15 percent, and 20 percent). Even though long-term capital gains tax rates apply, qualified dividends are still classified as ordinary income (as distinguished from capital gains).

Computation of Taxable Income

As previously stated, a deduction is an item of expense that reduces the amount of the taxpayer's income that is subject to tax. There are many different items that are deductible for federal income tax purposes. However, before some of these items are listed and explained, the concepts of *adjusted gross income (AGI)* and *taxable income* should be understood.

Adjusted Gross Income

adjusted gross income   Adjusted gross income is an intermediate calculation that is made in the process of determining an individual's income tax liability for a given year. Why is such an intermediate calculation necessary or useful? For purposes of the tax law, adjusted gross income is used as a base amount to determine how the taxpayer must treat certain other items for tax purposes. For example, adjusted gross income is used to calculate the maximum amount of charitable contributions that may be deducted by an individual in a given year (generally 50 percent of the individual's adjusted gross income).

The Determination of Adjusted Gross Income

**adjusted gross
income (AGI)**

Calculation of Adjusted Gross. The calculation
of an individual taxpayer's *adjusted gross income (AGI)*
is an intermediate step in the process of calculating
taxable income. To calculate adjusted gross income, certain deductions are
subtracted from the individual's gross income.

**above-the-line
deductions**

**below-the-line
deductions**

There are two fundamental categories of deductions for
individual taxpayers: deductions allowable in determining
adjusted gross income and deductions allowable in
determining taxable income. Deductions subtracted
from gross income in determining adjusted gross income
are referred to as *above-the-line deductions*. Deductions subtracted from
adjusted gross income in determining taxable income are referred to as
below-the-line deductions.

Although the calculation of AGI is an intermediate step, it is an important one.
Two of the most significant reasons why are as follows:

- Above-the-line deductions allowable in determining adjusted gross
  income are available regardless of whether the taxpayer claims
  "itemized" deductions. As explained below, the taxpayer claims
  itemized or below-the-line deductions only if the total of such
  deductions exceeds the available standard deduction. For this
  reason, above-the-line deductions are often more valuable to the
  taxpayer.

- Many tax benefits are currently reduced if the taxpayer's AGI
  exceeds certain specified amounts. Certain other deductions are
  available only to the extent that the amount of such deductions
  exceeds a specified percentage of AGI (a deduction "floor"). Also,
  the deduction for charitable contributions is allowed only to the
  extent that contributions do not exceed a specified percentage of
  AGI (a deduction "ceiling").

The reduction of an individual's AGI results in the increased availability of
other tax benefits. In fact, the maximum allowable reduction of an individual's
AGI is one of the most important individual tax planning objectives.
Above-the-line deductions reduce AGI, while below-the-line deductions do
not.

With a few exceptions, above-the-line deductions generally relate to business
or income-producing activities of the taxpayer. On the other hand, the

majority of the taxpayer's itemized or below-the-line deductions are expenses or losses of a personal nature for which Congress has provided income tax deductions for social and economic policy reasons.

Above-the-Line Deductions. The following expenses are some, though not all, of the more important deductions that are claimed above the line by individual taxpayers. They include:

- all deductions attributable to a trade or business carried on by the taxpayer, if such trade or business does not consist of the performance of services by the taxpayer as an employee
- certain business expenses of employees, including expenses reimbursed by the taxpayer's employer, business expenses of performing artists, and business expenses of certain public officials
- losses from the sale or exchange of property subject to limitations described in the taxation of gains from capital and business assets
- deductions attributable to rents and royalties
- deductible contributions to pension and profit-sharing plans of self-employed individuals
- deductible contributions to IRAs
- penalties or other forfeitures resulting from premature withdrawals from time savings accounts or deposits (including certificates of deposit)
- deductible alimony payments
- the portion of jury duty pay remitted to the taxpayer's employer
- deductible moving expenses
- contributions to medical savings accounts or health savings accounts
- deductible interest payments made on qualified education loans
- qualified tuition and related expenses through 2013
- the deduction for legal costs paid in connection with certain civil rights actions

Deductions

The Standard Deduction and Itemized Deductions

standard deduction

itemized deduction

The standard deduction is a fixed amount that the individual may claim in lieu of claiming *itemized deductions* on Schedule A of Form 1040. Itemized deductions, or deductions taken on Schedule A, include charitable contributions, deductions for interest payments, taxes, casualty losses, certain business expenses of employees, and other items. The amount of the standard deduction depends on the individual's filing status; that is, whether the individual is filing the return as a single taxpayer, an unmarried head of household, a married taxpayer filing jointly, or a married taxpayer filing separately. The 2014 standard deduction for an individual taxpayer is $6,200 and $12,400 for taxpayers that are married filing jointly.

If the individual is entitled to claim itemized deductions that, when added together, are more than the amount of his or her standard deduction, then the individual should deduct his or her itemized deductions and not claim the standard deduction. The standard deduction amounts are indexed annually for inflation.

All itemized deductions are below-the-line deductions (deductions taken in calculating taxable income). However, if these items were above-the-line deductions (deductions taken in determining adjusted gross income rather than taxable income), the taxpayer would deduct these items regardless of whether he or she claims the standard deduction. The standard deduction can be taken in addition to above-the-line deductions. This is the second important difference between above-the-line and below-the-line deductions. The first type are deductible regardless of whether the individual claims the standard deduction. The second type may be claimed only in lieu of the standard deduction.

Categories of Deductions

Before we discuss the various types of deductions that are allowable under federal tax law, it is important to remember that a deduction may be claimed only if there is a specific provision in the Internal Revenue Code that allows it. If there is no provision in the Code regarding a given item, no deduction may be claimed for that item.

Stated broadly, there are three basic categories of deductions allowable to individual taxpayers. The first category includes deductions for expenses that are incurred in the course of carrying on a trade or business. For example, the cost of employees' salaries or advertising would fall into this category. These are referred to as business deductions. The second basic category includes deductions for expenses that are incurred in the course of an activity that is not a trade or business, but is engaged in for the purpose of producing income and making a profit. An example of a deduction falling into this category is an expense incurred in connection with the maintenance of a taxpayer's investments, such as a fee for investment advice. The third basic category includes deductions for expenses that are simply personal, family, or living expenses. Although the Code provides as a general rule that these expenses are nondeductible, there are several important exceptions to the general rule. Personal expenses that are deductible within limitations include charitable contributions, taxes (including state, local, and real estate taxes), out-of-pocket medical expenses, interest payments for home mortgages and home equity lines of credit, and certain student loan interest. However, many of these personal deductions are subject to limitations as to what and how much can be deducted.

Whenever the client or advisor is determining whether a given item of expense is deductible, certain questions should always be asked. Obviously, the first and most basic question is whether the Code allows a deduction for the item. A second important question is what basic category the expense falls under; in other words, whether it is a *business expense,* an *expense for the production of income,* or a *personal expense.* A third question is whether the deduction is an above-the-line or below-the-line deduction. It is always important for tax planning purposes to know where an item will appear on the individual's tax return.

A fourth question that should be asked is whether there is a particular restriction or limitation on the deductibility of the item. For example, certain deductions such as the medical expense deduction and the casualty loss deduction are subject to a floor. This floor is based on a percentage of the taxpayer's adjusted gross income. If the taxpayer's expenses in a given category are less than the applicable floor, no deduction will actually be allowed for the expenses.

EXAMPLE
Trish has medical expenses of $5,000 in 2013. Medical expenses are deductible, but only to the extent they exceed 10 percent of the taxpayer's adjusted gross income. Trish's adjusted gross income this year is $70,000. Although Trish has $5,000 of medical expenses, her deduction for these expenses is zero because the amount of the expenses ($5,000) is less than 10 percent of her adjusted gross income ($7,000).

Other types of restrictions may apply to particular deduction items. For example, cash contributions to a public charity are generally deductible, but only up to a maximum of 50 percent of an individual's adjusted gross income for any given year. Contributions in excess of that amount must be carried over to future taxable years. In the case of charitable contributions, the individual's adjusted gross income provides a ceiling for the deduction, rather than a floor.

Another type of restriction that may apply to a deduction is a dollar-amount restriction. An example of this restriction is the rule for deducting interest payments on a taxpayer's first mortgage on his or her principal residence. Generally such payments are deductible, but only with respect to a maximum of $1 million of loan principal. If the first mortgage exceeds $1 million, a corresponding portion of the interest deduction is disallowed. Note that in the case of the deduction for home mortgage interest, the dollar amount limitation is based on the amount of the loan principal, not the amount of the interest expense itself. Another example of a dollar-amount limitation is the limitation on deductible contributions to a traditional individual retirement account (IRA) that may be available to individuals who are not covered by employer-provided retirement plans and by certain other individuals whose income falls within specified ranges.

Yet another type of restriction on the deductibility of certain expenses is a percentage limitation. For example, business entertainment expenses are generally deductible, but the deduction is limited to 50 percent of the actual expenses. There are many other ways in which the Internal Revenue Code limits the claiming of deductions.

Impairment-Related Work Expenses. Any expense incurred that is necessary for a disabled person to work may be deductible. These expenses are called impairment related work expenses. These expenses are considered business expenses, therefore they are not subject to the 10 percent AGI limit that applies to medical expenses.

Impairment-related expenses defined. Impairment-related expenses are those ordinary and necessary business expenses that are:

- necessary for you to do your work satisfactorily
- for goods and services not required or used, other than incidentally, in your personal activities, and
- not specifically covered under other income tax laws

Medical Expense Deductions. Individuals can claim an itemized deduction for the unreimbursed medical expenses for themselves and their dependents in excess of 10 percent of adjusted gross income. The more typical expenses which qualify for deduction are payments to health-care providers, treatment facilities, prescription drugs, therapies, and health care premiums.

Medical Conferences and Seminars. Parents of special needs children often attend medical conferences and seminars in order to learn more about their child's disability. The amounts paid for the registration fees and travel expenses are deductible as medical expenses (*Revenue Ruling 2000-24, 2000-19 I.R.B. 963*). However, parents should obtain the recommendation of their child's doctor to insure their medical deduction. In addition, the deduction may not extend to any meals and/or lodging costs incurred while attending the conference. Furthermore, the conference or seminar must deal specifically with the medical condition from which the child suffers, not just general health and well-being issues. As with the special instruction and other medical expenses, the aggregate amount of all medical expenses incurred must exceed 10 percent of the taxpayers' AGI to be deductible.

Special Instruction Qualifying as Medical Expense Deductions. In general, costs related to providing a child's traditional education are not considered medical care and, therefore, are not deductible. However, the unreimbursed cost of attending a *special school* for a neurologically or physically handicapped individual is deductible as a medical expense if the principal reason for the individual's attendance is to alleviate the handicap through the resources of the school or institution (Treasury Regulation 1.213-1(e)(1)(v)). This deduction may also include amounts paid for lodging, meals, transportation, and the cost of ordinary education incidental to the special services provided by the school. Also, any costs incurred for the supervision, care, treatment and training of a physically and/or neurologically handicapped individual are deductible if provided by the institution.

Under U.S. law, all children are entitled to an equal and appropriate (public) education. However, many public schools do not have special programs and/or facilities to handle the needs of neurologically and/or physically handicapped children. As a result, it is sometimes necessary for neurologically or physically handicapped children to attend special schools where the focus is not only on education, but also on alleviating the handicap of the child. The cost of these special schools is not always covered by the government or the school district and, therefore, the parents must pay for all or a portion of the tuition. If the school qualifies as a special school, the entire unreimbursed cost (subject to the 10 percent AGI limitation) incurred by the parents is deductible as a medical expense. Parents who are eligible to participate in tax-advantaged plans through work for funding medical expenses, such as flexible spending accounts or health savings accounts can set aside limited amounts of money to finance medical care expenses on a pretax basis while bypassing the 10 percent AGI limitation.

A *special school* is distinguishable from a regular school by the substantive content of its curriculum. A special school may offer ordinary education, but it must be incidental to enabling the student to compensate for or overcome a handicap so that he or she will be prepared for future normal education or normal living. A special school is not determined by the institution as a whole, but by the nature of the services received by the individual for whom a medical care deduction is sought. The IRS considers the medical facilities and therapeutic orientation of a school as critical factors in determining whether a school is a special school for a qualifying medical care deduction. Case law and IRS administrative rulings reveal a litany of examples considered special schools by the IRS:

- schools for teaching Braille to the blind or lip reading to the deaf
- schools for training the mentally retarded
- a military school that accepted a physically and mentally handicapped student (the school gave personal daily attention to the student to improve upon the student's low attention span)
- a boarding school recommended by a psychiatrist (the school had psychiatrists, psychologists, and social workers who developed a special program for each student)
- schools for average and above average students with learning disabilities which provide an environment in which they can adjust to a normal competitive classroom situation, and

- a regular school's curriculum that is specially designed to accommodate the needs of handicapped children with IQ scores ranging from 50 to 75

Furthermore, regular schools with special curricula can be classified as a special school for an individual. For example, in one Revenue Ruling, the school in question had a special curriculum for neurologically disabled children with the special curriculum representing a separate component of the school's activities. Since the school's special education curriculum was a severable aspect of the school's activities, the IRS ruled that the special curriculum was a special school (*Rev. Rul. 70-285,* 1970-1 CB 52).

In another case, the IRS specifically ruled that a taxpayer whose child suffers from severe learning disabilities caused by a neurological disorder (that is, autism spectrum disorder) may deduct as a medical expense amounts paid for tuition and related fees for the child's education at a special school that has a program designed to "mainstream" these children so they can return to a regular school (*Rev. Rul. 78-340,* 1978-2 CB 124). The Ruling further held that amounts paid for private tutoring by a specially trained teacher (that is, therapeutic and behavioral support services) qualified to deal with severe learning disabilities is also deductible. However, both the special school and tutoring need to be recommended by a physician.

In another case, the IRS expanded the definition of special schooling to include tuition for programs enabling dyslexic children to deal with their condition. The IRS ruled that a medical expense deduction was justified when children were attending the school for the principal purpose of obtaining medical care in the form of special education. The special education was required for the years in which the children were diagnosed as having a medical condition (including dyslexia) that impaired their ability to learn (Letter Ruling 200521003).

Reimbursements for Medical Expenses. A taxpayer may be reimbursed by an insurance company or other institution for deductible medical expenses. If a reimbursement is received in the year of the medical expense, the itemized medical expense deduction is simply reduced by the amount of reimbursement. If the reimbursement is received in a year after medical expenses were incurred and deducted, some or all of the reimbursement may be included in income for the year in which the reimbursement was received. The amount included in income for the year is the lesser of:

- the reimbursement amount;

- the excess of total itemized deductions over the standard deduction, or
- itemized medical deductions for the prior year

Personal and Dependency Exemptions

Each individual taxpayer is allowed to claim a *personal exemption* for himself or herself. A married couple filing jointly may claim an exemption for each spouse. The amount of the exemption or exemptions is subtracted from adjusted gross income in the process of computing taxable income. Personal exemptions are not itemized deductions claimed on Schedule A of Form 1040, however. Therefore, either the standard deduction or itemized deductions may be claimed in addition to the taxpayer's exemptions.

Individual taxpayers are also permitted to claim a *dependency exemption* for each dependent individual who is supported by the taxpayer. There are strict rules regarding whom a taxpayer may claim as a dependent and under what circumstances. Usually, the IRS requires that a dependency exemption may only be claimed by a taxpayer if the dependent meets the following requirements: The dependent must be (a) under age 19 at the end of the year and younger than you (or your spouse, if filing jointly), (b) under age 24 at the end of the year, a student, and younger than you (or your spouse, if filing jointly), or (c) any age if permanently and totally disabled. The definition of permanently and totally disabled for a dependency exemption is the same as that used for a qualifying child.

The personal and dependency exemption for 2014 is $3,950. The exemption amount changes annually by way of an inflation adjustment.

The Dependency Exemption

qualifying child   In order to claim a dependency exemption ($3,950 for 2014), a taxpayer must satisfy a five-prong test—support, relationship, gross income, joint return, and citizenship. Briefly stated, the taxpayer must provide more than half of the dependent's support. The dependent must be a "qualifying relative" or member of the taxpayer's household for the entire year. The dependent's gross income cannot exceed the exemption amount ($3,950 for 2014). If married, the dependent cannot file a joint return for the year unless the only purpose for the return is to claim a refund. The dependent must be a U.S. citizen or resident or resident of Canada or Mexico. With passage of the Working Families Tax Relief Act of 2004 (taking effect for 2005 and years thereafter), the definition of a "qualifying child" and "qualifying relative" was clarified to provide a uniform definition for purposes of dependency exemptions, child tax, dependent care, and earned income tax credits. Under this definition, in addition to meeting the relationship test [taxpayer's child, stepchild, eligible foster child, or descendent (for example, grandchild) or taxpayer's brother, sister, or descendent (for example, niece, nephew)], a "qualifying child" must meet any ONE of the following three requirements. Either the "child" must be under the age of 19 at year end; or the "child" must be a full-time student under the age of 24 at the end of the year (qualifying "students" must be enrolled as a "full-time" student during any part of five calendar months during the year); or *the individual must be totally and permanently disabled at any time during the year.*

It is important to note that grandparents, uncles, aunts, brothers and sisters satisfy this "relationship" test and, therefore, may be allowed to claim the dependency exemption for a "qualifying child" who is totally or permanently disabled, regardless of the age of that child. Furthermore, while Section 152(c)(3) was amended for tax years beginning in 2009 to require that the qualifying child be younger than the individual claiming the dependency exemption, this does not apply to a child who is permanently and totally disabled. Age is simply not a relevant factor in determining the dependency exemption of an individual who is totally or permanently disabled. The AGI phaseout for exemptions goes from at $254,200 to $376,700 for individual taxpayers and from $305,050 to $427,550 for married taxpayers filing jointly.

Tax Rates and Brackets

Once the taxpayer's gross income has been determined, all deductions allowable in determining adjusted gross income are subtracted from gross income. Next, all deductions and exemptions allowable in determining taxable income are subtracted from adjusted gross income. The resulting figure is the taxpayer's taxable income. This is the figure to which the income tax rates are applied to determine the amount of income tax payable for the year.

Under the law currently in effect, the income tax on ordinary income (as distinguished from capital gain) is imposed under a seven bracket system with the lowest bracket's rate being 10 percent. The next five brackets' rates are 15 percent, 25 percent, 28 percent, 33 percent, and 35 percent, respectively. The highest bracket's rate is 39.6 percent. The tax rate applicable to each income bracket is called the *marginal tax rate.* The amount of taxable income subject to each marginal tax rate for each *filing status* is referred to as a *tax bracket*. The brackets are indexed annually for inflation.

These brackets of taxable income to which the various rates are applied depend on the individual's filing status. As previously mentioned, an individual taxpayer is categorized within one of four filing status categories: a single taxpayer, a married taxpayer filing jointly, a married taxpayer filing separately, or an unmarried head of household. The amount of taxable income that will fall into each tax bracket varies according to the individual's filing status.

It should be noted that an upper-income taxpayer's *effective marginal tax rate* may be higher than his or her statutory marginal rate. This can happen as a result of the rules that limit or reduce certain deductions and/or exclusions as a taxpayer's adjusted gross income increases. The effective marginal rate for an upper-income taxpayer depends on a number of factors, including the level of adjusted gross income and the nature and amount of exclusions, deductions, and exemptions claimed by the taxpayer. A specific calculation of the effective marginal rate is beyond the scope of this reading. However, the reader should be aware of the potential distinction between a statutory marginal tax rate and an effective marginal tax rate.

2014 Federal Tax Brackets				
Tax Rate	Single	Married Filing Jointly and Surviving Spouses	Married Filing Separately	Head of Household
10%	$ - - $ 9,075	$ - - $ 18,150	$ - - $ 9,075	$ - - $ 12,950
15%	$ 9,076 - $ 36,900	$ 18,151 - $ 73,800	$ 9,076 - $ 36,900	$ 12,951 - $ 49,400
25%	$ 36,901 - $ 89,350	$ 73,801 - $148,850	$ 36,901 - $ 74,425	$ 49,401 - $127,550
28%	$ 89,351 - $186,350	$148,851 - $226,850	$ 74,426 - $113,425	$127,551 - $206,600
33%	$186,351 - $405,100	$226,851 - $405,100	$113,426 - $202,550	$206,601 - $405,100
35%	$405,101 - $406,750	$405,101 - $457,600	$202,551 - $228,800	$405,101 - $432,200
40%	over $406,750	over $457,600	over $228,800	over $432,200

Unearned Income Medicare Contributions Tax

Effective 2013, some individuals will be subject to the Unearned Income Medicare Contribution tax on unearned income. This tax applies to single taxpayers with a modified adjusted gross income (MAGI) in excess of $200,000 ($250,000 for taxpayers married filing jointly, or $125,000 if filing a separate return). For most individuals, MAGI will be their adjusted gross income unless they are U.S. citizens or residents living abroad and have foreign earned income. The tax is 3.8 percent of the lesser of net investment income or the amount by which MAGI exceeds the applicable threshold. Net investment income includes certain types of interest, dividends, annuities, royalties, and rents, and income from a passive activity or a trade or business of trading in financial instruments or commodities. Net gain realized on the disposition of property other than property held in an active trade or business is subject to this tax. The taxable gain on the sale of a personal residence in excess of the Sec. 121 exclusion would be included.

Tax Credits

Families with special needs individuals may be eligible for tax credits. As opposed to tax deductions, which work by lowering taxable income, tax credits directly reduce the amount of tax due on a dollar-for-dollar basis.

Child Tax Credit

Certain credits may be available to parents of special needs children. The most common of these credits is the $1,000 Child Tax credit which is allowed for the taxpayer's "qualifying child" under the age of 17. The definition of a "qualifying child" used for purposes of claiming a dependency exemption under IRC Sec. 151 is the same as that used for purposes of claiming the child tax credit. Consequently, the taxpayer claiming the dependency exemption for the child is the individual entitled to the credit. Prior to 2009, a child qualifying for the child tax credit was not required to be claimed as a dependent. *The Fostering Connections to Success and Increasing Adoptions Act of 2008* added this additional condition. This is important to consider in cases involving divorced, separated, or unmarried parents.

Phaseout of the Tax Credit for Children. The credit is phased-out for upper-income taxpayers. The phaseout occurs based on the taxpayer's adjusted gross income (AGI) with certain minor modifications ("modified adjusted gross income"). The phaseout begins at the following levels of modified AGI:

Married filing joint return	$110,000
Married filing separately	$ 55,000
Unmarried taxpayers	$ 75,000

The otherwise allowable credit is phased out by $50 for each $1,000 (or fraction thereof) by which modified AGI exceeds the threshold amount. For example, a married couple filing jointly with one child this year would have no child credit if their modified AGI was more than $129,000. This is because their AGI exceeds $110,000 by $19,000 plus a fraction of $1,000. Therefore the credit is phased out by 20 x $50, or $1,000, the total amount of the credit.

The credit is phased out sequentially (rather than simultaneously) per child for taxpayers with more than one child. Therefore, taxpayers with more than one child will have a larger "phaseout range" for the credits.

In addition, the child tax credit is partially refundable to the extent of the greater of:

1. 15 percent of earned income above $3,000, or
2. for taxpayers with three or more qualifying children, the excess of the taxpayer's Social Security taxes for the tax year over the earned income credit for the year, or the 15 percent method from above (IRC Sec. 24(d)).

Child and Dependent Care Credit

Note

Sources for Child Care Credit and Child and Dependent Care Credit: IRS, Instructions for Form 1040, Form 2441, and Form 8812, and IRS Revenue Procedures 2007-66 and 2008-66.

The Child and Dependent Care credit applies to expenses paid by individual taxpayers for the care of their dependents. Its purpose is to provide a tax credit for working parents with children in day care facilities. The amount of the credit currently ranges from 20 to 35 percent of qualifying expenses based on the taxpayer's income level. The qualifying expenses upon which the credit percentages are based are subject to certain dollar amount limitations as explained below.

Eligible Expenses for the Credit. As stated above, the expenses must be incurred to allow the taxpayer to be gainfully employed for the credit to be available. The expenses must be paid by a taxpayer who has a household in which one or more "qualifying individuals" resides for more than half of the taxable year. Expenses must be paid either for household services or specifically for the care of a qualifying individual. A qualifying individual must fall within one of the following definitions:

1. the taxpayer's "qualifying child" who is under the age of 13

2. an individual who is *physically or mentally incapable of caring* for himself or herself and is also the taxpayer's dependent for tax purposes

3. the taxpayer's spouse who is *physically or mentally incapable of caring* for himself or herself.

As a general rule, the expenses must be paid for services rendered inside the taxpayer's home, unless the services are for the care of either the taxpayer's dependent child who is under the age of 13 (that is, day care services), or for the care of another qualifying individual who regularly spends at least 8 hours per day in the taxpayer's household. If the child has a disability and requires supervision, the age limit is waived. For example, a 16 year-old child with autism and behavioral disorders who is incapable of self-care and cannot be left unattended would qualify his or her parents for this credit. In no event, however, will expenses paid for an overnight camp be eligible expenses for the credit.

In addition, child-care related expenses are disallowed if paid to certain related individuals. Eligible expenses do not include payments for care provided by a child of the taxpayer who is under the age of 19 (such as a sister or brother of the qualifying individual). Also, eligible expenses do not include those paid for services rendered by any individual who is a dependent of the taxpayer for dependency exemption purposes. The purpose of this rule is to prevent child-care payments made to certain family members from generating a tax credit.

There is a limit on the amount of expenses that can be counted in calculating the allowable credit. For taxpayers caring for one qualifying individual, the maximum amount is $3,000 per year. If there are two or more qualifying individuals, the maximum amount is $6,000. As an additional limitation, qualifying expenses may not exceed the amount of the taxpayer's earned income for the year.

Calculation of the Credit. The allowable credit currently ranges from 20 to 35 percent of eligible expenses. The allowable percentage is reduced by one percent for each $2,000 (or fraction thereof) of adjusted gross income in excess of $15,000. The credit is fully reduced to 20 percent once the taxpayer's AGI exceeds $43,000.

Coordination with Dependent-Care Assistance Programs. The same eligible expenses cannot be used for both the dependent-care credit and the income tax exclusion for amounts received from an employer-provided dependent-care assistance program. In addition, if a taxpayer is a participant in such a program, the maximum amount of qualifying expenses for credit purposes is reduced dollar for dollar paid from the employer program and excluded from the taxpayer's gross income. As a result, taxpayers are often forced to choose between the income tax exclusion for such plans and the dependent-care credit. Generally speaking, if a married taxpayer or head of household is in a marginal tax bracket of 25 percent or higher, the exclusion provides a more effective method of funding dependent-care expenses than the otherwise available credit amount.

Additional Rules for Married Couples. Special rules apply to married couples claiming the dependent-care credit, and include:

- Married couples must generally file a joint return to be eligible for the credit. However, if the spouses live apart for the last 6 months of the taxable year, the credit may be available even if separate returns are filed.

- Eligible expenses are limited to the earned income of the spouse with the lower earned income. Therefore, generally speaking, both spouses must be working to claim the credit, although there is no requirement of full-time employment.

- A significant exception to the rule just described involves spouses who are either full-time students for at least 5 calendar months during the year or who are incapable of self-care during the year. Such spouses are currently deemed to have a monthly earned income of $250 for each month during which they are students or incapable of self-care. If there are two or more qualifying individuals in the household, then such spouses are currently deemed to have $500 per month of earned income.

Tax Credit for Adoption Expenses

An Adoption Credit was signed into law in 2002. This credit of up to $13,190 per eligible child (for 2014) is available for qualified expenses paid in the course of adopting a child. This figure is subject to annual inflation adjustments. The limit on the credit is a cumulative limit per child. In other words, no more than the maximum amount may be claimed for any one child regardless of the number of years for which the credit is claimed for that child. Nevertheless, an additional credit may be claimed for the adoption of more than one child. Similar to other credits, the adoption credit is phased-out for upper-income taxpayers. However, the phaseout income level is significantly higher than other credits. More important in the context of this discussion, the credit has a unique application for adoptions of children with special needs.

Definition of an "Eligible Child". An *eligible child* is a person who is either under the age of 18 or is physically or neurologically incapable of self-care. A *child with special needs* is defined as a citizen or resident of the United States who is determined by state authorities to be unable to be placed for adoption without adoption assistance. Requirements for such a determination by state authorities include findings that the child should not be returned to his or her biological parents, and that there is a specific factor or condition that makes the child unable to be placed without adoption assistance.

Qualified Adoption Expenses. It is important for individuals considering adoption or in the process of adoption to understand what expenses qualify for the credit. *Qualified adoption expenses* include legal fees, court costs, attorney fees, and other related fees and costs that have the principal purpose of a taxpayer's legal adoption of an eligible child or a child with special needs. However, costs associated with the adoption of a child of the taxpayer's spouse or costs for surrogate parenting arrangements are not qualified expenses for purposes of the credit.

Special Rule for Adoptions of Children with Special Needs. For adoptions of children other than special needs children, the amount of the credit depends on the amount of qualified expenses. By contrast, the full amount of the adoption credit is allowed to taxpayers adopting a special needs child regardless of the amount of qualified adoption expenses paid by the taxpayer. This means that taxpayers will be eligible for the maximum credit even if they have little or even no actual adoption expenses. Special needs adoptions are typically less expensive than other adoptions. Congress enacted this provision to help taxpayers who have decided to adopt special needs children and to encourage these adoptions.

When to Claim the Adoption Credit . For tax years in which an adoption becomes final, the taxpayer is allowed to claim the credit for expenses paid during that year. For years in which qualified expenses are paid but in which the adoption does not become final, the taxpayer must claim the credit for those expenses for the tax year following the year in which the expenses are paid. If expenses are paid in a year following the year the adoption becomes final, the expenses may be claimed for the year in which they are made.

Foreign adoptions or adoptions of a child with special needs qualify for the credit only if the adoption becomes final and must it be claimed in that year even if paid in a prior year.

There is a 5-year carryover period available for taxpayers whose allowable adoption credit exceeds their tax liability for the year the credit is first allowable.

Phaseout of Credit. The adoption credit is phased-out for taxpayers with adjusted gross income exceeding $197,880 for 2014. The credit is completely phased-out at $40,000 above the threshold. Adjusted gross income for this purpose is determined with certain minor modifications similar to those used for the tax credit for children.

To calculate the amount of the credit that is phased out, divide the amount of the taxpayer's adjusted gross income in excess of $197,880 by $40,000. Then multiply the resulting percentage by the otherwise allowable amount of the credit.

Related Income Exclusion. In planning for the adoption credit, it is important to note that an *income exclusion* is available for amounts paid by a taxpayer's employer for qualified adoption expenses on behalf of the taxpayer/employee. Such amounts must be furnished under a nondiscriminatory adoption assistance program. However, the exclusion for adopting a special needs child applies regardless of whether the employee has qualified adoption expenses. The rules defining and limiting this exclusion for adoption assistance payments are similar to the rules just described for application of the adoption credit. For example, the dollar amounts of the available exclusion are the same as the dollar amounts of the credit. Any amounts excluded from gross income under such a program are not eligible to be treated as qualified adoption expenses for purposes of the adoption credit.

The Alternative Minimum Tax (AMT)

alternative minimum tax (AMT)

The *alternative minimum tax (AMT)* is a separate and parallel system of income taxation to the regular system. It applies to any taxpayer whose tax liability under the parallel system is greater than the liability for that year under the regular income tax system. In other words, the taxpayer pays the AMT amount if the AMT is greater than the regular tax. Therefore, it follows that the computational process for determining the AMT is a different process from that used in determining the regular tax. The deduction rules are different. The credit rules are different. The tax rates and brackets are different.

The purpose of the AMT is to make certain that taxpayers who enjoy certain tax benefits will not be permitted to reduce their tax liability below a minimum amount by claiming certain tax deductions. For example, one thing that the AMT rules do is to add back certain deductions (such as personal exemptions and state and local taxes) for AMT purposes that are allowable to the taxpayer for regular tax purposes. These items that are deductible for the regular tax, but face different rules under the AMT, are referred to as *tax preference items.* These items generally produce no benefit or a lesser benefit to the taxpayer under the AMT system as compared to their treatment under the regular tax system.

Items of Tax Preference

Some of the more significant tax-preference (and adjustment) items that are handled differently in computing AMTI as compared with taxable income for regular tax purposes are as follows:

- Some itemized deductions allowable on Schedule A of Form 1040 for regular tax purposes cannot be claimed for AMT purposes; that is, they are tax-preference items. Deductions for state and local taxes or sales taxes, real estate taxes, and miscellaneous itemized deductions are examples of itemized deductions not allowable for AMT purposes. However, certain itemized deductions of individuals *are* permitted to be claimed as deductions in calculating AMTI. These include:
  - charitable contributions
  - casualty and theft losses
  - interest on indebtedness used to acquire or improve a qualified residence of the taxpayer
  - investment interest not in excess of qualified net investment income
  - the deduction for estate taxes attributable to income in respect of a decedent
  - medical expenses deductible for regular tax purposes. Note, however, that the deduction "floor" for medical expenses under the AMT rules is 10 percent as distinguished from the 7.5 percent floor that applies for

        regular tax purposes for taxpayers who are 65 and older at the close of a tax year

The overall limitation on itemized deductions does *not* apply in calculating AMTI.

- The standard deduction is not allowable in computing AMTI. If an individual taxpayer uses the standard deduction for regular tax purposes, the amount of the standard deduction is added back to taxable income in calculating AMTI.

- Personal and dependency exemptions are not allowable in computing AMTI. Like the standard deduction, any exemption amounts claimed for regular tax purposes must be added to the taxpayer's regular taxable income in calculating AMTI .

- When the actual value of an incentive stock option at the time the option holder's rights become nonforfeitable exceeds the price paid for the option, the excess must be included in calculating AMTI.

- Certain research and experimental costs paid by individuals who own interests in a business in which they do not materially participate and have deducted must be capitalized and amortized over a 10-year period in computing AMTI.

- Certain publishing circulation expenses that individuals incur are not allowable in computing AMTI.

- A portion of certain deductions for depreciation allowable for regular tax purposes is not allowable for AMT purposes. For example, in claiming deductions for depreciation on real property, only straight-line depreciation using a 40-year recovery period is allowable in calculating AMTI. Any excess of that amount claimed for regular tax purposes is disallowed. Also, with respect to depreciable personal property placed in service after 1998, the 150 percent declining-balance method (switching to straight-line depreciation) must be substituted for property that qualifies for the 200 percent declining-balance method for regular tax purposes. Certain different adjustments were made to depreciation deductions for personal property placed in service before 1999. These adjustments apply to both individuals and corporations. However, "bonus" depreciation is allowed in full for purposes of the AMT.

- Interest on nongovernmental purpose bonds (that is, private activity bonds) issued after August 7, 1986, that is excludible from gross income for regular tax purposes must be included in the calculation of AMTI by both individuals and corporations (except for bonds issued in 2009 and 2010).

- Other deductions allowable for regular tax purposes are disallowed or otherwise partially restricted for AMT purposes for both individuals and corporations. These preference items include:
  - – amortization of pollution-control facilities
  - – mining exploration costs
  - – certain intangible drilling costs incurred by businesses engaged in the extractive industries

The AMTI Exemption

After AMTI is calculated, it may be reduced by an exemption amount. The applicable exemption amount is determined by the taxpayer's filing status and is phased out for upper-income taxpayers. The phaseout of the AMTI exemption is determined by calculating the amount of the taxpayer's AMTI that is in excess of a specified threshold amount and then multiplying that excess by 25 percent. The resulting figure is the amount of the AMTI exemption that is disallowed. If the amount disallowed is more than the AMTI exemption, then the exemption is zero.

For the tax year 2014, the exemption amounts and the threshold amounts for phasing out the exemption are shown in the following table:

Filing Status	Exemption Amount	Phaseout Threshold
Married filing jointly	$82,100	$156,500
Single and head of household	52,800	117,300
Married filing separately	41,050	78,250
Estate or trust	23,500	78,250

AMT Tax Rates

Once the taxpayer's AMTI has been reduced by the applicable exemption amount, the amount of the remaining AMTI, or tentative minimum taxable income (AMT base) is multiplied by the applicable alternative minimum tax rate to arrive at the tentative minimum tax (TMT). The applicable rates are shown in the following table:

Taxpayer	AMT Tax Rate
Individuals other than married filing separately	26 percent of the first $182,500
	28 percent of the excess over $182,500
Married filing separately	26 percent of the first $91,250
	28 percent of the excess over $91,250
Corporations	20 percent

Individuals who have net long-term capital gains or qualified dividends for regular tax purposes receive the benefit of a lower maximum tax rate on such gains and dividend income. Those lower maximum rates also apply to those categories of income for AMT purposes. Therefore, if a taxpayer has long-term capital gains or qualified dividend income, the AMT will not result in a higher tax rate on those items. *Note: the inclusion of net long-term capital gains and qualifying dividend income in the AMTI calculation can result in loss of the AMT exemption by increasing AMTI.*

Tax Credits

The tax credit for children and the adoption credit may be used to offset AMT liability as well as liability for the regular tax. Also, any foreign tax credit allowable in computing the regular tax may be used to offset AMT liability. However, the overall credits cannot exceed the sum of both the regular tax liability (less the foreign tax credit) and the excess of the Tentative Minimum Tax (AMT amount multiplied by the applicable tax rate) over the regular tax (the AMT).

Chapter Review

Review questions are based on the learning objectives in this chapter. Thus, a [3] at the end of a question means that the question is based on learning objective 3. If there are multiple objectives, they are all listed.

Key Terms and Concepts

gross income
deduction
tax-exempt
tax-deferred
nonrecognition transactions
capital losses
taxable gain
taxable loss
basis
ordinary gain or loss

capital gain or loss
qualified dividends
adjusted gross income
adjusted gross income (AGI)
above-the-line deductions
below-the-line deductions
standard deduction
itemized deduction
qualifying child
alternative minimum tax (AMT)

Review Questions

1. Describe how a taxpayer's basis on a piece of property is relevant in a tax computation. [1]

2. Describe a limitation in the use of capital losses to reduce a taxpayer's tax due. [1]

3. What is the purpose of Adjusted Gross Income (AGI)? [2]

4. Describe the relationship between above-the-line deductions, below-the-line deductions, and itemized and standard deductions. [2, 3]

5. Describe the restrictions that may be imposed on a deduction. [3]

6. A 28-year-old special needs female lives with her parents full time. She is totally and permanently disabled. Her parents provide 100 percent of her financial support. The female is not married, earned $2,000 of income for the year, and is a U.S. citizen. Can her parents claim a dependency exemption for her in 2014? [5]

7. Mary has an autistic child and wants to attend a conference on autism. What expenses will be deductible, and what requirements must Mary meet in order to deduct those expenses? [4]

8. What requirements must be met for a taxpayer to deduct the cost of his child's special education? [4]

9. How should a taxpayer treat a reimbursement for medical expenses received in the year after he deducted those medical expenses on his tax return? [4]

10. A taxpayer has a 20-year-old child with a disability and hires a caretaker to care for the child for 10 hours during the day while he is at work. May the taxpayer claim the dependent care credit on his tax return for the cost of these services? [4]

11. A married couple adopted a special needs child from the state agency who is a U.S. citizen. The adoption became final in 2014. The couple has incurred $10,500 in qualified expenses relating to the adoption in 2013 and $2,000 in 2014. How much can the couple claim for the adoption credit in 2014? [6]

Learning Objectives

An understanding of the material in this chapter should enable you to

1. Describe the purpose of essential documents used in the estate planning process.

2. Consider the impact of estate planning tools on a client's estate, such as the federal estate tax exemption, marital deduction, trusts, and gifts.

3. Describe how life insurance can be used advantageously in planning a client's estate.

4. Describe the residential care alternatives for a special needs individual, and describe the factors for choosing among these alternatives.

5. Explain the purpose and significance of a letter of intent.

6. Identify the important government benefits available to families with members who have disabilities.

7. Explain how an individual's disability is established within the rules of the Social Security system.

8. Understand the operation of the Social Security Disability Income (SSDI) and Supplemental Security Income (SSI) systems.

9. Explain the basics of the Medicare and Medicaid government programs.

10. Describe the impact of gifts to a special needs individual through UGMA or UTMA accounts.

11. Describe the methods that might be used to transfer assets from a special needs individual.

12. Describe the purpose and types of special needs trusts (SNTs) in relation to qualification for SSI or Medicaid.

13. Discuss the unique considerations of an ILIT intended to be designed as a third party supplemental needs trust benefitting a special needs family member.

Estate Planning Documents

The estate plan is a road map directing how the client's wealth will be assembled and disposed of during the client's life or at his or her death. The plan itself is useless unless the documents of the plan have been drafted appropriately. The documents must be drafted carefully to avoid hidden traps and to provide direction to the appropriate personal representatives, fiduciaries, and beneficiaries of the client. These directions must be drafted according to the principles of state law and should unambiguously state the intent of the client. Since these documents necessarily involve compliance with state law, they should be prepared by an attorney who specializes in estate planning in the local jurisdiction.

The Client's Will

Despite the importance of the will in a client's estate plan, it is estimated that seven out of ten Americans die without a valid will. Unfortunately these individuals have left the disposition of their estates to the provisions of state intestacy law. In addition, the estates of these individuals will be handled by a court-appointed administrator. In many cases the estate will be subject to unnecessary taxes and administration expenses. In any event, a valid will is necessary for the implementation of a cohesive estate plan.

What Can a Valid Will Accomplish?

The client's will is the centerpiece of the estate plan. Although its primary function is to direct the disposition of the client's wealth, it serves other purposes as well. A properly drafted will can accomplish the following objectives:

- direct the disposition of the client's probate assets
- nominate the personal representative of the testator, known as the executor, who will handle the administration of the client's estate
- nominate the guardians of any minor children of the testator
- create testamentary trusts that will take effect at the testator's death to hold the property of the testator for the benefit of named beneficiaries
- name the trustee of any trust created under the will
- provide directions to the executor and/or trustees named in the will indicating how these fiduciaries will manage assets contained in the estate or testamentary trust. (The directions could be quite specific or provide broad powers to the fiduciaries.)

- provide directions for payment of the estate's taxes and expenses. (Care should be taken in naming the components of the estate that will be responsible for taxes and expenses. Incorrect designation of the component obligated to pay such expenses could result in increased death taxes or inappropriately diminished shares of specific beneficiaries.)
- establish the compensation of executors and/or trustees named in the will

Requirements for a Valid Will

Although the requirements for wills are provided by the laws of the various states, several items are universal. With some minor exceptions for rare circumstances the following are required for a valid will:

- The will must be in writing.
- The testator, or creator of the will, must sign the will at the end of the document, usually in the presence of witnesses.
- A number of witnesses (generally two or three) must sign the will after the testator's signature. The witnesses are attesting that the signature of the testator is in fact his or her signature.

Planning for the Federal Estate Tax

All individuals who are citizens or residents of the United States at the time of their deaths are subject to the federal estate tax. However, each decedent is permitted to transfer an "exemption amount" free from federal estate taxes due to the applicable credit. This exemption amount shelters $5 million from tax for deaths after 2009. The exemption amount is indexed annually for inflation ($5,340,000 2014 indexed amount). With appropriate planning, this exemption would result in significant estate-tax savings. This tax savings could even be greater if the funds exempted at the death of the first spouse appreciate in value before the death of the surviving spouse.

Flexibility is Critical

The tax savings provided by the exemption are too good to pass up for most families. However, most people are resistant to tak significant steps that might be irrevocable in implementing an estate plan. The uncertainty of the future for federal estate tax law has provided an additional motive to procrastinate. It is essential that any plan can be altered to adapt to potential tax changes.

More importantly, flexibility is critical to meet the family's needs since trust planning could be implemented to last for the surviving spouse's lifetime and maybe much longer in the case of generation-skipping trusts. We need to ensure that the support needs of the beneficiaries will be met over the intended time horizon.

Coordinating the Marital Deduction and the Estate Tax Exemption

Congress provided a complete estate-tax exemption for property transferred during life and at death to the transferor's spouse through an estate or gift tax marital deduction. However, the property is included in the transferee-spouse's estate and subject to applicable estate taxes at that time. At the first death, the deceased spouse will waste the estate tax exemption if all property is transferred to the surviving spouse under the protection of the marital deduction. This enhances the value of the second estate and the tax savings discussed in the previous paragraph will be unavailable.

To provide for optimal tax planning, it is essential that the first spouse to die leaves as much as possible up to the exemption amount ($5,340,000 2014 indexed amount) in a manner that fails to qualify for the estate tax marital deduction. Here are some transfer choices that would permit the use of the unified credit:

- bypass the surviving spouse entirely and leave the exemption amount ($5,340,000 2014 indexed amount) to other heirs
- create a trust that benefits both the surviving spouse and other heirs under the discretion of the trustee
- create a trust that provides income only to the surviving spouse while he or she is alive with the remainder passing to heirs selected by the transferor
- create a trust that provides the surviving spouse with all income and as much principal as necessary for the support, education, and maintenance of the surviving spouse while he or she is alive with the remainder passing to heirs selected by the transferor

The Unified Credit Trust

The exemption trust bypasses estate taxes in both estates for a married couple. The normal strategy is to provide a significant growth element to this trust. Discretionary gifts or expenditures by the surviving spouse should be made from the survivor's funds or the marital share left to the survivor by the first-to-die since these assets will be subject to estate taxes at the second death. For this reason, it is generally recommended that qualified retirement plans or IRAs should not be used to fund the exemption (bypass) trust except as a last resort. These assets are subject to income tax and must be withdrawn under required minimum distribution rules over the surviving spouse's life expectancy. Thus, these assets would cause shrinkage in the exemption (bypass) trust at the marginal income tax rate applicable to the distributions.

One option is to use the funds of the exemption (bypass) trust in a manner that would minimize distributions and provide for growth. Of course, this strategy would be recommended only if the surviving spouse or other beneficiaries won't need the current distributions. If the trust terms don't permit accumulation of income (as defined by the state's principal and income act), the trust could be structured to avoid unnecessary accounting income. Investment advice should be consulted to minimize accounting income and provide growth and the trust terms and state law must permit the investment choices made by the trustee.

If the survivor has a substantial estate and associated tax problems, life insurance could be purchased on the surviving spouse's life inside the exemption (bypass) trust using some or all of the funds. Life insurance provides no accounting income as the cash surrender value accumulates in the policy, and it provides for growth as a result of the death benefit. Only when the proceeds are received and reinvested after the death of the insured-surviving spouse will accounting income begin to accrue. In addition, there are estate and gift tax advantages to this choice. First, the life insurance proceeds will avoid inclusion in the surviving spouse's gross estate and pass to the heirs free of any estate tax. Of course, the surviving spouse should not be the trustee (a resignation is always possible) when the insurance is purchased or the trust should be designed with an independent cotrustee to hold the incidents ownership on the life insurance policy on the life of the surviving spouse. Second, there are no gift tax consequences to paying the premiums because the transfer taxes were avoided by the use of the estate tax exemption of the first spouse to die when the exemption trust was funded. Again, flexibility is available. If funds are needed by the surviving spouse, the trustee could take money out of the life insurance policy through policy loans. The policy could also be surrendered or settled and the proceeds reinvested in other opportunities if the circumstances indicate making such a change.

Trusts

A trust is a relationship (generally in the form of a written document) that divides the ownership of property. Legal title to the trust is held by one party, known as a trustee. The beneficial or equitable interest in the trust property is owned by the beneficiaries of the trust. The trustee has the duty to manage the trust property provided by the grantor of the trust for the benefit of the beneficiaries. The trust is used to provide for beneficiaries when, for one reason or another, they are unable to administer the trust assets for themselves. For example, a trust may be created to provide for minor beneficiaries. Minor beneficiaries are incapable under state law of holding property in their own name and perhaps lack the necessary experience and financial acumen to manage the trust property. In the case of a beneficiary with special needs, specialized trusts may be indicated to preserve the beneficiary's qualification for needs-based public assistance. In any event, the trust is an excellent tool for handling and/or consolidating accumulations of wealth.

The trustee manages the trust property under the terms of the trust. The trust terms are the directions and intentions of the grantor with respect to the management of the trust. For example, there may be directions with respect to the investment of trust assets. More importantly, there are directions with respect to providing for the beneficiaries of the trust. The trust terms may be restrictive and provide the trustee with very little discretion. For example, the terms may provide for specified distributions of income and/or principal to designated beneficiaries at various points in time. Or the trustee may be provided with "sprinkle" powers permitting the trustee to determine when distributions of either income or principal are appropriate for the various beneficiaries. The trustee has the legal obligation to manage the trust prudently and, to the extent the trustee has discretionary powers, to act impartially with respect to the beneficiaries.

Since the trust terms describe the intentions of the grantor, a trust should be drafted carefully under the direction of an attorney who specializes in such matters. In addition, the grantor should select the trustee, whether a private individual or a corporate trustee, with great care.

Testamentary Trust

A testamentary trust is created under the will of the testator. Since the will can be changed as long as the testator retains legal capacity, the testamentary trust is never irrevocable until the client's death (or permanent legal disability). A testamentary trust does not receive property until the client dies and the proceeds are transferred to the trust by the executor. Since the trust is contained in the client's will, it is subject to probate. In a simple will testamentary trusts are often drafted to provide for the testator's children should the spouses die in a common disaster. In a more complex estate plan testamentary trusts are often the vehicles for the marital and family trusts described earlier in this chapter.

Estate Planning Documents
• Will
• Trusts
• Durable powers of attorney (including health care power of attorney)
• Living will

Living (Inter Vivos) Trust

A trust can be created during the lifetime of a grantor. It could be created for several reasons. The trust could hold property and operate prior to the death of the grantor. Or a trust could be created during the lifetime of the grantor simply to receive assets at the grantor's death. Such a trust is known as a *pour-over* trust.

A trust could be either revocable or irrevocable. A revocable trust is created when the grantor transfers trust property to the trust but reserves the power to alter or revoke the agreement. Since the revocable trust is an incomplete transfer, the creation of a revocable trust has no effect on the client's income, estate, or gift tax situation. The revocable trust gives the grantor the ability to observe the management of the trust assets without relinquishing ultimate control of the assets. Thus the grantor can reclaim the trust assets at any time. The revocable trust becomes irrevocable only when the grantor modifies the trust to become irrevocable or dies and therefore is no longer able to modify the trust.

The revocable trust has gained popularity in recent times as an estate plan in itself. It is drafted to provide the dispositive directions normally contained in a client's will. The client will then transfer all appropriate assets to the trustee to be retitled in the trustee's name. At the grantor's death the trust becomes irrevocable and all property contained in the trust is managed or disposed of under the terms of the trust. The revocable trust is popular as an estate plan since property disposed of by the revocable trust avoids the publicity, delay, and some expenses associated with the probate process.

A living trust can also be designated as irrevocable by the grantor. Since the irrevocable trust is a completed gift, it is effective for gift and estate tax purposes. A properly designed irrevocable trust can receive property from the grantor which, as a completed gift, will avoid the gross estate of the grantor at his or her death. In addition, funds placed in the irrevocable trust become the property of the trustee and are exempt from the claims of the grantor's creditors. The irrevocable trust is an effective estate planning tool for older grantors who face substantial estate tax burdens. One type of irrevocable trust, a Special Needs Trust, is a trust created to hold the assets of a special needs individual.

Estate Planning Documents

Durable Power of Attorney

A power of attorney is a written document that enables the client, known as the *principal,* to designate a holder of the power, known as the *attorney-in-fact,* to act on the principal's behalf. The attorney has the power to act in behalf of the principal only with respect to powers specifically enumerated in the document. A *durable* power of attorney is an estate planning document that is not terminated by the legal disability of the principal. Since this document provides the attorney-in-fact with the potential to abuse the privileges granted by the document, these documents are construed very narrowly in transactions with third parties. Thus any powers that the principal wishes to grant to the attorney-in-fact should be specifically enumerated. The document should also clearly specify whether or not the legal disability of the principal has any effect on the power of attorney.

A power of attorney should be drafted prudently for the specific circumstances of the client. Care should be taken as to the choice of the attorney-in-fact, the powers granted to him or her, and when the powers take effect. The advantages of a durable power of attorney include these:

- An older client can execute a durable power of attorney and avoid the necessity of having a guardian or a conservator appointed should the client lose legal capacity.
- The attorney-in-fact can be given the power to manage the principal's assets should the principal suffer a permanent or

temporary loss of legal capacity. This is particularly important for owners of a closely held business.

- The durable power can replace or complement a revocable trust. The attorney-in-fact can manage the client's assets subsequent to a client's legal disability and, if empowered, continue the client's dispositive scheme. For example, the attorney-in-fact could continue to make annual exclusion gifts or contributions after the legal disability but prior to the death of the principal.

- Most states allow a *health care power of attorney* in which the attorney-in-fact can make medical care decisions on behalf of the principal.

Living Wills (a/k/a Advance Medical Directives)

A living will is a document indicating the client's intentions should the client become disabled and lack the legal capacity to make decisions for himself or herself. Generally speaking, the living will deals with the health care measures that the client wants imposed should he or she become legally disabled. If a living will is desired, the document should carefully spell out whether or not the client desires that heroic measures be taken should he or she experience a life-threatening accident or illness. Living wills are not valid in all states, and local counsel should be obtained if the client wishes to state his or her intentions in this regard.

Letter of Intent

The purpose of the Letter of Intent is for family members or caregivers to memorialize in writing their wishes and vision for the special needs individual after the caregiver or parent passes away. The letter of intent is not a legally binding document. The Letter of Intent reflects in writing the goals and information of the special needs individual. A typical letter of intent may include information about residential living situations, education, employment, religion, medical care, final arrangements, and social settings. The letter should be signed by all persons that are involved in the care of the special needs individual. The letter should be reviewed each year to ensure it remains current, and should be revised immediately if the circumstances change, such as a change in medication or an improvement or decline in cognitive function.

Residential Care Alternatives

Choosing among residential care alternatives is an intensely personal decision for the parents of a special needs child. There is parental preference for the size of the home, the level of privacy, and availability of recreational, employment and educational opportunities to name but a few. Any facilities meeting initial criteria need on site investigation. In the end, parental intuition, "gut," or "feel" will be a major factor in how to decide. Given the waiting lists for many types of facilities, it is advisable to apply to more than one. For the severely disabled, institutional care may be the best option given its capability for custodial supervision, evaluation, treatment and training. However, for those special needs individuals without severe disabilities, there are six (6) options.

The first is a family-type living arrangement. Here the special needs individual lives with family members or friends at the passing of both parents. The arrangement can be either at the home of the parents or the caregiver. Parents will want to be sure sufficient resources exist to permit continued residence at their home. But, as is the case for this and the other five (5) arrangements described below, choice of the caregiver is likely the most critical in making any living arrangement successful.

The second is an adult-foster care arrangement in a family-like setting. Unlike the family-type living arrangement, the caregiver is not a family member. Accordingly, more will be required than an interview with a caregiver. There should be references and interviews with the sources of references. The goal is minimizing the risk a caregiver will not be up to the responsibilities.

The third is a group home which houses several unrelated individuals with disabilities. The group home may be either publicly or privately owned (whether for profit or not). It is often advisable for the special needs individual to enter the group home before the death of both parents. Doing so will be less traumatic for the child. And as a practical matter, it may be necessary given that waiting lists for such facilities may require move-in whenever space is available.

The fourth is a community residential setting often known as community care homes or community residences. The level of care is generally geared to those with less severe disabilities. Typically care is provided by a house manager, a rotating staff, or combination of both.

The fifth is an intermediate care facility. Like community residences, these facilities may be large complexes of buildings or smaller community residences. They are designed for those with moderate to severe disabilities. Since the facilities cover a continuum of disability levels, these facilities can permit the special needs individual to graduate to a lower level of supervised care or even independence.

The sixth and final arrangement is independent supported living for those needing limited supervision. Often these special needs individuals live in a home or apartment and near those with relatively mild disabilities. Adult service agencies can be a source to locate these independent living arrangements.

Government Benefits

Individuals with disabilities may be eligible for various government benefit programs. Government benefits will play a pivotal role in the family's finances, due to the high cost of care for individuals with disabilities. Few families are financially able to pay out-of-pocket for a disabled individual's medical care, housing costs, physical and mental therapy, and transportation costs. Therefore, incorporating government benefits into a family's estate plan is essential.

Government programs for individuals with disabilities are primarily designed to cover life's basic necessities such as food, shelter, clothing, and medical care. Government programs can be needs-based or part of a social insurance program. Individuals are eligible for needs-based programs, such as Supplemental Security Income (SSI) and Medicaid, based on the individual's "resources." Resources include an individual's income and assets. Individuals with resources below a certain threshold will be eligible for needs-based programs. Individuals are eligible for social insurance programs, such as Social Security and Medicare, if they are considered to be disabled. Unlike needs-based programs, an individual's income has no bearing on eligibility for a social insurance program. As long as an individual or their parents have paid premiums into the social insurance programs, such as the Social Security and Medicare taxes garnished from payroll, an individual will be eligible for these programs.

Government benefits may be run by the federal government, state governments, or a combination of both. Therefore it can be very confusing to determine what benefits and individual is entitled to under each program.

If a person's resources are limited, they may be eligible for Supplemental Security Income at age 18, or even younger depending on the individual and family's resources. The timing of a child's disability is irrelevant for Supplemental Security Income. Most individuals that are eligible for Supplemental Security Income are also eligible for Medicaid.

Disabled individuals may be eligible to reside in a government-funded residential home. If so, any Social Security or Supplemental Security Income benefits the individual receives will be substantially reduced.

Resources

Parental Resources

For disabled children under 18, the parents income and resources will be counted as the child's resources and income when determining eligibility for SSI, even if those resources are not readily available to the child. This often results in children whose parents live above the poverty level being denied government benefits as their resources exceed the income and resource thresholds. The child must wait until age 18 to become eligible for these government benefits.

Excess Resources

Estate Planning for Excess Resources. Sometimes, individuals or their families try to meet the resource and income eligibility thresholds by transferring resources out of the disabled individual's name. This is not recommended. Both Medicaid and SSI have "look back" periods of between 36 – 60 months. Any property transferred out of the disabled individual's name within the look back period will be counted as a resource of that individual.

Estate planning tools can be used to help an individual who has resources and income that exceed the SSI and Medicaid thresholds to become eligible for these programs.

The first method of reducing resources and income is called spend down. This is simply spending the excess resources down to the desired eligibility level. The resources must be spent for the child's benefit. This method can also be used if the child's assets are in a UGMA account. Spend down of the UGMA trust assets lowers the amount of assets eventually disbursed to the individual upon reaching the age of majority.

If the individual is of majority age and sufficient mental capacity, the individual can choose how to spend his or her excess assets. However if the individual cannot make those decisions on his/her own, parents or family members can petition a court to get approval to spend the individual's funds.

A second method of reducing resources and income is to place those excess resources into a trust. Special Needs Trusts are discussed above.

When an Individual Has Excess Assets. Recall that Medicaid and SSI are needs-based programs and that individuals only qualify if their income and resources do not exceed the designated thresholds. Since these income and resource thresholds are quite low, an individual can easily find himself or herself in a situation where he/she has income and resources that exceed the thresholds, but does not have the funds available for pay for the variety of costly expenses related to a disability.

Gifting. For the above stated reasons, outright gifting money or property to a disabled individual can easily disqualify that individual from SSI and Medicaid assistance. Gifting to a disabled individual can be made into a joint account with the disabled individual or through the Uniform Gift to Minors Act (UGMA). Any property gifted into a joint account will be considered that individual's property for income and resource determination unless the other joint account holder can prove that the property is actually theirs.

Gifting under the UGMA involves gifted property that is placed into a trust for the benefit of the disabled individual. The donor makes an irrevocable gift of the trust property to the disabled individual, who is the beneficiary of the trust. The gift and any income earned by the trust is under the control of the trustee until the beneficiary reaches the age of majority. The trustee has the discretion to spend the trust funds for the benefit of the beneficiary. Upon reaching the age of majority, all assets in the trust are disbursed to the beneficiary. While the property in the trust is under the control of the trustee, it is not counted as income or resources of the disabled individual. When the trust property is disbursed to the individual upon reaching the age of majority, or if cash distributions are made to the beneficiary prior to the termination of the trust, the property is then counted as income in the month of disbursement and a resource in the month following disbursement.

Social Security Insurance

An individual may qualify for government benefits if he or she meets the definition of disability per the Social Security regulations. The Social Security Administration defines "disability" as:

> • [T]he inability to do any substantial gainful activity by reason of any medically determinable physical or mental impairment which can be expected to result in death or which has lasted or can be expected to last for a continuous period of not less than 12 months.

In a practical sense, disability is determined if an individual is not able to earn more than the threshold amount per month after deducting impairment work related expenses and employer subsidies ($1,900 indexed for 2014). The threshold amount is adjusted annually for inflation. To establish disability, the Social Security Administration will perform an analysis to determine whether the individual can perform a "substantial gainful activity" to earn income.

Social Security Disability Insurance

Social Security Disability Insurance (SSDI) provides cash benefits to disabled individuals. Individuals can qualify for SSDI in two ways:

1. Working individuals who become disabled prior to retirement age (65). The individual's work history must satisfy Social Security requirements. Most individuals who have worked for at least a few years will have a history that satisfies these requirements. The amount of benefit paid out to the individual is based on the individual's past earnings.

2. Disabled children of retired, disabled, or deceased individuals who participated in Social Security. The child must have become disabled before age 22. The amount of benefit paid out to the child is based on the benefit the parent is eligible for. The child receives one half of the benefit paid out to disabled or retired individuals receiving Social Security, and three-fourths of the benefit of a parent receiving Social Security that is now deceased. Benefits may be reduced if more than one child claims the parent's benefits. A child may no longer be eligible for benefits if they marry an individual who does not also qualify for Social Security benefits.

If an individual has received Social Security benefits for at least 2 years, they are likely eligible for Medicare.

Supplemental Security Income

Supplemental Security Income (SSI) is considered a needs-based benefit. SSI is available to individuals who are disabled, blind, elderly, or to those whose resources fall below the SSI resource threshold. SSI is a monthly cash benefit ($721 indexed for 2014) to these individuals to provide a minimum amount of income. Some states supplement SSI with state monthly benefits as well.

"Disability" under the SSI program is defined in the same way as under the SSDI program. The major difference between eligibility for SSI and SSDI is that a person is not required to be working, or to have become disabled before age 22, in order to receive SSI benefits.

SSI Benefits

The SSI monthly benefit ($721 indexed annually for 2014) may be reduced if the child earns income, receives unearned income (such as Social Security), lives in a private home but does not contribute proportionally towards household expenses, receives financial assistance from Medicaid, or if the child lives in a home that is not funded by Medicaid and the home does not qualify as an educational school, vocational school, or eligible community residence.

SSI Resource Determination

In addition to the income limitation, an individual must also qualify under SSI's resource limitation. In order to be eligible for SSI, an individual's resources must not exceed $2,000 ($3,000 for couples). Resources include cash, liquid assets such as stocks and bonds, and any property that the individual owns and could convert to cash to pay for his or her needs.

The following items are specifically excluded from the SSI resource determination:

1. the principal place of residence, including the land it sits on and any other buildings on that land
2. funds from the sale of a home if they are reinvested in a new home in a timely manner
3. one vehicle used for transportation
4. burial plots or spaces held for the individual, the individual's spouse, or family members
5. certain prepaid burial contracts

6. household goods and personal items

SSI Income Threshold

SSI has a strict resource threshold that individuals must not exceed in order to be eligible for SSI benefits. SSI requires a person to be denied benefits in any month in which the person's income exceeds the SSI threshold. The threshold is usually the same amount as the SSI monthly benefit ($721 for 2014, adjusted annually for inflation).

An individual's income, for purposes of determining the SSI threshold, is defined very broadly as anything an individual can use to provide food or shelter. Income includes all income earned, unearned (such as government benefits), and *in kind* income (food and shelter provided for free).

The following income items are specifically excluded from SSI's income determination:

1. the first $20 of unearned income received each month
2. the first $65 of earnings received in a month, and one-half of earnings over $65 per month
3. the value of food stamps
4. income tax refunds
5. food or shelter provided by private nonprofit agencies, if needs-based
6. cash loans
7. amounts expended by a third party on behalf of the disabled individual for nonfood or shelter expenses
8. the value of medical care and services provided at no cost or paid for by a third party directly to the medical provider
9. room and board during a medical confinement
10. gifts for tuition and education costs
11. amounts excluded under Social Security Disability's work supports, such as impairment related work expenses

Medicaid

Medicaid, also known as *Medical Assistance,* is available to pay for medical expenses of low income individuals who are blind, disabled, elderly, or who have dependent children. Medicaid can supplement Medicare income by covering expenses that are not covered by Medicare.

In most states, individuals who are eligible for SSI are also eligible for Medicaid.[12] However, an individual is not required to meet SSI eligibility requirements in order to qualify for Medicaid. Individuals whose resource and eligibility make them ineligible for SSI may nonetheless qualify for Medicaid if they qualify under the *spend down* rule. The spend down rule dictates that if an individual's income and resources may be reduced by medical expenses in order to determine eligibility for Medicaid. Most state have adopted the spend down rule.

If an individual is receiving both SSI and Medicaid and loses eligibility for SSI due to increased earnings, the individual does not automatically lose eligibility for Medicaid as well. Eligibility for Medicaid is only lost once the government determines the individual has earned enough additional income to afford their own medical insurance. The income threshold varies by state.

Under the Affordable Care Act, all individuals under age 65 with incomes at or below 133 percent of the Federal Poverty Level (FPL) will be eligible for Medicaid. (In 2014, the FPL for an individual is $11,670.)

Medicare

Medicare is a government benefit provided for individuals aged 65 and older, disabled individuals under 65, and individuals with end stage renal disease. Individuals are eligible for Medicare if they entered the United States legally and have lived in the U.S. for at least 5 years.

Medicare is composed of several parts. Medicare Part A is called Hospital Insurance. Medicare Part A provides payments for inpatient medical services. If an individual or their spouse paid Medicare taxes while employed, no monthly premium is required for Medicare Part A benefits. Medicare Part B is called Medical Insurance. Medicare Part B provides payments for outpatient care and preventive services. Part B requires a monthly premium ($104.90 indexed for 2014) from most individuals.

Eligible individuals can choose between Original Medicare, Medicare Advantage, and Medicare Part D Coverage. Original Medicare allows individuals to choose coverage by Part A, Part B, or coverage by both Part A and Part B. Medicare Advantage requires some kind of coverage under

---

12. Certain states, known as Section 209(b) states, have imposed stricter financial requirements for SSI than for Medicaid. These states are Connecticut, Hawaii, Illinois, Indiana, Minnesota, Missouri, New Hampshire, North Dakota, Ohio, Oklahoma, and Virginia.

Original Medicare, however additional services are covered. Part D coverage over Prescription Drugs can be added to any Medicare Plan for an additional cost.

Special Needs Trusts

The Special Needs Trust (SNT) is a trust device designed to provide for benefits that are not available through public assistance programs. The benefits of the trust are limited to payments for benefits not otherwise provided by Medicaid. The benefits are discretionary and are explicitly not to be used for the basic health, maintenance and support of the special needs beneficiary. The properly drafted SNT will not cause disqualification from SSI or Medicaid.

Self-Settled Special Needs Trusts (SNTs)

The special needs individual that has independent assets or will receive a personal injury award will normally have all nonexempt assets and income counted against the asset or income tests of SSI and Medicaid. Thus, the outright ownership of these assets is a problem for the purposes of qualifying for these public assistance programs. Because of this problem, we recommend that gifts or inheritances to the special needs individual be handled carefully as provided for in the upcoming assignments. It is very risky to attempt to defer planning transfers to the special needs individual by relying on the power of attorney or guardianship. For example, disclaimers of the gift or inheritances by the special needs individual (or an attorney-in-fact or guardian representing the special needs individual) may not be permitted. Our discussion here is limited to the assets owned or to be received by the special needs individual that cannot be avoided.

There is a misconception that all SNTs are provided for by the family of the special needs individual. However, the law permits SNTs to be self-settled by the special needs individual. Without the self-settled SNT, the receipt of an injury settlement or judgment in excess of $2,000 will disqualify the special needs individual from receiving public assistance. Technically, the self-settled SNT cannot be created by the special needs individual directly, but must be created for the special needs individual by a family member, an attorney-in-fact, or a guardian.

There are several forms of self-settled SNTs. The self-settled SNTs were initially authorized by the Omnibus Budget Reconciliation Act of 1993 (OBRA) and have been further explained by the Health Care Financing Administration (HCFA). The "safe harbor" self-settled SNTs fall into three categories. First, the *"(d)(4)(A)" SNTs* were designed to permit the special needs individual to place an injury award or inheritance into a trust that will qualify as an exempt resource. That is, transfers to the trust will not be treated as transfers for the purposes of SSI or Medicaid disqualification look-back rules.

The (d)(4)(A) SNT must (1) be for a beneficiary under 65 years of age, (2) provide for a "disabled" beneficiary, (3) be established by the special needs individual's parents, grandparents, guardian, or a court, and (4) provide for the recovery by the state for Medicaid benefits received by the beneficiary. Hence, the (d)(4)(A) trust is also known as a payback SNT from the requirement to pay back funds received from Medicaid. Although the payback requirements sound harsh, there is the distinct advantage that the funds used to reimburse the state's Department of Welfare for Medicaid payments are reduced by the actual amounts expended by Medicaid. Of course, the Medicaid reimbursement rate is significantly less than a private pay rate that would otherwise apply to the special needs individual's funds. Hence, the self-settled payback SNT does provide significant asset protection for the special needs individual's funds. Any trust funds remaining at the time of the special needs beneficiary's death that are not used to reimburse Medicaid can pass to designated family beneficiaries.

Before the trust terminates, the benefits are provided or not provided to the special needs beneficiary at the discretion of the trustee. This form of trust could be funded with the special needs individual's assets, such as a settlement from a personal injury award, or can be a receptacle to receive assets from third parties, such as the special needs individual's parents or grandparents. Because of the payback requirement, the funds provided for the special needs individual by family members should be placed in a third-party supplemental needs trust that will be discussed in a later chapter.

A second form of SNT is the *"(d)(4)(C)" SNT* which is a *pooled trust* for the benefit of disabled beneficiaries. The (d)(4)(C) SNT must (1) be established and maintained by a nonprofit association and (2) maintain a separate account for each special needs beneficiary of the pooled trust. The funds are pooled for investment management purposes. The assets remain in the trust for the other beneficiaries at the time the special needs individual dies. (Some states may require some part of the decedent's funds to be used to reimburse Medicaid.) The pooled SNT can be funded by the beneficiary (or by his or her attorney in fact or guardian) or the pooled SNT can be funded by the beneficiaries family through third-party gifts or bequests. The benefits of the pooled SNT are twofold. First, there is the ability to use the pooled SNT with smaller amounts than would be appropriate for a private individual trust. Second, the nonprofit trust provides for continuity and management after family caregivers have grown too old or have passed away.

A third form of SNT is the so-called *Miller Trust*. This trust is specific to the "income cap" states discussed earlier. The trust is designed to hold excess income above the SSI limit to permit the special needs beneficiary to qualify for long-term care and medical benefits under Medicaid. The Miller trust is created by the court to hold the Social Security, pension, or other income of the beneficiary. The trustee is directed to pay the required sum to the institution providing the special needs beneficiary's care and remaining principal is available for estate recovery purposes to the Department of Welfare to the extent of medical assistance provided by Medicaid.

In the case of self-settled SNTs, state rules often require a corporate trustee unless it is unfeasible. In the pooled form of SNT, the nonprofit association is the trustee. In the other forms of SNTs, a corporate trustee may be required (for example, PA Rules of Civil Procedure), particularly with a minor or incompetent special needs beneficiary. In the case of a smaller settlement, the Courts have permitted a noncorporate fiduciary. A family member could be used but should be capable and prepared to handle the normal duties of trustee along with the unique aspects of the SNT.

The trustee of the self-settled SNT will determine the distributions that will be made to or for the benefit of the special needs beneficiary. The trusts are carefully drafted and administered to avoid making distributions for expenses that would otherwise be provided by Medicaid. In addition, distributions should not be made that would reduce or eliminate the beneficiary's qualification for SSI or Medicaid. The types of expenditures that are typically appropriate for the benefit of the special needs beneficiary as determined by the discretion of the SNT's trustee include:

- automobile/van
- clothing
- accounting services
- appliances (TV, VCR stereo, microwave, stove, refrigerator)
- bottled water or water service
- bus pass/public transportation costs
- camera film, recorder and tapes, development of film

- clubs and club dues (record clubs, book c1ubs, health clubs, zoo, advocacy groups, museums)
- computer hardware or software
- courses or classes (academic or recreational)
- dental work not covered by Medicaid, including anesthesia
- down payment on home/security deposit on apartment
- laundry service
- elective surgery
- fitness equipment
- funeral expenses
- furniture, home furnishings
- gasoline and/or maintenance of auto/van
- haircuts/salon services
- holiday decorations, parties, dinner dances, holiday cards
- home alarm and/or monitoring/response system
- home improvements, repairs, and maintenance (not covered by Medicaid), including tools to perform home improvements, repairs, and maintenance by homeowner
- home purchase (to the extent not covered by benefits)
- house cleaning services
- insurance (automobile, home and/or possessions)
- legal fees/advocacy
- massage
- musical instruments (including lessons)
- nonfood grocery items (laundry soap, bleach, personal hygiene products, paper towels, and any household cleaning products)
- over-the-counter medications (including vitamins and herbs, etc.)
- personal aid services not covered by Medicaid
- pet supplies/veterinary services
- physician specialists not covered by Medicaid
- private counseling not covered by Medicaid
- repair services (appliance, automobile, etc.)
- snow removal/landscaping service
- sporting goods
- stationary, stamps, etc.
- storage facilities

- taxicab
- telephone service and equipment, including cell phone, blackberry, etc.
- therapy (physical, occupational, speech) not covered by Medicaid
- tickets to concerts or sporting events (for beneficiary/accompanying companion)
- transportation
- utility bills
- vacations (including paying for personal assistant to accompany the beneficiary)

The types of distributions that the SNT trustee should avoid include those that would reduce the beneficiary's SSI benefits or make the trust potentially available to Medicaid. The following types of distributions should be avoided:

- basic shelter-related expenses
- food
- cash for any purpose
- paying for a service already paid for by another source
- distributions not in the best interest of the beneficiary (made primarily for the benefit of another person)

Special Needs Trusts Settled by Third Parties

Third party SNTs are created and funded with the assets of a person other than the disabled beneficiary. These trusts are not counted as a resource if the beneficiary has no control over trust distributions and no ability to revoke the trust. The trusts can be revocable, irrevocable, or a life insurance trust. The great advantage of a third party trust over one funded with the disabled individuals' assets is that there is no Medicaid payback requirement. The trust may be funded by assets during grantor's life or at grantor's death, and can be funded with property, investments, retirement accounts, and life insurance. The trust corpus remaining at the death of the disabled beneficiary passes to remainder beneficiaries selected by the donor or testator. The disabled beneficiary has only a lifetime interest.

Special Needs ILIT

Provisions to Supplement and Not Replace Public Benefits Available to the Special Needs Beneficiary. Under current law, funds provided to a special-needs beneficiary by a third-party will not be treated as an available asset to the beneficiary if placed in the supplemental needs trust. Of course, funds from life insurance covering the life or lives of a parent or parents of the special-needs beneficiary placed in an ILIT with appropriate supplemental needs dispositive provisions would be exempt from current attachment or future Medicaid estate liens of the special-needs beneficiary.

The dispositive provisions of the trust would grant the trustee the purely discretionary powers. There would be a prohibition for the trustee to provide cash directly to the special-needs beneficiary or make distributions for the purposes of the beneficiary's basic food and shelter requirements. There will often be permissible purposes for distributions. For example, the trustee of the supplemental needs trust should be given the powers and directions to distribute to pay the expenses of any caregivers or professional advisers of the special-needs beneficiary. Although the self-settled SNT normally would have a corporate trustee, it is possible to have individual trustees of the third-party supplemental needs trust. Even if a corporate trustee's used, it is possible to create a committee of trustee advisors from the family members or other advisors of the special-needs beneficiary to provide a more personal touch with respect to advising the trustee with respect to distributions.

Other Beneficiaries of the Third-Party Supplemental Needs ILIT.
The third-party supplemental needs ILIT should have other beneficiaries besides the special-needs beneficiary. However, the special-needs beneficiary is generally the sole beneficiary during his or her lifetime. The other beneficiaries have a vested remainder benefit from the third-party supplemental needs ILIT. The remainder beneficiaries could be individuals, such as other heirs of the insured(s), or could be a charitable organization. It is important to have remainder beneficiaries and trust provisions that emphasize the preservation of the principal of the trust, to the extent possible, for the remainder beneficiaries. This places the remainder beneficiaries in a position to have legal standing to object if the principal of the trust is jeopardized. For example, the remainder beneficiaries could file suit to prevent the state from attempting to force distributions to the special-needs beneficiary to prevent the beneficiary from taking advantage of public benefits from programs such as SSI or Medicaid.

It is generally not recommended to provide benefits to other family members from a third-party supplemental needs ILIT concurrently with the special-needs beneficiary. The trust distribution provisions would certainly become confusing if the trustee had to exercise the discretion to make current benefits available to other family members along with the special-needs beneficiary. If the grantor of the third-party supplemental needs ILIT wanted to make funds available immediately to other beneficiaries at the grantor's death, he or she should consider creating a separate ILIT for this purpose since the provisions for the other heirs would be significantly different. For example, in an ILIT not designed as a supplemental needs trust for a special-needs beneficiary, it is possible to provide immediate guaranteed income or principal to the other family members who do not have a requirement to qualify for SSI, Medicaid, or other creditor problems.

   Provisions to Amend or Terminate the Third-Party Supplemental Needs Trust. The third-party supplemental needs ILIT will be in place for a potentially lengthy period of time. There could be changes to the law that render the trust ineffective for its purpose. Or, changes to the health and disability status of the special-needs beneficiary might dictate a different type of trust. It is imperative that the third-party supplemental needs ILIT provide for the potential to revise or terminate the trust. A trustee could be given the power to amend the trust with some specific directions. For example, the trustee could be given the power to amend the trust to ensure qualification for public benefits. Of course, the trustee is a fiduciary with responsibility to all beneficiaries of the trust including the remainder beneficiaries. It may be difficult to expect the trustee to act quickly to changes of circumstance when the relative interests of the beneficiaries of the trust might be altered. Another approach is to include a trust protector with specific directions with respect to changes in the laws associated with the qualification of the beneficiary for public benefits. The trust protector does not have the same fiduciary responsibility to the beneficiaries of the trust.

The Advantages of Lifetime Gifts

Nontax Advantages of Lifetime Gifts

Clients give away property during their lifetime for many reasons. The advantages of making lifetime gifts are as follows:

- The donor can provide for the support, education, and welfare of the donee.
- The donor gets the pleasure of seeing the donee enjoy the gift.
- The donor avoids the publicity and administrative costs associated with a probate transfer at death.
- The donated property is protected from the claims of the donor's creditors.

Tax Advantages of Lifetime Gifts

Although the federal gift and estate taxes are unified for tax purposes, there are some distinctions that make lifetime gifts favorable from a tax standpoint. The tax advantages of lifetime gifts include these:

- The annual gift tax exclusion for gifts of $14,000 or less (2014 indexed amount) provides a complete loophole from federal gift and estate taxes. Each year any number of $14,000 gifts ($28,000, if the spouse joins in them) can be made to reduce the ultimate transfer tax base of a donor.

- The gift tax is imposed on the value of the gift at the time a completed transfer is made. Thus any posttransfer appreciation on the property avoids all transfer tax.

- The gift tax payable on gifts made more than 3 years prior to the donor's death is excluded from the donor's estate tax base.

- The income produced by gifted property is shifted to the donee for income tax purposes. Lifetime gifting may be used to move taxable income from a high-bracket donor to a lower-bracket donee. (This advantage is somewhat limited by special rules related to "kiddie" tax.)

- Unlimited qualifying transfers can be made between spouses without incurring gift taxes. Spouses can advantageously shift assets between themselves to meet the needs of the estate plan of each spouse.

The Opportunities Created by the Annual Gift Tax Exclusion

As discussed above, the annual exclusion allows the donor to make up to $14,000 (2014 indexed amount) worth of gifts tax free to any number of donees each year. If the donor's spouse elects to split gifts with the donor for the tax year, the annual exclusion is increased to $28,000 (2014 indexed amount) per donee. If the client has a substantial estate and several individuals to benefit, the systematic use of annual exclusion gifts can cause the transfer of substantial wealth free of transfer tax.

The annual exclusion is available only for gifts that provide the donee with a present interest. For example, an outright transfer of property provides a present interest. Since the outright transfer is often unfavorable (for example, the donee is a minor), significant planning is often necessary to design gifts that restrict the donee's current access to the funds while qualifying for the annual exclusion.

Gifts to Minors

Quite often annual exclusion gifts will be made to minor children or grandchildren as part of the estate plan of a wealthy client. This creates problems for the donor and donee. First, there are restrictions on a minor's ability to hold or otherwise deal with property under state law. In addition, the donor will naturally be concerned about the safety of the funds if the minor has significant access rights. Fortunately there are several methods for making annual exclusion gifts to minors with restrictions on the minor's access to the property.

Transferring Assets to Minors: Techniques That Restrict Access
• Uniform Gifts to Minors Act (UGMA)
• Uniform Transfers to Minors Act (UTMA)
• Sec. 2503(b) Trust
• Sec. 2503(c) Trust
• Irrevocable Trust with Current Withdrawal Powers

Uniform Gifts to Minors Act (UGMA) or Uniform Transfers to Minors Act (UTMA)

The UGMA and UTMA statutes are model laws that have been adopted in various forms in individual states. They permit the transfer of funds to a custodial account for the benefit of a minor. The custodian of the UGMA or UTMA account manages the property under the rules provided by state law. There are restrictions on the type of property permissible as an investment for these purposes. The original model act, UGMA, has been expanded in most states to increase the types of permissible investments. In a majority of states the newer model act, UTMA, has been adopted, and relatively few restrictions exist in these states on the permissible investments. A UGMA or UTMA transfer is particularly favorable for smaller gifts because it provides for the protection of the assets without the expense of the administration of the trust. The provisions for distribution from the UGMA are provided under the various state laws. Generally speaking, the UGMA funds can be accumulated during the minority of the donee, but the custodial assets must be distributed to the beneficiary upon majority.

Sec. 2503(b) Trust

A Sec. 2503(b) trust is an irrevocable trust created by a donor during his or her lifetime to receive annual exclusion gifts. The trust requires that income be distributed at least annually to (or for the benefit of) the minor donee. The minor would receive distribution of the trust principal whenever the trust agreement specifies. A distribution of principal does not have to be made at the majority of the donee. The annual gift tax exclusion is limited to the value of the income interest provided by the trust. The Sec. 2503(b) trust should be invested in income-producing property and is less favorable in some respects than the UGMA gift because income cannot be accumulated.

Sec. 2503(c) Trust

A Sec. 2503(c) trust is another type of irrevocable trust designed to receive annual exclusion gifts for a minor. This type of trust requires that income and principal be distributed to the minor at age 21. However, the trust is allowed to accumulate current income prior to the termination of the trust.

The Role of Life Insurance in the Estate Plan

Life insurance can serve either as an estate liquidity or estate enhancement tool. The most appropriate use of life insurance in the estate plan depends upon the age, family circumstances, and financial status of the particular client.

Life Insurance for Estate Liquidity Purposes

For older clients with larger estates, estate liquidity becomes a primary focus in the use of life insurance. Older clients have generally completed or nearly completed the heaviest support and educational expense years for dependent children. These individuals are usually well along in the funding of their retirement plans and have fewer years of employment ahead of them.

Since these clients may have accumulated substantial wealth, the protection offered by the marital deduction and lifetime exclusion may be inadequate to shelter their estates. Although the marital deduction will generally shelter all of the estate from tax at the death of the first spouse, the second death creates a substantial tax problem in the foreseeable future (if the spouse is of similar age). In addition, an affluent client may have accumulated substantial wealth that is not liquid. For example, an interest in a closely held family business is often assigned a high value for the purposes of the federal estate tax. However, the business interest may be unmarketable to purchasers outside the family group. If the heirs are to remain in the business, they must discover a method to pay any estate taxes due.

Under the circumstances described above, life insurance is quite useful in providing for estate liquidity. Life insurance can be secured by a client to provide death proceeds equal to the size of the wealth lost in the form of the substantial state death taxes and federal estate tax. In addition, the life insurance proceeds provide cash, which, as opposed to illiquid estate assets, is more readily available to provide for the liquidity needs of settling the estate.

The estate tax treatment of the life insurance selected by these individuals is critical. Since affluent clients are hoping to solve liquidity problems rather than add to a tax burden, life insurance should be purchased and owned in a manner that keeps the death proceeds out of the gross estate if at all possible. Thus these individuals often have ownership arrangements for the life insurance that provide the insured with no incidents of ownership. This can be accomplished by having either the spouse or children of the insured apply for and own the life insurance policy. Or, as discussed below, a trust can be designed to own the life insurance policy. However, the estate or the executor should never be the beneficiary of the proceeds since this beneficiary designation would place the proceeds in the gross estate for tax purposes.

Life Insurance for Estate Enhancement

Life insurance is generally used for estate enhancement for (1) younger clients, (2) clients with dependent family members, and (3) clients with small to moderate-sized estates. Clients in these categories generally have protection as the primary need for their life insurance coverage. These individuals need to protect their families from the loss of future earnings with which to support the family members. These clients are either in or are headed toward their peak earning years, and their families rely on these future earnings for such things as the educational and medical needs of the children, the support needs of the client and his or her spouse, and the eventual retirement needs of the client and his or her spouse. In a family with a special needs child or grandchild, the support needs might well continue beyond the death of the child's parents. In this instance, the estate enhancement need will continue beyond the parents' working years.

The death taxes facing a younger client with a small to moderate-sized estate are relatively minor. The applicable exclusion amount and marital deduction will generally remove the danger of federal estate taxes for these individuals. Thus estate liquidity is not the primary concern. It is highly improbable, however, that these individuals have accumulated enough wealth to replace future income and support of a prematurely deceased breadwinner. Life insurance is the perfect estate enhancement tool to replace some or all of the financial loss created by the premature death.

Life Insurance Trusts

Revocable Trusts

A revocable life insurance trust is designed to own and/or be the designated beneficiary of life insurance coverage on the grantor's life. The revocable life insurance trust serves no estate tax planning purposes. Since the trust is revocable, the insured is treated as the owner of the policy and the death proceeds will be included in the insured's gross estate. The revocable trust is ordinarily used when a specific, perhaps temporary, protection need exists.

The revocable trust is an excellent method for providing life insurance benefits for the protection of young children. If the insured dies, the trust becomes irrevocable and the children can be provided for by the beneficial terms of the trust. The revocable life insurance trust is also an excellent method of providing protection for children following a divorce.

Irrevocable Life Insurance Trusts (ILITs)

ILIT

Advantages of the Irrevocable Life Insurance Trust.
Since the *ILIT* is generally regarded as the most powerful estate planning technique available today, it merits special treatment in this reading.

Gift Tax Advantages. There are numerous advantages in making lifetime gifts. The ILIT is a particularly advantageous vehicle for making a lifetime gift. Properly designed and administered, the ILIT can permit the grantor to make significant cash gifts for premium payments that are sheltered entirely by the grantor's annual gift tax exclusions.

The annual exclusion is limited to gifts of a present interest up to $14,000 per donee (as indexed for 2014). If the grantor is married and his or her spouse elects to split gifts, the annual exclusion can be increased to $28,000 per donee. Thus, the grantor is able to contribute up to $28,000 for each beneficiary of the ILIT without any gift tax consequences. The annual-exclusion gift is the single most beneficial estate planning technique because the cash or other property that is transferred through the annual exclusions is forever removed from the donor's transfer-tax base.

The donor's applicable credit amount (gift tax exemption) will shelter up to $5,340,000 (2014 indexed amount) cumulative taxable transfers for amounts contributed to an ILIT in excess of the grantor's annual exclusions. If it is feasible for the donor's spouse to contribute to the ILIT (for example, the ILIT will invest in a survivorship life insurance policy on the donor and his or her spouse), a second applicable credit amount is available. Thus, a married couple can contribute to an ILIT as much as $10,680,000 million in premiums in excess of the donor's annual gift tax exclusions without incurring gift taxes.

In the largest estate planning cases, the annual exclusions and applicable credit amount(s) will not entirely shelter the required premium gifts to the ILIT. Nevertheless, the ILIT continues to be a useful planning technique in these cases. Gift taxes paid on taxable gifts made more than 3 years prior to the grantor's death will be removed from the donor's gross estate—that is, the gift tax system is tax-exclusive. This means that the donor will not have to pay transfer taxes on gift taxes paid on gifts made more than 3 years before his or her death. The payment of gift taxes on lifetime gifts in excess of the annual exclusions and applicable credit amount might be beneficial.

Compare this either to transfers made within 3 years of death or that are transfers made at death. For these transfers, the transferor will pay tax not only on the property transferred but also on the tax payable on the transfer. Thus, the transfer-tax system is tax-*inc*lusive for gifts that are made within 3 years of death and for transfers that are made at death. Since lifetime gifts decrease the ultimate size of the taxable estate, even if they are taxable, lifetime gifts will be an effective transfer-leveraging technique.

Estate Tax Advantages. The ILIT is a safe way to avoid estate taxes with a uniquely appreciating asset. If the ILIT is properly designed and administered, the death benefits payable to the trustee will be completely free of estate taxes.

The ILIT gives the grantor a tremendous transfer-tax-leveraging advantage. As discussed above, the ILIT can be funded with lifetime gifts sheltered by a variety of gift-tax-sheltering techniques. Thus, the trust could be entirely funded with no transfer-tax costs. Since the death benefits are not subject to estate taxes, both the premium payment gifts and the death benefits received by the trust can avoid all transfer taxes.

Of course, the grantor could transfer virtually any property to an irrevocable trust with the same transfer-tax results. However, the unique nature of the life insurance product offers an appreciation potential that exceeds that of all other investments. This is particularly true if the grantor-insured dies prematurely. Even if the grantor-insured lives to or beyond his or her life expectancy, competitive life insurance products will provide a favorable return.

Probate Expenses and Publicity Are Avoided. The death benefits paid to the ILIT avoid the expenses of probate when the grantor-insured dies. In addition, the ILIT is a private nonprobate document, and the beneficial provisions of the ILIT are known only by the grantor, trustee, and trust beneficiaries. Thus, the grantor of the irrevocable life insurance trust has the ability to create a completely private estate that avoids the scrutiny of the grantor's other heirs.

Trust Terms Give Grantor Dispositive Flexibility. The ILIT is a private document that directs a trustee to manage the trust according to its specified terms. To succeed in meeting the transfer-tax planning goals for the ILIT, the grantor can retain no control over the disposition of the trust after the trust is created. However, the trust terms can be designed to give an independent trustee significant flexibility in managing the trust. The ILIT permits the grantor to defer distributions to beneficiaries and empower a mature, competent trustee to make dispositive decisions for the grantor after the grantor's death.

For example, the trustee can be given discretionary powers to sprinkle trust income or principal among the various beneficiaries after the death benefits are paid to the trust. The grantor can specify that his or her children have merely an income interest in the trust during their lives. The remainder of the trust corpus can be distributed according to the dispositive terms specified by the grantor at the time the ILIT is created, or it can be distributed under powers of appointment granted to the trustee or beneficiaries of the trust.

Compare an ILIT's dispositive flexibility with the outright payment of death benefits to the insured's beneficiaries. With an outright payment nobody but the beneficiary is responsible for managing the death proceeds. The proceeds could be consumed or given away quickly by the beneficiary or assigned to the beneficiary's creditors. A large death benefit designed to last a lifetime or into the next generation, therefore, could be wasted in a short period of time.

If the life insurance is instead acquired by an ILIT, the grantor's specified terms will provide for the disposition of the asset. Thus, the death proceeds from the life insurance policy will be invested and managed by a selected individual or institution. The payment of any income or principal could be limited by the predetermined terms of an ILIT or placed in the hands of a responsible and reliable trustee.

Irrevocability Concerns Can Be Addressed. The irrevocability of the ILIT is, of course, a disadvantage from the grantor's standpoint. The possibility for the permanent repeal of the federal estate tax will certainly create concerns about the adoption of an irrevocable trust. However, if the gift and estate tax advantages are to be achieved, the ILIT must be a no-strings-attached transfer. The grantor must not have the express ability to control the actions of the trustee or to reacquire the life insurance policy.

Fortunately, the grantor can, through careful trust drafting, give the independent trustee a great deal of flexibility in managing the trust. If it is desirable, the independent trustee can transfer the policy from the ILIT. For example, the policy can be distributed to beneficiaries or it can be sold to anyone, including the grantor, provided the trustee exercises independent judgment. Or the grantor can provide a limited power of appointment for another individual to invade the ILIT. This power of appointment can give access to the policy's cash surrender value or provide for the distribution of the life insurance policy.

Income Tax Consequences Are Minimal. The income tax consequences of the typical ILIT are negligible. Under the grantor-trust rules, the grantor is taxed on any portion of the income of the trust that is or may be applied, without the approval of an adverse party, to the payment of premiums on policies insuring the life of the grantor or his or her spouse. This means under most circumstances the ILIT will be a grantor trust. Therefore, any taxable income of the ILIT will be reported on the grantor's individual return. This rule will affect only trusts that have taxable income. In the typical ILIT the grantor will contribute amounts sufficient merely to cover the premium payments and trust expenses. Thus, the "unfunded" trust will not cause the grantor to incur income taxes.

In the case of a funded ILIT, the grantor has contributed substantial income-producing principal to the trust, and the income from the trust can be used to make the premium payments. The grantor is personally responsible for income taxes created as a result of such trust income. But these taxes can be minimized if the grantor funds the trust with tax-exempt securities or the trustee chooses such investment for the trust principal.

The principal of the unfunded ILIT will be the policy itself. If the policy is permanent insurance, cash surrender value buildup will occur. However, the income tax advantage of life insurance is that this policy buildup is tax free. If the policy is overfunded and fails the modified endowment contract (MEC) rules, taxable income will be incurred only to the extent that the trustee actually withdraws or borrows cash from the cash surrender value of the policy.

For the beneficiaries of the ILIT, there are some income tax issues that are more complicated. After the death benefits are received and the funds are reinvested in income-producing assets, the income has to be taxed to either the trustee or the appropriate beneficiaries, depending on the terms of the ILIT, and the income distributed to beneficiaries. If the beneficiaries have withdrawal powers (as they often do as an ILIT is funded), they become the income tax owners of a corresponding portion of the trust for any withdrawal powers that are lapsed by the beneficiaries.

Estate Liquidity Is Enhanced. An ILIT should not be designed to directly benefit the insured's estate or to pay estate expenses. Under the rules of Sec. 2042, proceeds payable to or for the benefit of the estate will be included in the insured's gross estate. However, the trustee of the ILIT can use the policy death benefits indirectly to enhance the liquidity of the estate. But the trustee should exercise caution when using this technique. It is important to note that estate liquidity issues will need to be addressed even if the federal estate tax is repealed.

Gift Tax Planning for ILITs. The gift tax planning involved in creating and funding an ILIT is the most complex aspect of such trusts. It is essential that the trust be created and managed properly to benefit from the available gift-tax-avoidance provisions of the tax rules. For example, the donor should take advantage of every available annual exclusion. The applicable credit amount should be used only as necessary; if the credit is used to avoid gift taxes, it must be used as efficiently as possible.

Most individuals considering an ILIT have substantial estates. They also are generally older on the average than people who purchase life insurance outright. They usually have significant unearned income, their estates are growing larger all the time, and they are using the ILIT to save estate taxes. In many cases, they own closely held businesses or professional practices. These individuals should be considering the use of every gift-tax-saving avenue for the remainder of their lives. If the premium gifts to an ILIT are not designed in the most gift-tax-efficient manner, the grantor will be wasting estate planning opportunities. Any inefficient use of the gift tax shelters will ultimately result in increased estate tax costs and decreased family wealth for the next generation.

annual exclusion   The *annual exclusion* was created to prevent taxation of *de minimis* gifts to family members through the gift tax system. Think of the compliance difficulty that would occur if every birthday or holiday present to a child or grandchild were subject to gift tax reporting. However, the annual exclusion creates an estate planning opportunity that goes far beyond *de minimis* gifts. A wealthy donor can transfer up to $14,000 (2014 indexed amount) to any number of individuals without gift tax consequences. Annual-exclusion gifts are not defined as taxable gifts under the unified estate and gift tax system. Thus, such gifts *never* become part of the donor's transfer-tax base.

Taxable gifts (gifts in excess of the annual exclusions and marital deduction) are, on the other hand, returned to the donor's estate tax base as adjusted taxable gifts, even if the taxable gifts were fully sheltered by the applicable credit amount. Therefore, annual-exclusion gifts represent a rare opportunity to avoid the federal tax system entirely. If the grantor makes systematic annual-exclusion gifts to his children and/or grandchildren over a number of years, a significant estate tax savings will result. If the donor is married and his or her spouse elects to split gifts each year, the transfer tax savings can be doubled by increasing the annual exclusion to $28,000 per donee.

EXAMPLE
Tom Taxplanner, a widower aged 65, has two children and four grandchildren. In 2014, Tom can make up to $84,000 of total qualifying gifts annually to his children and grandchildren without ever subjecting this property to the transfer tax base. If Tom lives another 20 years, he can give away a total of $1,680,000 at a minimum (ignoring further inflation adjustments to the annual exclusion) to these donees. If there is a federal estate and/or state death tax imposed on his estate, the tax savings could be significant. The savings are further enhanced because the appreciation of the property transferred through annual-exclusion gifts is also removed from Tom's estate tax base.

The example above demonstrates tremendous potential estate tax savings if the annual exclusion is used effectively. The savings demonstrated above could be even greater if the annual exclusion gifts are made to an ILIT and invested in a life insurance policy covering the donor's life (or perhaps the lives of the donor and his or her spouse).

gifts of a present interest

Unfortunately, annual exclusion from gift taxes is not available for all gifts. The rules of Sec. 2503 state that the annual exclusion is available only for *gifts of a present interest*. That is, an annual-exclusion gift must give the donee a present right of enjoyment. Certainly, all outright transfers of cash or property to a donee qualify for an annual exclusion. Even property such as life insurance, which provides for death benefits at a later date, will qualify as a present interest if it is transferred directly to the donee.

A problem arises in creating a present interest when a gift is made to a trust for the benefit of the donee-beneficiaries. If the trust does not provide for immediate benefits and delays income and principal distribution to a future date, the trust provides a future interest to the beneficiaries. An ILIT is a future-interest trust. The grantor-insured of an ILIT has no intention of providing any current benefits to the ILIT's beneficiaries. The beneficiaries are not expected to benefit until the grantor-insured's death when the death proceeds are received by the trustee. Can irrevocable trusts that defer beneficiaries' receipt of benefits be designed to qualify as present-interest gifts sheltered by the annual exclusion? The answer is given below.

Crummey withdrawal powers

"Crummey" Withdrawal Powers. Fortunately, gifts to trusts can qualify for the annual exclusion if they are appropriately designed. However, the trust must provide current enjoyment rights to the donee-beneficiaries. With an ILIT this is accomplished by giving each donee who will receive annual-exclusion gifts the right to receive the gift outright immediately. These withdrawal powers (referred to as Crummey powers) are a powerful planning technique.

As long as a trust contains a power to demand distribution, a present-interest gift will be considered to have been made. This guarantees the availability of the annual exclusion. Therefore, since there will be a possible federal gift tax created (1) by transferring existing life insurance policies into a trust and/or (2) by gifting premiums to the trustee, the availability of the annual exclusion becomes very important because it is a method to reduce or even eliminate federal gift tax liability. Thus, qualifying gifts to an ILIT for the annual gift tax exclusion is essential if the grantor hopes to maximize his or her potential gift and estate tax savings.

A clause that allows the beneficiary to demand distribution must be included in the ILIT. This is true regardless of whether or not minors and a guardian are involved. As long as the named beneficiaries of the trust have been given ample notice of their right to demand distribution, a present-interest gift is deemed to exist. Therefore, the annual exclusion will be available.

EXAMPLE 1

Marvin has created an ILIT and has transferred a life insurance policy into the trust. The face amount of the policy is $300,000, and its gift tax value is $4,700 on the day of the transfer. Premiums of $903 are payable annually on March 1. The beneficiary of the policy is the ILIT, and the beneficiary of the ILIT is Marvin's daughter, Ellen, aged 28. Because Ellen is not a minor, there is no guardian involved. There is a provision in the ILIT that Ellen, as beneficiary, will be notified within 60 days of receipt if Marvin makes any gifts to the ILIT. Furthermore, Ellen has been given the "power to demand distribution" of this gifted property.

When Marvin's next annual premium is due, he makes a gift of an amount roughly equal to the premium amount to the trustee. The trustee notifies Ellen in writing that she has the right to demand this gift. She, of course, does not demand it. The federal gift tax annual exclusion is available for both the policy's value of $4,700 when it was originally transferred and for the premium payment of $903. Therefore no federal gift tax liability is triggered.

EXAMPLE 2

John has created an ILIT and has transferred a life insurance policy into the trust. The face amount of the policy is $100,000, and the policy's fair market value is $3,100 on the day of the transfer. Premiums of $811 are payable annually on January 14. The beneficiary of the policy is the ILIT, and the beneficiary of the ILIT is John's daughter, Jennifer, aged 3. John's brother, Ed, is named guardian on behalf of Jennifer, and under the terms of the ILIT, Ed is given the power to demand distribution on Jennifer's behalf when John transfers funds to the ILIT.

When John's next annual premium is due, he makes a gift of an amount equal to the premium amount plus anticipated expenses of the trust to the trustee. The trustee notifies Ed that he has the right to demand this gift as guardian for Jennifer. Ed does not demand it. The federal gift tax annual exclusion is available for both the policy's value of $3,100 when the policy was originally transferred and for the premium payment. Therefore no federal gift tax liability exists.

Although it is generally considered important to shelter gifts to an irrevocable trust by the use of the federal gift tax annual exclusion, the provision of a Crummey power for a special-needs beneficiary should be avoided. A Crummey power is a general power of appointment and the beneficiary provided with this right must have no legal impediments that would prevent the withdrawal of any funds subject to the power.

A special-needs beneficiary of a third-party supplemental needs trust should not be provided with any type of power of invasion. The ability to take any principal or income from the trust would be treated as an available asset to the holder of a Crummey power. In applying the test for SSI and Medicaid, the state would consider any assets subject to a Crummey power to be an available asset for the beneficiary. This would be true even though the Crummey power is temporary and subject to lapse in a short period of time. A lapsing Crummey power would be treated as income to the extent of the withdrawal power in any month that the special-needs beneficiary held the power. This would cause the beneficiary to exceed the SSI income limitations for the respective months and cause disqualification from Medicaid. The failure to exercise the power and make the asset available would be subject to challenge by the Department of Welfare whether the powers held directly by the special-needs beneficiary or by a guardian or other representative.

A third-party supplemental needs trust will certainly have other family members as vested remainder beneficiaries. It probably is appropriate to provide Crummey powers for other beneficiaries of the supplemental needs ILIT who do not have SSI and Medicaid concerns or other creditor problems. The trust provisions granting the Crummey powers should be drafted carefully to explicitly avoid providing a Crummey power to a special needs beneficiary. If the beneficiaries are forced by the state to withdraw under the Crummey provision, the life insurance policy funding the supplemental needs ILIT could be jeopardized by the reduced funds available to pay the annual premium.

 Keeping ILIT Proceeds Out of Grantor's Estate. Life insurance is included in the gross estate under the rules of Sec. 2042 in conjunction with the special rules of Sec. 2035. Under Sec. 2042, life insurance proceeds are included in the gross estate of a decedent-insured if (1) the policy proceeds are payable to the decedent's executor (that is, for the benefit of the decedent's estate), or (2) the decedent-insured owned incidents of ownership in the policy at the time of his or her death. The special rules of Sec. 2035 also cause inclusion in the decedent-insured's estate if he or she made a gratuitous transfer of the policy within 3 years of his or her death.

Dispositive Provisions of ILIT. The grantor has full control over the terminology in his or her ILIT. A significant advantage of using an ILIT to own a life insurance policy is the ability to control the disposition of the proceeds after the insured's death. Compared with outright payment of proceeds or the use of policy settlement options, an ILIT places an independent decision maker selected by the grantor in the role of controlling the disposition of policy proceeds. Thus, the management of the disposition of life insurance policy proceeds can be left, within reasonable limits, in the hands of the trustee after the insured's death.

The amount of dispositive discretion left to the trustee is determined by the grantor when the ILIT is created. The grantor can direct the trustee to pay specific amounts of principal and/or income to the ILIT's beneficiaries. Outright disposition of the entire principal can be deferred until such time as the grantor feels is appropriate (for example, the 30th birthday of the youngest beneficiary). In other instances, the trustee can be given broad discretionary powers to sprinkle funds. Under these circumstances, the trustee can use his or her discretion in determining the timing and amounts of income and/or principal to distribute to each beneficiary. The trustee's discretion can be based on a specified standard, such as the support of the beneficiary, or it can be unlimited. The grantor should select which dispositive terminology to use, based on his or her feelings about each beneficiary's needs and the trustee's ability to handle discretionary authority.

ILIT Terms Should Avoid Directly Benefiting Insured's Estate. In the typical ILIT, the trustee is the owner and named beneficiary of the policy held by the ILIT. The ILIT terminology instructs the trustee on how investments should be managed and how the death proceeds will ultimately be provided to the beneficiaries. The proceeds could be payable to the ILIT beneficiaries outright at the decedent's death. In most circumstances, however, the ILIT will continue beyond the life of the insured and provide income and/or principal gradually to the beneficiaries. In many instances, the trustee is given a discretionary power to choose the size and timing of distributions to the beneficiaries.

Caution should always be exercised in drafting the terminology of an ILIT. Sample ILIT documents received from insurance companies, banks, or law libraries should be examined carefully to ensure that the terminology will not cause tax problems for the insured. In particular, the ILIT terminology should not direct the trustee to use policy proceeds to pay the expenses of the insured's estate. If the trustee is directed to pay the expenses of the estate, the IRS will deem the policy payable to the executor, and the proceeds will be included in the insured's estate. If the trustee is given the mere discretionary power to pay estate expenses with the proceeds, this should not cause the proceeds to be treated as "payable to the executor" under Sec. 2042(1). However, any amounts so used will be included in the insured's gross estate. Since the typical ILIT is designed to remove the death proceeds from the insured's gross estate, terminology that directs the trustee to use the death proceeds to pay estate expenses would be a costly mistake, while terminology that permits the trustee to use the death proceeds for estate expense purposes should be used only after careful consideration of all the tax consequences.

Following the decision in *Headrick v. Commissioner of Internal Revenue,* the IRS indicated that it will no longer litigate the Sec. 2035 3-year-rule implications of life insurance policies newly acquired by an ILIT. Thus, a client will be within a safe harbor if an ILIT is created and administered according to the facts of the *Headrick* case. If the ILIT is created and administered in a more aggressive manner, there is a risk that the IRS will deem that the policy newly acquired by the ILIT was, in fact, transferred to the ILIT by the grantor-insured and thus subject to the Sec. 2035 3-year rule. If the IRS is successful in this endeavor, the grantor-insured of the ILIT could have the full amount of proceeds included in his or her gross estate if the grantor dies within 3 years of the acquisition of the policy. Since the facts of *Headrick* give us careful guidance, it is important to review the events of the *Headrick* case in detail here.

EXAMPLE

Eddie Headrick, an attorney, approached a local bank and trust company and explained his plan to create an irrevocable trust. The trust was executed the same day and funded by a check Eddie wrote to the bank as trustee. The terminology of the trust permitted many types of investments, including the purchase of life insurance on the grantor's life. The trust terminology did not, however, direct the trustee to purchase such insurance.

The following day, the bank, as trustee, applied for a life insurance policy on the life of the grantor—Eddie Headrick. Within 10 days, Eddie submitted to a physical examination for the purpose of securing the insurance. Eddie was found to be insurable, and the trust paid the first premium. Within one month after the trust was created a policy was issued.

Mr. Headrick died approximately 2 years later, and the IRS attempted to treat the transaction as if Eddie controlled the trustee and, in effect, caused a transfer of a policy on his life in which he had incidents of ownership to the trust. Thus, Sec. 2035 would require that the proceeds be included in Eddie's gross estate since he died within 3 years of this "deemed transfer." The court held for the estate of Mr. Headrick, based on the grounds that no transfer had actually taken place. The trustee was merely investing trust funds irrevocably transferred to the trust by the grantor. Therefore, the policyowner of the life insurance at the time of its purchase was established unequivocally to be the ILIT and not Mr. Headrick.

The facts of the *Headrick* case can be listed in the following steps that are recommended to anyone establishing an ILIT:

Step 1: The ILIT is executed before the final policy application is made and any premium is paid.

Step 2: The grantor transfers funds to the ILIT (and makes further gifts, as necessary, when premium payments are due).

Step 3: The trustee sends notice to the beneficiaries of their Crummey withdrawal rights. (This step is repeated each time additional gifts are transferred to the ILIT.)

Step 4: The trustee applies for the policy on the grantor's life and is named as owner and beneficiary of the policy. (The insured participates in the transaction only for the purpose of establishing his or her insurability and signs only the "insured" signature block on the policy application.)

Step 5: The trustee pays the policy's annual premium to the insurance company when the Crummey powers lapse.

If an ILIT is created and/or administered in a manner different from the steps described above, the insured is increasing the risk that the IRS will attempt to attribute incidents of ownership to him or her.

To summarize the material discussed above, the insured should employ the following defensive strategies:

- The insured should not pay the policy premium before the ILIT is created.
- The terms of the ILIT should authorize but not direct the purchase of life insurance on the life of the grantor.
- The insured should retain no contractual rights, and there should be no trust provisions permitting him or her to acquire the policy held by the ILIT.
- The insured should not be the trustee and should not retain the power to become the trustee.
- The trustee should exercise clearly independent decision-making authority over the investment and disposition of trust assets.

Policies owned by the insured are subject to the 3-year rule regarding gratuitous transfers. That is, the proceeds will be included in the insured's gross estate if the insured's death occurs within 3 years of the policy's gratuitous transfer to a third party. This 3-year rule, of course, applies to transfers of existing policies to ILITs. Regardless of this rule, transferring an existing life insurance policy to an ILIT is an appropriate planning technique under certain circumstances.

Transferring an existing life insurance policy to an ILIT created by the insured is recommended when the estate planning objectives for the transfer are more important than other goals. The transfer of a policy to an ILIT should not be made until after the insured feels comfortable that he or she will not require further access to the policy's cash value. The grantor-insured should be relatively older and financially more secure. Furthermore, he or she should be certain of his or her ILIT beneficiary selections before implementing the transfer. After the transfer, the trustee will become the owner and named beneficiary of the policy, and the proceeds will be distributed according to the ILIT's terms. Since the trust is irrevocable, the grantor-insured will not be able to retrieve the policy or change the trust's terms.

To achieve estate tax advantages a grantor-insured will have to survive more than 3 years following the transfer of his or her life insurance policy to an ILIT. However, this transfer is still a useful planning technique since the full amount of policy proceeds will avoid estate taxation if the grantor-insured survives the 3-year period. Even if the grantor-insured does not survive the 3-year period, his or her estate will be no worse off than if the transfer had not been made. That is, absent the gift of a policy to an ILIT, the insured's estate would already have included the full proceeds because the insured would have continued to hold incidents of ownership in the policy until the time of his or her death.

Life insurance can serve either as an estate liquidity or estate enhancement tool. The most appropriate use of life insurance in the estate plan depends upon the age, family circumstances, and financial status of the particular client.

Chapter Review

Review questions are based on the learning objectives in this chapter. Thus, a [3] at the end of a question means that the question is based on learning objective 3. If there are multiple objectives, they are all listed.

Key Terms and Concepts

ILIT   gifts of a present interest
annual exclusion   Crummey withdrawal powers

Review Questions

1.   Describe how receiving a general power of appointment can impact a client's estate. [1]

2.   Describe both the nontax and tax advantages of lifetime gifts for estate planning purposes. [2]

3.   Describe the following estate planning tools that escape federal gift taxation:
     a. UGMA gifts [2]
     b. Sec. 2503(c) trusts [2]

4.   Describe the type of client for whom life insurance may be particularly appropriate for purposes of
     a. estate enhancement [3]
     b. estate liquidity [3]

5.   Explain why government benefits play an important role for most families with a disabled child. [6]

6.   Explain the significance of the threshold amount as applied to substantial gainful activity for purposes of establishing a disability under Social Security. [7]

7.   When is Social Security Disability Income (SSDI) generally available? [7]

8.   Describe the nature and purpose of the Supplemental Security Income (SSI) program, and how its qualification rules differ from those applicable to the SSDI system. [8]

9.   Describe the impact of a gift to a joint account with a special needs individual who is applying for SSI or Medicaid? [9]

10. Describe the circumstances where it might be advisable to expend a special needs child's funds for his or her benefit? [11]

11. Discuss the alternatives if the special needs individual has been made beneficiary of an inappropriately designed trust providing for distributions for support. [11]

12. Under what circumstances should a self-settled SNT be considered for a special needs individual? [12]

13. Describe the purpose and terminology of a self-settled payback SNT. [12]

14. What is a pooled SNT and under what circumstances is it indicated? [12]

15. How does a self-settled SNT affect the beneficiary's qualification for benefits from SSI or Medicaid? [12]

16. Who are the remainder beneficiaries of a self-settled SNT at the time of the beneficiary's death? [12]

17. Identify the estate-planning advantages of an ILIT. [13]

18. Discuss the potential benefits to other family heirs from an ILIT designed as a supplemental needs trust for special needs beneficiary. [13]

Learning Objectives

An understanding of the material in this chapter should enable you to

1. Develop a plan for providing for special needs family members based on financial data about a client family's personal situation.

Children with Special Needs

Greg and Donna Ford are the parents of two children with special needs, ages 16 and 24. Their 16-year-old special needs child, Thomas Ford, began attending the Vanguard School in the Philadelphia area for special needs children this past January. Thomas currently functions at a 4-year-old level and is incredibly rigid with regard to his schedule. The slightest deviation from his schedule creates anxiety and significant frustration. Thomas is currently under the care of a team of medical professionals, including a developmental pediatrician and a psychiatrist. Thomas was diagnosed with autism at age 3 and has now received extensive therapeutic assistance for over a decade.

Gregory is 24 and has been diagnosed with Asperger's Syndrome. Although Gregory functions at a much higher level than Thomas, it is unlikely that he will be able to obtain regular employment. Although bright, he suffers from extreme anxiety and is very uncomfortable in social settings. He currently works part time in the afternoons and weekends for a local supermarket and spends many hours in an adult day care facility. The Fords incur day care facility costs in excess of $3,000 annually for Gregory and impairment related work expenses of $1,750 annually to assist their son in his employment at the supermarket. Gregory also receives therapeutic assistance and daily medication for his anxiety.

Mr. and Mrs. Ford also have a younger child, Andrew, who is 15, and attending high school and an older child, Shannon, who is 27, married and living with her family. Greg Ford, who is 55, works as a corporate lawyer for a Fortune 500 Company and has underutilized many of the benefits available to him (that is, flexible spending account). Donna, age 52, works minimally outside the home due to the amount of time required to manage Thomas and Gregory's daily schedules. She rarely earns more than $3,500 to $4,000 annually. However, when both are in school and at work, she volunteers within the special needs community.

The Fords are also considering adopting a special needs child and have attended the required "foster to adopt" program to initiate the process.

For the current year, Mr. and Mrs. Ford will have an AGI of $150,000. They anticipate the following medical expenses for Thomas and Gregory during the year: $51,300 for the Vanguard School for Thomas (a "Special School"), $8,750 in out-of-pocket costs for prescription medication, and physical, speech, and therapeutic/behavioral services for both boys, $5,750 for unreimbursed physician recommended vitamin therapy for Thomas, and $1,000 for out-of-pocket medical expenses for Andrew, Greg, and Donna. This is in addition to health care insurance which is partially paid for by Greg's employer (single coverage). Greg is out of pocket $750 a month after-tax for the family component of the coverage. The Fords' have traditionally itemized their deductions.

Greg and Donna Ford are often assisted financially by Greg's parents. Greg's father, Tom, was a successful stock broker and has accumulated a net worth in excess of $6 million. He established UGMA accounts for all four grandchildren several years ago. Each account currently has a value in excess of $50,000. In addition, Tom and his wife supplement the family "income" by providing monthly gifts for their grandsons' ongoing medical care. Greg's parents routinely provide monthly assistance of $4,000 or more for Thomas and Gregory's ongoing medical and therapeutic care.

The Fords' are also considering the sale of significantly appreciated stock that was inherited many years ago from Greg's grandparents and has a very low basis ($35,000). The potential sale at $285,000 will defray some of the ongoing medical expenses. Unfortunately, the family will have a long-term capital gain of $250,000 if they currently sell the stock.

In addition, the Ford family has currently maximized their $100,000 home equity line of credit, and will incur interest expense on the line of $4,850 this year. Other itemized deductions will include: state and local taxes of $8,500; real estate taxes of $8,800 on their primary residence; mortgage interest expense of $11,500; and charitable contributions of $3,500. Donna Ford also attended a medical conference on autism during the year and incurred a registration fee of $250 for the one-day conference and travel related expenses of $50.

As a result of hiring a special needs lawyer this year, the Fords' anticipate receiving a $50,000 reimbursement from the township either this year or next for the Vanguard School since the township was unable to provide an appropriate education for Thomas.

Further, Thomas was seriously injured in a recent automobile accident as a passenger. Although Thomas is expected to recover fully from the injuries he suffered in the accident, his autism represents a lifelong disability. A personal injury settlement in the amount of $550,000 has been obtained for Thomas. Following satisfaction of liens, costs, and attorney fees, the net recovery for Thomas will fall somewhere between $450,000 and $500,000. The family's personal injury attorney is very concerned about the award, and has advised the family to seek appropriate representation (that is, an advisor specializing in working with families with special needs children) regarding the award.

Currently, Thomas, Gregory, and Andrew have their own mutual fund accounts with approximately $3,500 each in their names.

Greg and Donna Ford also believe that both Thomas and Gregory could require a group home in the future. However, they are hopeful that with some significant private funding, Shannon and her husband will accept both Thomas and Gregory into their home so long as sufficient resources exist to provide care and assistance to the brothers without straining Shannon's own home environment. Shannon is 27 years old, a married mother of twins, and has completed both her undergraduate and graduate education in special education. Her husband, Fred, is a successful engineer. Although Andrew adores his brothers, Andrew is already too aware that Thomas will ultimately require 24/7 care and Gregory presents unique challenges on a daily basis.

Greg and Donna own a primary residence worth $375,000, an existing mortgage of $250,000, and taxable/tax-free investments of $15,000. In addition, Greg's retirement plan has assets slightly in excess of $300,000; whereas, Donna's retirement plan is currently valued at $55,000. Greg has an ABA term life insurance policy with a death benefit of $1,000,000 (premium of $4,000) and Donna has a term life insurance policy with a death benefit of $150,000 (premium of $750). Greg also has a group-term life insurance policy thru work with a death benefit of $200,000. In addition, Greg has disability insurance thru his employer, but has not acquired any long-term care insurance.

Case Study Questions

1. Prepare an income tax projection (with and without the long-term capital gains of $250,000). Please remember to consider all potential exemptions, deductions, and credit (that is, child tax, adoption, and child and dependent care credits) opportunities in your analysis. Also, are there any potential alternative minimum tax (AMT) implications?

2. How will the Fords' treat the $50,000 settlement from the township (with and without long-term capital gains)?
   a. Will the year of receipt make a difference?

3. Discuss the tax implications in adopting a special needs child.

4. Do the mutual funds or UGMA investments present any potential issues?
   a. What is the impact on federal and state assistance?
   b. Will Thomas and/or Gregory qualify for SSI, and if so, when?
   c. Are the grandparents "helping" with their monthly assistance?

5. How will the Ford family handle the personal injury award? What types of trusts, if any and why, would you recommend to the Ford family?

6. Broadly speaking, are there any life or estate planning issues? What are the overall planning opportunities that exist for the Fords?

Answers to Case Study Questions

1.

AGI ($150,000 AGI + $250,000 LT Capital Gains)		
Schedule A		
Medical Expenses		
$76,100 – (10% AGI = 40,000) =	$36,100	
SALT	8,500	
R/E Taxes	8,800	
Mortgage Interest	11,500	
Home Equity Interest	4,850	
Contributions	3,500	
Impairment Related Work Expenses (not subject to 2% of AGI)	1,750	
		–75,000
Add-back ($400,000 – $305,050 @ 3%)		2,849
Exemptions (5)		–19,750
Add-back ($400,000 – $305,050 divided by $2,500 times 2%) 76% lost		15,010
Taxable Income		$323,109
10% 18,150; 15% on up to $73,800 ($323,109 less $250,000 LTCG) Reg. Tax		10,059
15% Long-Term Capital Gains Tax (15% x $250,000 LT Capital Gains)		37,500
Child Tax Credit (Neither child under 17 qualifies for the credit with AGI of $400,000)		
Child and Dependent Care for Gregory: Credit $3,000 @ 20%		–600
Unearned Income Medicare		
Contributions Tax (3.8% x $150,000 net investment income)		5,700
Net Tax Due		$52,659
Alternative Minimum Tax		
AMT: Taxable Income		$323,109
Adjustments:		
SALT + R/E Taxes	17,300	
Home Equity Interest	4,850	
Less: Add-back	–2,849	19,301

Exemptions (5)	19,750	
Less: Add-back	−15,010	4,740
AMTI		$347,150
Exemption		−34,437
($347,150 − $156,500 @ 25% = $47,663. $82,100 less $47,663 = allowable exemption of $34,437)		
TMTI		$312,713
TMT ($62,713 @ 26% plus $250,000 @ 15%)		53,805
Reg. Tax		−47,559
AMT		**$6,246**

Analysis:

The following deductions result in 2014 AMT "add-back" items: home equity interest expense of $4,850; state and local taxes of $8,500; real estate taxes of $8,800 on their primary residence; and exemptions of $19,750 ($3,950 times 5).

The disallowed itemized deductions and exemptions due to the phase-out rules serve to reduce the add-back for the AMT calculation. Personal credits, such as the child tax credit of $1,000 and the child and dependent care credit of $600 (in our case) will reduce both the regular tax and AMT.

Itemized deductions are phased-out for individuals with AGI in excess of these same thresholds. The disallowed amount of the allowable itemized deductions is the lesser of 3% of the excess of AGI over these thresholds, or 80% of the total amount of otherwise allowable itemized deductions. For 2014, the beginning point for phase-out threshold is the same for both the exemptions and itemized deductions: $305,050 for married couples filing jointly and $254,200 for single filers. In our case, the add-back represents the excess of $400,000 in AGI over the threshold of $305,050 at 3% or $2,849, which is less than 80% of the otherwise allowable itemized deductions of $75,000.

For 2014, in computing the regular tax, personal exemptions of $3,950 begin to phase-out at an adjusted gross income (AGI) level of $305,050 for married couples filing jointly ($254,200 for single filers) and are completely phased out at an AGI level of $427,550 for married couples filing jointly ($376,700 for single taxpayers).

In our case, the add-back is calculated as follows: $400,000 AGI – $305,050 threshold divided by $2,500 ($1,250 if married filing separately) times 2%, resulting in a loss of 76% of the available exemptions, or $15,010.

The Alternative Minimum Tax (AMT) exemption is also phased-out in our case study. The 2012 American Taxpayer Relief Act not only permanently increased the AMT exemption, but also indexed the exemption for inflation for the first time. For 2014, the AMT exemption is $82,100 for married couples filing jointly and $52,800 for single filers. However, similar to the deductions for exemptions and itemized deductions, the AMT exemption is phased-out at higher levels of income. The AMT exemption is reduced by 25% of the amount by which alternative minimum taxable income exceeds $156,500 for married couples filing jointly ($117,300 for single taxpayers). In our case, alternative minimum taxable income of $347,150 exceeds the beginning of the threshold of $156,500 by $190,650. As a result, an exemption of 25% of this amount or $47,663 is lost. The reduced exemption is $82,100 less $47,663, for an allowable exemption of $34,437. For 2014, the 28% AMT rate applies to alternative minimum taxable income above $182,500 ($91,250 for married taxpayers filing separately). The rate applicable to capital gains and qualifying dividends is the same 15% for both the regular tax and AMT calculations for our case study (since the taxpayers are not in the highest income tax bracket of 39.6%).

The 3% Unearned Income Medicare Contribution tax on net investment income applies because the couple's MAGI exceeds the applicable threshold, or $250,000 for couples married filing jointly.

2. The tax treatment of the reimbursement of $50,000 from the township for past medical expenses varies depending on the timing of the receipt and if the couple sold their stock during the year, thereby incurring long-term capital gains.

   If a reimbursement for medical expenses is received in the year of the medical expense, the itemized medical expense deduction is simply reduced by the amount of reimbursement. If the reimbursement is received in a year after medical expenses were incurred, some or all of the reimbursement may be included in income for the year in which the reimbursement was received. The amount included in income for the year is the lesser of:

- the reimbursement amount
- excess of total itemized deductions over the standard deduction; or
- itemized medical deductions for the prior year

If the couple does not sell their stock and incur capital gains and the reimbursement is received in 2014, the itemized medical expense deduction would be reduced to $11,100 ($61,100 total medical expenses minus 50,000 reimbursement). If the reimbursement is received in 2015, all or part of the reimbursement may have to be included in income. The amount includible in income is the lesser of:

- the total reimbursement ($50,000)
- the excess of the total itemized deductions ($100,000) over the standard deduction (assuming the couple is married filing jointly, the 2014 standard deduction is $12,400), or $87,600, or
- the amount of itemized medical expense deduction taken in the prior year ($61,100)

Therefore the total reimbursement of $50,000 will be included in income in 2015.

If the couple sells their stock and realizes a $250,000 long-term capital gain, their itemized medical deductions will decrease due to the AGI phase out. If the reimbursement were received in 2014, their medical expense deduction would be reduced to zero, because the total reimbursements exceed the total itemized medical expense deductions ($36,100). If the reimbursement is received in 2015, all or part of the reimbursement may have to be included in income. The amount includible in income is the lesser of:

- the total reimbursement ($50,000)
- the excess of the total itemized deductions ($75,000) over the standard deduction (assuming the couple is married filing jointly, the 2014 standard deduction is $12,400), or $62,600, or
- the amount of itemized medical expense deduction taken in the prior year ($36,100)

Therefore, part of the reimbursement, $36,100 will be included in income in 2015.

3. **Special Needs Adoption Considerations:**

A taxpayer may take the full amount of the adoption credit ($13,190 per child in 2014) for adoption of a special needs child, regardless of actual adoption expenses paid by the taxpayer. To qualify as a special needs child, the child must be a U.S. citizen or resident and must be requiring adoption assistance.

The credit is a dollar-for-dollar reduction against both the regular tax and AMT owed. The credit may be taken for qualifying expenses such as legal fees, court costs, and other related adoption costs. The credit is limited to a total amount per child. Therefore if part of the credit is claimed in one year for some qualifying expenses, only the unused portion of the credit may be claimed in future years. The credit is nonrefundable and is subject to 5-year carryover rules. The credit is claimed in the year adoption becomes finalized regardless of actual expenses paid or incurred in the year the adoption becomes final.

The credit is phased-out for taxpayers with adjusted gross income exceeding $197,880 for 2014, and is completely phased-out at $40,000 above the threshold. Therefore, if the Fords sell their stock in 2014 with a capital gain of $250,000, they will not qualify for the adoption credit.

4. **Supplemental Security Income:**

In order to qualify for Supplemental Security Income (SSI), the individual claimant(s) (both Thomas and Gregory) must have "countable resources" of $2,000 or less upon application ($3,000 for couples). According to Social Security Administration (SSA), countable resources include: cash; bank accounts, stocks, U.S. savings bonds; land; life insurance; personal property; vehicles; anything else owned which can be changed to cash and used for food or shelter; and deemed resources (that is, a portion of the resources of a spouse, parent, parent's spouse, sponsor of an alien or sponsor's spouse are deemed to belong to the person filing for SSI if the child is under age 18).

Countable resources do NOT include: a personal residence; household goods and personal effects; burial spaces for you or your immediate family; burial funds for you and your spouse (each valued at $1,500 or less); life insurance policies with a combined face value of $1,500 or less; one vehicle, regardless of value (if it is used for transportation); retroactive SSI or Social Security benefits for up to 9 months after you receive them; grants, scholarships, fellowships, or gifts set aside to pay educational expenses for 9 months after receipt.

To be eligible for SSI benefits according to SSA, a child must be either blind or disabled. The medical standards for disability are the same for both SSI and SS for individuals age 18 or older. There is a separate definition of disability under SSI for children from birth to age 18.

An individual age 18 and older is "disabled" if he or she has a medically determinable physical or mental impairment, which results in the inability to do any substantial gainful activity; and can be expected to result in death; or has lasted or can be expected to last for a continuous period of not less than 12 months.

An individual under age 18 is "disabled" if he or she has a medically determinable physical or mental impairment, which results in marked and severe functional limitations; and can be expected to result in death; or has lasted or can be expected to last for a continuous period of not less than 12 months.

A child may be eligible for SSI disability benefits beginning as early as the date of birth; with no minimum age requirement.

SSI provides a monthly stipend for individuals that are financially needy, elderly, blind, and/or disabled. Qualifying individuals can receive up to $721 monthly ($8,652 for 2014). Couples can receive up to $1,082 monthly for 2014. However, if a claimant has income, the monthly benefit generally will be lower than the maximum federal SSI payment. For example, the first $20 of most income received in a month is excluded, as well as the first $65 of earnings and one-half of earnings over $65 received in a month. Some states also supplement the federal SSI payment.

In applying for SSI, parental income and resources will be deemed available for children under 18 living with parents (resources of siblings not counted). In our case, Thomas will be ineligible to apply until at least age 18 (and should immediately consider utilizing his assets for medical care and the special school). Gregory can apply, but will need to spend down the mutual fund of $3,500 and the UGMA account of approximately $50,000. In addition, the monthly assistance of $4,000 provided by the grandparents for food and shelter will disqualify Thomas and Gregory from receiving SSI.

In planning, those who qualify for SSI automatically receive Medicaid. The Fords should apply immediately for Gregory upon qualification and when Thomas reaches 18.

5. **Special Needs Trusts/Estate Considerations:**

In order to protect Thomas's entitlement to Medical Assistance and SSI, two special needs trusts should be created for him. The personal injury award of between $450,000 and $500,000 represents Thomas's own money and is not subject to income taxes. Therefore his personal injury recovery should be placed into a self-funded special needs trust which would need to 1) include a "payback provision" to the State Department of Public Welfare, and 2) be approved by the court, as all claims involving a minor or an incapacitated person require court approval. Depending upon the state and/or county in which the personal injury action is brought, prior approval by the State's Department of Public Welfare may, or may not, also be necessary to obtain court approval of the special needs trust. In most situations involving a substantial recovery, the court will require a corporate fiduciary to act as the trustee. Self-funded special needs trusts must be created by a parent, grandparent, guardian, or the court.

Thomas will also require a supplemental third party funded special needs trust as part of Greg and Donna Fords' estate plan. Under current law, no payback is required from such a trust. The supplemental third party funded special needs trust should generally be created in a document separate from the parents' wills (but can be incorporated in their will as a testamentary supplemental special needs trust). Because Greg and Donna do not own assets in excess of 5 million dollars each in 2014, it does not appear that a credit shelter trust (CST) must be included in their wills, although CSTs could be provided in order to hedge against the possibility of increased value in family assets and/or a reduction in the federal estate tax threshold. If CSTs are used, it would be important to advise the family of the need to place at least some assets that pass under the will into individual names. (It is always possible that the protection currently afforded special needs trusts will change.) However, it appears that Greg's parents may have a taxable estate for federal estate tax purposes and will require careful planning, especially in terms of transfers to Thomas and Gregory.

In addition, in order to protect Gregory's entitlement to Medical Assistance and SSI, a supplemental third party funded special needs trust should be created for him (similar to Thomas). The case study does not indicate whether Gregory has assets independent of the mutual fund or UGMA accounts and the amount of his current earnings. Both Gregory's assets and earnings may disqualify him from receiving SSI.

If Greg and Donna decide to acquire more life insurance (or assign Greg's ABA term policy for example) to provide additional resources for the supplemental third-party funded special needs trust, the family should be advised to consider the use of an irrevocable life insurance trust (ILIT) to own any new policy at the outset, so as to avoid the 3-year look-back period for existing life insurance which is placed into an irrevocable life insurance trust. In addition, an ILIT may be a good planning tool for Greg's parents to utilize in providing for both Thomas and Gregory. However, a word of caution is in order. If Greg and/or his parents intend to fund a supplemental third party funded special needs trust with life insurance, the ILIT should be drafted to avoid providing Crummey withdrawal powers for the special needs beneficiaries since such withdrawal rights could affect the beneficiary's eligibility for Medical Assistance (that is, Medicaid) and SSI benefits. A second-to-die life insurance policy may be a good vehicle to fund the ILIT.

6. **Some General Estate Considerations:**

Greg and Donna have sufficient life insurance and disability insurance coverage. In addition, the couple has prepared for their future by saving for retirement. However, the couple's assets are threatened by their lack of long-term care coverage. With recent and developing medical technology, people are living longer and longer lives. A person's assets can be quickly depleted if they incur a long-term illness in their post-retirement years. The couple should purchase long-term care insurance to protect their assets against loss in case of chronic illness in old age.

As part of their estate plan, Greg and Donna should also consider powers of attorney for financial and medical considerations, as well as an advanced medical directive for each child with special needs.

Overall, a team of advisers will need to be retained by the Ford family, and should include: a family advocate, a guardian, an attorney in fact (agent) under a power of attorney, a lawyer specializing with families of children with special needs, trustee(s), a trust protector, a CPA aware of the income tax implications in working with families having children with special needs, and a financial services professional.

In addition, the Ford family should have a "letter of intent" prepared at all times to supplement their will. The "letter" will provide a daily "blue print" to assist in managing the lives of Thomas and Gregory.

However, as previously discussed, Thomas and Gregory should not have "countable resources" in excess of $2,000. Both boys currently have mutual funds with a balance of over $3,500. Further, the grandparents have established UGMA accounts for all of the children. Each account currently has a balance in excess of $50,000 and will disqualify both Thomas and Gregory from Medical assistance and SSI. Greg and Donna will need to carefully spend down the accounts of Thomas and Gregory to ensure eligibility. Both Greg and Donna will need to work with Greg's parents in funding the supplemental third party funded special needs trusts and perhaps creating ILITs on behalf of Thomas and Gregory. Obviously, both Greg and Donna will need to coordinate their estate plan with Greg's parents to ensure ongoing and continuous eligibility of public benefits for both Thomas and Gregory.

Further, the Ford family will need to consider housing issues and ongoing adult day care for Thomas when he reaches the age of 22. Hoping that both Thomas and Gregory ultimately reside with Shannon and Fred may be unrealistic.

> ## Learning Objectives
>
> **An understanding of the material in this chapter should enable you to**
>
> 1. Describe the agency parties and unique aspects of working with members of the lesbian, gay, bisexual and transgendered (LGBT) community.
>
> 2. Discuss the ethical principles ChFC® professionals must adhere to when working with members of the LGBT community.
>
> 3. Explore financial planning topics and their applications when working with LGBT clients.

Introduction

Chartered Financial Consultant®

A Chartered Financial Consultant® (ChFC®) is charged with competently practicing elements of financial planning. Competence requires professionals to understand the legal and cultural scaffolding of their recommendations. When working with a single consumer, a financial services professional is presented with a clear framework of established financial planning techniques based on relatively consistent federal and state tax regulations. The addition of a partner, regardless of the partner's gender, presents additional challenges to the financial planning process and understanding of legal and cultural expectations.

In a single-client framework, financial service professionals serve as conduits between the interests of principals (clients), the interests of financial service firms, and any interests of the financial planner (agents). A financial service professional must constantly balance between those three groups. The addition of a partner or spouse makes planning even more complex. Considering two principals (client and partner, client and spouse, or client and client) expands the number of relationships a financial professional must navigate. When working with a couple, financial professionals make recommendations concerning agents, multiple principals, and their own interests.

The pressures on a ChFC® working with same-sex clients are complicated even further by the addition of ever-changing rules, discriminatory legal frameworks, and potentially hostile parties.

EXAMPLE

Doug meets with Elisabeth, a ChFC® professional. Doug has asked Elisabeth to review his current life insurance and investment positions. Doug currently has a universal life policy at a strongly rated insurance company with a $1,000,000 death benefit and $300,000 cash value. Additionally, he has $250,000 in a brokerage account comprised of mutual funds and stocks. Elisabeth is exclusively contracted with BIG insurance company and carries the appropriate securities licenses. Doug would like to leave his insurance policy to charity at his death and may need to access the cash value when he retires. He discloses he is comfortable with volatility in his brokerage account and will need the funds in fifteen years.

Elisabeth must balance the interests of Doug, herself, her broker, and her insurance agency when developing recommendations for him. Doug is relying on Elisabeth to work in his best interest and meet his planning needs of charitable giving, portfolio growth, and open access to his assets. Elisabeth is an agent for BIG insurance who contractually expects her to profitably represent the company, and Elisabeth represents a brokerage firm who likely has given Elisabeth minimum production and sales goals to maintain her contract. Elisabeth must also navigate her own revenue and profit through her recommendations to Doug. In this example, Elisabeth must balance the interests of four parties in her decision making.

After working together for a year, Doug introduces his partner Jamal to Elizabeth. Jamal becomes a client as well, and Doug's goals change. Elisabeth must now consider the needs of Jamal in her process of making recommendations.

Instead of navigating between the interests of four parties in her decision making, Elisabeth must consider additional interests when making financial planning recommendations. She must look at Jamal's interest, Jamal and Doug's relationship dynamics, as well as existing responsibilities to Doug, BIG Insurance, and her broker/dealer. When advising a couple, Elisabeth must balance the interest of six entities in her decision making, as opposed to the four entities she must consider when working with only a single individual.

Working with any couple complicates the financial planning process by increasing the number of "best interests" a financial service professional must navigate between. Additional agency pressures require more sophisticated planning techniques and advanced knowledge to meet the needs of all parties involved.

same-sex

transgendered

Same sex couples present additional challenges to financial service professionals navigating between best interests, due to inconsistency and uncertainty in legal scaffolding. While federal income, gift, Social Security, Medicare, and estate tax regulations evolved in 2013 and 2014 to reflect the needs of married same-sex couples, state regulations remain less uniform and concrete. Navigating these challenges requires in-depth knowledge of financial planning techniques across financial planning disciplines. Professionals working with same-sex and transgendered couples can benefit from learning applied techniques designed to clarify inconsistencies or alleviate uncertainty in the financial planning process.

This chapter will discuss the application of techniques that financial service professionals should apply to help their clients meet their financial planning goals. Students will survey financial planning techniques organized by major planning topic areas. This is not intended to be a comprehensive guide to working with same-sex or transgendered couples, but should provide students with a background in additional techniques needed to plan for same-sex couples rather than those of opposite genders. Major planning topic areas are intended to guide professionals through the decision-making and recommendation process, but are not likely to be effective in every state or city. Practicing financial service professionals must build teams of experts who have specific knowledge of local rules and customs.

This chapter addresses the technical financial planning differences financial service professionals face when working with lesbian, gay, bisexual, and transgendered (LGBT) clients. The section is not all-inclusive, but it does address reoccurring themes which require unique approaches, additional time, or amended skills. The section is broken into financial planning topic areas covered in The American College course curriculum to become a ChFC®.

Ethical Considerations

eight ethical canons

professional pledge

CLU and ChFC® professionals agree to abide by eight ethical canons and a professional pledge. The professional pledge requires professionals to agree to the following rule of conduct: "I shall, in light of all conditions surrounding those I serve, which I shall make every conscientious effort to ascertain and understand, render that service which, in the same circumstances, I would apply to myself." Two words stand out when working in communities who require additional expertise: ascertain and understand.

ascertain

understand

Professionals working with members of the LGBT community have pledged to ascertain which financial planning techniques are effective or ineffective and when to bring additional legal, tax, and insurance experts into the planning conversation. CLU and ChFC® professionals pledge to apply the same best practices to financial planning for their LGBT clients that they would apply to their personal financial planning. These practices often require atypical solutions, counseling, and training. Secondly, professionals pledge to understand their clients. Understanding requires an objective assessment of clients' goals and intentions, without overlaying existing notions or value propositions from advisers.

ChFC® professionals must not develop the mindset that all gay or lesbian clients have the same financial planning goals or needs, any more than they would presume all heterosexual clients focused on the same planning outcomes. A lesbian couple raising a 5-year-old child has more financial planning goals in common with a different-sex couple raising a 5-year-old child than with a lesbian couple with no interest in having children. The pledge to ascertain and understand clients mandates objectivity and competence in fact finding and making client recommendations.

In addition to abiding by an ethical pledge, professionals holding a CLU or ChFC® Certification agree to abide by eight ethical canons:

1. Conduct yourself at all times with honor and dignity.
2. Avoid practices that would bring dishonor upon your profession or The American College.
3. Publicize your achievement in ways that enhance the integrity of your profession.
4. Continue your studies throughout your working life so as to maintain a high level of professional competence.
5. Do your utmost to attain a distinguished record of professional service.
6. Support the established institutions and organizations concerned with the integrity of your profession.
7. Participate in building your profession by encouraging and providing appropriate assistance to qualified persons pursuing professional studies.

8. Comply with all laws and regulations, particularly as they relate to professional and business activities.

The first two canons are particularly relevant to professionals working in the LGBT community. CLU and ChFC® professionals agree to treat clients with honor and dignity. Adhering to ethical canons compels professionals to take one of two actions with any prospect they encounter. Advisers can either choose not to work with a prospect and leave him or her unhindered to pursue other financial representation or embrace the prospect as a client. No middle ground exists for a CLU or ChFC®. Haphazardly or negligently representing a client from lack of competence or objectivity is a violation of honor to the client, a disservice to The American College, and contrary to at least two ethical canons.

Technical Aspects of Financial Planning in the LGBT Community

This section cannot address every circumstance that may arise when working with members of the LGBT community. Rather, it will focus on recurring themes that require tailored approaches, additional time, or amended skills. The section is broken into financial planning topic areas covered in the curriculum to become a ChFC®. Working in the LGBT community requires ChFC® professionals to master the general financial planning techniques that will allow them to appreciate, diagnose, and understand the differences in strategies and techniques to successfully help their clients succeed. The following section provides an overview of financial planning topic areas relevant to LGBT clients which may require advisers to draw upon additional resources and expertise, and approach with more care and understanding than they typically do with their non-LGBT clients. Financial planning topics can generally be broken down into the following categories:

- general principles
- risk management
- estate planning
- tax planning
- investment planning
- retirement planning

General Principles of Financial Planning

Hard technical skills, such as time-value-of-money calculations and a thorough understanding of the steps in the financial planning process, are consistent across any type of family. However, communication between LGBT clients and financial service professionals who are unfamiliar with gay and lesbian issues can create roadblocks. Understanding relevant and current communication norms within the LGBT community is the first step to building and maintaining rapport. Kapp and Burkholder (2008) suggest reviewing the *Stylebook Supplement on Lesbian, Gay, Bisexual and Transgender Terminology,* available through the Association of Lesbian, Gay, Bisexual, and Transgendered Journalists, as a starting point in developing appropriate communication skills and vernacular for an unfamiliar adviser to the LGBT community. In 2013, an emerging rubric of "LGBTQIA" (Lesbian, Gay, Bisexual, Transgendered, Queer, Intersex, and Allies) became more common on college campuses. This text will use the abbreviation LGBT to address lesbian, gay, bisexual and transgendered clients; however, advisers are cautioned to stay in touch with common cultural terms and norms. Understanding communication preferences can help financial advisers present a clear message and better uphold the ethical canons of The American College.

Kapp and Burkholder (2008) advise financial service professionals to stay up to date with continuing education and create an environment as free from prejudice and judgment as possible. Some prospective clients may not be out and open with their sexual orientations while others may. This can lead to initial inconsistencies in gathering data and building a strong planning relationship. Offering an open and friendly office environment can help mitigate inconsistencies.

Confidentiality is important in any planning relationship. Financial service professionals, particularly those who are certified as CLU, ChFC® and CFP® professionals, have agreed to limited levels of confidentiality regarding their client relationships. Generally, client files are subject to regular internal and external audits and are not excluded from review as are attorney/client relationships. Discretion is relevant in any client relationship, but acknowledging limits to confidentiality helps build rapport with clients from any background.

A study by MetLife (2010) found that one-fourth of older LGBT clients reported that having faced discrimination over their lifetimes made them feel more resilient when developing financial and long-term care relationships than their control group counterparts. This resilience can help clients build rapport with financial advisers willing to ask the right questions. Half of the older participants in the same study reported their sexual orientation makes positive outcomes more difficult, reinforcing the need for dignity and honor in financial planning relationships.

fact-finding
When working through the financial planning process, ChFC® and CLU professionals must consider the multiple stakeholders involved in the outcome of planning within the LGBT community. Unfortunately, an increased possibility of antagonistically engaged family members and institutions may persist when working with gay, bisexual or transgendered clients, which creates a greater need for careful attention to fact finding and detail than with heterosexual clients. Family members may not be accepting of the client's financial planning objectives and may actively work to undermine hard-planned outcomes. The fact-finding process must include questions about relationships and openness with both immediate family (siblings, parents, and children) and indirect relationships (in-laws', grandparents, aunts, uncles, or cousins). Standard financial planning fact finders may lack the correct questions for assessing those who could later act against the client's wishes. While adding printed questions to a fact finding document may be insensitive, asking questions in person about gender self-identification as well as supportive and potentially negative family members and business partners will enhance communication between the adviser and client.

Fact-finding documents and financial planning questionnaires may not be equipped to assess the risks government institutions (municipal and state) pose to a client's goals and wishes. The year 2013 brought a Supreme Court challenge to and repeal of sections of the Defense of Marriage Act (DOMA), which lessened most federal elements of legal discrimination against same-sex married couples. However, this repeal did not eliminate state and local prohibitions against marriage or workplace discrimination. A review of the various states' current laws and their positions on marriage equality will be included in the following chapter. The fact-finding period can be a time in the planning relationship to engage clients in a discussion of their concerns, as well as an opportunity to assess clients' needs and assemble a team with the appropriate experience and knowledge to meet them.

bankruptcy

credit management

General principles of financial planning typically include bankruptcy planning and credit management. This area is reserved for consumers who are financially strained and have exhausted other options of debt management. Different-sex spouses in legally recognized marriages can file bankruptcy (Chapter 7, 13, or 11) either individually or jointly. A Chapter 7 bankruptcy allows for a release of unsecured personal liability from debts but may require the permanent forfeiture of the debtor's (or debtors') property. Chapter 13 bankruptcy restructures debts, and Chapter 11 is generally reserved for small business or sole proprietorship operations. Students wishing to learn more about the dynamics of bankruptcy should visit the US Bankruptcy Court's Bankruptcy Basics.

An individual bankruptcy considers the income, debt, and assets of the filing spouse, while a joint bankruptcy considers the income, debt, and assets of both spouses. Prior to the repeal of DOMA, same-sex couples, either married or unmarried, were unable to file joint federal bankruptcies. This limited the ability of a couple who had incurred joint debt (such as debt from a foreclosed mortgage on a property purchased joint tenants in common) to clear the debt through one bankruptcy process.

With the repeal of DOMA, the options for same-sex couples looking to file bankruptcy have grown more complicated. Unmarried partners, including those in some state civil unions, are restricted to filing bankruptcy as individuals. Same-sex married couples can file joint or individual bankruptcies based on the character of debt or accounts. Opacity abounds if a married same-sex couple resides in a state that does not recognize their marriage. State recognition of marriage is not concrete or federally protected and is subject to change over time. Financial service professionals should encourage gay and lesbian clients to find qualified and experienced legal counsel to help with their specific needs during the bankruptcy process.

community property

Community property further complicates the bankruptcy process. Community property is a function of state recognition, which would indicate that income produced in the course of a marriage is treated as income of both spouses. Personal and real property purchased with community income become community property, which is owned equally by both spouses. Nine states are considered community property states: Arizona, California, Idaho, Louisiana, Nevada, New Mexico, Texas, Washington and Wisconsin. As of the spring of 2014, California, New Mexico and Washington recognize same-sex marriages and treat same sex-couples with the same community property laws as different-sex couples. The remaining states do not, but may in the future.

Community property and income may be subject to recognition in the bankruptcy process even if titled in separate accounts.

EXAMPLE
Kirk and Gary, both men, marry in 2013 in California. They open a checking account in Gary's name after their wedding and fund it with $25,000 of nonpartitioned community income. If Kirk later files for bankruptcy, a portion of these assets may be considered in his bankruptcy estate. Assume Kirk and Gary wed in California but move to TX. Assume an identical set of facts as above. Texas would not recognize Kirk and Gary's marriage or the community property character of their income. If Kirk files bankruptcy in Texas, Gary's checking account would not be forfeitable.

adoption   Adoption advice is not often associated with financial planning advice; however, financial professionals are uniquely suited to help a family prepare their personal finances before having or adopting a child. Individuals or couples wishing to adopt a child are subject to local and state oversight, home visits, and possible financial audit. State and local law shape the impact (if any) sexual orientation has on the adoption process. Some states may ask about and prohibit cohabiting or married same-sex couples from adopting. Those same states may allow noncohabiting gay and lesbian individuals to adopt. Some states do not solicit information about sexual orientation as part of the adoption process. Financial advisers are encouraged to research the laws of their state and states with similar laws to help clients considering adoption locate appropriate legal representation and to assist with the planning process.

LGBT couples adopting children is a polarizing political issue and, as with most polarizing issues in financial planning, is subject to legislation, judicial challenge, and change. Understanding change and how to plan in a fluid environment is critical to helping clients going through this deeply personal process. Competent assistance to same-sex couples trying to adopt children will likely require a team of experts. Compassionate assistance in this area requires empathy and open communication.

As of 2013, legally married couples or individuals of any gender can take advantage of the adoption tax credit. State recognition of marriage is irrelevant to a taxpayer's ability to take the credit. This credit is nonrefundable and allows a taxpayer (or married taxpayers) to deduct adoption fees, attorney fees, court costs, travel expenses (including meals and lodging) while away from home, and adoption expenses of a foreign child. The credit does not allow a deduction for any amounts otherwise reimbursed by federal, employer, or local programs or expenses relating to surrogate parenting. For 2014, the credit is limited to $13,190 per child and begins being phased out for taxpayers with an adjusted gross income (AGI) above $197,880; the credit is completely phased out at an AGI over $237,880. The credit can be claimed for domestic, international, or failed adoptions which incurred qualified expenses. In the case of a domestic adoption of a child who a state has qualified with special needs, the maximum credit may be taken, even if the taxpayer did not incur adoption costs. IRS Tax topic 607, available at www.irs.gov, further details this tax credit.

divorce   Divorce takes on new meaning when working in an atmosphere of fluid and uncertain state recognition, regulation, and political processes. The number of states allowing same-sex marriage has increased by ten over the past decade, while the number of states constitutionally banning same-sex marriage has also increased. This conflict of state rules, resistance, and recognition complicates divorce and separation. Take the following example of Charlie and Brad as they move across the country.

EXAMPLE

Charlie and Brad were legally married in Delaware in 2013. Brad is the primary wage earner, making $200,000 annually to Charlie's $50,000 annually.

Scenario One: Charlie and Brad adopt a child as a couple in Delaware. (Both are legal parents; Delaware recognizes their marriage.) In 2014, Brad files for divorce, and Charlie maintains custody of their child. Brad will likely be subject to the same child-support payments and alimony payments as would a different-sex couple.

Scenario Two: Charlie and Brad move to Alabama, which prohibits same-sex marriage. Brad is unable to file for divorce in Alabama: The state does not recognize their marriage and will not permit such a filing. Brad would have to file for divorce in a state where he is not a resident, which may be difficult and require moving for a period of time to establish residency. Charlie would be at a legal disadvantage for receiving alimony or child support. To file and finalize divorce proceedings, either Charlie or Brad would need to relocate to another state. Relocation may not be feasible for either spouse

> Scenario Three: Charlie and Brad move to Oregon, which, as of October 2013, recognizes their marriage but does not allow same-sex marriage. Brad may be able to file for divorce, but custody may become complicated, and support payments would likely be dictated by a less-experienced judiciary process.

As shown in scenarios two and three, divorce can be particularly complicated for same-sex couples. Financial professionals working in the area of same-sex divorcing couples must become involved in legal networking organizations to help their clients find appropriate representation during an emotionally difficult and legally uncertain time.

financial aid   Other general principles of financial planning which may require additional expertise or training when working with members of the LGBT community include college funding. Private funding models would not vary between single or married couples of any gender, but the federal financial aid process known as FAFSA (Free Application for Federal Student Aid) has been built on a two-parent chassis. The website www.studentaid.ed.gov provides helpful tools and resources to help families determine college funding. Federally, FASFA considers a couple either legally married or not legally married and is not sensitive to gender issues.

In the FAFSA process, students must calculate their expected family contribution (EFC). The EFC is a function of student income, student assets, parent income, and parent assets. The EFC may not consider domestic partner income or assets, but would include accounts and revocable trust assets owned jointly by a parent and partner. The higher a student's EFC, the less need-based financial aid he or she will likely be able to receive in the form of grants and subsidized loans through the public financial aid process. Financial advisers may discover domestic partner couples have an advantage over married couples when planning for the education of a child.

This advantage is potentially overshadowed by the inability of a domestic partner to make penalty-free withdrawals from 401(k) or IRA accounts to provide for the child of their partner. Unlike domestic partners, LGBT couples who were legally married would not experience any restriction on utilizing retirement accounts for the educational planning of children of their spouses. As of December 2013, the IRS had not issued formal guidelines about the specific issue of educational planning and same-sex couples. Financial advisers should consult with a local tax professional who specializes in same-sex planning.

Federally, legally married same-sex spouses are subject to identical legal protections as those of their different-sex counterparts, including federal pension survivor benefits, the right to refuse to testify against a spouse in a federal trial, and prison visits. These rights may be challenged over time and advisers should maintain relevancy.

Risk Management

McCarran-Ferguson Act of 1945   The insurance industry is currently regulated through state governments. While federal oversight, such as the McCarran-Ferguson Act of 1945, places some limits on insurance company activities, insurance company underwriting, rate setting, and reserve requirements are generally left up to state law, suggestions from the National Association of Insurance Commissioners, and regional customs. Given the unique circumstances of the marketplace, financial advisers should consider this section as an outline of potentially difficult topics. Insurance challenges can be overcome by developing a deep knowledge of specific insurance company offerings and brokers who cater to the LGBT community.

life insurance   Life insurance challenges fall within questions of ownership, beneficiary distribution, control, and evidence of insurability. Life insurance policies may provide living benefits (such as cash value, ability to borrow against a contract, and ability to escalate death benefits in case of a terminal illness) and fundamentally provide proceeds at the death of an insured person. The owner of an insurance policy has the authority to make living- and death-benefit decisions (such as appointing a beneficiary or requesting policy proceeds) while the insured is living. Advisers working with members of the LGBT community frequently use estate planning techniques to consolidate family assets; in order to limit the influence of unsupportive parties or plan for estate taxation, financial advisers may transfer the ownership of an insurance policy into a revocable or irrevocable trust. When insurance policies are owned by a trust, the trustees of the policies, rather than outright owners, then guide living and death benefits.

Financial advisers should paint a clear picture of client vision, particularly in trust-owned contracts. The trustees (individuals who manage trust assets, including insurance policies) name policy beneficiaries, which may not be the trust itself. Flowcharts or diagrams are useful tools in understanding ultimate death benefit distribution within a trust arrangement. The following example is a snapshot illustration of a complicated arrangement. Clients may find illustrations depicting how insurance policies work to meet their goals beneficial. The trust illustrated below would not shield the client and domestic partner from potential estate taxes, but would allow the control of insurance policies and assets to remain unquestioned.

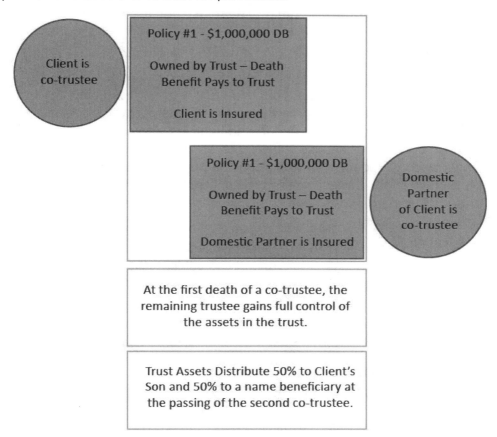

Life, health, and disability insurance require evidence of insurability between the policy owner and the insured individual at the time a policy is issued by an insurer. State law sets the basis for insurance regulation, and in states which are unfriendly or have constitutionally banned same-sex marriage, gay or lesbian clients may have difficulty stating a recognized insurable interest. Financial advisers can help their clients by shopping insurance companies and using brokers who are familiar with insurance companies that are more likely to recognize a valid interest and do not discriminate against sexual identity.

**property
and casualty
insurance**
Property and casualty insurance generally extends liability coverage for the owners of property, their spouses, and their children. Financial advisers should contact property/casualty insurance companies with their clients to ensure the property of domestic partners, or that of same-sex spouses in states which do not allow same-sex marriage, will be covered.

Homeowners and auto policies can be problematic in states that do not give legal recognition to married partners. Homeowners policies generally extend protection to the individual or individuals listed on a policy, their relatives, unrelated children aged 21 or under, and relatives who previously lived in the house but now reside elsewhere (such as college students). Same-sex couples who live together may find only the property owner is extended protection through a homeowner's policy. Adding a non-property owner spouse or civil partner can be accomplished with a phone call and eliminates this risk.

Automobile insurance may not require spouses to be listed on a policy, even if they have regular access to an underlying vehicle. Same-sex couples may need to add themselves as authorized users of each other's vehicles to prevent accidental uncovered loss. Umbrella insurance follows a similar pattern, and specifically adding an individual to a homeowners and umbrella policy can eliminate headaches and potential strife.

health insurance
Health insurance is an area of risk management that varies widely by state of residence and marriage status. Most employers include the option of covering domestic partners and their children; some states mandate minimum coverage levels while others do not. Court challenges will likely continue to shape the health insurance landscape as it applies to same-sex partners and spouses. Financial advisers should remain well read and up-to-date when following health insurance rules and regulations. Legally married same-sex spouses who were married before 2013 likely paid income tax on dollars used to pay premiums for spousal coverage in 2011 and 2012. They may be able to file amended tax returns to claim refunds but should consult with a professional tax adviser or CPA.

Cash flow planning for insurance premiums will differ for same-sex couples. Two men will face higher aggregate life insurance premiums than a male and female couple would. Two women will likely have lower aggregate premiums. Premium differences extend to other types of insurance coverage, such as long-term-care and disability premiums. Insurers may offer long-term-care spousal discounts to same-sex couples, and savvy insurance brokers can help shop for appropriate client coverage.

Estate Planning

Estate planning conversations are often twofold: estate tax and purpose. When working with same-sex clients, federal estate tax planning is a function of legal recognition of marriage. Examples of federally recognized spousal benefits include an unlimited marital deduction at the death of the first spouse, QTIP trusts, portability of any unused exclusion, and gift tax splitting. Beginning in 2013, any couples who are in legal marriages are able to take advantage of the same federal tax benefits as different-sex married couples. IRS publications 590 and 559 shed insight into filing an estate tax return and taking advantage of the unlimited marital deduction and any unused exclusion for married couples.

intestate   In 2014, an individual's applicable exclusion is $5,340,000 and is scheduled to inflate in future years. Individuals typically do not pay estate tax if their adjusted gross estate is under this amount at death or the alternative valuation date. This amount is likely different than state inheritance tax exclusion limits, and while federally a married same-sex couple realizes the same tax recognition as a male and female couple, states may not recognize same sex-marriage. A lack of recognition is particularly problematic to assets passing through probate in the event a couple does not have a will and dies intestate.

EXAMPLE
Jennifer and Heather were married in Hawaii. They move to Alabama and purchase a $500,000 home in Jennifer's name. Neither Jennifer nor Heather has a will. If Jennifer and Heather were an opposite-sex couple, the house would pass to the surviving spouse.
However, Jennifer and Heather are both women. Therefore, Alabama does not recognize their marriage through constitutional amendment. If Jennifer predeceases Heather, the home will pass through Alabama's intestate laws, bypassing Heather and passing the home directly to Jennifer's siblings or parents. If Jennifer does not have siblings or parents, the home will pass to nieces, nephews, or cousins. Heather will not be included in the inheritance process

In a dynamic and potentially antagonistic legal framework, financial advisers must encourage LGBT clients to draft and execute legal documents such as wills and trusts. Potentially antagonistic family members add to the urgency of appropriate estate planning. Consider suggesting LGBT clients outline their intent before meeting with a qualified estate planning attorney who specializes in working with the LGBT community. Organization will help clients ensure their wishes are met and appropriate legal documents are drafted. Assets passing through title or contract (such as insurance policy death benefits, retirement accounts, and trust assets) are not subject to intestate rules and are more likely to pass according to the intent of the deceased.

medical directives

living wills

powers of attorney

Medical directives, living wills and powers of attorney are imperative for LGBT couples to not only draft but to maintain on their person if vacationing with a partner or spouse in a state that is antagonistic to LGBT rights. Financial advisers must strongly suggest LGBT clients carry relevant estate planning documents when travelling. Documents should ideally be carried in paper form to easily be shown in times of crisis.

EXAMPLE

Gary and Emir are driving through Georgia. They were married in New York and live in Florida. Gary and Emir are involved in a car accident, and Emir is critically injured. If Gary and Emir were a different-sex couple, they would be able to care for one another.

In Georgia, marriages of two men (or two women) are considered invalid by law. Without a valid general or durable power of attorney for health care, Gary may be unable to make immediate care decisions or visit Emir in the hospital.

The repercussions of improper estate planning for lesbian and gay clients are tangible and permanent. Antagonistic family members and government policy can drastically compound the stress and anxiety associated with end-of-life decisions. Financial advisers can serve as a sound source of advice to ensure the wishes of their clients are met.

While federal estate and gift tax is blind to the gender of a married couple, state inheritance taxes are not. Intermediate techniques, such as using trusts or life insurance policies, may be simple solutions to combat less friendly state inheritance taxation at the death of a first spouse. Financial advisers working with same sex couples should consider the use of lifetime gifting and trust arrangement to ensure testamentary wishes of both parties are met. Focus on planning before death, creating structures that accomplish the wishes of both spouses and offer protection from the ebb and flow of federal and state regulation as well as potential adversarial family members.

EXAMPLE
Peter and Alex are married in Delaware but move to Nebraska. Peter is a small business owner and in bad health. Peter predeceases Alex and has an adjustable gross estate of $8,000,000. From a federal estate tax perspective, the estate can pass to Alex free of taxation, as Alex would receive an exemption being Peter's spouse. Nebraska would not recognize the marriage under constitutional amendment and would subject anything Alex inherited from Peter to an inheritance tax of 18 percent ($1,440,000) as Nebraska would not define Peter as an immediate or remote relative.
If Peter and Alex lived in a state which recognized same sex marriage or in a state without an inheritance tax, they would avoid $1.4 million in taxation. Prior planning would have allowed an insurance solution to this tax issue or a trust arrangement which would allow the business to continue running well after Peter's death.

inherited IRA

five-year averaging

lump sum distribution

Upon inheritance of qualified retirement plans or individual retirement accounts, partners in a civil union are not able to open spousal IRA rollover accounts. Instead they have three options available:

1. Transfer proceeds into an inherited IRA beneficiary distribution account. These accounts are often referred to as "nonspousal IRA accounts" or "beneficiary IRA accounts." This allows a beneficiary to continue to benefit from tax deferral over time but is subject to minimum required distributions. If the deceased had not begun taking distributions, they are based on the age of the beneficiary and must begin the year following the passing of the decedent. If the deceased had begun taking minimum distributions, a client can choose between making distributions based on the deceased's age or their own age. These minimum withdraws are not subject to any early withdraw penalties.

2. Take advantage of five-year averaging. Five-year averaging allows the beneficiary of an IRA, 401(k), or select defined-contribution accounts to withdraw inherited proceeds from the account over a five-year period. This election eliminates any early withdrawal penalties. Any distributed gains or deferred contributions will remain taxable.

3. Distribute proceeds into a nonqualified account in a lump-sum distribution. Assets may be distributed out of the IRA but will likely incur a significant tax burden on the recipient. Lump-sum distributions may be appropriate to generate liquidity but are not eligible to continue tax-deferred growth.

Understanding the intersection of state inheritance and estate tax rules along with same sex-marriage recognition is critical when working with affluent same-sex clients.

Taxation

The Internal Revenue Service (IRS) has answered specific questions regarding filing status and challenges for same-sex spouses who are married, as well as couples who are in domestic partnerships. This guidance can only be applied to federal income tax issues. State income, inheritance, property, and gift tax issues are a function of state laws and may quickly become complicated.

EXAMPLE
Bill and Ted live in Georgia. They were married on a visit to New York and later returned to Georgia. Bill and Ted will follow federal rules and regulations when filing a federal income tax return, but they are subject to state laws and regulations when filing a state income tax return. Federally, they can elect married filing jointly or married filing separately filing statuses, but on a state level they are limited to filing as two single individuals.

The IRS has provided frequently asked questions and answers to tax questions for same-sex married couples and those in domestic partnerships. A subset of those questions relating to financial planning techniques is included below. Students can find the entire list of questions at http://www.irs.gov/uac/Answers-to-Frequently-Asked-Questions-for-Same-Sex-Married-Coupl

Frequently Asked Questions for Same-Sex Married Couples

lawfully married

Q1. When are individuals of the same-sex lawfully married for federal tax purposes?

A1. For federal tax purposes, the IRS looks to state or foreign law to determine whether individuals are married. The IRS has a general rule recognizing a marriage of same-sex spouses that was validly entered into in a domestic or foreign jurisdiction whose laws authorize the marriage of two individuals of the same sex even if the married couple resides in a domestic or foreign jurisdiction that does not recognize the validity of same-sex marriages.

federal tax returns **Q2.** Can same-sex spouses file federal tax returns using a married filing jointly or married filing separately status?

A2. Yes. For tax year 2013 and going forward, same-sex spouses generally must file using a married filing separately or jointly filing status. For tax year 2012 and all prior years, same-sex spouses who file an original tax return on or after Sept. 16, 2013 (the effective date of Rev. Rul. 2013-17) generally must file using a married filing separately or jointly filing status. For tax year 2012, same-sex spouses who filed their tax return before Sept. 16, 2013, may choose (but are not required) to amend their federal tax returns to file using married filing separately or jointly filing status. For tax years 2011 and earlier, same-sex spouses who filed their tax returns timely may choose (but are not required) to amend their federal tax returns to file using married filing separately or jointly filing status provided the period of limitations for amending the return has not expired. A taxpayer generally may file a claim for refund for three years from the date the return was filed or two years from the date the tax was paid, whichever is later. For information on filing an amended return, go to Tax Topic 308, Amended Returns, at http://www.irs.gov/taxtopics/tc308.html.

joint return **Q3.** Can a taxpayer and his or her same-sex spouse file a joint return if they were married in a state that recognizes same-sex marriages but they live in a state that does not recognize their marriage?

A3. Yes. For federal tax purposes, the IRS has a general rule recognizing a marriage of same-sex individuals that was validly entered into in a domestic or foreign jurisdiction whose laws authorize the marriage of two individuals of the same sex even if the married couple resides in a domestic or foreign jurisdiction that does not recognize the validity of same-sex marriages. The rules for using a married filing jointly or married filing separately status described in Q&A #2 apply to these married individuals.

Q4. Can a taxpayer's same-sex spouse be a dependent of the taxpayer?

A4. No. A taxpayer's spouse cannot be a dependent of the taxpayer.

Q5. Can a same-sex spouse file using head of household filing status?

A5. A taxpayer who is married cannot file using head of household filing status. However, a married taxpayer may be considered unmarried and may use the head-of-household filing status if the taxpayer lives apart from his or her spouse for the last 6 months of the taxable year and provides more than half the cost of maintaining a household that is the principal place of abode of the taxpayer's dependent child for more than half of the year. See Publication 501 for more details.

Q6. If same-sex spouses (who file using the married filing separately status) have a child, which parent may claim the child as a dependent?

A6. If a child is a qualifying child under section 152(c) of both parents who are spouses (who file using the married filing separate status), either parent, but not both, may claim a dependency deduction for the qualifying child. If both parents claim a dependency deduction for the child on their income tax returns, the IRS will treat the child as the qualifying child of the parent with whom the child resides for the longer period of time during the taxable year. If the child resides with each parent for the same amount of time during the taxable year, the IRS will treat the child as the qualifying child of the parent with the higher adjusted gross income.

Q7. Can a taxpayer who is married to a person of the same sex claim the standard deduction if the taxpayer's spouse itemized deductions?

A7. No. If a taxpayer's spouse itemized his or her deductions, the taxpayer cannot claim the standard deduction (section 63(c)(6)(A)).

Q8. If a taxpayer adopts the child of his or her same-sex spouse as a second parent or coparent, may the taxpayer ("adopting parent") claim the adoption credit for the qualifying adoption expenses he or she pays or incurs to adopt the child?

A8. No. The adopting parent may not claim an adoption credit. A taxpayer may not claim an adoption credit for expenses incurred in adopting the child of the taxpayer's spouse (section 23).

Q9. Do provisions of the federal tax law such as section 66 (treatment of community income) and section 469(i)(5) ($25,000 offset for passive activity losses for rental real estate activities) apply to same-sex spouses?

A9. Yes. Like other provisions of the federal tax law that apply to married taxpayers, section 66 and section 469(i)(5) apply to same-sex spouses because same-sex spouses are married for all federal tax purposes.

Q10. If an employer provided health coverage for an employee's same-sex spouse and included the value of that coverage in the employee's gross income, can the employee file an amended Form 1040 reflecting the employee's status as a married individual to recover federal income tax paid on the value of the health coverage of the employee's spouse?

A10. Yes, for all years for which the period of limitations for filing a claim for refund is open. Generally, a taxpayer may file a claim for refund for three years from the date the return was filed or two years from the date the tax was paid, whichever is later. If an employer provided health coverage for an employee's same-sex spouse, the employee may claim a refund of income taxes paid on the value of coverage that would have been excluded from income had the employee's spouse been recognized as the employee's legal spouse for tax purposes. This claim for a refund generally would be made through the filing of an amended Form 1040. For information on filing an amended return, go to Tax Topic 308, Amended Returns, at http://www.irs.gov/taxtopics/tc308.html. For a discussion regarding refunds of Social Security and Medicare taxes, see Q&A #12 and Q&A #13.

EXAMPLE

Employer sponsors a group health plan covering eligible employees and their dependents and spouses (including same-sex spouses). Fifty percent of the cost of health coverage elected by employees is paid by Employer. Employee A was married to same-sex Spouse B at all times during 2012. Employee A elected coverage for Spouse B through Employer's group health plan beginning Jan. 1, 2012. The value of the employer-funded portion of Spouse B's health coverage was $250 per month.

The amount in Box 1, "Wages, tips, other compensation," of the 2012 Form W-2 provided by Employer to Employee A included $3,000 ($250 per month x 12 months) of income reflecting the value of employer-funded health coverage provided to Spouse B. Employee A filed Form 1040 for the 2012 taxable year reflecting the Box 1 amount reported on Form W-2.

Employee A may file an amended Form 1040 for the 2012 taxable year excluding the value of Spouse B's employer-funded health coverage ($3,000) from gross income.

IRS Question and Answer: Registered Domestic Partners

**registered
domestic partners**

Q1. Can registered domestic partners file federal tax returns using a married filing jointly or married filing separately status?

A1. No. Registered domestic partners may not file a federal return using a married filing separately or jointly filing status. Registered domestic partners are not married under state law. Therefore, these taxpayers are not married for federal tax purposes.

Q2. Can a taxpayer use the head-of-household filing status if the taxpayer's only dependent is his or her registered domestic partner?

A2. No. A taxpayer cannot file as head of household if the taxpayer's only dependent is his or her registered domestic partner. A taxpayer's registered domestic partner is not one of the specified related individuals in section 152(c) or (d) that qualifies the taxpayer to file as head of household, even if the registered domestic partner is the taxpayer's dependent.

Q3. If registered domestic partners have a child, which parent may claim the child as a dependent?

A3. If a child is a qualifying child under section 152(c) of both parents who are registered domestic partners, either parent, but not both, may claim a dependency deduction for the qualifying child. If both parents claim a dependency deduction for the child on their income tax returns, the IRS will treat the child as the qualifying child of the parent with whom the child resides for the longer period of time during the taxable year. If the child resides with each parent for the same amount of time during the taxable year, the IRS will treat the child as the qualifying child of the parent with the higher adjusted gross income.

Q4. Can a registered domestic partner itemize deductions if his or her partner claims a standard deduction?

A4. Yes. A registered domestic partner may itemize or claim the standard deduction regardless of whether his or her partner itemizes or claims the standard deduction. Although the law prohibits a taxpayer from itemizing deductions if the taxpayer's spouse claims the standard deduction (section 63(c)(6)(A)), this provision does not apply to registered domestic partners, because registered domestic partners are not spouses for federal tax purposes.

Q5. If registered domestic partners adopt a child together, can one or both of the registered domestic partners qualify for the adoption credit?

A5. Yes. Each registered domestic partner may qualify to claim the adoption credit for the amount of the qualified adoption expenses paid for the adoption. The partners may not both claim a credit for the same qualified adoption expenses, and the sum of the credit taken by each registered domestic partner may not exceed the total amount paid. The adoption credit is limited to $12,970 per child in 2013 [$13,190 in 2014]. Thus, if both registered domestic partners paid qualified adoption expenses to adopt the same child, and the total of those expenses exceeds $12,970 [$13,190 in 2014], the maximum credit available for the adoption is $12,970 [$13,190 in 2014]. The registered domestic partners may allocate this maximum between them in any way they agree, and the amount of credit claimed by one registered domestic partner can exceed the adoption expenses paid by that person, as long as the total credit claimed by both registered domestic partners does not exceed the total amount paid by them. The same rules generally apply in the case of a special needs adoption.

Q6. If a taxpayer adopts the child of his or her registered domestic partner as a second parent or coparent, may the taxpayer ("adopting parent") claim the adoption credit for the qualifying adoption expenses he or she pays to adopt the child?

A6. Yes. The adopting parent may be eligible to claim an adoption credit. A taxpayer may not claim an adoption credit for the expenses of adopting the child of the taxpayer's spouse (section 23). However, this limitation does not apply to adoptions by registered domestic partners because registered domestic partners are not spouses for federal tax purposes.

Q7. Do provisions of the federal tax law such as section 66 (treatment of community income) and section 469(i)(5) ($25,000 offset for passive activity losses for rental real estate activities) that apply to married taxpayers apply to registered domestic partners?

A7. No. Like other provisions of the federal tax law that apply only to married taxpayers, section 66 and section 469(i)(5) do not apply to registered domestic partners because registered domestic partners are not married for federal tax purposes.

Q8. Is a registered domestic partner the stepparent of his or her partner's child?

A8. If a registered domestic partner is the stepparent of his or her partner's child under state law, the registered domestic partner is the stepparent of the child for federal income tax purposes.

Publication 555, Community Property, provides general information for taxpayers, including registered domestic partners, who reside in community property states. The following questions and answers provide additional information to registered domestic partners (including same-sex and opposite-sex registered domestic partners) who reside in community property states and are subject to community property laws.

Q9. How do registered domestic partners determine their gross income?

A9. Registered domestic partners must each report half the combined community income earned by the partners. In addition to half of the community income, a partner who has income that is not community income must report that separate income.

Q10. Can a registered domestic partner qualify to file his or her tax return using head-of-household filing status?

A10. Generally, to qualify as a head-of-household, a taxpayer must provide more than half the cost of maintaining his or her household during the taxable year, and that household must be the principal place of abode of the taxpayer's dependent for more than half of the taxable year (section 2(b)). If registered domestic partners pay all of the costs of maintaining the household from community funds, each partner is considered to have incurred half the cost and neither can qualify as head of household. Even if one of the partners pays more than half by contributing separate funds, that partner cannot file as head of household if the only dependent is his or her registered domestic partner. A taxpayer's registered domestic partner is not one of the specified related individuals in section 152(c) or (d) that qualifies the taxpayer to file as head of household, even if the partner is the taxpayer's dependent.

These frequently-asked questions were provided in September of 2013. As court challenges and constitutional amendments continue to shape policy, these rules will evolve. Financial advisers must maintain relevant readings and a current understanding of dynamic tax planning for members of the LGBT community.

Investment Planning

Investment planning is likely the area of financial planning with the fewest differences between different-sex and same-sex couples. Any client may be interested in adopting a social investing style which favors firms who are friendly to the LGBT community. The evidence of this investing style resulting in any appreciable differences in returns compared to investing in the overall market is mixed.

Credit Suisse has created a Corporate Equality Index, which ranks and tracks companies based on pro-LGBT policies. More about the index can be found at http://www.hrc.org/campaigns/corporate-equality-index. Brokerage firms with outdated systems may have difficulties listing same-sex individuals as married, and advisers should perform diligence to ensure their clients will be properly accounted for.

Marrying a registered domestic partner allows for accounts which were titled jointly to be titled joint with rights of survivorship. Additionally, as mentioned in the tax section, community income generated from investment property may belong equally to both spouses. Community and jointly-held assets can have meaningful impacts on spouses' estates and their ability to receive public assistance and benefits. Financial advisers should consider consulting with tax advisers and CPA professionals before retitling investment accounts.

risk tolerance Risk tolerance should be measured across all clients in a financial planning relationship who are titled on an account. Account titling may be limited due to state recognition of marriage, but generally, pay-on-death accounts, joint accounts titled tenants in common (JTIC), and trust accounts are available regardless of geographical limitation. These types of accounts protect a surviving spouse or member of a civil union upon the death of an account holder.

Annuity contracts used to assist in retirement planning may present challenges to LGBT clients. Annuity contracts are composed of owner(s), annuitant(s), and beneficiary. As insurance law is governed on a state level, some states may not recognize a same-sex marriage and limit the types of contracts available (such as joint life annuitants) to a couple. Financial advisers should seek out insurance companies who regularly do business with same-sex couples to prevent unusual limitations or pricing structures.

Retirement Planning

Retirement planning for LGBT clients contains more unknowns (as of February 2014) than other financial planning topic areas. The 2013 repeal of the Defense of Marriage Act has led to immediate income tax reforms, but Social Security and Medicare reforms will likely face court battles. Medicaid and Medicare planning are hybrid programs, and as such, their reforms will pose a unique set of hurdles. Financial advisers must maintain a working knowledge of current regional, state, and national issues when addressing potentially irrevocable retirement planning decisions.

Same-sex couples face retirement planning decisions similar to those of their different-sex counterparts. Common questions include: When should retirement occur? How will retirement be structured? Where will we live? Will we work part time? Which assets should we pull resources from and in what order? How much should we spend? What happens if one of us is sick?

Complicating the conversation of retirement for same-sex couples is an issue of domestic partnership or marriage. The Social Security Administration and veterans' benefits programs have traditionally not recognized domestic partnerships as eligible for benefits but have adopted guidelines for legally married couples. As of 2013, same-sex married couples are treated in the same manner as different-sex married couples for the following federal benefits, even if their marriage is not recognized in their home state or they were legally married outside of their home state:

- Social Security retirement benefits
- Social Security survivor benefits
- Social Security disability benefits
- Medicare Parts A and B
- Medicare Part C
- Medicare Advantage Plans
- Medicare Part D
- Medicaid (with some state exceptions)
- federal housing programs
- veterans benefit programs

The Social Security Administration has created a guide of specific questions relating to same sex couples; it can be found at http://www.ssa.gov/same-sexcouples/. This resource contains material about the claims process, frequently asked questions, and application guidelines.

Domestic partnerships are not likely to qualify for these benefits. Additionally, same-sex couples may face additional discrimination hurdles imposed by regional, state, or local institutions and governments. Nursing homes and retirement communities are state regulated, and most are privately owned and operated, which leads to unequal experiences for many Americans. Financial advisers working with LGBT clients must keep in mind the challenges their clients face in addition to the complexities of planning for retirement.

Conclusion

This chapter is intended to introduce nuances in planning for LGBT clients while emphasizing the importance of building a capable and competent team to navigate a complicated state-by-state planning environment. ChFC®s working with members of the LGBT community must spend time learning about their state of practice as well as states in which their clients own property or regularly travel. Those who do not regularly work within the LGBT community can develop partnerships with planners who do, and they can ensure their clients are met with competence and understanding.

Bibliography

Douglas, P. (2007, October). Diversity and the gay and lesbian community: More than chasing the pink dollar. Ivey Business Journal. 1-8.

Kapp, J., & Burkholder, N. (2008, March). A guide to serving the estate and financial planning needs of gay men, lesbians, and same sex couples. The Journal of Financial Planning, 54-64.

Still out, still aging: The Metlife study of lesbian, gay, bisexual, and transgender baby boomers. (2010, March). MetLife Mature Market Institute & The American Society on Aging. Retrieved from https://www.metlife.com/assets/cao/mmi/publications/studies/2010/mmi-still-out-still-aging.pdf

Chapter Review

Review questions are based on the learning objectives in this chapter. Thus, a [3] at the end of a question means that the question is based on learning objective 3. If there are multiple objectives, they are all listed.

Key Terms and Concepts

Chartered Financial Consultant®	life insurance
same-sex	property and casualty insurance
transgendered	health insurance
eight ethical canons	intestate
professional pledge	medical directives
ascertain	living wills
understand	powers of attorney
fact-finding	inherited IRA
bankruptcy	five-year averaging
credit management	lump sum distribution
community property	lawfully married
adoption	federal tax returns
divorce	joint return
financial aid	registered domestic partners
McCarran-Ferguson Act of 1945	risk tolerance

Review Questions

1. Why does working with two same-sex clients present challenges not found when working with different-sex clients? [1]

2. How does the professional pledge of The American College apply to a ChFC® professional working with a same-sex couple but unfamiliar with the legal framework of the couple's home state? [2]

3. What are the six topics of financial planning which present differences when working with members of the LGBT community? [3]

4. What type of questions should be included in fact finding when working with clients who are members of the LGBT community? [3]

5. How can divorce become complicated for same sex couples who are legally married? [3]

6. Why are medical directives and powers of attorney potentially more important for clients in same-sex relationships than married, different-sex clients? [3]

7. When are individuals of the same sex lawfully married for federal tax purposes? [3]

8. Can a taxpayer and his or her same-sex spouse file a joint return if they were married in a state that recognizes same-sex marriages but they live in a state that does not recognize their marriage? [3]

9. Can registered domestic partners file federal tax returns using a married filing jointly or married filing separately status? [3]

10. Where can a financial adviser find more information about companies who have pro-LGBT policies? [3]

Learning Objectives

An understanding of the material in this chapter should enable you to

1. Identify the major impact of *Windsor v. U.S.* on LGBT clients and financial services professionals.

2. Identify the primary impediment(s) to LGBT clients achieving traditional financial planning goals.

3. Distinguish the differences between state and federal laws regarding same-sex marriages.

4. Discuss a number of considerations a financial services professional must make when deciding to include LGBT clients in their practice.

Introduction

LGBT

Windsor v. United States

In this chapter, practical applications of the changes brought about by *Windsor v. United States* and how they actually impact planning professionals and their lesbian, gay, transgendered and bisexual clients (LGBT) will be considered. In addition, the results of a number of interviews conducted with planners serving the LGBT community, as a part of their day-to-day professional practices, are included, This material will assist the reader in recognizing and better understanding a number of issues facing financial advisors when they are working with LGBT clients. Lastly, a list of resources identified by practicing planners in the LGBT community that will be beneficial to planners deciding whether to include LGBT clients in their practices, is included.

By now, practicing financial services professionals will have undoubtedly noticed that working with nontraditional clients and couples, be they LGBT or heterosexual, unmarried couples, requires a knowledge base and skill set that are different from those required to competently serve traditional clients and couples.

In almost every area of planning, the reasons for LGBT couples requiring alternative planning tools and techniques are based, primarily, on each state's definition of marriage. Despite the precedent-setting ruling by the Supreme Court of the United States in *Windsor v. United States*, financial planning issues remain primarily a state issue, since marriage remains a state issue. Although *Windsor* established the right of legally married, same-sex couples to have access to previously denied federal benefits; it did nothing to clarify the issue for same-sex couples involved in a myriad of other legally recognized relationships, not defined as marriage. In addition to the issue of marriage recognition, are the values, beliefs, goals and objectives of the LGBT client. The purpose of this chapter is to provide a greater understanding of the challenges that face LGBT clients, as they seek to secure their financial future, through financial planning. In addition, it is hoped that this material, especially the insights gained through planner interviews and the research conducted by Prudential Financial, Inc., will also serve as the catalytic thought for a financial planner to decide, "Do I want to serve the LGBT community in my practice?"

Brief History

DOMA

same-sex marriage

An often quoted statistic, attributed to the Government Accounting Office, is the 1,138 federal benefits that were available to married heterosexual couples but denied married, same-sex couples. This was the essence of what the Supreme Court of the United States struck down by their ruling in *Windsor v. United States*. In the case *Windsor v. United States*, the Supreme Court, in a 5-4 ruling, struck down Section 3 of the Defense of Marriage Act (DOMA). DOMA was legislation passed in 1996 by a bipartisan congress and signed into law by then President Bill Clinton. Section 3 of DOMA restricted federal recognition of same-sex marriage for the purposes of federal benefits.

Specifically, *Windsor v. United States* dealt with the case of Edie Windsor and the estate tax bill she faced upon the death of her legally married, same-sex spouse, Thea Spyer. Windsor and Spyer had been life partners since 1963, registered domestic partners in the State of New York since 1993, and legally married under Canadian law since 2007.

Thea Spyer died in 2009. Upon her death, Thea left her estate to her life partner and spouse of 46 years, Edie. As Spyer's executrix, Windsor completed her federal estate tax return claiming the marital deduction for the amounts she inherited. The IRS rejected the return and Windsor was left with a tax bill of $363,053. Windsor filed suit in New York State's Southern District Court, seeking a refund of the taxes paid.

The court granted Windsor's petition and ordered a refund for Windsor, based on finding Congress's intention in excluding same-sex marriages from the definition of marriage for federal purposes failed under equal protection grounds. This ruling followed the precedent set in *Massachusetts v. U.S. Health and Human Services*, by the First District Court of Massachusetts in its ruling on this matter, May 31, 2012. The lower court's ruling was appealed and, by a 2-1 decision, the Second District Court of Appeals held that DOMA was unconstitutional under the Equal Protection Clause of the Fifth Amendment.

The Supreme Court of the United States (SCOTUS) accepted the case for review and heard oral arguments on March 27, 2013. On June 26, 2013, SCOTUS handed down its ruling and, as of that date, granted same-sex couples access to the 1,138 benefits formerly available only to traditionally defined married couples. This ruling further prohibited the federal government from using any classifications on the recognition of marriage and further determined that marriage, per se, is a state issue. (Karbijanian, 2013)

So, what does all that have to do with the practice of being a financial services professional? As implied in the opening paragraphs of this chapter, the world of financial services professionals has changed. Financial planners now face planning issues many have never faced before, especially those with lesbian, gay, bisexual and transgendered (LGBT) clients.

Let us begin by considering some of the effects this court ruling will have on LGBT clients. What are some of the 1,138 benefits available to LGBT couples today that have never been available to them before on the federal and, in many cases, the state level as well?

The first and most obvious benefit is the ability to file a joint federal income tax return. Additional considerations in the financial planning area include:

- claiming marital deductions for gift and estate taxes
- splitting lifetime gifts
- naming a spouse as beneficiary under a qualified retirement account
- allowing rollover of qualified accounts at the death of a spouse
- simplifying rules related to joint ownership of property;
- granting of Social Security, Medicare and Medicaid benefits

- strengthening federal provisions relating to hospital visitation rights.

These are but a few of the more important considerations on which advisors and planners will need to educate themselves going forward, and depending upon the scope and nature of their practice, they may have to do so for more than one set of state laws. (GAO, 2004)

While this ruling may be thought to have "regularized or normalized" the issue relating to financial services on the federal level, the situation is very different on the state level where licensed financial advisors and insurance professionals live their daily professional lives At present, eighteen states, and the District of Columbia, recognize same-sex marriage. In addition, there are other states that recognize some form of same-sex partnership for state tax and benefits purposes. These other relationships, however, do not presently meet the standard of the definition of marriage. Therefore, they do not benefit from *Windsor v. United States*.

The lack of formal education, in the financial tools and techniques needed to ethically perform the tasks required, is one of the first obstacles financial planners will face, when deciding to serve LGBT community. The primary courses found in the standard CFP educational curricula programs do not adequately prepare a planner to accomplish the mission of ethically and professionally providing financial planning advice to this community. A specialized program developed by the College for Financial Planning that does partially address the needs of nontraditional families and LGBT clients, is the Accredited Domestic Partner Advisor. This is a self-study program with four modules: Wealth Transfer, Federal Taxation, Retirement Planning, and Planning for Financial Medical and End of Life Issues (CFP Board, 2014). Because of the lack of professional education resources in this area, most financial professionals servicing the LGBT community have had to cobble together their own unique set of affiliated professionals, to address each of the areas mentioned. Affiliated professionals include attorneys, CPAs, insurance professionals and financial planning professionals who are educated in the needs and issues facing the LGBT community.

Until now, the standard courses within the ChFC® Designation Program also failed to meet the educational needs of advisors desiring to serve the LGBT community. Filling that need is one of the primary purposes of including this material in the newly revamped ChFC curriculum of The American College for Financial Services.

Where Do We Stand Today?

As one of the interviewed financial planners stated, the world is evolving almost daily, in this arena. During the time spent researching and writing this material, three additional states approved recognition of same-sex marriage. (The information contained herein reflects the status of recognized same-sex-marriage states, as of December 31, 2013.)

Below are the states that ban same-sex marriage, by constitutional amendment and state law, with the year the amendment passed and the year their state law passed.

States Banning Same-Sex Marriage		
State	**Constitutional Amendment**	**State Law**
Alabama	2006	1998
Alaska	1998	1996
Arizona	2004	1997
Arkansas	2004	1997
Colorado	2006	2000
Florida	2008	1997
Georgia	2004	1996
Idaho	2006	1996
Kansas	2005	1996
Kentucky	2004	1998
Louisiana	2004	1999
Michigan	2004	1996
Mississippi	2004	1997
Missouri	2004	1996
Montana	2004	1997
North Carolina	2012	1995
North Dakota	2004	1997
Ohio	2004	2004
Oklahoma	2004	1996
South Carolina	2006	1996
South Dakota	2006	1996
Tennessee	2006	1996
Texas	2005	1997
Virginia	2006	1997
Wisconsin	2006	1979

These states ban same-sex marriage by constitutional amendment only:		
Nebraska	2000	
Nevada	1997	
Oregon	2004	
These states ban same-sex marriage by state law only:		
Indiana		1997
Pennsylvania		1996
West Virginia		2000
States having *no ban* on same-sex marriage:		
New Mexico		

A number of states recognize same-sex marriage today. These states came to permit same-sex marriage through three different approaches to the issue: by court decision, by state legislature and by popular vote. Here is a breakdown of those states and the manner by which same-sex marriage became legal in each:

Breakdown of Recognition States, by Method Granting Recognition:		
State	**Year**	**Method**
California*	2013	Court Decision
Connecticut	2008	Court Decision
Iowa	2009	Court Decision
Massachusetts	2004	Court Decision
New Mexico	2013	Court Decision
Utah**	2013	Court Decision
New Jersey	2013	Court Decision
Delaware	2013	State Legislature
Illinois***	2014	State Legislature
Minnesota	2013	State Legislature
New Hampshire	2010	State Legislature
Rhode Island	2013	State Legislature
Vermont	2009	State Legislature
Maine	2012	Popular Vote
Maryland	2013	Popular Vote
Washington, DC	2012	Popular Vote

*On Feb. 7, 2012, the Ninth Circuit Court of Appeals affirmed that California's anti-gay marriage initiative known as Proposition 8 was unconstitutional. That case was appealed to the U.S. Supreme Court. On June 26, 2013, in a 5-4 decision, the Supreme Court ruled that defenders of Proposition 8 lacked "standing" to represent the case. As a result, the Ninth Circuit Court of Appeals lifted its stay blocking same-sex marriages on June 28, 2013 (gaymarriageprocon.org).
**Utah became the 18th state to recognize same-sex marriage, December 22, 2013, on 14th Amendment Grounds. The federal court judge's decision is currently under appeal.
***Illinois became the 15th state to permit same-sex marriage on November 5, 2013. The law will go into effect June 1, 2014.

Source: gaymarriageprocon.org.

For a time line of the information covered in this section, see Supplement A.

Where Does this Leave Financial Services Professionals Today?

The art and science of advising same-sex couples today remains a challenge. Some of the issues remaining to be clarified include:

- the marriage penalty? Should same-sex couples marry or not?
- what about divorce?
- state of celebration vs. state of residence
- states recognition of out-of-state marriages

state of celebration

state of residence

While this material will not answer these questions, it does point out some of the areas where differences exist between advising LGBT versus non-LGBT clients. It is clear that marriage equality laws, or the lack thereof, are the primary impediment to equality in financial planning solutions as well. This issue is very complicated. For example, the difference between the *state of celebration* and the *state of residence* is a meaningful issue and serves as the aforementioned example. Effective with taxes filed for tax year 2014, the IRS will adopt the state-of-celebration standard. That is, where did the marriage take place? If the marriage was performed in a state recognizing the marriage, then the couple is considered married and will be required to file tax returns accordingly. On the other hand, for purposes of receiving OASDI (Social Security benefits), Medicare, and other federal benefits, the state of residence is the determining factor as to whether or not benefits will be payable to a surviving spouse. Therefore, as mentioned earlier, despite the changes at the federal level, state laws remain a determining factor in serving and advising clients.

One of the planners interviewed for inclusion in this material spoke at the Financial Planning Association Convention in September 2013. During one of his presentations, he gave a practical example of how these differences in marriage equality laws affect real people. A legally married couple from Maryland drove into Virginia to do some shopping at a store that did not have locations in Maryland. In Virginia, their marriage was not recognized. The couple was involved in a serious auto accident and one spouse was taken to the hospital, critically injured. Under Virginia law, the other spouse had no rights to assist in the medical decision-making normally ascribed to legally married spouses. The husband was forced to locate his spouse's mother, from whom he was estranged, and get her to make medical decisions for a son with whom she had severed all ties. This is just one example of the issues with which LGBT couples have to deal, that are not issues in the non-LGBT community. Another example of a same-sex couple affected similarly, in the state of Florida, is included in one of the interviews incorporated into this material.

Methodology

The 2013 Financial Planning Association (FPA) Conference was held in Orlando, FL in September, 2013. Preceding the conference, Pride Planners held a preconference, which featured an update on the after effects of the partial repeal of DOMA, as well as presentations by nationally recognized LGBT-centric financial planning professionals. After returning from Orlando, FL in September, a letter was drafted to Pride Planners, requesting access to their membership, for the purposes of gaining responses to a "practice questionnaire." The Board of Pride Planners agreed to distribute the request for participation and 12 responses were received indicating a willingness to be interviewed. After various scheduling issues, nine practice questionnaires were completed, all of which are included herein. These interviews will provide the reader with some of the information needed for them to decide whether or not they are willing to acquire the education needed to serve the LGBT community, as well as whether or not they have the desire to "advocate and not just tolerate."

The Interviews

During November and December of 2013, the aforementioned outreach to a number of practicing planners was conducted, requesting completion of a practice standards questionnaire. Only 2–3 responses had been anticipated but nine responses were received. Eight of the nine participants were members of Pride Planners, an organization of "financial professionals serving the gay and lesbian community." (www.prideplanners.org) The ninth participant was a referral from a Pride Planners member.

The group of planners who volunteered to participate in this project had the following characteristics:

- Most are in their 50s.
- Eight of the nine are gay or lesbian.
- All have college degrees; four have advanced degrees and all hold multiple professional designations.
- They vary in practice size and scope; all classify themselves as comprehensive planners.
- Six of nine have a higher percentage of LGBT clients than non-LGBT clients.
- Six of nine have nationwide practices.
- All participate in local LGBT community service organizations. At least three serve on national boards as well.

The nine interviews are presented, in alphabetical order, preceded by the practice standards questionnaire attached to the email, sent to each participant, prior to the interview.

The materials presented herein, reflect the status of same-sex marriage laws in effect as of December 31, 2013. Changes in marriage equality laws will undoubtedly continue to occur, as there are numerous court challenges presently being contested.

Practice Standards Questionnaire

I would like to conduct interviews with 3-6 practicing planners who serve the LGBT community. Ideally, they would be willing to be quoted, in print, in a text book I am co-editor/authoring. I will also accept planners who, for personal or professional reasons, do not care to be quoted.

Those electing not to be quoted will have their contributions attributed as, "According to one financial services practitioner, serving the LGBT community…"

Here is the script I will be following when conducting your interview.

1. "How did you come to be a financial planner? When did you decide to include the LGBT Community in your practice?
2. What is the scope of your practice? Modular, specific, focused or comprehensive? Solo shop or team based? Do you affiliate with other professionals to provide "full service?" (Attorneys, CPAs, Insurance Professionals, etc.)
3. What are the issues you face in providing financial planning advice to LGBT clients that are different than issues you address for your non-LGBT clients?
4. What are the three most important things you would say to a planner considering serving the LGBT community?
5. What are the "top LGBT resources" you would recommend for inclusion in a planners digital rolodex?
6. Demographic Data: Age, gender, marital status, area of the country where you practice, years in the business, etc.

Thank you for your time and for your contributions!

Kevin M. Lynch, ABD, CFP, ChFC, CLU, RHU, REBC, CASL, CAP, LUTCF, FSS
Asst. Professor of Insurance and Charles J. Zimmerman Chair of Insurance Education
The American College of Financial Services

Stuart Armstrong II

"How did you come to be a financial planner? When did you decide to include the LGBT Community in your practice?"

Before I became a financial planner, I wanted to be a doctor and I actually went to medical school, after getting an undergraduate degree in Biology. Once in medical school, however, I determined that it was not for me so I went into the Bio Tech field. After a downturn in that industry, I serendipitously saw an ad from a predecessor company of Ameriprise, IDS, and looked into the field of financial services. Although I did not join IDS, it did open my eyes to possibilities in the field and I entered the field in 1985.

As a gay man, I was open to working in and serving the LGBT community from the very beginning of my career. My employer hired me, with the knowledge that I intended to serve the LGBT community. Today I have a book of business that is approximately 40/60 gay-straight.

"What is the scope of your practice? Modular, specific, focused or comprehensive? Solo shop or team based? Do you affiliate with other professionals to provide "full service?" (Attorneys, CPAs, Insurance Professionals, etc.)"

I am one of 70 financial advisors in my firm. Each of us has an independent practice. My practice is comprehensive in nature, with a heavy focus on aspects of wealth management. My investment and insurance work is done in-house and I work with associated professionals, including Attorneys, CPAs, and Property & Casualty Insurance Professionals, in order to provide a full slate of services to my clients.

Although I do not focus solely on minimums for accepting clients, I do have clients mainly with $250,000 or more to invest. I consider my clients more holistically, however, considering the entire relationship potential and not just AUM (assets under management) potential.

My focus is on families and individuals, as well as small business owners. I use a fee based compensation system, with fee-only plans available as well as plans with fees adjusted to reflect additional relationships services. I also accept some clients on an "hourly, as needed" basis as well as insurance or investment advisory only clients.

"What are the issues you face in providing financial planning advice to LGBT clients that are different than issues you address for your non-LGBT clients?"

My practice is based in Massachusetts, which was one of the states that recognized same sex marriages early on. This has caused a recent focus on revisiting planning that was done over the past few years, to make sure that with the recent changes at the federal level, plans are still providing the protections to clients for which they were designed. Areas of focus for review include taxes, estate planning and survivorship issues.

In addition to same-sex marriage issues, there are now issues with divorce for same-sex couples.

On the insurance side of the ledger, there are planning issues in long term care insurance planning.

In the area of titling of property, there are any number of machinations required to achieve goals that non-LGBT clients do not have to endure. As an example, just to purchase a home together, some clients have to execute partnership agreements and deal with gifting issues.

"What are the three most important things you would say to a planner considering serving the LGBT community?"

In addition to establishing that anyone in the financial planning industry must have adequate education and experience, there are additional considerations when dealing with LGBT clients.

To begin with, you must be genuine! You must genuinely have a desire to serve the community and to be of service to the community. You have to be sensitive when discussing planning as well as personal issues.

In addition to traditional financial planning education, you must be committed to researching and learning the challenges faced by members of the LGBT community. As a baseline, you will want to have at least the additional knowledge of having completed the ADPA (Accredited Domestic Partner Advisor) program through the College for Financial Planning.

"What are the "top LGBT resources" you would recommend for inclusion in a planners digital rolodex?"

As a start, you will want to be a member of Pride Planners, for the professional connections. Then, educationally, you will want to complete the Accredited Domestic Partner Advisor Program (ADPA).

As far as organizations are concerned, The National Gay and Lesbian Taskforce is an important organization to be aware of. Another great resource is the Human Rights Campaign. Their website has a number of resources all planners serving the LGBT community will find beneficial.

As far as printed materials go, Nolo Press publishes material from multiple authors including Frederick Hertz, an attorney in Oakland, CA who wrote Making it Legal. There is another great new book out by Scott Squillace, an attorney from Boston. It is titled, Whether to Wed.

"Demographic Data: Age, gender, marital status, area of the country where you practice, years in the business, etc."

I am 54 years old, a legally married gay man, with a nationwide practice. I have been in the business since 1985 and my spouse is an accounting professional.

Nan Bailey

"How did you come to be a financial planner? When did you decide to include the LGBT Community in your practice?"

About age 30 I had completed by MBA in Accounting and I was working in a small firm that had extensive ties to the Interior Design World. The owner of the firm died of AIDS and I found myself in the midst of making a career decision. While speaking to a "headhunter" about my employment future, he planted the seeds of the idea of becoming a financial planner and after coming across a brochure for The College for Financial Planning at the New York Public Library, I was hooked on the idea.

I began in the business with Mutual Benefit Life, and I built my business through "warm calling" clients I had worked with at my old firm. A significant number of those former clients were gay and my business naturally grew through those contacts. My employer was aware I was a lesbian, and while it was not something I hid, neither did I make a point of announcing it to prospective clients.

Through my work and networking, I was introduced to the president of Lambda Legal and was asked to become their treasurer and sit on their board. I served from about 1988 through 1995.

Today my client based is 60-75% LGBT and I am still in contact with my peers at Lambda Legal.

"What is the scope of your practice? Modular, specific, focused or comprehensive? Solo shop or team based? Do you affiliate with other professionals to provide "full service?" (Attorneys, CPAs, Insurance Professionals, etc.)"

I am an independent financial planner associated with Commonwealth. I run a solo shop, using Commonwealth back office support or virtual staff through other services. I build the foundation with each of my clients based upon financial plans exclusively. I charge fees for my plans and offer my clients choices as to other compensation for other services. I especially enjoy the investment planning and investment management aspects of my job. I use *Money Guide Pro* as my primary planning software and my client base consists of predominantly older clients, needing retirement and estate planning services.

Support for all my financial planning product needs is run through Commonwealth, as their service and platform are especially supportive and broad based. I consider them to be "top notch" in all the areas I need their services. When I need outside assistance with taxes, legal documents or insurance and investments, I lean on my group of what I call professional associates.

I maintain relationships with approximately thirty financial, tax and insurance and investment professionals. These relationships also serve to provide me with convenient meeting places, e.g. conference rooms, where I can meet clients in NYC, without having to rent space.

"What are the issues you face in providing financial planning advice to LGBT clients that are different than issues you address for your non-LGBT clients?"

The number one thing you must bring to the table when serving the LGBT community is "sensitivity to your assumption base."

When you have a straight couple come into your office, you can safely assume that they represent one economic unit, where financial matters are concerned. That is not a safe assumption when meeting with an LGBT Couple. In the case of LGBT clients, you would be more accurate to assume you are dealing with two independent economic units, even though there may be some degree of joint ownership or joint spending.

Another area where you will need to gain specialized knowledge is in the area of "workarounds." LGBT clients, depending on their state of residence, may have to use legal documents to achieve end results that straight couples will not need. These documents can include those needed for co-adoption, asset ownership and titling, estate planning, and other related documents. With the recent court decision of *Windsor v. United States*, you will also need to look back on workarounds you have designed for clients previously, to adjust them, where needed.

The mere act of a legally married, same-sex couple traveling state-to-state, presents myriad problems with spousal and marriage recognition. One couple in Florida went on a Disney Cruise with their child and one spouse became seriously ill. The hospital in Florida refused to recognize the married spouse's rights, as they were non-existent under FL law. The spouse died, with the other spouse having no input in treatment and no ability to participate in end-of-life decision-making. Lambda Legal pursued this case and its resolution resulted in a Presidential Executive Order allowing for same-sex couples having hospitalization related access rights.

While marriage is a big issue in the LGBT community, divorce is becoming one as well. Personal experience and $150,000 in legal bills taught me the cost of divorce lesson. In addition, I was one of the first lesbians to go through co-adoption, helping in the drafting of the legal documents when my daughter was co-adopted by my spouse in 1996. The aforementioned divorce was able to benefit from the co-adoption allowing both parents to stay a part of the lives of the children involved.

These are but a few of the issues which make advising LGBT clients more demanding than advising straight clients. Other areas of concern involve, income and gift taxes, estate planning, family dynamics and issues, etc.

"What are the three most important things you would say to a planner considering serving the LGBT community?"

First and foremost, if you are a straight planner, find a way to become involved with the community, in a manner which allows you to contribute, or "pay back" those who spent the 30–40 years sacrificing to gain the progress achieved to date.

Recognize the areas that have had tremendous changes occurring in the last few decades, including those achieved legislatively, through the courts and through the media. One way I contributed was by being on the board of "In the Life," a weekly PBS program which featured stories of LGBT people. From 1992 until today, this group worked tirelessly to present gays on TV in a positive manner. While some believe their goals have been achieved, there remains work to be done.

To educate yourself and to keep current, use social media. Facebook, Linked In, Twitter, etc. can all help you be "in the know." If you are not up to speed on these tools today, "suck it up" and force yourself to learn, to benefit from them. It will make you a better, more informed, and more aware planning professional, in the issues impacting the LGBT community.

"What are the "top LGBT resources" you would recommend for inclusion in a planners digital rolodex?"

I am somewhat biased in my first choice, but Lambda Legal is a tremendous resource. Other excellent websites include FreedomtoMarry.org and the NRC.org. Also, your peers in the LGBT community and the associated professionals who also serve the community are excellent resources.

"Demographic Data: Age, gender, area of the country where you practice, years in the business, etc."

I am a 57-year-old legally married lesbian and the mother of two children. I live in Larchmont, NY and I have been in the business since 1985. In addition to the years I spent with Mutual Benefit Life, I have been associated with Commonwealth for 10 years and 12 years with Nathan & Lewis Securities.

Lori Cannon

"How did you come to be a financial planner? When did you decide to include the LGBT Community in your practice?"

I came to the financial planning industry through a nontraditional route, through the "death care industry." I was a commissioned sales person in the business of selling headstones and memorials to families who had recently lost loved ones. I worked in the field for 10 years, for a family owned business, and when they sold the business to a larger, national company, they "changed the deal on me," basically lowering my commissions. At the time, I was an Edward Jones client and my Jones advisor recruited me into the business. The two of us believed that with my people skills and my ability to work with people who are making emotional decisions, the career path made sense. Fortunately, we were right. I have been with Jones for 10 years.

As a member of the LGBT community, it was natural for me to begin my business prospecting in that community, among others. I have made an attempt to solicit clients from the LGBT community since day one. Early on, I advertised in gay publications but most of them are no longer around. I also supported local LGBT causes and programs. One of my prospecting methods involved partnering up with gay friendly affiliated professionals and offering workshops to educate LGBT prospects in various aspects of financial, investment and estate planning.

Today, about 25% of my clients are gay.

"What is the scope of your practice? Modular, specific, focused or comprehensive? Solo shop or team based? Do you affiliate with other professionals to provide "full service?" (Attorneys, CPAs, Insurance Professionals, etc.)"

I am a traditional Edward Jones Financial Advisor. I operate a storefront office location with a full-time Branch Office Administrator. My primary business is investment planning and investment management. We have a commission and an AUM platform available to us and I use both of them. My business is 80 percent investments and 20 percent insurance, including life insurance and long-term care insurance.

Most of my planning tends to be more modular vs. comprehensive. My software is proprietary to Jones and it allows me to plan in different segments of the planning spectrum, individually or in combination with other segments. About 50 percent of my clients have requested planning versus investments only.

Yes, I do maintain relationships with a stable of affiliated professionals, including insurance professionals for property & casualty planning, attorneys for estate planning issues, and CPAs for tax advice and tax planning. I am not compensated for referrals to these fellow professionals but they are integral in my delivering the service levels my clients deserve.

"What are the issues you face in providing financial planning advice to LGBT clients that are different than issues you address for your non-LGBT clients?"

LGBT clients have a need for more legal documents than my straight clients do, and these legal documents need to be drafted by attorneys knowledgeable about LGBT issues. The most important documents are those needed at death.

Family relationships are another area where I spend more time with my LGBT clients. It is important to know what the relationship is between LGBT clients and their families. Do they have supportive families or have they been disowned? Answers to these questions will dictate the need for additional legal protections to insure their wishes for their assets are honored at death.

From an investments standpoint, other than for my clients wishing to engage in socially responsible investing, there is little difference in selection and management of investment assets. (Some clients do not wish to own stocks from intolerant or gay hostile companies.) The same is basically true for insurance, although the amounts of insurance might be higher, to meet related but different needs of LGBT clients.

"What are the three most important things you would say to a planner considering serving the LGBT community?"

After meeting all licensing and educational requirements and assuming competence in those areas, some important areas to consider are:

Be prepared to discuss marriage issues with your LGBT clients. Although there are opportunities to marry today that have not existed before, there are also tax and benefit choices impacted by the decision to marry…or not to marry.

Stay current on the myriad tax changes that seem to be changing daily. Know the effects of these laws on tax filing, Social Security and other federal benefits.

Understand the impact of living together with a partner, with respect to P&C insurance.

"What are the "top LGBT resources" you would recommend for inclusion in a planners digital rolodex?"

Locate and support local community-based LGBT organizations – like Equality Toledo, as well as statewide LGBT organizations – like Equality, OH. These organizations can direct you to affiliated professionals to build upon in order to establish your network to serve your LGBT clients.

They can also direct you to the resources you would most benefit from serving LGBT clients.

On a personal level, when you are prospecting within the LGBT community it is important to serve members where they are. Some are still "in the closet." You have to respect their decisions on these matters.

"Demographic Data: Age, gender, marital status, area of the country where you practice, years in the business, etc."

I am a 52-year-old lesbian, partnered for 24 years, but not legally married (we are a registered domestic partnership in Toledo) with my office in Toledo, OH. I have clients in 20 states.

Educationally, I hold a BS in Education and the AAMS designation. I will be starting my studies for the CFP® in March of 2014.

Joshua Hatfield-Charles

"How did you come to be a financial planner? When did you decide to include the LGBT Community in your practice?"

Out of college with my Industrial Psychology degree, I intended to follow a path toward Masters and then PhD in Psychology, but life happened. I got a job in health insurance and that led to a job with a family friend's dad, in finance. During this same period, I was involved in a serious relationship and when we looked for advice on financial matters, the advisors we were meeting with, although competent to assist straight clients, were not that well versed in issues important to a couple who were legally, strangers.

To compensate for the lack of quality advice I was able to access, I began doing research on my own and discovered The Certified Financial Planning Program and pursued it, working first in financial planning as an employee, and then on my own.

As far as my decision to work with LGBT clients, that was a natural outgrowth of my own personal pursuit of planning advice. Living in the greater DC area, I knew the need was there and I simply included LGBT clients from day one in my business. Today I would estimate 60-70 percent of my clients are members of the LGBT Community.

"What is the scope of your practice? Modular, specific, focused or comprehensive? Solo shop or team based? Do you affiliate with other professionals to provide "full service?" (Attorneys, CPAs, Insurance Professionals, etc.)"

My practice is very comprehensive and is teamed based. In addition to a COO who is a JD and has an extensive compliance background, including having been employed by FINRA, I have another CFP on staff and assorted support staff, including insurance specialists. While we do not provide Property & Casualty (Liability) Insurance directly, we do refer for P & C as well. Our compensation model is fee and commission.

Our firm is associated with outside CPAs, attorneys and estate planning attorneys as well. I operate as often as possible as the quarterback of my client's financial planning team.

"What are the issues you face in providing financial planning advice to LGBT clients that are different than issues you address for your non-LGBT clients?"

The primary focus of my practice is to help client couples who are living lives out of sync with the laws that govern them. Basically, many of my clients have to face the fact that until there is marriage equality in all 50 states, they will be fighting with issues of recognition and in some cases, continued social stigma.

Recent changes in the military's *Don't Ask Don't Tell* regulations and more importantly, recent changes at the federal level with DOMA, have caused large numbers of LGBT couples to be in need of updated documents for a variety of needs.

Estate planning issues and family dynamics continue to be a primary focus for LGBT clients, especially in states without marriage equality. This is an area where I stress to my clients, you do not want to try to minimize your spending in this area. Cut back somewhere else if you want to save, and get quality documents and legal advice. Estate planning documents are what will speak on your behalf, after you are gone and can no longer speak for yourself, or your partner.

Providing the right advice to get the right protections is one of my primary responsibilities to my clients.

"What are the three most important things you would say to a planner considering serving the LGBT community?"

Making the assumption that you are educated and appropriately licensed to provide financial advice, I would say the first order of business before you decide to serve the LGBT community is to understand that LGBT clients need you to know how to use existing laws to provide the required workarounds needed to provide the right protections for them.

In addition, remember that you do not know what you do not know. Avail yourself of the training and education available to financial services professionals, especially through membership in professional organizations like the FPA and Pride Planners.

Realize that you do not want to be the specialist. You want to be the relationship manager and the quarterback of a team of associated professionals who are focused on providing the right protections for your clients.

"What are the "top LGBT resources" you would recommend for inclusion in a planners digital rolodex?"

Competent associated professionals, currently serving the needs of the LGBT community today, are always your first best bet, but there are other resources as well.

Organizations like:

- HRC
- ACLU
- Pride Planners
- The William's Institute
- College for Financial Planning's APDA Program

"Demographic Data: Age, gender, marital status, area of the country where you practice, years in the business, etc."

I am a 43-year-old, married, gay man. I live in the MD/DC area and I have been in the business since 1995. I have a client base that is national and international.

Diane Hack Gould

"How did you come to be a financial planner? When did you decide to include the LGBT Community in your practice?"

From the time I was 8 years old, I always wanted to be a teacher; however, while engaged in student teaching as a senior in college, I came face to face with politics in education. That experience changed my life forever. At the time, working my way through college, I worked at a State Farm office and my agent encouraged me to consider life insurance as a career. My agent told me my income would be unlimited and I would still be teaching, just a different subject!

I applied to ten different companies and the only one who turned me down was New York Life. Being as determined as a single, female, recent college graduate can be, I worked for three months to make the manager at New York Life realize the error of his ways…and he relented. I was one of the last hires he ever made, as he retired shortly after I started with the company.

Early on in my career, I became ill and I was not able to work in the evenings. This, of course, led me to calling on those who you can reach in the daytime, business owners. My natural marketing area was the Georgetown area of Washington, DC and in those days, the area was populated with a large number of gay business owners. As I assimilated into the community, I built a rapport with my clients and they introduced me to other gay and lesbian friends and business owners.

For my first thirteen years in the business, I focused on employee benefits and executive benefits. My clients considered me a value-added resource, as I became involved in educating their employees on their benefit programs. As this field became more and more commoditized, with benefit program selection based primarily on cost alone, I naturally migrated to other areas of planning. I was not a spreadsheet person and I did not relate to that kind of service. Although I changed the focus of my services to other areas of financial planning, I remained close to my gay and lesbian clients and they continued to be a large part of my practice.

"What is the scope of your practice? Modular, specific, focused or comprehensive? Solo shop or team based? Do you affiliate with other professionals to provide "full service?" (Attorneys, CPAs, Insurance Professionals, etc.)"

I specialize in delivering an integrated estate, retirement and financial planning experience to my clients. Although I operate as a solo practitioner, I work closely with the other professionals who serve the legal, accounting, and property and liability insurance needs of our mutual clients.

My niche is the deep question! My clients expect to answer questions that reveal their value system. What are the values they hold dear? What is important to them in their lives, and why? What values have they developed over their lifetimes that they want perpetuated? Which values handed down to them from their parents and family, do they no longer wish to embrace and include in their lives? An example of this last value is one I find in "trust fund babies." As their parents age, they see traits within their children being taught to their grandchildren that they do not wish to leave as a family legacy.

"What are the issues you face in providing financial planning advice to LGBT clients that are different issues you address for your non-LGBT clients?"

In many ways, there is more similarity than difference when serving both groups, especially when you focus on needs, wants and desires. As human beings, we all have similar needs, wants and desires. Where the differences come in are in the areas of solutions available to address the goals of the LGBT client.

Another difference I observe is between how gay couples and lesbian couples respond when fact-finding and recommendations are addressed. While equality is a paramount value for the vast majority of my LGBT clients, the interpersonal dynamics exhibited by lesbians differs markedly from their gay counterparts. I find lesbian couples to be far more focused on collaboration in goal setting and solution selection. On the other hand, gay couples tend to mimic straight couples, with there being a dominant partner in the relationship. They are equal partners, but one partner is just a little more equal.

It is important to keep these dynamics in mind as you serve the means of the three entities with whom you are dealing...each of the two members of the partnership and the partnership itself.

"What are the three most important things you would say to a planner considering serving the LGBT community?"

Number One is Education! It goes without saying you need to be formally educated as a financial services professional, but as important, if not more important, that you be educated on LGBT issues, the needs of the LGBT community and specifically the laws of the land.

Number Two is honesty and personal integrity. You must be a genuine person, with sincere motives and a desire to serve. If you are a straight financial advisor, be who you are, period. Do not try to be someone you are not, because you think that's what an LGBT client wants. What LGBT clients want are ethical, educated and experienced professionals, eager to treat them with respect and with a strong desire to serve their individual needs. Closely tied to this is **openness and the lack of being judgmental**. The LGBT lifestyle might be strange to a straight planner, but it is not strange to the LGBT clients. It is important that you accept their lifestyle and their needs, wants, desires, and goals, without being judgmental. If you cannot or will not, you should reconsider serving the LGBT Community. Remember, you do not have to agree with and embrace the lifestyle yourself. You need only to understand it and understand the unique challenges your LGBT clients face, every day of their lives.

Number Three is to ask questions. You only gain insight and understanding of your clients, gay or straight, by asking questions. The basic questions are those about assets, liabilities, etc. The truly important questions revolve around feelings, values, dreams, desires, and lifetime goals.

One important question you have to be very careful in asking is "Are you a gay man or a lesbian?" I do not usually ask that question, rather, if the client does not volunteer the information, I ask if he or she has a partner? The longer you work in the LGBT community, the more well known you become within the LGBT community, the less challenging this question will become.

"What are the "top LGBT resources" you would recommend for inclusion in a planners digital rolodex?"

Many of my clients are seniors or are approaching senior citizen status. Therefore, a number of my favorite resources reflect that age cohort. One of my favorite resources is The National Resource Center on LGBT Aging. (www.lgbtagingcenter.org)

In order to understand the global perspective on LGBT issues, specifically lesbian issues, I like to refer to ASTREA. This site focuses upon international issues of justice for the lesbian community.

My last resource recommendation is the digital library at The American College. EBSCO and PROQUEST give the advisor access to journal articles from academia, the popular financial press, dissertations from learned scholars, etc. As a graduate of TAC, I have access to these tools through the college. If you are not a TAC graduate, these resources are available through other college and public libraries, nationwide.

"Demographic Data: Age, gender, area of the country where you practice, years in the business, etc."

I will soon be 60 years old and I am in my 39th year in this industry. My offices are in the DC area, but I have clients all along the East Coast. Because DC is a transient area, I also have a number of clients on the West Coast as well.

I hold the CLU, ChFC, CAP, CLTC professional designations and Master of Science in Financial Services. I am also a member of the first cohort of the PhD program in Financial and Retirement Planning at The American College.

Jill Hollander

"How did you come to be a financial planner? When did you decide to include the LGBT Community in your practice?

I have always been in finance. In my prior life, I worked at Levi Strauss and Wells Fargo. I actually came into the business because of a friend, Melvin Gladstone, who had lost his job in a hostile takeover. He was the Director of Human Resources and part of the pension committee. He enjoyed investment selection and management and when he lost his job, he opened an investment advisory firm. In 1993, he was looking to expand his business, and invited me to join his firm.

He retired 12/31/99 at 80 years of age and I bought the firm. I migrated from investment management as a primary focus to financial planning as my primary focus, retaining investment management as a secondary focus.

Mel had a number of LGBT clients when I joined the firm, and I expanded the business in the LGBT community, primarily through word of mouth. Today, I am Managing Partner of the firm, *Financial Connections*, and roughly 1/3 of our clients are LGBT.

"What is the scope of your practice? Modular, specific, focused or comprehensive? Solo shop or team based? Do you affiliate with other professionals to provide "full service?" (Attorneys, CPAs, Insurance Professionals, etc.)"

My practice is based on a model I call "Project Based Financial Planning." That means I accept clients based on their needs, as long as I have the ability to serve those needs. I am a member of the Garrett Planning Network, which focuses on "hourly, as needed" financial planning. My firm, which includes 6 financial professionals, also manages about $175 million in assets.

When permitted to act as the quarterback for my client's cadre of related professionals, I do. I am particularly adept in providing coordination in the areas of estate planning and taxes, and I make it a point to serve as the primary educator for my clients in these areas of the financial planning process. This does entail working with attorneys and CPAs. It is a little more challenging working with property and liability insurance professionals, as I have not been fortunate enough to find adequate numbers of them in my area. However, I do make referrals on occasion, for my clients' financial well-being.

"What are the issues you face in providing financial planning advice to LGBT clients that are different than issues you address for your non-LGBT clients?"

With the overturn of DOMA and the subsequent reversal of Marriage Equality bans here in California, there have been numerous changes in planning practices this year. Advising many LGBT couples is now much more similar to advising straight couples.

That being said, however, the most important things for a new advisor to consider, as he or she evaluates whether or not to serve the LGBT community are:

1. **Begin by having a long talk with yourself.** If you are going to "tolerate" LGBT clients, do not make the move to serve the LGBT community. On the other hand, if you are prepared to "advocate," you will be appreciated and welcomed into the community.

Abandon pre-conceptions about LGBT clients. Put your notions of how finances are handled in a box and lock them away.

2. **Do not assume!** Just as all straight couples are not the same, neither are LGBT couples. There are differences in the manner in which LGBT couples manage their finances. Some partners commingle their finances, but some do not. Some partners co-own property, but some do not. Some partners have separate accounts but also have a joint account. An excellent idea when establishing a new client relationship with an LGBT couple is to simply ask, "How do you handle your finances?"

3. **Do not assume!** Just because LGBT partners can now legally marry, it is not necessarily the best option for them. One of my clients was recently advised by his CPA that getting married would create an additional $30,000 a year in taxes.

"What are the three most important things you would say to a planner considering serving the LGBT community?"

Be open and non-judgmental. This relates to the first point in the prior section. Be prepared to ask questions and truly learn about your clients. A good temperature-taking opening question to use when working with LGBT client couples is, "How does your family feel about your relationship?" Be prepared to listen and learn to read between the lines.

In order for a new planner to become familiar with where he or she needs to build professional education and competence, I suggest using a spreadsheet. On one side of the sheet, list all the financial planning concerns of straight Married Couples. Then, on the other side of the sheet, identify those areas where "legal strangers" would experience a statutorily different treatment. (Legal Strangers is a term to describe those partners residing in states that do not have legal recognition of same-gendered couples. This exercise will identify the areas where your LGBT clients will need specialized legal, accounting, tax and estate planning assistance. (Where Estate Planning issues and documents are involved, use specialized, customized forms. Commonly available forms tend not to be appropriate for LGBT clients.)

Know your state laws as well as applicable federal laws. Be aware of differences in ownership and titling. Know the difference between joint ownership with rights of survivorship (JTWROS) and tenants in common (TIC). I operate in a community property state. If you do too, that presents another entire spectrum of issues with which to deal. Remember to become familiar with local laws and ordinances as well. Property taxes on residences can be a major consideration for LGBT couples.

"What are the "top LGBT resources" you would recommend for inclusion in a planners digital rolodex?"

Your professional library should include books by Frederick Hertz, Sheryl Garrett and Debra Newman.

Organizations whose materials I turn to regularly include the National Center for Rights (NCLR), Horizons Foundation and Marriage Equality. I also use materials and research from The Human Rights Campaign. (HRC)

"Demographic Data: Age, gender, area of the country where you practice, years in the business, etc."

I am a 63-year-old, legally married lesbian. I have been in the industry since 1993. My practice is located north of San Francisco, in Marin County.

Lorraine Johnson

"How did you come to be a financial planner? When did you decide to include the LGBT Community in your practice?"

As an undergraduate, I was interested in Trust Management and Estate Planning. When I graduated from college in the mid 1980s, I joined a firm, pursued my Chartered Financial Analyst designation (CFA), and eventually grew into a position managing a $100,000,000 portfolio.

Although I loved the management of the money, I eventually preferred more face to face interaction. This led me to a career with The Principal Financial Group, where I learned their financial planning process and flourished.

Being a lesbian and having a number of lesbian friends, my practice grew initially by word of mouth and by sponsoring events in the LGBT Community. I literally "put my money where my mouth was," sponsoring countless events, and becoming known through my website and mission statement as a financial planner serving the LGBT Community.

In addition to my sponsorships of events in the LGBT Community, I also worked to meet the needs of other nontraditional families, as many of their planning needs were similar to those of my LGBT clients.

"What is the scope of your practice? Modular, specific, focused or comprehensive? Solo shop or team based? Do you affiliate with other professionals to provide "full service?" (Attorneys, CPAs, Insurance professionals, etc.)"

I operate as a solo advisor with a support staff. I have an office manager, a part-time assistant for her, and I also have a para-planner. Our Broker Dealer is Royal Alliance Associates, Inc. and I would classify our practice as comprehensive. With my background in portfolio management, I do manage money for clients, and my typical client minimum is $250,000. Because of my experience with The Principal, I also recognize the importance of insurance as a part of a true comprehensive plan.

I have a network of CPAs, Attorneys and P&C professionals I rely on for their areas of expertise. While I am basically flat-fee based, I occasionally do some work hourly, as needed. One hallmark of my practice is not being "pushy" when it comes to services beyond the initial financial planning engagement.

"What are the issues you face in providing financial planning advice to LGBT clients that are different than the issues you address for your non-LGBT clients?"

Many of the issues are related to recent changes in federal law. As of this interview, the Supreme Court has overturned Section Three, of the Defense of Marriage Act. However, Section Two is still in place. This means that the federal government *has to* recognize couples as married on a federal level if they are recognized by the state. The Supreme Court ruling, however, does not say that the federal government must recognize married couples in non-recognition states. Also, one state does not have to recognize same-gender marriages performed in another state.

The federal government has different departments, with varying regulations. Some of these regulations are determined by state of celebration, and others are determined by state of domicile. The result is that all departments do not treat the couple similarly.

As of the date of this interview, the U.S. Treasury and the IRS have announced that couples who are legally married will be treated as married for federal tax purposes, regardless of the state they live in. So federal tax law is now determined by state of residence rather than state of celebration. It can be difficult to advise clients who, from an income tax perspective, are treated as married at the federal level, but not married on the state level. Social Security, however, is following state of residence.

1. One of the worst issues for legally married same-gender couples residing in a non-recognition state is multiple tax filings. Currently in North Carolina, for instance, a legally married same-sex couple residing there must file their federal returns either as married filing jointly or married filing separately. The state, however, requires them to file as individuals, and submit proforma federal returns that are completed *as if* they had filed as individuals. So members of a couple who are married filing separately at the federal level, have to prepare a total of six returns: One each at the federal level; one each at the state level; and two additional pro-forma federal returns to be filed with the state returns. This is ridiculous.

2. LGBT couples face a possible challenge when they are legally married in one state, then travel to and through others, where their marriage is not recognized. They must carry their powers of attorney and living wills with them. In the event that they need medical attention, this can be crucial in determining whether one spouse can visit the other in the hospital, or even whether they make life-and-death decisions for one another.

3. State inheritance tax and beneficiary laws are another area where my heterosexual married clients have greater clarity.

4. Social Security and other benefits are sometimes adversely affected by marriage, and sometimes improved by marriage. All unmarried couples should consider this when contemplating "tying the knot," regardless of gender. This is particularly complicated for same-gender couples now. As of the date of this interview, the Social Security Administration is paying spousal benefits to legally married same-gender couples *who reside*

in states that recognize their marriages. In non-recognition states, Social Security spousal benefits are not paid. This goes for spousal retirement, spousal survivor, and spousal disability. I'm not certain exactly how ex-spouse benefits fit in. Social Security Disability benefits for children are also affected. In a family where the non-biological parent is disabled, the children do not receive benefits.

5. Should a couple in a non-recognition state move to a recognition state, if doing so will improve their financial situation? For people who are financially comfortable, this is less likely to be a consideration. But for a retired same-gender couple on a limited income, for instance, a spousal retirement benefit might mean a significant increase in their monthly income. Should they have to leave their families, doctors, and friends in order to be treated equally from a Social Security standpoint? This is a disgrace.

6. Having children can be very expensive for LGBT couples. Becoming parents for these couples by definition involves adoption, in vitro fertilization, surrogacy, etc. All of these are very expensive. When a heterosexual couple says they want to have children, we're talking about day care and college. For a same-gender couple, we're *literally* planning for the cost of having children.

"What are the three most important things you would say to a planner considering serving the LGBT community?"

- Get educated, not only as a financial planner, but in the specific issues of the LGBT community.
- Sponsor everything. Get yourself known in the community.
- SHOW UP! Volunteer. Contribute to the community.
- Be comfortable with and in the presence of your LGBT clients.

Most important, as I said in a recently published article in *Investment News*, is this: if the only reason you are "targeting" the LGBT community is because of the reputation we have as being affluent with extra disposable income, don't bother. It's very offensive, and we do not need you. If you don't genuinely care about us, please target someone else!

"What are the "top LGBT resources" you would recommend for inclusion in a planners digital rolodex?"

The ADPA program from The College for Financial Planning is a good beginning. If you plan to work with older LGBT clients, I recommend SAGE.

Other good resources would include:

- Lambda Legal
- Human Rights Campaign
- Pride Planners
- Depending on where you practice, your state's affiliate of the Equality Federation. Here, for instance, I support Equality North Carolina.

"Demographic Data: Age, gender, area of the country where you practice, years in the business, etc."

I am 51 years old, female, bisexual, have been with my partner for 18 years, and my practice is NC centric. I have a few clients living in other states, but most of them first became clients here in NC. I came into the business in 1985 and established my individual practice in 2007.

Diane Ouellette

"How did you come to be a financial planner? When did you decide to include the LGBT Community in your practice?

I graduated from college with a degree in biology, but I spent my first 24 years working, in corporate America. I was an employee of Western Electric and throughout my career I absorbed all the changes…from Western Electric to AT&T to Lucent etc…. until I received a retirement buyout, at age 50. Along the way, I earned an MBA and was exposed to finance and investments.

As I considered what I wanted to do with the rest of my life, I was drawn to investments and investment management. As I learned more about the industry, I knew I had no further desire to be engaged corporately, so I researched becoming a Registered Investment Advisor (RIA). I began my practice in 2002, in Provincetown, MA. From the very beginning I knew I wanted to be present in the LGBT community and serve the LGBT community so I set up my practice to do exactly that. I was not going to hide who I was, as I had to do in my corporate career. My practice today consists of 65 percent LGBT clients and 35 percent straight clients. Of my gay clients, 90 percent are lesbians.

In 2004, after becoming legally married in Massachusetts, my partner and I relocated to Arizona. I am dually registered in Massachusetts and Arizona, and I have clients in 10 states.

"What is the scope of your practice? Modular, specific, focused or comprehensive? Solo shop or team based? Do you affiliate with other professionals to provide "full service?" (Attorneys, CPAs, Insurance Professionals, etc.)"

I run a solo, comprehensive, holistic planning practice. I offer comprehensive planning to all of my prospective clients, but only about 20% use that level of service. My primary software is *Money Guide Pro*. Most of my engagements are for investment planning and management. My client base is primarily Middle Class. I have no asset or income minimums, but the majority of my clients have [about] $200,000 in assets under management (AUM).

I maintain an informal network of affiliated professionals, consisting of estate planning attorneys, family law attorneys, CPAs, tax attorneys etc. to whom I make referrals, without compensation. These affiliated professionals are actively supportive of LGBT community issues and are considered "gay friendly."

Although as I said earlier, I have no asset or income minimums, I do have a minimum annual fee, payable quarterly. On occasion, I will also accept, "hourly as needed" compensation projects.

"What are the issues you face in providing financial planning advice to LGBT clients that are different than issues you address for your non-LGBT clients?"

This is an ever-evolving area.

Income tax planning is one area of significant difference. For my LGBT clients, there are new sets of issues, as the result of changes to DOMA. These are state-by-state specific, and with clients in 10 different states, present a challenge, as the landscape is constantly changing.

Social Security and retirement planning issues are now also important issues for my gay clients. IRAs, Pension Benefits, Health Care issues…all of these areas pose significantly different problems for my LGBT clients.

Healthcare documentation is particularly challenging, when couples married legally in one state travel to states without same-sex marriage recognition.

More Life insurance is required to meet LGBT needs, than would be required by straight couples, due to pension benefit and survivor benefits difference, and the need to balance incomes for some couples.

One newly developing area within the LGBT Community is the need for advisors who have a fiduciary standard in their practice. There are concerns about some planners having conflicts of interest in serving clients. One area of professional development and accreditation is the AIF program (Accredited Investment Fiduciary.) I see this as an area of growth within the advisor community serving the LGBT community.

"What are the three most important things you would say to a planner considering serving the LGBT community?"

Once we assume all required licensure and education is in place, building trust and friendships within the LGBT community is critical to the new advisor-planner. Getting involved in community organizations serving the community is essential. Supporting LGBT friendly non-profits is an excellent entrée into serving the community. This is where your referral base will come from.

Establishing connections with gay friendly strategic partners and affiliated professionals would be step two. One way to do this is to cosponsor education events with your strategic partners.

In our case our website is our primary form of marketing. Our site, www.goldcanyonFP.com is where most of our referrals find out about us, and our services. I could not imagine not having a web presence today.

"What are the "top LGBT resources" you would recommend for inclusion in a planners digital rolodex?"

There are a number listed on our website. These are some I would recommend for consideration:

- PLAG
- HRC
- Pride Planners
- FPA Diversity Group
- freedomtomarry.org
- DOMA Project
- Family Equality Council
- EqualityAZ.org

"Demographic Data: Age, gender, marital status, area of the country where you practice, years in the business, etc."

I am a 57-year-old married lesbian. I have been in practice since 2002 and lived in AZ since 2004, and my practice is here. I have clients in 10 states and I remain dually registered in AZ and MA. I hold an MBA and my professional licenses include the CFP® certification and the FINRA Series 65.

Sharon Rich

"How did you come to be a financial planner? When did you decide to include the LGBT Community in your practice?"

While a doctoral graduate student, I was studying women's psychology, and decided that the best way to empower women was through helping them understand finance and money. That led me to found my company, WOMONEY. I was specifically interested in helping women with inherited wealth and socially responsible investing and I had a natural desire to work with non-traditional clients.

While working on my dissertation, I pursued a Diploma in Financial Planning at Boston University and followed that up with teaching the CFP curriculum at Northeastern University for a few years.

I sought out LGBT clients from the very beginning of my practice in 1984. In addition to word of mouth, I advertised in local papers that served the community and networked within those organizations comprised of LGBT clients or who served the LGBT community.

"What is the scope of your practice? Modular, specific, focused or comprehensive? Solo shop or team based? Do you affiliate with other professionals to provide "full service?" (Attorneys, CPAs, Insurance Professionals, etc.)"

I am a solo practitioner. My business model is Fee Only, "hourly planning, as needed." Although I am not a member, my practice was the model Sheryl Garrett used when founding the Garrett Planning Network.

As Fee-Only, I provide advice and follow-up to assure client implementation, but I do not personally sell insurance or financial products or earn any income from referrals, commissions, or assets under management.

I do make referrals for insurance and investment needs as well as to attorneys for estate planning purposes, but again, these are done to serve my planning clients, not for compensation.

"What are the issues you face in providing financial planning advice to LGBT clients that are different than issues you address for your non-LGBT clients?"

The landscape has changed considerably since the DOMA ruling, in June of this year. I practice solely in the Commonwealth of Massachusetts, where marriage equality was already state law, but with the DOMA ruling, everything changed. Now same-sex marriage is not only recognized under state laws, but under federal law as well.

While the changes are welcome, they introduce a series of issues that still require planning decisions for LGBT clients that most traditional clients do not face when they travel out of state.

Examples include:

- Co-adoption of children issues
- Residual planning issues looking back for three years
- Re-evaluation of all the "workaround" documents designed for clients previously, to determine what, if any, updates are required.
- State specific questions, especially if legally married MA residents are considering relocating to a state where marriage equality is not the law.

And for LGBT clients in non-recognition states …

- Tax implications of marriage
- Gifting issues

"What are the three most important things you would say to a planner considering serving the LGBT community?"

1. Assuming all necessary education and licensing is already in place, I would say that the number one goal for a new planner would be to get his or her team in place. Attorneys, insurance professionals, investment professionals, and tax professionals, all of whom must be knowledgeable in LGBT issues, have to be identified and put into place.

2. Networking with existing LGBT planners in your area. Know who your peers are and know whom you can call on for competencies outside of your own skill set.

3. Network in general to get yourself known in the community for business development purposes. Teaching is one method I used to network in my early years.

"What are the "top LGBT resources" you would recommend for inclusion in a planners digital rolodex?"

There are any number of websites you can Google and lots of information available. I use the GLAD website a lot because it is very active in my area.

Of course I recommend Pride Planners, even if one day, soon, our reason for being will no longer be as critical as it was when we started in the late 90s.

HRC has a number of good resources on their website as well.

"Demographic Data: Age, gender, marital status, area of the country where you practice, years in the business, etc."

I am a 57-year-old married lesbian female and I have been in the business since 1984. I practice only in the state of MA.

The Interview—Conclusions

While there were similarities in the responses to most of the questions in these interviews, the question that gives the planner the most information needed to consider whether or not to serve the LGBT Community was, "What are the three most important things you would say to a planner considering serving the LGBT community?"

The responses that manifested themselves almost universally were:

- **Be Educated.** Not only as a qualified Financial Services Professional, but in the issues most important to the LGBT Community.
- **Be Sincere.** Be genuinely interested in the needs of the client, first and foremost.
- **Be Authentic.** Be true to yourself and to those you serve. Be open and respectful of your LGBT Clients.

Although verbalized in these exact words by only one participant, the spirit of the following response was almost universally implied. It bears consideration by all planners considering whether to include the LGBT Community in his or her practice:

"...if the only reason you are "targeting" the LGBT community is because of the reputation we have as being, as a group, "Affluent," don't bother. We do not need you! Please go do something else!"

Supplemental Information

Supplement A: Time Line of Same-Sex Marriage Bans and Legalizations by Effective Date of Laws

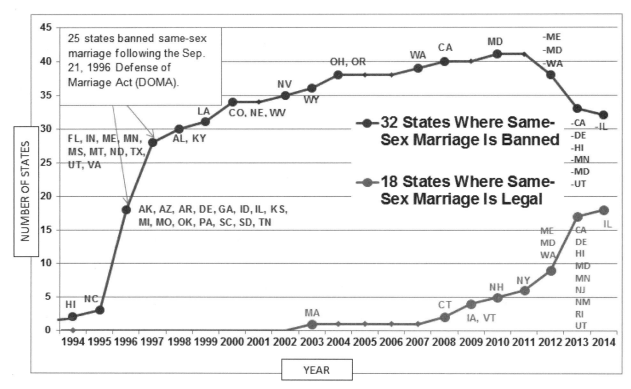

*DC legalized same-sex marriage on Mar. 10, 2012.
Wisconsin banned same-sex marriage in 1979.

Sources:

1. Joseph Ax and Edith Honan, "New Jersey Judge Allows Same-Sex Marriage," Reuters, Sep. 27, 2013
2. David Bailey, "Minnesota Governor Signs Bill Legalizing Gay Marriage," Reuters, May 14, 2013
3. Eve Batey, "Farewell Prop 8: SF City Attorney Vows to Litigate Aggressively to Ensure Marriage Equality for California," www.sfappeal.com, June 26, 2013

4. Cindy Carcomo, "New Mexico Becomes Latest State to Legalize Gay Marriage," latimes.com, Dec. 19, 2013

5. Doug Denison, "Gay Marriage in Delaware to Become Legal July 1," www.delawareonline.com, May 7, 2013

6. Erik Eckholm, "Same-Sex Marriage Gains Cheer Gay Rights Advocates," www.nytimes.com, Nov. 7, 2012

7. Andrew M. Francis, Hugo M. Mialon, and Handoe Peng, "In Sickness and in Health: Same Sex Marriage Laws and Sexually Transmitted Infections, Appendix: Legal References and Notes," Emory Law and Economics Research Paper No 11-97, www.emory.edu (accessed Aug. 10, 2012)

8. Human Rights Campaign, "Marriage Center," www.hrc.org (accessed Aug. 10, 2012)

9. Rachel La Corte, "Washington Voters Approve Gay Marriage," Associated Press, Nov. 9, 2012

10. Lambda Legal, "In Your State," www.lamdbalegal.org (accessed Aug. 10, 2012)

11. William P. LaPiana, "Domestic Partnership Chart," www.actec.org (accessed Aug. 10, 2012)

12. Marriage Law Foundation, "Marriage Statutes," www.marriagelawfoundation.org (accessed Aug. 10, 2012)

13. National Conference of State Legislatures, "Child Support and Family Law," www.ncsl.org (accessed Aug. 10, 2012)

14. Katharine Q. Seelye, "Rhode Island Joins States That Allow Gay Marriage," www.nytimes.com, May 2, 2013

15. Elizabeth Weise, "Federal Judge Allows Gay Marriages to Continue in Utah," usatoday.com, Dec. 23, 2013

Source: gaymarriageprocon.org

For an interactive, informative breakdown of this state by state map, visit:

http://www.marriageequality.org/sites/default/files/National%20Map%20%2319%20%2820-Dec-2013%29.pdf

The following statement is presented along with this map:

"Although **39%** of Americans live in 19 states that have adopted full, state-level equality (CA, CT, DC, DE, HI, IA, IL, MA, MD, ME, MN, NH, NM, NJ, NY, RI, UT, VT, WA), and more live in cities, counties, or states with partial equality (mainly CO, NV, OR, WI), **50%** live in 33 jurisdictions that still ban all types of unions except one-man-one-woman couples."

Source: marriageequality.org

An additional view from FreedomToMarry.Org:

Winning the Freedom to Marry: Progress in the States

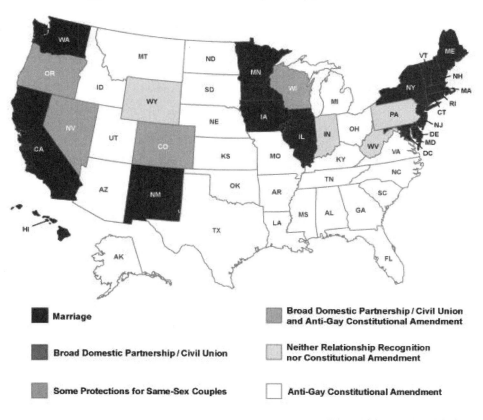

Marriage

Broad Domestic Partnership / Civil Union

Some Protections for Same-Sex Couples

Broad Domestic Partnership / Civil Union and Anti-Gay Constitutional Amendment

Neither Relationship Recognition nor Constitutional Amendment

Anti-Gay Constitutional Amendment

Last Updated December 20, 2013

Eighteen states—CA, CT, DE, HI, IA, IL, ME, MD, MA, MN, NH, NJ, NM, NY, RI, VT, UT, and WA—plus Washington, D.C. have the freedom to marry for same-sex couples.

Three states offer broad protections short of marriage. CO allows civil union, while OR and NV offer broad domestic partnership. WI has more limited domestic partnership.

With these advances, a record number of Americans live in states that recognize relationships between same-sex couples:

- **Over 38%** of the U.S. population lives in a state that either has the freedom to marry or honors out-of-state marriages of same-sex couples.
- **Over 41%** of the U.S. population lives in a state with either marriage or a broad legal status such as civil union or domestic partnership.
- **Over 43%** of the U.S. population lives in a state that provides some form of protections for gay couples.

Source: freedomtomarry.org/states

Supplement B: Other Maps of Import to LGBT Clients

The Human Rights Campaign has a number of maps on their website that show the status of various issues, by state. One of those maps includes hospital visitation laws referred to earlier in this material.

Map of Hospital Visitation Laws

Since January 8, 2011 federal regulations have required hospitals participating in the Medicare and Medicaid programs to adopt written policies and procedures regarding patients' visitation rights, including a prohibition on discrimination in visitation based on sexual orientation and gender identity (January 18, 2011).

Hospital visitation laws can be in the form of relationship recognition laws (marriage, civil unions, and domestic partnerships) or separate visitation statutes.

States extending equal hospital visitation rights to same-sex spouses or partners through marriage equality or statewide relationship recognition (20 states and D.C.):

California, Connecticut, Colorado, Delaware, District of Columbia, Hawaii, Illinois, Iowa, Maine, Maryland, Massachusetts, Minnesota, Nevada, New Hampshire, New Jersey, New Mexico, New York, Oregon, Rhode Island, Vermont and Washington.

States extending equal hospital visitation rights to same-sex spouses or partners through specific provisions as part of a limited relationship recognition statute (1 state): Wisconsin.

States extending hospital visitation rights through a designated visitor statute (5 states): Kentucky, Nebraska, North Carolina, Virginia and West Virginia.

Healthcare Agent Statute: Two states extend hospital visitation rights to a designated health care agent by statute: Georgia and South Carolina.

Additional maps are available at this site dealing with marriage equality and employments issues, as well as issues important to LGBT youth.

Source: Human Rights Campaign | 1640 Rhode Island Ave., N.W., Washington, D.C. 20036 | www.hrc.org/statelaws

Supplement C: Resources for the Financial Advisor Serving the LGBT Community

The following are resources mentioned by the participants in the interviews, as well as others that may serve to benefit those financial planners interested in serving the LGBT Community.

SAGE	http://sageusa.org
GLAAD	http://www.glaad.org
PFLAG	http://www.pflag.org
The LGBT Aging Project	http://www.lgbtagingproject.org
The Human Rights Campaign	http://www.hrc.org
The Gay Straight Alliance Network	http://www.gsanetwork.org
Gender Equity Resource Center	http://geneq.berkeley.edu
Freedomtomarry.org	http://www.freedomtomarry.org
Marriage Equality USA	http://www.marriageequalityusa.org
The College for Financial Planning	http://www.cffpdesignations.com/Designation/ADPA
Lambda Legal	http://lambdalegal.org
ACLU	https://www.aclu.org/lgbt-rights
The Williams Institute	http://williamsinstitute.law.ucla.edu/category/research/
Pride Planners	http://www.prideplanners.comastrea
ASTREA	http://www.astraeafoundation.org
DOMA Project	http://www.domaproject.org
National Center for Lesbian Rights	http://www.nclrights.org
Horizons Foundation	http://horizonsfoundation.org
FPA Diversity Group	http://www.fpanet.org/professionals/Connect/diversity/
Family Equality Council	http://www.familyequality.org
Google.com	https://www.google.com

This is but a short list of resources available to financial professionals desiring to serve the LGBT Community. Also included are a number of related Google Searches. Google.com searches for the following words provided indicated results:

Gay Rights	693,000 hits
LGBT	19,300,000 hits
Marriage Equality	80,000 hits

Financial Planning in The LGBT Community	2,990,000 hits

Company names identified with this last search included:

Raymond James	Prudential	Ameriprise
Metlife	Merrill Lynch	Northern Trust
Wells Fargo	New York Life	Morgan Stanley

Is your company represented on this list?

Supplement D: The LGBT Financial Experience

The following material is reprinted with permission[13] of Prudential Financial, Inc. and its affiliates, Newark, NJ. It will provide you with some of the most current research on the financial beliefs, values, goals and objectives of the LGBT client.

---

13. *Copyright © 2012, Prudential Financial, Inc. Reprinted with permission. Further reproduction is prohibited without written permission of the publisher.*

FOREWORD

THE LGBT FINANCIAL EXPERIENCE

Over the last decade, many companies have paid increasing attention to the Lesbian, Gay, Bisexual and Transgender (LGBT) market. While much of this attention has been focused on buying power and consumer behavior, little information has been available about the financial experience of the LGBT community.

At Prudential, we wanted to take an in-depth look at the current financial landscape for LGBT Americans to better understand the financial challenges and concerns of the community as a whole, same-sex couples and LGBT parents.

The research findings are eye opening and dispel common perceptions. While we found people to be largely optimistic about the future, the LGBT community, like most Americans, was affected by the recession and is very concerned about being able to retire.

The study demonstrates the diversity of financial experience among LGBT people. Financial health and decision-making vary significantly by gender, generation, ethnicity, state of residence and relationship status. The research also highlights financial concerns and challenges related to the legal status of LGBT relationships that are unique to the community.

This is an important baseline study that provides a snapshot of the financial lives and experience of LGBT Americans today. We hope that its insights will enable both Prudential and the financial services industry to better meet the LGBT community's financial needs.

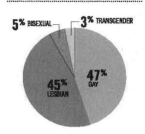

Figure 1.   **LGBT Participant Breakdown**

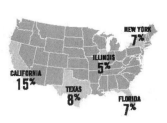

Figure 2.   **Geographic Breakdown**

Survey participants represented all 50 states plus Washington D.C. Regions are balanced to 2010 U.S. Census data for same-sex households. Top five states indicated by percentage.

CHARLES F. LOWREY
Executive Vice President
Chief Operating Officer, U.S. Businesses

SHARON C. TAYLOR
Senior Vice President, Human Resources
Chair of The Prudential Foundation

Learn more at Prudential.com/LGBT

METHODOLOGY

During August 2012, a diverse group of 1,401 Lesbian, Gay, Bisexual and Transgender (LGBT) Americans participated in an online survey about their financial health and experiences. To assure broad representation, participants needed only to define themselves as part of the LGBT community, and to be aged 25 to 68. The study reached both people who are "completely out" (64%) and those who are still at least somewhat "in the closet" (36%). LGBT Americans from every state and the District of Columbia participated in the survey. Survey respondents' state of residence closely reflected the same-sex couple distribution captured during the 2010 U.S. Census.

The survey contained more than 70 multiple choice and write-in questions, which yielded more than 6,000 written comments about participants' financial experience. Community Marketing, Inc. administered the study, and participants were members of its LGBT Research Panel.

General population statistics are from the U.S. Census or from a Prudential financial study in early 2012.

Charts showing participant demographics are included in this introduction (Figures 1-6) and throughout the report. The margin of error for results reported at the total sample level (n=1,401) is +/- 2.6% (95% confidence level).

More information and study results can also be downloaded at Prudential.com/LGBT.

Figure 3. **Ethnicity**

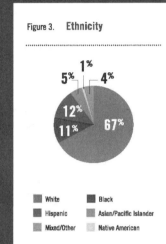

- White
- Hispanic
- Mixed/Other
- Black
- Asian/Pacific Islander
- Native American

Figure 4. **Age and Generation**

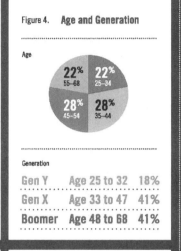

Age

Generation

Gen Y	Age 25 to 32	18%
Gen X	Age 33 to 47	41%
Boomer	Age 48 to 68	41%

Figure 5. **How out are you?**

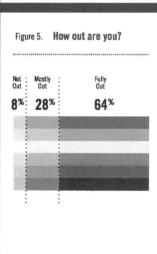

Not Out	Mostly Out	Fully Out
8%	28%	64%

Figure 6. **Where do you live?**

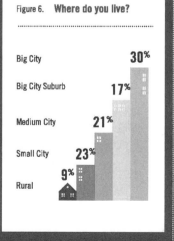

Big City	30%
Big City Suburb	17%
Medium City	21%
Small City	23%
Rural	9%

SUMMARY

THE LGBT FINANCIAL EXPERIENCE

A Community Not on the Edges

Overall, we found the LGBT community solidly in the middle in their financial attitudes and actions. Attitudes toward investing, savings, home ownership and debt are more moderate compared to Prudential general population research. LGBT Americans earn a Prudential LGBT Financial Confidence Index score of 48 out of 100, right in the middle. While individual LGBT income falls across the economic spectrum, as a whole, the LGBT community is largely in the middle class.

The L, G, B and T Have Different Needs

The LGBT community is made up of groups who share common struggles yet retain distinct traits, outlooks and characteristics. For example, lesbian couples are far more likely to have children than gay men. The bisexual community is comprised of both opposite-sex and same-sex couples, while transgender people often face increased economic discrimination compared to the rest of the community. Based on this diversity, financial companies cannot assume they can apply the same outreach and strategies to serve the financial needs of lesbians, gay men, bisexuals and transgender people.

Lesbian Financial Power

While the media typically focuses on the buying power of gay male couples, the study indicates that lesbians are also a significant economic force. Lesbians have a higher median individual income than women in the general population, and their overall household income is on par with gay men because the majority live in a dual-income household.

Equality Trumps Economy

The LGBT community is far more concerned about issues related to legislation affecting LGBT financial rights and the lack of Social Security survivors benefits for same-sex couples than they are about the national debt and inflation. Equality policy trumps economic policy.

Financial Independence

Same-sex couples value financial independence far more than the general population, often keeping separate accounts and financial plans. The financial services industry needs to understand and appreciate this important difference.

More LGBT Parents and Elders

Over the next decade, the demographics of the LGBT community will change dramatically, affecting its financial health and needs. The number of lesbian, gay, bisexual and transgender parents has been growing steadily over the past decade and is expected to increase significantly with Generation Y. At the same time, Baby Boomers are and will continue to enter retirement in record numbers, which will focus the community on caring for the financial, health and housing needs of LGBT elders.

The Retirement Confidence Gap

Retirement is the top financial concern in the LGBT community. Like most Americans, the LGBT community has a significant confidence gap in whether they will have enough money to last a lifetime. Retirement planning will be among the major financial issues facing the community over the next decade.

Optimistic About Their Future

Despite retirement concerns, the LGBT community is more confident about the future than the present, especially as it relates to making strides toward LGBT equality and their own household finances.

Financial Industry Needs to Improve

Despite some outreach by the financial services industry to the LGBT community, study participants rank the industry's attention to their financial needs low. In write-in questions, many participants state that financial institutions do not have the expertise to address the complex financial concerns of same-sex couples and LGBT parents.

LGBTs Need Financial Planning Assistance

The study shows that LGBT Americans are less confident in financial planning than the general population. Their finances as well as tax, retirement and estate planning remain complicated because of the intricacy of tax and family laws affecting LGBT couples and parents. Many indicate that they need help with financial and estate planning. Those who receive financial planning assistance from a qualified professional feel more confident about their finances.

CONFIDENCE

PRUDENTIAL LGBT FINANCIAL CONFIDENCE INDEX

The Prudential LGBT Financial Confidence Index establishes a baseline of the LGBT community's financial confidence that can be tracked over time. Survey participants answered 10 questions about their current financial status and future prospects. Each question has a score of 0–10 for a total potential score of 100.

Highlights

- The Prudential LGBT Financial Confidence Index shows mid-range financial confidence, with gay men more confident than lesbians, Gen Ys more confident than Baby Boomers, those living in big city metro areas more confident than those living in rural America and those working with financial professionals more confident than those who are not.

- The LGBT community is most confident about their household finances, followed by their local economy. They are less confident about current LGBT equality and the state of the national economy. Notably, the community is least confident about the financial industry's attention to LGBT Americans.

- Compared with the general population, the LGBT community feels less prepared to make wise financial decisions for a variety of unique legal, economic and social reasons.

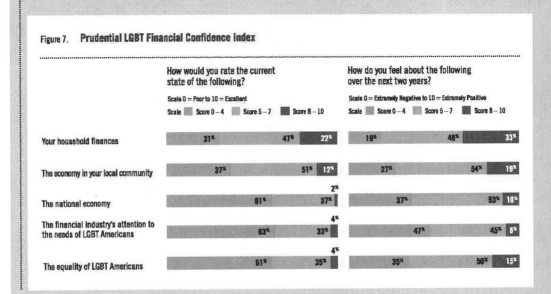

Figure 7. **Prudential LGBT Financial Confidence Index**

	How would you rate the current state of the following?			How do you feel about the following over the next two years?		
	Scale 0 = Poor to 10 = Excellent			Scale 0 = Extremely Negative to 10 = Extremely Positive		
	Score 0–4	Score 5–7	Score 8–10	Score 0–4	Score 5–7	Score 8–10
Your household finances	31%	47%	22%	19%	48%	33%
The economy in your local community	37%	51%	12%	27%	54%	19%
The national economy	61%	37%	2%	37%	53%	10%
The financial industry's attention to the needs of LGBT Americans	63%	33%	4%	47%	45%	8%
The equality of LGBT Americans	61%	35%	4%	35%	50%	15%

Confidence Index Year One Results

The baseline Prudential LGBT Financial Confidence Index indicates that the LGBT community has a mid-range financial confidence score of 48 out of 100 (Figure 8). Certain groups within the community score higher on the confidence index than others: Gay men are statistically more confident than lesbians (51 vs. 45), Gen Ys are more confident than Baby Boomers (50 vs. 46), those living in big city metro areas are more confident than those living in rural America (50 vs. 44) and those working with financial professionals are more confident than those who are not (50 vs. 46). LGBT residents of states with same-sex marriage are more confident than LGBTs living in states with civil union, domestic partnership or no legal relationship status (51 vs. 47).

Figure 8.   Confidence Score for Select Demographics

The Prudential LGBT Financial Confidence Index score is calculated by adding the average response from 10 separate questions (see Figure 7 for questions).
The 10 questions each have a potential score of 10 points for a maximum score of 100. The overall LGBT score of 48 indicates the community is mid-range in their confidence.
Some segments of the community scored higher than the overall LGBT confidence score, while others scored lower.

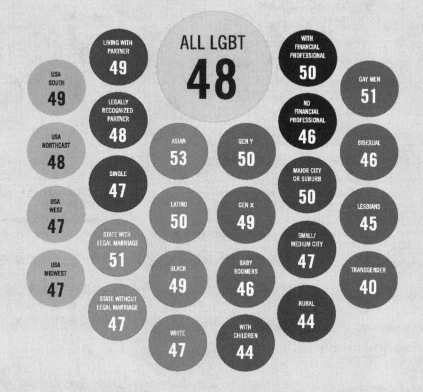

CONFIDENCE

We found major differences in how the community ranked the response categories within the Index. The LGBT community is most confident about themselves and their household finances, followed by their local economy (now and over the next two years). They are less confident about current LGBT equality and the state of the national economy. Notably, the community is least confident about the financial industry's attention to LGBT Americans.

The LGBT community is optimistic about their future, ranking all categories significantly higher when asked to project two years from now.

Need for More Financial Education

Compared with the general population, LGBT Americans are far less confident about their financial preparedness, with only 14% indicating they are well prepared, compared with 29% of the general population (Figure 10). LGBT community members using a financial professional have significantly higher confidence with 66% feeling either well prepared or needing help in only a few selected areas, compared to 49% of those without a financial professional.

Unique Financial Concerns

To further understand the concerns affecting participants' ability to achieve their financial goals, we asked them about 12 economic issues, some general and some LGBT-specific. LGBT Americans are much more concerned about economic equality issues than they are about the general state of the economy. About two-thirds rate the following issues as top financial concerns (Figure 9):

1. Lack of Social Security or pension survivor benefits for same-sex couples.

2. Legislation that negatively affects LGBT financial rights.

3. Tax treatment of same-sex couples.

In contrast, they are less worried about issues such as recession, inflation and the national deficit.

> "I am now, for the first time, working on building a life that includes financial considerations with my wife. We were able to file our taxes together, and I have more faith that our joint accounts are more secure for each of us."
>
> — Lesbian, 51, New York

"Until we achieve total financial equity in taxes, employment, etc., we need advisors who can help create air-tight financial plans for our families."

— Gay man, 26, Vermont

Figure 9. How concerned are you about the following issues affecting your ability to achieve your financial goals?

Scale 0 = Not at all concerned to 10 = Extremely concerned
Percentage rating very concerned (8 to 10)

Issue	%
Lack of Social Security or pension survivor benefits for same-sex couples	69%
Legislation negatively affecting LGBT financial rights	67%
Tax treatment of same-sex couples	64%
Benefit inequality for LGBT employees	60%
Inheritance rules for same-sex couples	60%
Lack of protection of joint assets if you or your partner become disabled	59%
Lack of employment protection for LGBT individuals	54%
Recession	50%
Loss of your or your partner's job	45%
Inflation	43%
Low interest rates impacting savings growth	43%
National deficit	39%

Figure 10. Need for More Financial Education

	LGBT	GENERAL POPULATION
I'M A BEGINNER AND NEED TO GAIN A LOT OF KNOWLEDGE AND EXPERIENCE	15%	11%
NEED TO CATCH UP MY KNOWLEDGE IN MANY AREAS	30%	22%
NEED HELP IN A FEW SELECTED AREAS OR TOPICS	41%	38%
VERY WELL PREPARED	14%	29%

DYNAMICS

LGBT FAMILY, MARRIAGE AND COUPLE COMMUNICATION

Highlights

- Lesbians are far more likely than gay men to live in a dual-income household.

- Within the LGBT community, 15% are already parents, and the number of LGBT parents is projected to dramatically increase as the majority of Gen Y plan to have children.

- Gay male couples are especially likely to have open communication about finances, but maintain separate accounts to retain financial independence.

Same-Sex Couples and Financial Rights

Financial planning for LGBT couples and parents can be complex, requiring the need to maneuver through widely varying state laws that govern relationship status and adoption. Just over one-third (34%) of study participants live together with no legal protections, and another 17% are in a legally recognized relationship: married, civil union or domestic partnership, all with different rights and responsibilities affecting their household finances (Figure 11). Lesbians are far more likely to live with a partner in a dual-income household than gay men (62% vs. 40%). However, gay men are more likely than lesbians to have been together with their partner for more than 10 years (50% vs. 38% of those living with their partner).

We found in the responses that it is difficult to make assumptions about relationships when navigating the LGBT financial landscape. Bisexuals might be in an opposite-sex or same-sex relationship. Some transgender people consider themselves to be both part of the LGBT community and heterosexual. Some same-sex couples are legally married, yet live in a state that does not recognize the relationship. Financial institutions and advisors need to understand their clients' unique relationships and legal status.

Open Communication, Separate Accounts

Across the LGBT community, many same-sex couples desire to maintain financial independence while in the relationship, a striking difference compared to the general population. While same-sex couples tend to have equal and open communication about financial concerns (at similar levels to general population couples), they often maintain separate financial accounts. Three-quarters (75%) of same-sex couples indicate keeping some separate accounts and 44% of gay male couples maintain completely separate accounts (Figure 12). The majority of gay men (60%) and half of lesbians (50%) living with their partner say they keep separate accounts mainly to retain financial independence, followed by simpler tax preparation (32% for LGBT) and different viewpoints on money and credit (24% for LGBT).

> "Do what is right for the individual. The financial industry needs to understand that they work for the individual investor no matter how they identify."
>
> — Transgender person, 50, Nebraska

"Right now, we're planning to have a child, so our financial goal is to save up a 'nest egg' to help ease the financial burden of getting pregnant, hospital costs, second-parent adoption and other costs associated with having a child."

— Lesbian, 36, Pennsylvania

LGBT Parents Have Added Expenses

The number of LGBT parents continues to grow and is expected to increase significantly starting with Gen Y. Already 23% of lesbians and 7% of gay men are financially responsible for a child under age 18 (Figure 13). Among Gen Y study participants, 11% already have children and an additional 49% plan to have children in the future.

LGBT parents report being financially secure. However, they also report needing to spend significant household income on legal and financial protections for their families because of the lack of legal protections in most states. LGBT parents have a low Prudential LGBT Financial Confidence Index score (44), expressing their largest concerns about the equality of LGBT Americans and the financial industry's attention to their needs.

Singled Out

Almost half of the LGBT study participants are single with different financial needs. LGBT singles are more likely to be younger and earn less income because of their age; 24% live with roommates. While they have less disposable income than those in relationships, they are much more likely than older LGBTs to spend on entertainment, fitness and personal care items. Many LGBT parents are single with 24% of the children in LGBT families being raised by single parents, parallel to the general population.

Caring for Parents

Nearly 1 in 10 LGBT participants report financially caring for a parent or other elder, with 4% having elders living in their home. Care for an elder is spread equally across generations with approximately 10% of Gen X, Gen Y and Baby Boomer participants. However, we did find significant differences by ethnicity, with greater numbers of Asian American (21%), Hispanic (18%) and African-American (15%) participants caring for an elder.

Figure 11. **Relationship Status**

	Legally recognized relationship*	Living with partner, no legal status	Single
LGBT	17%	34%	49%
LESBIAN	19%	43%	38%
GAY	13%	27%	60%
BISEXUAL	17%	21%	62%
TRANSGENDER	33%	22%	45%

* Includes Married, Civil Union and Domestic Partnership

Figure 12. **How do you and your spouse/partner organize your finances?**

	Completely separate account and investments	Separate and joint accounts and investments	All savings and investment accounts shared
LGBT	36%	39%	25%
LESBIAN	31%	45%	24%
GAY	44%	32%	24%
GENERAL POPULATION	18%	33%	49%

Figure 13. **How many children do you have under age 18 for whom you are financially responsible?**

	Parents	1 Child	2+ Children
LGBT	15%	10%	5%
LESBIAN	23%	15%	8%
GAY	7%	5%	2%

60% OF GEN Y ARE PARENTS OR PLAN TO HAVE CHILDREN

FINANCES

THE LGBT COMMUNITY IS IN GOOD FINANCIAL HEALTH

Highlights

- The LGBT community has a higher median income compared to the general population, likely a result of education levels and a tendency to live in states with higher median income.

- While gay men earn higher individual incomes than lesbians, lesbians have higher median household incomes as they are far more likely to live in a dual-income household.

- The LGBT community has high discretionary income, with 40% of gay men and 25% of lesbians spending more than $500 a month on discretionary items.

Spending Power of the LGBT Community

What is the spending power of the LGBT community? The reality is much more nuanced than typically reported in the media.

The median household income of study participants is $61,500 compared with $50,000 for the average American household. This difference reflects several factors, most notably education levels (50% indicate attaining at least a bachelor's degree) and where the LGBT community chooses to live (tending toward "LGBT-friendly" states with higher median incomes).

Individually, gay men earn more money than lesbians ($49,900 vs. $43,500 median income) – not surprising in a country where men earn more on average than women. However, the income gap between gay men and lesbians is smaller than the gender income gap in the general population. Among those employed full-time, lesbians earn 84% of what gay men earn, compared to the 77% female to male ratio among the total population.

While gay men earn more than lesbians individually, household income is another story. Lesbian household income is actually higher than gay household income ($63,700 vs. $62,300) because lesbians are far more likely to live in a dual-income household than gay men.

LGBT households with financial responsibility for a child report a median income of $71,100.

Gay male couples have the highest median household income ($103,100), but they are a minority of LGBT households (only 19% of participants). While many companies focus on the spending power of gay male couples, they actually make up a minority of the overall LGBT community.

General population income data from 2011 United States Census Bureau reports.

> "LGBT is a bit of a unique minority in that we encompass the entire spectrum of humanity, yet a good number of us are college educated with decent discretionary income. LGBT needs to be wooed. We have money to spend."
>
> — Gay man, 35, Tennessee

Figure 14. **In general, how would you describe your current financial situation?**

	LGBT	GENERAL POPULATION
Upscale – I'm doing what I want, when I want, where I want	2%	5%
Doing Well – I'm not part of the 1%, but things are good	20%	19%
Adequate – I'm living modestly, paying the bills and staying independent	47%	40%
On Edge – I'm making ends meet, but it's a struggle	25%	27%
Falling Behind – No longer able to keep up with expenses	6%	9%

Figure 15. **Discretionary income**

Top items for discretionary income spending

	GAY	LESBIAN
Dining out	75%	71%
Entertainment	67%	62%
Travel / vacation	52%	53%
Personal care items	46%	43%
Pet care items	33%	54%
Donating to charities	34%	36%
Clothing	38%	27%
Fitness	37%	26%
Home decoration or improvement	34%	30%
Children's items	4%	18%

A Pulse on Financial Health

The majority of LGBT participants are upbeat about their financial health. Twenty-two percent indicate they are "upscale or doing well," and 47% indicate they are "paying their bills and staying independent." In contrast, 31% say they are "on the edge or falling behind." These percentages are similar to those of the general population, according to a study conducted by Prudential earlier in 2012 (Figure 14). Although the community sees itself as more mid-scale, 4-in-10 households have income above $75,000 and 3-in-10 have investable assets of more than $100,000, both traditional definitions of a more "mass-affluent" community.

Significant Discretionary Income

Because the LGBT community is comprised of many dual income households without children, they have a substantial amount of discretionary income. About 40% of gay men and 25% of lesbians spend more than $500 a month on discretionary items, and 5% of the LGBT community spends $2,000 per month or more. The leading items for discretionary spending are dining out, entertainment and travel (Figure 15).

Home Ownership, Savings and Debt

LGBTs owning a home have a median home equity of $77,000. LGBT median household savings is $28,000 (not including employer-sponsored retirement plans), and median household debt is $14,000 (not including home mortgages or home equity loans).

Relatively Low Unemployment

Seven percent of LGBT participants define themselves as "unemployed and looking for work." There is no significant difference in unemployment rates by generation; however, lesbians have the lowest unemployment rate at 5%, and transgender people have the highest at 12%.

RETIREMENT

RETIREMENT IN THE LGBT COMMUNITY

Highlights

- Not outliving their money and maintaining lifestyle in retirement are the most pressing financial concerns of the LGBT community.

- The largest concentration of wealth and retirement preparedness is within the Baby Boomer generation; however, LGBT Baby Boomers face a unique set of financial obstacles.

- While most LGBT Baby Boomers are financially secure, about one-third describe their financial situation as "on the edge" or "falling behind."

A Gap in LGBT Retirement Confidence

Concerns around retirement are top of mind in the LGBT community. Not outliving their money and maintaining lifestyle in retirement are not only some of the most pressing financial concerns, but they are also areas with the largest LGBT financial confidence gaps (Figure 16). Related issues such as lack of Social Security benefits for same-sex survivors only add to retirement concerns. As a write-in question, we asked participants to name their most important financial goal. "Retirement" was the most frequently mentioned word. With this significant personal focus on retirement, it is not surprising that we found that 78% of all LGBT participants are already saving for retirement.

Baby Boomers' Unique Retirement Challenges

Among LGBT study participants, Baby Boomers are the generation most concerned about retirement. Many have been hard-hit by the recession, losing assets in the stock market and real estate close to their retirement age. In written responses, many report losing jobs and finding it hard to recover employment at the previous level. While these recession concerns are not unique to the LGBT community, many LGBT Baby Boomers indicated other challenges specific to being an LGBT person of that generation. For example, some discussed facing a lifetime of employment discrimination that has suppressed their savings potential. Especially among gay men of this generation, the HIV epidemic has left many survivors taking early retirement through disability, leaving them economically challenged for the rest of their lives. Currently, 23% of LGBT Baby Boomers report being retired, or living on income from disability or Social Security.

Despite Challenges, Baby Boomers Are Well Positioned for Retirement

Regardless of their unique challenges, the Baby Boomer generation has the greatest concentration of wealth in the LGBT community with a median household income of $70,000. More than half (53%) of Baby Boomers report living with a partner, and of those with partners, 56% have been with their partner for 10 years or more and 7% for 30 years or more. Few (8%) are financially responsible for a child, leaving them with added discretionary income. Boomer couples are much more likely to have joint bank accounts, and 71% share the responsibilities of financial planning. About 70% own their homes, and 52% of homeowners have more than $100,000 in home equity. Boomers indicate they are better prepared to make financial decisions than other generations, with 65% saying they are "very well prepared" or "only need help in a few selected topics." Fifty-seven percent work with some type of financial professional.

While most LGBT Baby Boomers are doing financially well, there are some struggling to make ends meet. Just under a third describe their financial situation as "on the edge" or "falling behind."

A Boomer Trend Toward Self-Employment

It should also be noted that 14% of LGBT Baby Boomers report being self-employed or small business owners with unique financial needs, compared to 9% of Gen X and 5% of Gen Y.

"I have a financial planner who is excellent, and my challenge is to create more wealth and have peace of mind in retirement."

— Lesbian, 63, California

Figure 16.   **Confidence Gap: Importance of goals vs. Confidence about achieving goal**

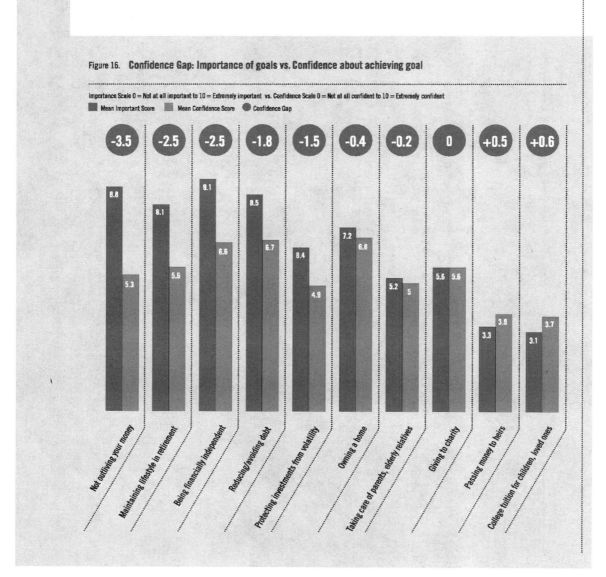

Importance Scale 0 = Not at all important to 10 = Extremely important vs. Confidence Scale 0 = Not at all confident to 10 = Extremely confident
■ Mean Important Score   ■ Mean Confidence Score   ● Confidence Gap

Goal	Gap	Mean Important	Mean Confidence
Not outliving your money	-3.5	8.8	5.3
Maintaining lifestyle in retirement	-2.5	8.1	5.6
Being financially independent	-2.5	9.1	6.6
Reducing/avoiding debt	-1.8	8.5	6.7
Protecting investments from volatility	-1.5	6.4	4.9
Owning a home	-0.4	7.2	6.8
Taking care of parents, elderly relatives	-0.2	5.2	5
Giving to charity	0	5.6	5.6
Passing money to heirs	+0.5	3.3	3.8
College tuition for children, loved ones	+0.6	3.1	3.7

PRODUCT OWNERSHIP

PRODUCT OWNERSHIP AMONG LGBT AMERICANS

Highlights

- LGBT people tend to maintain three core financial products – life insurance, an employer-sponsored retirement account and a savings account – adding others as they age, become parents or establish long-term partnerships.

- Within the LGBT community, same-sex couples in a legally recognized relationship and parents have the highest ownership of financial and estate planning products.

- More than half of LGBT Americans own a life insurance policy. Unlike the general population, where women are less likely to have life insurance, lesbians own life insurance equally to gay men.

Increased Need for Financial and Estate Planning Products

Within the LGBT community, same-sex couples in a legally recognized relationship and parents have the highest ownership of financial and estate planning products (Figure 17). In contrast, single LGBTs are least likely to own these products.

LGBTs own an average of four types of financial and insurance products. Product ownership increases with age and with each successive generation.

- Gen Ys begin with a core set of three products: a savings account, an employer-sponsored retirement plan and a life

insurance policy. Older generations maintain these three core products while adding others.

- Gen Xs are significantly more likely than their Gen Y counterparts to add mutual funds and stocks held outside of retirement accounts, additional insurance products and estate planning products to their portfolio. Ownership of disability insurance and long-term care insurance is highest among Gen X.

- Boomers are significantly more likely to have products that can help produce retirement income streams, such as annuities and IRAs. Ownership of investment products is highest across the board among Boomers.

While LGBT Baby Boomers are significantly more prepared than younger generations for the legal complexities they face in estate and inheritance planning, many still do not have key documents in place.

Life Insurance Is a Core Product

More than half (52%) of LGBT Americans own a life insurance policy. Like the general population, ownership is higher among those who own a home, have a partner, have children, work with a financial professional or have at least $75,000 in annual income (Figure 18). However, unlike the general population, where women are less likely to have life insurance, lesbians own life insurance equally to gay men.

> "We have had to spend a large amount of money protecting our parental rights, and on intensive wills and agreements to protect spousal rights."
>
> – Lesbian, 35, Wisconsin

Figure 17. **Which of the following financial, insurance and estate planning products do you have?**

	GEN Y	GEN X	BOOMERS	LGBT PARENTS	LEGALLY RECOGNIZED COUPLES
Retirement					
Employer-sponsored retirement plan	49%	59%	49%	59%	58%
Employer-sponsored pension plan	13%	21%	28%	26%	29%
IRA	23%	30%	39%	34%	38%
Savings					
Savings accounts	51%	53%	57%	56%	65%
Individual bonds	7%	6%	12%	9%	14%
Individual stocks	10%	17%	23%	15%	28%
Mutual funds	9%	16%	27%	16%	32%
529 Education savings plan	2%	4%	3%	12%	4%
Insurance					
Life insurance	49%	53%	51%	62%	65%
Annuity	3%	4%	13%	7%	10%
Long-term care insurance	11%	19%	16%	19%	24%
Disability	20%	34%	21%	31%	33%
Estate Planning					
Will	15%	30%	52%	48%	52%
Trust	3%	9%	15%	16%	19%
Healthcare proxy	14%	28%	51%	45%	58%
Power of attorney	14%	25%	42%	40%	53%
Average number of products	**3**	**4**	**5**	**5**	**6**

Figure 18. **Most likely LGBT owners of life insurance**

$75,000 OR MORE IN ANNUAL INCOME	ARE IN A LEGAL RELATIONSHIP	HAVE CHILDREN UNDER 18	WORK WITH A FINANCIAL PROFESSIONAL	OWN HOME	LIVE WITH PARTNER
67%	**65%**	**62%**	**62%**	**59%**	**58%**

FINANCIAL SERVICES COMPANIES AND THE LGBT COMMUNITY

Highlights

- LGBTs perceive their financial planning needs to be different from those of the general population.

- The LGBT community feels underserved by financial services companies and the vast majority of LGBTs never had a financial professional contact them about LGBT financial planning.

- LGBTs do not require that financial professionals be part of the LGBT community, but they do need these professionals to have an understanding of their unique needs as LGBT individuals.

LGBTs View Their Financial Needs as Different

Only 25% of LGBT participants believe that their financial needs are similar to those of the population at large. Even fewer LGBT couples living together (21%) feel they share comparable needs (Figure 19).

Increased Relevance of Financial Professionals

More than one-third (38%) of the LGBT community and nearly half (49%) of LGBT couples in a legally recognized relationship work with some type of financial professional. Word of mouth is the top way they find a financial professional, with 45% relying on a referral from a friend, a family member or a co-worker. While LGBTs do not require that financial professionals be part of the LGBT community, they do need these professionals to have an understanding of their unique needs as LGBT individuals (Figure 21).

LGBTs feel underserved by financial services companies (Figure 20) and the vast majority of LGBTs (88%) have never had a financial professional contact them about LGBT financial planning. Even those with financial advisors needed to seek out the services of an LGBT-understanding professional.

Figure 19. **Opinion on how similar or different LGBT financial planning needs are vs. the general population**

Scale 0 = LGBT financial needs are extremely similar to the population at large to 10 = LGBT financial planning needs are extremely different than the population at large

	Similar to General Population (0-4)	Neutral (5)	Different than General Population (6-10)
LGBT	25%	14%	61%
SINGLE	29%	17%	54%
LIVING WITH PARTNER	21%	11%	68%

Figure 20. **What can financial services firms do better to meet the needs of LGBT individuals?**

Size of word corresponds to the number of times the word was mentioned in participant write-in responses.

"Provide tips and information that are not commonly known. Flashy advertising is nice, but I would prefer some substance over just seeing a firm march in a Pride parade."

— Bisexual woman, 32, Washington

Choosing Financial Services Companies

LGBTs indicate that sensitivity to their needs is paramount in their selection of a financial services company. The top three factors (out of 14) they look for when choosing a financial services firm are the strength and reputation of the company (77%), LGBT-friendly hiring practices (63%) and professionals who specialize in LGBT finances (61%). In a separate question, more than 70% of participants report that they would much more likely choose a financial services firm that publicly supports LGBT causes, equal job rights for LGBT employees, marriage equality and LGBT employee benefit equality. Among transgender participants, more than 90% say they would choose a company if it supports transgender rights in the workplace.

Figure 21. **How important is it for a financial professional you work or would work with to...**

Scale 0 = Not at all important to 10 = Extremely important

Percentage rating very important (8 to 10)

Understand the unique financial needs of LGBT individuals	75%
Work for a company that has demonstrated commitment to the LGBT community	55%
Support events/organizations within the LGBT community	40%
Have a large base of LGBT clients	34%
Advertise in LGBT media	29%
Personally identify as LGBT	23%

SERVING THE FINANCIAL NEEDS OF THE LGBT COMMUNITY

For financial services firms to succeed in working with lesbian, gay, bisexual and transgender clients, companies must understand and recognize LGBT specific financial and legal concerns as well as respect their unique life situations.

In particular, the study demonstrates that financial services companies need to make an increased effort to reach out to the community, gain expertise in laws affecting same-sex couples and LGBT parents, treat their own employees equally in the workplace and support LGBT non-profit organizations.

By understanding, anticipating and responding to the needs of the LGBT community, financial services firms have a significant opportunity to make an impact on their business as well as on the lives of this distinct yet diverse group of Americans.

Prudential

rock-solid eco-smart.
Produced with the environment in mind.

Printed on recycled paper with 30% post consumer waste

@ 2012 Prudential Financial, Inc. and its affiliates, Newark, NJ. Prudential, the Prudential logo and the Rock symbol are service marks of Prudential Financial, Inc. and its related entities, registered in many jurisdictions worldwide.

0234390-00001-00 Ed. 11/2012

Update

Utah

On January 6, 2014, the Supreme Court of the United States stayed a ruling from the U.S. Circuit Court of Appeals, which had issued a ruling declaring the ban on same-sex marriage in Utah to be unconstitutional. During the 17 days between the Circuit Court's ruling and the stay issued by the Supreme Court, over 1,300 couples had married in the state of Utah. The legality of those marriages are now undetermined. In 2004 and 2008, when same-sex couples in California had windows of opportunity to obtain marriage licenses and marry, court decisions on those marriages were inconsistent. The 2004 marriages were held to be illegal, while the 2008 marriages were later determined to be valid (Huffington Post, 2014).

Source:
http://www.huffingtonpost.com/2014/01/06/utah-gay-marriage_n_4548931.html

Oklahoma

On January 14, 2014 Federal Judge Terrance C. Kern ruled that Oklahoma's ban on same-sex marriage was unconstitutional. However, to avoid the results of a similar ruling in the State of Utah, less than 30 days earlier, Judge Kern immediately stayed his own ruling, until it had the opportunity to wind its way through the appeals process (NY Times, 2014).

Source:
http://www.nytimes.com/2014/01/15/us/federal-judge-rejects-oklahomas-gay-marriage-ban.html?rref=us&_r=0

U.S. Department of Justice

On February 10, 2014, U.S. Attorney General Eric Holder announced that the United States Government will be expanding recognition of same-sex marriages in federal legal matters. These matters will include bankruptcy protections, prison visitation and survivor benefits for police and firefighters. According to Holder, the Justice Department will recognize same-sex marriages, "to the greatest extent possible under the law."

In addition to the areas previously mentioned, the Justice Department announcement will also confer upon same-sex spouses the right to decline to give testimony in cases where doing so might incriminate their spouse.

Source:
http://politicalticker.blogs.cnn.com/2014/02/10/u-s-expands-legal-benefits-services-for-same-sex-marriages/?iref=allsearch

Virginia

On February 14, 2014 a federal judge in the Commonwealth of Virginia issued a ruling overturning the commonwealth's ban on same-sex marriage.

U.S. District Judge Arenda Wright Allen then issued a stay on her own ruling, while it is being appealed. This court's action followed similar action in the State of Oklahoma, when a federal judge there made a similar ruling on January 14, 2014, and also stayed the ruling, to avoid a repeat of events that occurred in Utah, in January 2014.

In the Utah case, over 1,300 LGBT couples took advantage of the lower court's ruling to rush into same-sex marriages, before the U.S. Supreme Court issued a stay. Currently, the legality of those marriages are in question.

Source:
http://ezproxy.theamericancollege.edu/login?url=http://search.proquest.com.ezproxy.theamericancollege.edu/docview/1491225339?accountid=46314

Illinois

On February 21, 2014 U.S. District Judge Sharon Johnson Coleman ruled that same-sex-marriages could begin in Cook County, Illinois largest county, which includes the city of Chicago, immediately.

The state legislature had passed legislation in 2013, allowing same-sex-marriages to begin in Illinois on June 1. 2014. A suit was filed however, by the American Civil Liberties Union and Lamda Legal, challenging the necessity of waiting until June 1, 2014, for couples who were terminally ill. That case resulted in the ruling by Judge Coleman, being celebrated by those in favor of same-sex marriage in Illinois.

Source:
http://news.yahoo.com/judge-gay-couples-wed-ill-39-cook-county-193951620.html;_ylt=AwrBJR7uRApT3S8AwoPQtDMD

U.S. Department of Justice

On February 25, 2014, U.S. Attorney General Eric Holder once again inserted himself into the same-sex marriage issue. In this instance he addressed his remarks to the fifty states attorneys general, pronouncing in a *NY Times* interview that his state counter parts were not obligated to defend state laws and bans in court, if they believe them to be discriminatory.

Source:
http://wtaq.com/news/articles/2014/feb/25/us-state-lawyers-dont-have-to-defend-gay-marriage-bans-holder/

Texas

On February 26, 2014 Federal District Judge Orlando Garcia ruled that Texas' ban on gay marriage unconstitutional. In the case of De Leon v. Perry, 5:13-cv-982, U.S. District Court, Western District of Texas (San Antonio), Garcia ruled for the plaintiffs. He said, "While acknowledging the state's argument that an injunction would be 'rewriting over 150 years of Texas law and radically altering the status quo,' keeping tradition and history intact is not a justification for the infringement of an individual's rights."

Garcia stayed his own ruling giving the state time to appeal, so same-sex marriages will not be performed in Texas, for the time being.

Source:
http://www.bloomberg.com/news/2014-02-26/texas-same-sex-marriage-ban-unconstitutional-federal-judge-says.html

Michigan

U.S. District Judge Bernard Friedman issued a ruling on March 21, 2014, striking down the state ban on same-sex marriage. The ruling was the result of a case brought by two Michigan lesbians, who originally challenged the states adoption code but later amended their suit to include the state ban on same-sex marriage.

State Attorney General Bill Schuette immediately appealed the decision to the U.S. Court of Appeals for the 6th Circuit, stating, "In 2004 the citizens of Michigan recognized that diversity in parenting is best for kids and families because moms and dads are not interchangeable. Michigan voters enshrined that decision in our state constitution, and their will should stand and be respected. I will continue to carry out my duty to protect and defend the constitution."

Unlike AG Schuette, a republican, the attorneys general of California, Pennsylvania, Illinois, Nevada and Oregon, all democrats, have refused to defend suits challenging same-sex marriage, in their states.

Approximately 300 Michigan couples married on Saturday, March 22, 2014, before a federal court issued a stay, and the state government is not weighing in on the issue of the validity of those marriages until the appeals court rules.

Source: http://news.yahoo.com/same-sex-marriage-court-shoots-down-yet-another-130331967.html;_ylt=A0LEViBTRzBTTH4AEIJjmolQ;
_ylu=X3oDMTBsa3ZzMnBvBHNlYwNzYwRjb2xvA2JmMQR2dGlkAw
–?ru=yahoo?mod=yahoo_itp

Oregon

On May 19, 2014, Oregon became the 18th state to recognize same-sex marriage. U.S. District Judge Michael McShane struck down Oregon State's constitutional amendment that prohibited recognition of same-sex marriage, ruling that it violates the U.S. Constitution. Unlike what has occurred in a number of other states when similar rulings have been handed down, McShane's ruling was effective immediately, allowing same-sex couples to begin getting married without any further delay.

Judge McShane, wrote the following in his ruling. "My decision will not be the final word on this subject, but on this issue of marriage I am struck more by our similarities than our differences. I believe that if we can look for a moment past gender and sexuality, we can see in these plaintiffs nothing more or less than our own families. Families who we would expect our Constitution to protect, if not exalt, in equal measure.

"With discernment we see not shadows lurking in closets or the stereotypes of what was once believed; rather, we see families committed to the common purpose of love, devotion, and service to the greater community.

"Where will this all lead? I know that many suggest we are going down a slippery slope that will have no moral boundaries. To those who truly harbor such fears, I can only say this: Let us look less to the sky to see what might fall; rather, let us look to each other ... and rise."

Source:
http://www.freedomtomarry.org/blog/entry/federal-judge-in-oregon-strikes-down-ban-on-marriage-for-same-sex-couples

Pennsylvania

On May 25, 2014, Pennsylvania became the 19th state to recognize same-sex marriage, when Judge John E. Jones III overturned the 1996 law defining marriage in Pennsylvania as between men and woman.

Jones wrote in his 39-page ruling, "That same-sex marriage causes discomfort in some does not make its prohibition constitutional. Nor can past tradition trump the bedrock constitutional guarantees of due process and equal protection. Were that not so, ours would still be a racially segregated nation according to the now rightfully discarded doctrine of 'separate but equal.'"

The State Attorney General, Democrat Kathleen Kane, refused to defend the law, based on her belief that the law was unconstitutional.

Source:
http://www.christianpost.com/news/republican-gov-decides-after-immense-struggle-not-to-appeal-striking-of-pa-same-sex-marriage-ban-120342/

Chapter Review

Review questions are based on the learning objectives in this chapter. Thus, a [3] at the end of a question means that the question is based on learning objective 3. If there are multiple objectives, they are all listed.

Key Terms and Concepts

LGBT	same-sex marriage
Windsor v. United States	state of celebration
DOMA	state of residence

Review Questions

1. Discuss the effect Windsor v. U.S. had on LGBT clients and financial services professionals.

2. Discuss three impediments to LGBT clients achieving traditional financial planning goals? [2]

3. Explain the difference in "state of celebration" and "state of domicile or residence." [3]

4. Which are the primary considerations enumerated in this chapter, as they relate to considerations a financial services professional must take when deciding to include LGBT clients in his or her practice? Which one is most important to you, and why? [4]

5. What, if any, trend does there appear to be developing for state-by-state recognition of same-sex marriage? [4]

Learning Objectives

An understanding of the material in this chapter should enable you to

1. Develop a set of recommendations that help LBGT clients meet their financial goals and to satisfy any unstated financial planning needs discovered through the financial planning process.

Introduction

Gary and Emir

Gary (48) is an executive with a major domestic airline. He is responsible for overseeing the human resources departments and is the management liaison to the pilot and flight attendants' union. You have been working with him for the past eighteen months and helped him design an investment portfolio and purchase a long-term care insurance policy. Gary was referred to you by another executive with the airline who is also your client. You met with Gary a handful of times before you met his partner, Emir (37). Gary and Emir are not married or in a legally-recognized civil union.

Emir and Gary have been together for the past 5 years. They reside in Gary's home. Emir works locally as an assistant manager in a community bank. Gary travels often on business; Emir joins him when he can. Gary actively supports his alma mater, the University of Virginia, and regularly attends college football games. Emir has a child, Candace, from a previous relationship. Candace is twelve years old and lives with her mother. Emir provides his daughter with monthly child support and spends time with her on some holidays and weekends. Candace's mother has remarried.

Both Emir and Gary have signed client agreements with your firm, though as of today you have opened investment accounts for only Gary. Gary is your primary point of contact in the client relationship. You enjoy working together and he is in the process of finalizing a referral to your firm.

Prior to your last meeting, Gary told you he was tired, losing weight, and having some medical tests done. He attended your last meeting without Emir and confided that a biopsy confirmed Gary has an aggressive prostate cancer. He was diagnosed at stage III, and Gary is considering his treatment options. Gary was composed but hopeful, and he wants to make sure Emir is secure while making amends with his own family. Gary's parents are no longer living, but he has become estranged from his sister. Emir is in good health and runs daily; Gary believes Emir will have an above average life expectancy.

Gary had a will drafted before he met Emir, leaving all of his property to his sister. He thinks his sister has a copy of it, but Gary is unable to locate the document. Emir drafted a will at his divorce leaving all of his property to Candace. Gary would like to leave Emir adequate assets to comfortably maintain his current lifestyle and home, provide a small college fund for Candace, and leave a substantial endowment at his alma mater.

Gary and Emir have provided you with an inventory of their assets, which is presented in a statement of financial position. Gary has extensive experience investing and completed a risk-tolerance questionnaire prior to his diagnosis. At that time he was comfortable with the risk associated with a portfolio comprised of 60 percent equities, 30 percent bonds, and 10 percent cash. Emir has far less experience with investments and has not filled out a risk-tolerance questionnaire. Neither Emir nor Gary has an existing relationship with an attorney.

Gary works with a local CPA to help prepare his taxes. The CPA also works with other airline executives. Both Gary and Emir have car insurance through one of Emir's friends, a licensed property/casualty agent. Emir and Gary both have strong credit scores (around 750), and neither has previously filed bankruptcy. Gary earns substantially more than Emir; they have provided you with a cash flow statement to assist in the planning process.

Neither Emir nor Gary has expressed an interest in having additional children. Gary enjoys spending time with Candace and Emir and often participates in holidays with Emir's family. Emir and Gary would love to get married, but considering their state's legal interpretation of same-sex marriage they are not sure if an out-of-state marriage would enhance or detract from their goals and objectives.

Stated Goals and Environment

Gary's Stated Goals and Objectives

1. Structure resources to allow Gary an extended leave of absence
2. Educate Emir about investment planning and risk management
3. Update beneficiary designations and estate planning documents
4. Maximize available employer benefits to Gary
5. Establish an endowment at the University of Virginia
6. Reconcile with Gary's sister

Emir's Stated Goals and Objectives

1. Provide for Candace in the event of Emir's death or disability
2. Allow for a leave of absence to provide support for Gary
3. Save for Candace's college
4. Continue saving towards retirement

Regulatory Environment

- Gary and Emir live in a state that has a constitutional amendment defining marriage as between a man and a woman.
- They reside in a state that is not a community property state.
- Gary and Emir live in a state that charges a graduated state income tax between 2.0 percent and 5.0 percent.

Economic Environment

- Investors can earn a 2.0 percent risk free rate.
- Inflation is estimated to be 3.5 percent.
- Housing prices have been stagnant the past three years.Unemployment is 8.0 percent nationally and 7.5 percent regionally.

Employee Benefit Information

Health Insurance: Gary and Emir

Gary and Emir are covered through Gary's health insurance policy at the airline. The policy meets or exceeds all federal guidelines for qualified coverage but is not considered a "Cadillac" plan. The plan has a $2,000 annual deductible per insured and a strong network of local doctors organized in a preferred provider network. After the deductible is met, 80 percent of qualified medical costs are covered through the plan for in-network physicians. Only 60 percent of costs for out-of-network physicians are covered. The plan has a maximum out-of-pocket family expense of $7,500. The plan provides reasonable prescription coverage. Gary pays $300 in monthly pretax payroll deductions for his personal participation in the plan; adding Emir increased the cost to Gary by an additional $400 monthly in after-tax premiums.

Short-Term Disability: Gary

Gary is covered under an executive short-term disability plan. He will receive 60 percent of his base salary for 6 months in the event of a short-term disability or catastrophic illness. This policy has a one month waiting period followed by 6 months of benefits. Gary has enough paid time off to provide his full salary during the waiting period.

Long-Term Disability: Gary

Gary is covered under an executive long-term disability plan. He will receive 55 percent of his base salary for up to 3 years in the event of a long-term disability. The policy will pay benefits if Gary is unable to perform his current job, which includes elements of travel and negotiation. The policy has a waiting period of 6 months and his disability or illness must be confirmed by a physician.

Employer Life Insurance: Gary

Gary has employer-provided life insurance with a death benefit of $500,000. Gary controls the beneficiary of this policy and has currently named Emir as the beneficiary.

Executive Benefits: Gary

Gary receives a monthly car allowance of $500 and unlimited guest airline tickets. Gary is seated in first class when flying on his employer airline for business or pleasure. His employer will reimburse him up to $5,000 annually for personal financial planning fees. Gary participates in a revenue sharing program and has outlined his previous year bonus on his income statement. He expects to receive a similar bonus at the end of this year.

Short Term Disability: Emir

Emir's employer does not offer short-term disability insurance.

Long Term Disability: Emir

Emir's employer does not offer long-term disability benefits.

Employer Life Insurance: Emir

Emir has employer-provided life insurance with a death benefit equal to three times his base salary, or $210,000.

Other Insurance Information

Long Term Care: Gary

Gary purchased a qualified long-term care policy from you last year. The policy will provide up to $250 in compounding, inflation-adjusted average daily benefits for up to 5 years. The policy will begin paying benefits if Gary is unable to perform two activities of daily living or becomes cognitively impaired. The policy will provide benefits for at-home or nursing-home care. The policy has a $300 monthly premium and is with an AA-rated insurance company.

Life Insurance: Gary

Gary owns a $50,000 single-premium whole life insurance policy he purchased 10 years ago. The policy currently has a cash value of $25,800. Gary no longer makes premium payments to the policy. The University of Virginia's Darden School of Business is the beneficiary.

Life Insurance: Emir

Emir owns a term life insurance policy with a $200,000 death benefit. The policy was initially a 20-year term policy and is 12 years into the term period. Candace is the beneficiary of the policy. Premiums are $30 monthly.

Auto Insurance: Gary and Emir

Gary and Emir are insured under separate policies through an AA-rated mutual insurance company. Their policies each have a $500 deductible and provide $100,000 of protection per bodily injury, $250,000 of aggregate bodily injury payments, and $100,000 of property damage protection per accident. Both policies also carry a new car replacement provision. Gary's premium is $200/month, and Emir's premium is $140/month. Emir is a personal friend of the representative from Mutual Insurance Company.

Homeowners Insurance: Gary

Gary's home is insured for its full replacement value of $750,000. Gary carries a HO-3 policy with a replacement cost rider on his personal property. The policy was sold to him by Emir's friend at Mutual Insurance Company and carries $100,000 of liability protection. Gary does not carry flood insurance and does not live in an area with a history of flooding. Annual premiums are $2,400.

Financial Statements

Statement of Financial Position: Gary Jones and Emir Leahy

ASSETS:[1]

Cash and Cash Equivalents

Checking Account - ABC Bank	$19,500	(JTIC)
Checking Account - XYZ Bank	7,000	(Emir)
Checking Account – ABC Bank	5,000	(Gary)
Money Market – ABC Bank	35,000	(Gary)
Total Cash and Equivalents	$66,500	

Investments

Growth Fund of America "A" Shares[2]	120,000	(Gary)
High Income Muni Bond "A" Shares[3]	50,000	(Gary)
Airline Executive 401(k) Plan[4]	380,000	(Gary)
Emir's 401(k) Plan[5]	45,000	(Emir)
IRA Rollover[6]	29,000	(Gary)
Total Investments	$624,000	

Personal

Home[7]	750,000	(Gary)
2011 Audi 3T	25,000	(Gary)
2008 Honda Accord	5,000	(Emir)
Personal property	75,000	(JTIC)
Single Premium Whole Life Policy CV	25,800	
Total Personal	$880,800	
	Total Assets	$1,571,300

LIABILITIES:

Mortgage[8]	390,442	(Gary)
Automobile loan[9]	12,200	(Gary)
Discover Card[10]	6,300	(Emir)
	Total Liabilities	$408,942

Net Worth

Total Liabilities and Net Worth	$1,162,358

Notes To Financial Statements:

[1] All assets are stated at fair market value. JTIC = Joint Tenants in Common.

[2] Purchased over the past eighteen months with an average cost basis of $100,000.

[3] Purchased over the past eighteen months with an average cost basis of $52,000.

[4] Gary's 401(k) plan is comprised of 40% airline stock, 50% Vanguard Target Date 2030 retirement fund at 10% guaranteed account currently earning 3%.

[5] Emir's 401(k) plan is comprised of 100% XYZ Bank Stock.

[6] Gary's IRA Rollover is 100% invested in the Vanguard Target Date 2030 Retirement Fund.

[7] The home was purchased for $550,000 10 years ago.

[8] Gary initially borrowed $480,000 at a 5% interest rate when he purchased his home. He makes monthly payments of $2,576.

[9] Gary's loan was at a promotional 0% APR. He pays $340 a month.

[10] Emir's Discover Card has a 12.99% APR. He makes regular payments on the balance and has a $12,000 credit limit. Gary also has an identical Discover card with no current balance and a $40,000 credit limit.

Statement of Cash Flow: Gary Jones and Emir Leahy for the Year 20XX

CASH INFLOWS

Salary – Gary	$235,000	
Bonus – Gary	42,800	
Executive car stipend	6,000	
Salary – Emir	70,000	
Bonus – Emir	10,000	
Interest and dividend income	2,000	
Gifts (Emir's Parents)	4,000	
Total Inflows		**$369,800**

CASH OUTFLOWS

Federal income tax (Gary)	$51,000
State income tax (Gary)	9,500
FICA taxes (Gary)	11,000
Federal income tax (Emir)	9,000
State income tax (Emir)	1,700
FICA taxes (Emir)	6,100
Property taxes	10,800
Health insurance (Gary & Emir)	8,400
Homeowners insurance	2,400
Auto insurance (Gary & Emir)	4,080
Life insurance (Emir)	360
Long-term care insurance (Gary)	3,600
Retirement plan savings[1]	35,000
Mortgage payment	30,912
Car payments	3,200
Auto Maintenance and repair	3,000
Child support (Emir)	6,000
Food (Groceries)	6,000
Food (Meals Out)	12,000
Entertainment	9,700

Utilities	6,800
Clothing	5,000
University of Virginia Annual Giving	20,000
Travel	10,000
Mutual fund savings	100,000

Total Outflows	$365,552
Discretionary Cash Flows	$4,248

[1] Gary and Emir are both maximizing contributions to their 401(k) plans. For this tax year, assume they could contribute $17,500 each into the plan on a pretax basis.

Further Considerations

This case focuses on holistic and technical planning elements. Students are encouraged to work through solutions on their own before reading the following case outcomes.

Two outcomes will be introduced. The first solution will be by Kevin Lynch, CFP®, ChFC®, CLU®, RHU®, REBC®, CASL®, CAP®, LUTCF. Kevin is an Assistant Professor of Insurance at The American College. Kevin holds the Charles J. Zimmerman Chair in Insurance Education and will bring an insurance background to this case study.

A second solution will be offered by Craig Lemoine, PhD, CFP®, a professor at The American College. Craig holds the Jarrett L. Davis Professorship in Financial Planning Technology. This case is modeled after that of a client Craig worked with, though the names, industry, and state of residence have been changed. Craig's solution will incorporate actual client outcomes.

The Case Study

Consider the financial planning process and help Gary and Emir develop a set of recommendations that meet their goals as well as any unstated financial planning needs discovered through the financial planning process.

The steps of the financial planning process are:

1. Establish and define the client-planner relationship.
2. Gather client data, including goals.
3. Analyze and evaluate the client's current financial status.
4. Develop and present recommendations and/or alternatives.
5. Implement the recommendations.
6. Monitor the recommendations.

Consider answering some of the following questions when preparing your case study. These questions are intended to guide the discovery process and help students craft comprehensive outcomes in line with the canon and pledge taken by all ChFC® professionals.

I. Establish and define the client-planner relationship

- Do you see any potential hurdles in continuing working with Emir and Gary?
- How would you be compensated for continuing to work with this couple?
- Do you have the resources in place to handle this client? If not, what steps do you need to take to work with the client?
- Does your business model place any limitations on your ability to work with this client? How can you overcome those limitations?

II. Gather client data, including goals

- What additional information can help you create a financial plan? How would you ask for the information?
- How would you gather information about Emir? About Gary?
- What questions are important to ask to further define the clients' goals?
- Based on the information provided, how would you prioritize and quantify client goals and objectives?
- What needs of the client may not be addressed in their goals?

III. Analyze and evaluate financial status

- What resources does the client have available for their goals?
- What types of retirement plans are appropriate for the client?
- As Gary may now be uninsurable, how might he be able to further provide for Emir?
- How would you calculate Gary and Emir's disability and retirement needs? Do these needs change in light of Gary's diagnosis?
- What would currently happen to Gary's assets if he were to die today?
- Do Gary and Emir need to reevaluate their estate plan? What suggestions would you make towards this financial planning area?
- Do you foresee any tax problems Gary or Emir might face this year? What changes can they make to limit audit risk?
- What are the financial planning advantages and disadvantages of marriage?

IV. Develop and present financial planning recommendations and alternatives

- How would you present your recommendations to Gary and Emir? Would you present your recommendations at a joint meeting?
- How would you prioritize your recommendations? Assuming Gary and Emir have a limited time to meet with you, which recommendations would you stress today?
- Would you involve other family members in the planning process?
- Which recommendations would you present alongside alternatives?
- How might your recommendations change if you were compensated under a different business model?

V. Implement recommendations

- Which implementation duties would you delegate to Gary, Emir, or your firm?
- How would you address competing recommendations made by Gary and Emir's property/casualty agent?
- How can Emir and Gary generate the cash flow necessary to put all elements of the plan in place?
- What products would you consider implementing?
- How are needs for liquidity and creditor protection satisfied?

VI. Monitor the financial plan recommendations

- What systems will you put in place to help prepare Emir as Gary's illness progresses?
- How will other professionals be involved in monitoring the plan?
- How does your business model compensate you for monitoring the plan?

Case Solution 1: Gary and Emir

Overview

Here are my thoughts regarding this case, written down as I read through the materials. Since I am not currently in practice, I do not have the fact finder forms, or the software I would traditionally be using to build a case like this. The process, however, is the same.

- First I will acknowledge a same-sex partnership, which does not currently enjoy the benefits of marriage, on the federal or state level. Gary and Emir have considered an out-of-state marriage, but have not yet decided if that would be worthwhile in their case.

- "They reside in Gary's Home." This piece of information is meaningful for two reasons: titling of property, and gifting challenges, depending on solutions pursued. It also brings up the need for renter's insurance for the nonowner resident.

- Gary has charitable intent as he supports his alma mater, the University of Virginia.

- Emir has a child from a previous marriage. This introduces two issues: providing for Candace, his daughter and the fact that her mother has remarried and has primary custody of Candace. Emir provides monthly child support.

- Both Gary and Emir are clients of the firm, with Gary as the primary point of contact. This information introduces the need to acknowledge to both clients that there are privacy and confidentiality issues in play here, with one FA serving the needs of two separate clients. Adequate disclosure is a must.

- **Gary has confided to you that he has Stage III Prostate cancer and is currently considering treatment options. This information is a "major red flag."** Estate planning needs, including various documents and agreements will now be moved to the forefront of any planning and implementation plans for this couple. (Gary is not aware of the location of his current will.) Gary has also introduced a number of estate planning goals here, which will need to be addressed. (Leave Emir adequate assets to comfortably maintain his current lifestyle and home, provide a small college fund for Candace and provide an endowment for his alma mater.)

- **Gary completed a risk tolerance questionnaire prior to his illness being diagnosed.** This needs to be readdressed, as does the initial review for Emir.

- Gary has assembled an assortment of professionals, including a CPA and a P&C Agent. No mention was made of a qualified estate-planning attorney being retained.
- Both Gary & Emir have excellent credit scores; 750 each.
- Marriage has been discussed but whether or not to marry out of state, with Virginia current marriage laws as they are, is seen as an impediment.

Provided Facts

The following individual items of information were provided in the case materials. I will comment on each, individually.

Health Insurance: Gary and Emir

Gary and Emir are covered through Gary's health insurance policy at the airline. The policy meets or exceeds all federal guidelines for qualified coverage but is not considered a "Cadillac" plan. The plan has a $2,000 annual deductible per insured and a strong network of local doctors organized in a preferred provider network. After the deductible is met 80 percent of qualified medical costs are covered through the plan for in-network physicians. Only 60 percent of costs for out of network physicians are covered. The plan has a maximum out of pocket family expense of $7,500. The plan provides reasonable prescription coverage. Gary pays $300 in monthly pretax payroll deductions for his personal participation in the plan; adding Emir increased the cost to Gary by an additional $400 monthly in after-tax premiums.

Comment: This appears to be an excellent policy. It is important to determine, through Gary's Human Resources Department, how Gary going on extended leave will affect this policy.

Short-Term Disability: Gary

Gary is covered under an executive short-term disability plan. He will receive 60 percent of his base salary for 6 months in the event of a short-term disability or catastrophic illness. This policy has a one-month waiting period followed by 6 months of benefits. Gary has enough paid time off to provide his full salary during the waiting period.

Comment: Once again, this is excellent coverage. Since the case doesn't mention the length of a proposed extended leave, and since it is ostensibly for Gary's treatment, this policy will provide a great start. Under most company policies, while an employee is on short-term disability leave, all pay and benefits continue under the status quo. In better plans, provisions include continuation of retirement benefit growth as well.

Long-Term Disability: Gary

Gary is covered under an executive long-term disability plan. He will receive 55 percent of his base salary for up to 3 years in the event of a long-term disability. The policy will pay benefits if Gary is unable to perform his current job, which includes elements of travel and negotiation. The policy has a waiting period of 6 months and his disability or illness must be confirmed by a physician.

Comment: This appears to be an own-occupation policy, which is a superior policy. Assuming Gary's prostate cancer is arrested and goes into remission, this should happen within the 3½ years provided by the disability policies provided through his employer.

Note: Gary is a high-income earner. Both of his short-term and long-term disability plans provide a severely reduced cash flow into the home. However, depending upon his contribution to the policies, some of those dollars can be received income tax free. Also, disability income dollars, at 60 percent and 55 percent of base salary, will be subject to much lower income taxes. This information also needs to be researched through Gary's human resources department and his CPA.

Employer Life Insurance: Gary

Gary has employer provided life insurance with a death benefit of $500,000. Gary controls the beneficiary of this policy, and has currently named Emir as the beneficiary.

Comment: This amount seems low, compared to his salary. Most companies permit executives to have 2-6 times annual income within a group life insurance program. This is something that needs to be explored immediately, as well as when the next open sign up period will begin.

Since Gary is currently diagnosed with cancer, he is not eligible for underwriting for a new policy. Should he go into remission, however, after 3–5 years, under most underwriting guidelines he will be a standard risk and be under 55 years of age. Additional insurance can be pursued at that time, as required by their current family circumstances.

Executive Benefits: Gary

Gary receives a monthly car allowance of $500 and unlimited guest airline tickets. Gary is seated in first class when flying on his employer airline for business or pleasure. His employer will reimburse him up to $5,000 annually for personal financial planning fees. Gary participates in a revenue sharing program and has outlined his previous year bonus on his income statement. He expects to receive a similar bonus at the end of this year.

Comment: Free air travel, a company provided auto expense account, and financial planning fees are tremendous perks. These types of benefits are usually extended to those on disability, so they should continue while Gary is on leave. Again, this information needs to be verified through Gary's human resources department.

Bonuses are usually handled differently however. Most bonus programs require you to be "actively at work," in order to be eligible for receipt of bonus dollars. Different companies treat this matter in different ways, depending on the nature of the bonus and the level of employee receiving the bonus. This will also need to be clarified through human resources.

Long-Term Care: Gary

Gary purchased a qualified long-term care policy from you last year. The policy will provide up to $250 in compounding inflation adjusted average daily benefits for up to 5 years. The policy will begin paying benefits if Gary is unable to perform two activities of daily living or becomes cognitively impaired. The policy will provide benefits for at-home or nursing home care. The policy has a $300 monthly premium and is with an AA-rated insurance company.

Comment: This appears to be a standard, quality, comprehensive long-term care insurance policy. Should Gary qualify for short-term or long-term disability with a prognosis of disability for 90 days or more, this policy should trigger benefits. These benefits are received income tax free, since Gary pays the premiums out-of-pocket and it is a qualified plan.

Life Insurance: Gary

Gary owns a $50,000 single — whole-life insurance policy he purchased 10 years ago. The policy currently has a cash value of $25,800. Gary no longer makes premium payments to the policy. The University of Virginia's Darden School of Business is the beneficiary.

Comment: As mentioned earlier, Gary has charitable intent and his alma mater is the target of this charity. This single premium policy is paid up and the University of Virginia is the beneficiary. There is no mention of the beneficiary being irrevocable, so in an emergency, Gary could use the cash values of this policy for other purposes. Also, depending upon the kind of policy it is—whole life, universal, etc.—it might be possible to use this same policy to increase the gift to the college, once Gary recovers, should that continue to be his desire.

Other insurance considerations in Gary and Emir's relationship are the auto and homeowner's polices currently in place.

Homeowners Insurance: Gary

Gary's home is insured for its full replacement value of $750,000. Gary carries a HO-3 policy with a replacement cost rider on his personal property. The policy was sold to him by Emir's friend at Mutual Insurance Company and carries $100,000 of liability protection. Gary does not carry flood insurance and does not live in an area with a history of flooding. Annual premiums are $2,400.

Comment: The case materials indicated that Gary wanted the home to stay with Emir. As currently owned, solely in Gary's name, there could be estate issues that arise upon Gary's death, because of the marriage inequality laws in Virginia. Although that is an estate planning issue, however, I wanted to make the point, and it is related to the homeowner's insurance.

The HO-3 policy, with full replacement on structure and contents, is a great policy. The liability coverage, however, needs to be increased to a minimum of $300,000 with a recommendation of $500,000. In addition, I would recommend a personal umbrella liability policy of at least $2,000,000. The cost is minimal and the protection, for a high net worth and high-income earner, is essential. (The increased liability coverage on the HO-3 will be a requirement for issuing the PUL.)

Another missing policy in this arrangement is a renter's policy, for Emir. Under the HO-3 policy, Emir, who is not legally related to Gary and is not an owner of the property, would not be covered by Gary's Homeowner's policy. The good news is, HO-4 (Tenant) policies are relatively inexpensive. The HO-4 will provide protection for Emir's personal property as well as liability coverage.

Auto Insurance: Gary and Emir

Gary and Emir are insured under separate policies through an AA-rated mutual insurance company. Their policies both have a $500 deductible and provide $100,000 of protection per bodily injury, $250,000 of aggregate bodily injury payments and $100,000 of property damage protection per accident. Both policies also carry a new car replacement provision. Gary's premium is $200/month and Emir's is $140 monthly. Emir is personal friends with the representative from Mutual Insurance Company.

Comment: In some states, even those with marriage inequality laws, insurance companies will permit domestic partners to be insured on the same policy. This is worth inquiring about.

As to the two existing policies, I recommend an increase in Gary's auto policy from $100/$250/$100 to $250/$500/$250. This will be required to gain access to the PUL policy previously mentioned. Emir's policy limits appear satisfactory. Both gentlemen might also inquire as to a $1,000 deductible vs. their current $500 deductible.

Emir's situation is not as complicated as Gary's. Emir has few benefits through his employer. Basically, he has only basic group life insurance, at what appears to be three times annual salary. In addition, he owns a $200,000 term policy.

Life Insurance: Emir

Emir owns a term life insurance policy with a $200,000 death benefit. The policy was initially a 20-year term policy and 12 years into the term period. Candace is the beneficiary of the policy. Premiums are $30 monthly.

Comment: This is an excellent small term policy and I am sure it was what Emir could afford 12 years ago. He might consider upgrading the policy to a permanent policy, perhaps a UL policy, with the same firm, using a conversion benefit. As an alternative, since he appears to be in good health, he could look into, at a minimum, a newer term policy with a 30-year fixed term, increasing the face amount. The policy could be initially earmarked for Candace, and once she has graduated college, could be split between Candace and any other purpose close to Emir's heart.

Short-Term and Long-Term Disability: Emir

Emir's employer does not offer short-term disability insurance.

Emir's employer does not offer long-term disability benefits.

Comment: Although personally purchased disability income insurance is more expensive than group coverage, since Emir's employer doesn't provide group coverage, ne needs to look into a personal policy. While an own-occupation policy might not be available, a hybrid policy, with 2–3 years own-occupation, followed by any-occupation might be affordable. This is especially true, if it is for a limited period, such as 5 years.

The Goals

Gary's Stated Goals and Objectives

1. Structure resources to allow Gary an extended leave of absence.
2. Educate Emir about investment planning and risk management.
3. Update beneficiary designations and estate planning documents.
4. Maximize available employer benefits to Gary.
5. Establish an endowment at University of Virginia.
6. Reconcile with Gary's sister.

Comments: Most of these goals and objectives have been addressed in the preceding comments, but I will now address any missed previously.

1. We need to define the term, "extended leave of absence." We also need to get a firm understanding of Gary's prognosis. Structuring resources for a terminal illness is far different than structuring resources for a 6-12 month illness and recovery period.
2. Educating Emir is a relatively easy task, depending on his time, talent and commitment to learning. I do not see this as a difficult challenge.
3. Updating beneficiaries and drafting estate-planning documents are actually a priority. As I indicated earlier, this needs to happen this week. It is the number one priority, in my opinion. It appears Gary doesn't have an estate-planning attorney, so it will be incumbent upon us to find a qualified estate-planning attorney.
4. Comments regarding maximizing Gary's benefits have been made throughout. An appointment with Gary's human resources department is in order.
5. An endowment for the University of Virginia is an important goal but I believe it is lower on the list of things to be addressed first. Once reached, this goal can be accomplished though insurance or annuities, depending on Gary's health situation.

6. Reconciling with his sister is a priority. A conversation with Gary is in order, but I would suggest an estate planning discussion as the catalyst for the meeting. Once his sister is aware of his prognosis, and sees Gary reaching out to her, chances are she will be amenable to meeting and reconciling. Although not specifically mentioned in the case material, reconciliation might also serve to forestall any challenges to Gary's will, by his sister. If she is his only living relative, there is precedent in some states and courts to set aside wills of LGBT citizens, in favor of family members.

Emir's Stated Goals and Objectives

1. Provide for Candace in the event of Emir's death or disability.
2. Allow for a leave of absence to provide support for Gary.
3. Save for Candace's college.
4. Continue saving towards retirement.

Comment:

1. Gary has indicated a desire to provide for Emir upon his death. In a way, this is helping Emir provide for Candace. In addition, Emir has insurance with Candace as the beneficiary. Emir currently has no disability insurance and needs to look into a personal policy. With a loss of income, he would be hard pressed to provide the child support he currently provides Candace.

2. Allowing for a leave of absence for Emir is a challenge in Virginia. Because Emir and Gary are not married, they do not have access to the federally mandated benefits of the Family Medical Leave Act. This is one argument for an out-of-state wedding in Maryland, for example. By so doing, they will become eligible for federal benefits in this area, as well as those outlined in earlier materials in this module.

3. Saving for Candace's college is a goal identified by Gary as well. A conversation on how best to accomplish this goal should follow and alternatives explored. There are life insurance alternatives, college funding plan alternatives, and other alternatives to be considered.

4. Saving for retirement is an ongoing process. In Emir's case however, it consists of a 401-k plan invested 100 percent in company stock. (See Notes to Financial Statements.) We are reminded of what happened to ENRON investors. Obviously, this needs to be addressed, and once the previously mentioned risk profile analysis is performed, a suitable asset allocation determined for his investments.

5. Once again, although Emir's divorce decree should have severed any rights to his assets by this ex-wife, as previously mentioned, there is precedent for the wills of LGBT citizens to be set aside, against their specified directives, in favor of living family members. It is important that Emir have his estate planning documents in order.

Taking a Look at the Financials

Both the Statement of Cash Flow and the Statement of Financial Position provide important information about this couple. Let's look at each one and see where planning issues might be identified.

Statement of Financial Position

In no certain order, are the following observations:

1. Pay off Emir's Discover Card. Why pay 12.99 percent interest when you have $66,000 in cash in checking accounts, earning less than 2 percent, if earning anything at all?

2. Investments identified as Gary's, with a cost basis of $150,000, do not appear to reflect Gary's stated investment risk profile. Based on his health issues, the entire portfolio needs to be reevaluated, assessed and reallocated appropriately. Of particular concern is the 40 percent holding inside his 401(k) of airline stock. While I am a fan of Vanguard, Gary has considerable holdings in Vanguard's 2030 Target Fund. Again, this needs to be readdressed, in light of current health issues.

3. As previously stated, Emir's 401(k) needs to be reallocated out of 100 percent company stock, to the degree permissible.

4. While the ideal time was 6–9 months ago, it might be worthwhile to investigate the benefits of refinancing the home. In addition, a discussion needs to take place regarding the ownership of the property.

5. Gary's auto loan is stated as a "promotional rate." Let's clarify that and make sure there is no possibility of a negative event occurring, should the promotional rate be of limited term.

Statement of Cash Flow

My only comments regarding the Cash Flow Statement are there are a number of opportunities to reduce spending, in the event it is required by an extended disability. At least $160,000 in outflows is "optional," and as stated previously, in the event of a disability, taxes will be reduced substantially as well.

Conclusions

These are the facts and observations I have gleaned from this case. This analysis may help you prepare your case study preparation. Below follows Craig Lemoine's analysis and actual case results.

Kevin M. Lynch, ABD, CFP, ChFC, CLU, RHU, REBC, CASL, CAP, LUTCF, FSS
Asst. Professor of Insurance and Charles J. Zimmerman Chair of Insurance Education
The American College of Financial Services

Case Solution 2: Gary and Emir

Gary and Emir represent actual clients. Craig Lemoine worked with the clients in 2005, well before many states recognized gay marriage. The case offers an opportunity for clients to review a comprehensive scenario and highlight the complexity of working with two same-sex clients living in a state with unfriendly policies. This case also highlights the need for uniform protections of married clients and how illness can drastically change the financial planning process.

The case will be broken into a discussion of actual consequences and outcomes as well as activities which may have created more positive circumstances.

Additional Case Facts

Gary became ill in the summer of 2005. His illness progressed quickly, but before his passing, he met with an attorney and drafted a simple will. The will left all Gary's property to Emir. Gary also made sure that the beneficiary of his 401(k) plan and IRA was Emir.

Emir was upbeat and positive about Gary's condition through the fall. He was in contact with our financial planning office through the winter. Emir spent most of his time taking care of Gary and took a leave of absence from his job at the bank. Gary passed away in December.

Final Wishes

Actual Outcome

Gary wished to remain in his home and enter hospice. However, he lost consciousness in early December and was taken to a local hospital. The hospital did not recognize Emir as a spouse and did not release Gary. Gary passed away in the hospital 2 weeks later.

Gary's sister initially threatened to challenge his new will and provided a copy of Gary's original will to Gary's attorney. She contended Gary was not competent when he executed his new will with Emir. The legal fight erupted after a misunderstanding between Gary's sister and Emir over his funeral: Gary's sister was grieving the lost opportunity to make amends, and Emir reacted strongly to what he considered the interference of an estranged family member.

The attorney who drafted Gary's new will reached out to the sister, and over time a settlement was arranged. Gary's will (leaving property to Emir) was probated, and Emir gave a gift of $50,000 to a charity dedicated to battling prostate cancer. The gift was given on behalf of Gary's sister, who has attempted to maintain a relationship with Emir.

Gary's gross estate was approximately $1,460,000, and the adjusted gross estate was just under $1,000,000, well below any federal estate tax thresholds at the time. However, an 8 percent state inheritance tax was assessed on the assets, causing Emir to sell mutual funds and write a check for $80,000. The inheritance tax was assessed due to Emir not being a legal spouse.

Possible Alternatives

Financial and health care powers of attorney would have allowed Emir to act on Gary's behalf and move him (if medically possible) into a hospice arrangement at home. This document could have been exercised at the time of his new will. Gary and Emir both felt the pressure of time, and, unfortunately, they had less time than they initially anticipated. This case reinforces urgency in planning. Evening meetings with an attorney and financial planner would have helped shape Gary's final wishes.

Had Gary and Emir drafted a living trust, Gary's final wishes would have been more concrete. His cash, home, and investment accounts could have been retitled into the trust with Emir and Gary as co-trustees. At Gary's death, the assets would have remained in trust, and Gary's estranged sister would have faced a higher bar for validating her accusations of wrongdoing. A trust would also have offered advantages to Emir after Gary's death. The revocable nature of the trust would become irrevocable at death and protect the assets from any of Emir's creditors.

An irrevocable trust may also have been appropriate. While "retitling" assets into the trust would have amounted to taxable gifts, the assets would have been removed from Gary's probate estate. Transferring other property by titling or beneficiary designation would have nullified Gary's sister's claim and avoided inheritance taxes.

Short of his moving to a state without inheritance taxes or gifting property into a trust, Gary was not positioned to easily escape this estate tax. Had Gary and Emir's relationship been recognized by their state of residence, Emir would have avoided this tax.

Inherited Assets — Distributions and Financing

Actual Outcome

Emir inherited both Gary's 401(k) and IRA (total proceeds of $409,000). He rolled the proceeds into a nonspousal inherited IRA. Emir began taking minimum required distributions in 2006. At the time, a 38-year-old person was required to take 1/45.6 of the prior year-end balance. His required distribution for 2006 was $8,969.30, all taxable income.

Emir sold Gary's car at his death and used the proceeds to pay off both car loans. While being settled, Gary's estate made mortgage payments using proceeds from cash and mutual fund accounts. After settlement, Emir was forced to use remaining mutual fund assets and a new $300,000 note to pay off the old mortgage. Emir did not have an income equal to Gary's and was unable to qualify for an evenly-matched mortgage. Gary's mortgage was not assumable.

After paying off debt, making contributions to charity, and paying inheritance taxes, Emir had exhausted the bulk of Gary's liquid nonqualified assets. Emir found himself making regular distributions out of the inherited IRA to sustain living expenses, child support, credit card debt, and debt incurred from the funeral.

Possible Alternatives

If Emir and Gary were legally married, Emir could have inherited Gary's IRA balance as a spousal IRA. He would not be subject to distributions until the year following his age 70½, and the assets would be better positioned to grow into retirement.

A trust arrangement or retitling the home prior to Gary's passing would have eliminated stress and the unnecessary use of liquid assets. Gary and Emir could have leveraged trust assets towards a joint mortgage, eliminating the need for Emir to seek refinancing after Gary's death. Liquid assets would allow Emir to provide for Gary's funeral without borrowing consumer debt.

While Gary and Emir were not in a relationship at the time of his home financing, an assumable mortgage may have have allowed Emir to continue making payments on the original note after Gary's death. This type of note provides more flexibility to a borrower and would have given Emir additional options.

Ongoing Relationship

Actual Outcome

Emir became dependent on his inherited IRA proceeds to provide for living expenses, travel expenses, and the charitable donations he wished to make on Gary's behalf. The financial planning team reached out to Emir monthly at first, and he attended two meetings in 2006. The first meeting focused on settling Gary's estate, and the second meeting focused on investment education. Emir continued living in Gary's home through 2008.

Emir's withdrawals totaled $50,000 in 2006 and $60,000 in 2007, well above his required distributions. By 2008, his relationship with the financial planning firm had become stale and he stopped returning calls. The relationship officially terminated after the market crashed in the fall of 2008, with Emir making a final distribution of the remaining assets in the account.

Possible Alternatives

Emir relied on Gary to make financial decisions while he was living. In the time between Gary's diagnosis and his illness's progressing, inviting Emir and Gary to discussions on investment allocation and cash flow planning may have strengthened the relationship between the financial planning firm and both clients.

Rationality flees in the face of grief. Providing professional counseling and customized communication styles in line with Emir's personality would better prepare Emir for life without Gary. Account withdrawals were symptomatic of overspending and a need for cash flow management and financial counseling.

Conclusion

This case did not end positively for the planning firm or Emir. Emir had the opportunity to plan for a comfortable retirement, though it would come at the expense of several years of careful spending. The financial planning firm had an opportunity to maintain a lifetime relationship and an ongoing revenue stream, though it would cost additional time and resources to provide Emir with the help he needed.

Clients and planners do not know what the future holds. Gary and Emir are an example of the need for financial planning before a crisis situation arises. Life insurance and estate planning would have created a fundamentally different outcome for Emir after Gary passed.

Craig Lemoine, PhD, CFP®

Assistant Professor of Financial Planning

Jarrett L. Davis Professor of Financial Planning Technology